ETHNICITY, MARKETS, AND

MIGRATION IN THE ANDES

ETHNICITY, MARKETS, AND

MIGRATION IN THE ANDES

At the Crossroads of History and Anthropology

EDITED BY BROOKE LARSON AND OLIVIA HARRIS

WITH ENRIQUE TANDETER

DUKE UNIVERSITY PRESS Durham and London

1995

Sponsored by the Joint Committee on Latin American Studies
of the Social Science Research Council and the American
Council of Learned Societies with funds from
the Andrew W. Mellon Foundation.

IN MEMORY OF OUR COLLEAGUES AND FRIENDS,

GUNNAR MENDOZA AND THIERRY SAIGNES

Contents

✤

Contents

Maps

✤

Acknowledgments

✤

As this project has evolved over the years and migrated between Europe, South America, and the United States, we have counted on the intellectual and editorial help of innumerable people on three continents. Many of those people who collaborated closely with us on the earlier Spanish edition (*La participación indígena en los mercados surandinos*) are mentioned in the preface to that book. But we would like to acknowledge here the early and enduring support of our Bolivian colleagues, as well as the generous support of the Joint Committee on Latin American Studies of the American Council of Learned Societies and the Social Science Research Council (SSRC). This book is part of a longer, collaborative research project in Andean history and anthropology, which has also yielded two other important volumes (see Chapter 1). Over many years, the Social Science Research Council has lent its financial and intellectual support to this project. Most recently, the council has provided funds to cover the costs of translation and manuscript preparation to bring out a greatly revised, updated, English-language version of the original book. We thank Eric Hershberg and other members of the staff of the Latin American program of the Social Science Research Council for their help in facilitating this funding.

Staff at our respective universities and research centers lightened the burdens of editorial work and typing, for which we are very grateful. The translation work was done by Anna Crowe, Judith Evans, Julie Franks, and José Gordillo. We are especially indebted to Julie Franks, who, in addition to translating the articles by Carlos Sempat Assadourian and Marisol de la Cadena (Chapters 4 and 11), found time to correct and style the book's bibliography and do the index. Problems of manuscript length and publication costs have compelled us to include a selected, though still lengthy, bibliography, but the interested reader will find extensive bibliographic discussions in the text and footnotes of the volume's introductory and concluding essays, as well as in the notes of most articles.

At different stages of this collaborative research project, each of us has assumed major responsibilities for conference organization and manuscript preparation. However, Brooke Larson coordinated the preparation of the manuscript for the revised, English-language book and did the liaison work with the SSRC and the publisher. She and Olivia Harris shared the editorial and translation work. Enrique Tandeter collaborated during the early stage of this project.

It has been a pleasure working with the editors at Duke University Press, including the former director, Lawrence Malley. Our biggest debt, however, is to Valerie Millholland, who rescued this manuscript and then shepherded it through the processes of editorial review. We also thank our copyeditor Cynthia Garver. Finally, we wish to thank all the historians and anthropologists who have been involved in this project through many years. We would have liked to include many more articles from the 1987 Spanish-language edition, but prudent editors persuaded us to publish a slim selection. In addition, we commissioned several new pieces for this book.

We thank all those people who have contributed in one way or another to this volume. In particular, we remember with gratitude and affection the enthusiasm and support that the late Gunnar Mendoza offered us when we held the 1983 conference on Indians and markets at the Archivo Nacional de Bolivia in Sucre. We dedicate this book to his memory and to the memory of our dear friend and colleague, Thierry Saignes, who went most of the way with us on this particular journey.

BROOKE LARSON, OLIVIA HARRIS, AND ENRIQUE TANDETER

I

Introduction

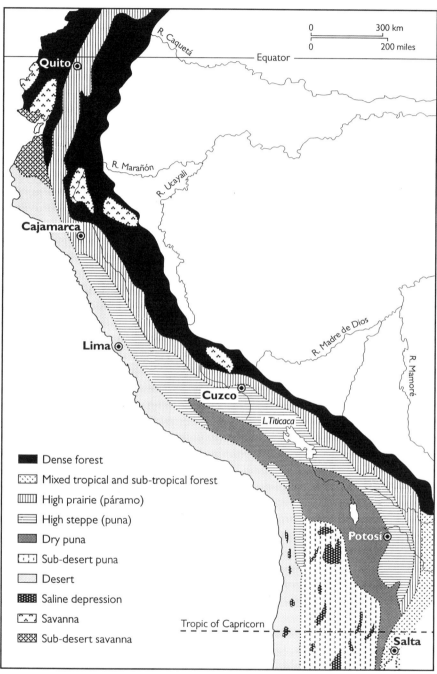

Map 1. Andean ecological zones.

Andean Communities, Political Cultures, and Markets: The Changing Contours of a Field

BROOKE LARSON

This book comes at the end of a long and gratifying intellectual journey. It is the final piece of a larger collaborative research project that began several years ago. If collective memory can be trusted, we trace its origins to a series of conversations in a favorite London pub around the turn of the 1980s. The exciting prospect of Manchester hosting the Congress of Americanists in 1982 promised to provide a forum for new and forthcoming research on the history of market expansion in the Andean highland regions, where Indian peasant production and labor sustained the evolving market economy over the course of five centuries of European rule. The goal was to provide fresh perspectives on the dynamics of economic and cultural change in the Andes, at both the local and global levels, by bringing together anthropologists and historians engaged in new research on the topic.[1]

On the other side of the Atlantic, about the same time, several Andeanists were invited by the Joint Committee on Latin American Studies (of the Social Science Research Council and American Council of Learned Societies) to consider how the councils might sponsor a collaborative research planning project to boost this field on the cusp of development. Our original intention was to create three nested research projects in Andean studies that embraced major overlapping themes and harnessed some of the new scholarship.[2]

We have largely accomplished that endeavor. The two companion Andeanist projects (one on Andean resistance and rebellion, the other on the local social and cultural processes within Andean kin groups and com-

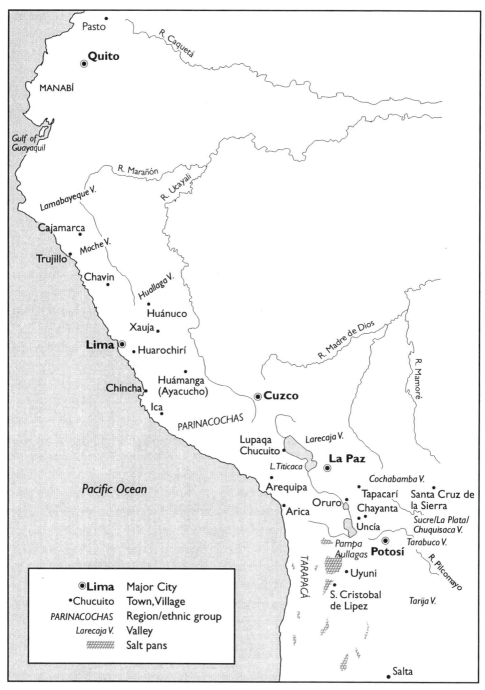

Map 2. Andean sites of study.

munities) have yielded important volumes over the past several years.[3] In the meantime, this project on Andean peasant engagement in market relations began to take shape as the first of the three council-sponsored Andean research projects, designed to stimulate interdisciplinary conversations and to nurture the promising, though still extremely young, field of Andean studies. Our interest in developing a conference on the theme of "Andean peasant responses to the penetration and expansion of the market" coincided with plans for the Manchester panel on "Indian market participation in the Andes." It made sense to merge the transatlantic efforts. What we thought then would be a conference carried out with an admirable economy of effort, thanks to the forum and funding offered by both the council and the Americanist Congress, turned out to be a rather inauspicious beginning of a long-term project. The war over the Islas Malvinas/Falkland Islands destroyed all prospects of a strong Latin American presence at the congress and forced us to organize a new conference in "neutral" territory. It was decided then to transport the project to Bolivia, open it as much as possible to Bolivian and other Andean scholars, and commit the conference volume to a Bolivian research institute for publication in Spanish. Logistical nightmares, local political tensions, and last-minute, long-distance negotiations added texture and color to the otherwise dull task of conference organizing. But at last the conference took place, in July 1983. It was held at the National Archive in Sucre, to honor the life's work of its director, the late Gunnar Mendoza. Thanks to the ongoing collaboration of our Bolivian colleagues, the conference volume was published there in 1987.[4]

This book meets our long-standing commitment to bring out a substantially revised, updated English-language edition. The theme of indigenous communities and markets in Andean history is more timely now than perhaps ever before. The climate of neoliberalism and current political efforts to reify the free market, amidst the human pain of "structural adjustments" among the rural and urban poor, has brought issues of markets, rural poverty, migration, and petty commerce (the so-called "informal sector") back into sharp focus. In spite of the passing of variant developmentalist paradigms from the current intellectual scene, the enduring problems of peasant poverty, proletarianization, and capitalist development in agrarian-based and export economies are still salient—indeed, high-stake—issues among politicians, international agents of the proliferating nongovernmental organizations (NGOs), and grassroots activists alike. And never more so than after the January 1994 uprising of Chiapas peasants in southern Mexico, exquisitely timed to coincide with the beginning of the North American Free Trade Agreement (NAFTA). Among scholars of the Andes, those more likely to pick up this book, there is continuing interest in the problems and prospects of commercial expansion and endemic rural poverty. Yet recent scholarship in anthropology, rural sociology, and history has tended to turn away from earlier efforts at building models and from structural approaches to agrarian change in order to pose a new set of questions to indigenous history and society.

This book is part of that effort to experiment with poststructuralist, ethnohistorical approaches to global historical processes—in this case, the integration and subordination of Indian peasantries to market forces since the sixteenth century. It draws on the ongoing work of historians and anthropologists who have helped revitalize and reshape the field of Andean social and ethnohistory over the past decade and a half. The project's original formulation in 1981 came out of the perceived need to bridge the conceptual gap between cultural anthropology and political economy, which seemed to be working at cross-purposes. The theoretical and disciplinary tensions between these two research traditions posed a central paradox in Andean history, which focused our collective attention: namely, the long-term historical resilience and adaptation of indigenous peasant economies, organized around reciprocal norms, in the midst of powerful and evolving commodity markets that swirled around the mining export economy of the southern Andes. As late as the 1970s, much research on the theme of Indians and markets seemed fragmented, even insular: anthropologists focused on Indians, political economists on markets. This book encompasses both perspectives in an effort to open insights into the social, cultural, and political ramifications of this apparent historical paradox of the southern Andes.

The scope and aims of this book are deeply informed by the cross-disciplinary conversations in Andean history and anthropology that have been ongoing over the past decade or so. So we begin this essay by setting the book in its broader intellectual context. With broad strokes, I want to trace parallel research trends in Andean anthropology and history / political economy that set the parameters of scholarship and debate about indigenous economies and the formation of markets during the 1960s and

1970s. Then I will turn briefly to highlight several important field advances during the 1980s, which have framed some of the overarching issues and perspectives developed in this book.

Traditions in Andean Anthropology and History

The southern Andes, particularly the high plains stretching to the north, west, and south of Lake Titicaca, were the spectacular setting of highly developed societies. Hundreds of years before the Europeans set foot on the altiplano in the mid-sixteenth century, Andean civilizations harnessed the resources of geographically dispersed ecological tiers to support highly dense settlements. To sustain dense populations in fragile, high-altitude alpine environments, they extended their reach across the vast, broken landscape down to the irrigated valleys of the western desert coast and into the eastern tropical valleys and basins of the Amazon (see Map 1). They settled colonists in these widely dispersed and contrasting ecological zones to gain simultaneous and direct access to the whole register of agricultural and livestock products offered by this spectacular vertical land. From small ethnic groups to powerful, confederated ethnic chiefdoms, Andean social organizations developed around the cultural ideals and practices of ecological complementarity. The great marketplaces of Mesoamerica had no Andean counterpart before the Spanish Conquest (see Chapters 2 and 5 in this volume).

This uniquely Andean solution to the problem of subsistence in a territory broken up by altitude, aridity, and extreme diurnal temperature contrast represents a major "human achievement" that permitted the florescence of high civilizations—including the empire of Tawantinsuyu—in the last centuries before the European invasion. On the eve of that invasion, ethnic authorities and the Inca state raised revenues sufficient to support imperial elites, bureaucracies, and armies in the process of pushing the frontiers of empire along a 5,000-mile stretch of the Andes. The capacity of the Inca state to accumulate surpluses, sustain its empire, and redistribute surpluses through symbolic gestures of reciprocity to its subject population has challenged the Western imagination ever since—from sixteenth-century European observers to twentieth-century anthropologists and archaeologists. Through the centuries, scholarship on the pre-

Hispanic Andes has sought to discover the distinctive characteristics of Andean civilization, given the striking absence of market and tribute institutions, money and merchants, property relations and impoverishment familiar to precapitalist Western societies.[5]

Yet within a half century of the Spanish Conquest, the southern Andes was the site of the world's richest and most legendary silver mine. Potosí sprang up in the mountainous interior of Alto Perú and by the 1580s became the principal source of silver for Europe and America. Its treasures, forged into specie, lubricated the economies of Western Europe and hastened the dissolution of feudalism, fanned the flames of inflation across Iberia, and quickened the tempo of commercial capitalism on a global scale. It became a mecca for treasure seekers and an industrial pit for Andean miners struggling to stay alive. Potosí mushroomed into a town of some 100,000 people by the turn of the seventeenth century. The concentration of human capital, inflationary price history, and dependence on imported goods from both Europe and surrounding Andean regions forged an enormous marketplace in the southern Andes. Out of the imperatives of the silver economy, and the preexisting capacity of Andean ethnic groups to produce surplus goods and services, markets took root and spread throughout the Andes, where money and mercantilism had never before existed.

This dramatic historical contrast—between the culminating achievements of Andean civilization before the European arrival and the rapid, post-Conquest organization of a mercantile colonial economy in the same geocultural space—gradually came to light in parallel research currents of anthropology and history during the 1950s, 1960s, and 1970s. As we shall see shortly, an emerging literature in history and historical sociology on the political economy of commercial capitalism and European expansion looked at the power of the conquest state and mercantile capital to suck the Andes, and other parts of America, into the whirlpools of the global economy. Andean historians thus tended to approach their region of study from the outside: as part of a larger field of force that interconnected events and cultures of local origin with the global forces of European expansion.[6] In contrast, anthropologists paid scant attention to the impact of markets or other exogenous forces of change on the Andes; instead, they searched for cultural specificity and continuity of Andean economic strategies and social organization. In the postwar decades, the dominant research tradition on the Andes, indeed the very font of Andean area studies, was the emerging body of ethnohistorical and archaeological research on Tawantinsuyu and the transition to colonial rule, as well as the contemporary ethnographic literature.[7] Whereas historical studies of the Andes remained fragmented and disparate until the late 1970s, Andean anthropology flourished in the 1950s, 1960s, and 1970s in Peru, North America, and Europe. The pioneers—such as, Hermann Trimborn, John Murra, John Rowe, and later R. Tom Zuidema—combined the methods and insights of archaeology and ethnohistory to shatter Eurocentric categories and polemics about the nature of the Inca empire and to gain fresh insights into Inca statecraft and local cultural forms before and after the European invasion in the sixteenth century. They set the research agenda for Andean ethnology, which matured rapidly in the 1970s. By the end of that decade, the ethnographic literature on the Andes had a density and unity that made it comparable to that on Mesoamerica.[8]

Among these pioneers, John Murra has had the most far-reaching impact on the overlapping fields of Andean ethnography and ethnohistory during the last thirty years. This synoptic overview can hardly do justice to the manifold ways that Murra's work and teaching have shaped the contours of these fields, but it is worth mentioning here several of Murra's more important contributions. To begin, Murra's seminal 1955 doctoral thesis on the economic organization of the Inca state was almost immediately appreciated for its penetrating insights into the internal economic and ideological workings of the Inca empire.[9] Shattering the old polemical stereotypes of the Incas, Murra's study revealed the processes of cultural hegemony at work. He showed how the rulers of Tawantinsuyu grafted labor demands onto local institutions and cultural practices, which left a considerable margin of cultural and economic autonomy to recently colonized ethnic groups and yet allowed the Inca lords to accumulate vast amounts of stored energy and wealth. The Incas balanced state demands against material and symbolic forms of "generosity" that respected and reinforced many of the rights and traditions of ethnic groups subject to Inca rule.

Murra's later work explored other aspects of economy, statecraft, colonization, and warfare under the Incas.[10] It also moved in a new direction, toward the study of native Andean peoples under early colonial rule. This was a natural outcome of his early research, as well as his pursuit of ethnohistorical sources. For while he used colonial documents to glean insights into Inca society and local social formations before the Spanish arrival, he also scrutinized those documents for information about the adaptive vitality of local Andean society under early colonial rule.[11] A crucial contribution to Andean ethnohistory, however, was Murra's effort to find and edit the writings of literate Andeans, other than the famous Garcilaso de la Vega. This pursuit of Andean voices and visions of the Inca past and of Spanish colonial rule culminated in 1980 with the publication of a new, critical edition of the vast and stunning work of Felipe Guaman Poma de Ayala [1613], coedited by Murra and Rolena Adorno.[12] Murra's emphasis on colonial texts as potential ethnohistorical sources bridged the conventional disciplinary divide between "prehistory"—once the presumed precinct of anthropologists and archaeologists—and "history" where mainly historians attended to the problems of European colonization.[13] From early on, Murra's own research crossed the divide, as he made plain that Andean peoples possessed a rich, complex history and a highly developed civilization, uniquely adapted to its mountainous environment, long before literate Europeans came to observe it and alter the course of its history. Yet his ethnohistorical work also revealed Andean cultural tradition as an adaptive, creative force that endured the cataclysms associated with European conquest and colonization.

Most illuminating in this regard was Murra's ethnohistorical reading and publication of two early colonial reports of local ethnic polities in the sierra of central Peru and the high plains of the Titicaca basin area, known as the *visitas* of Huánuco and Chucuito, respectively.[14] On the basis of these sources, dating from the 1560s, Murra further developed his study of the cultural logic of Andean settlement patterns and political organization that extended the reach of ethnic groups across several ecological tiers of the broken, mountainous landscape. His model posited a centralized political organization (at the level of ethnic chiefdom, or *señorío*) that colonized different productive zones—spanning the high-altitude puna, the middle-altitude range *quichua* valley, and the low-altitude tropical slopes of the eastern escarpment, as well as the western Pacific coastal region. The most compelling evidence of this "vertical archipelago" pattern was drawn from the visita of Chucuito. The source revealed the far-flung colonies of the rich agropastoral, altiplano chiefdom of the Aymara-speaking Lupaqas, who directly controlled lands as far away as a week's journey in the low-altitude tropical zone of the eastern slopes of the Andes, as well as along the river valleys that sliced through the arid coast to the west. The Lupa-qas constructed their social and spatial organization around the ideals of ecological complementarity, self-sufficiency, and reciprocity, thus gaining direct access to a rich variety of resources (salt, tubers, fuel, wool, llamas, and alpacas from the highlands; maize from the valleys; chili peppers, cotton, and other products from arid coastal areas; coca leaves and fruits from the tropical forests) without recourse to tribute in goods or to monetary exchange.

Murra's study of the archipelago strategy of subsistence, adapted by the Incas to suit their own imperial aims, became a central motif of a decade or more of anthropological scholarship in pursuit of the enduring cultural specificities—even uniqueness—of Andeanness (sometimes referred to, as *lo andino*).[15] Indeed, Murra inspired a new generation of anthropologists in the 1970s to blend ethnohistorical perspectives on Andean political culture and economy with local ethnography of rural communities. Working on small-scale units of social organization, many anthropologists explored the variations and permutations of the vertical archipelago model in diverse regional and cultural contexts in the contemporary Andes. In the view of Frank Salomon, these studies in ethnoecology gave "broad ethnographic confirmation" of Murra's model and "proved a dramatic demonstration of the continuing distinctiveness and viability of the Andean adaptive repertory."[16] They showed how many contemporary peasant communities solved the subsistence problem through a variety of kin-based strategies, as local peasantries tried to diversify agricultural and pastoral production in different ecological niches (particularly combining pastoralism and agriculture in the high- and middle-range altitude tiers) and to coordinate communal work efforts for certain agricultural tasks. Some of this ethnographic literature was less insular in approach and explored the intersection of market and kinship forms of exchange, or the insertion of local communities into larger fields of force,[17] but these studies sailed against the ethnological currents of the 1970s. Most cultural anthropologists focused their attention inward toward communal social and symbolic organizations.[18]

In this volume, John Murra (Chapter 2) returns to one of the unifying themes of his life's work: the social achievements of Andean peoples in harnessing the resources of their mountainous environment and creating highly integrated societies that were uniquely different from Western mercantilist economies and states. In a retrospective glance at the archaeological and historical evidence to date, Murra reexamines his long-standing premise that Tawantinsuyu mobilized and circulated goods and services without relying on protomarkets, circulating media, or tribute institutions (based on the extraction of goods). Two decades of ethnohistorical and ethnographic literature have tested, critiqued, revised, or elaborated Murra's model of Andean economic and political organization. As he reflects on that literature, Murra confirms the basic premise of his original work and goes on to raise fascinating questions about the cultural significance of long-distance exchanges and labor prestations, which continuously moved goods and people east and west across the cordillera, as well as north and south, linking far-flung colonies and kingdoms in a variety of commercial contexts. He draws particular attention to the scale and significance of Andean maritime traffic in precious things, a topic still largely unexplored in the anthropological literature.

While Murra and his fellow anthropologists drew attention to the enduring and adaptive cultural forms and practices that were singularly Andean, many historians were beginning to engage interdisciplinary issues about global political economy and, more specifically, the transition-to-capitalism question that was the theoretical seedbed of Andean historiography of the late 1960s and 1970s. These theory-driven debates encompassed all of Latin America, of course, and they engaged universal questions about the nature of the agrarian class structure, precapitalist and capitalist modes of exploitation, imperialism, and social movements.[19] In both mainstream developmentalist and critical Marxian traditions, scholars searched for the political and programmatic implications of their research to encourage conditions favorable to capitalist or socialist transition.[20] One stream of political economy of the Andes engaged debates about agrarian class relations in the Peruvian countryside and the prospects of ameliorating rural poverty through government intervention.[21] Many of these studies on the nature of Andean peasant economies and the hacienda regime set themselves the task of assessing the potential of peasants as revolutionaries. At base, critical Marxist research on the "agrarian question" interrogated the political possibility of peasants to transcend their presumed political naïveté and parochial concerns to forge an alliance with progressive sectors of the working class and intelligentsia. While some of these studies were grounded in local or regional Andean cases, their theoretical agendas gave priority to the universalizing issues and language of class, effectively effacing culture, ethnicity, and gender from the picture.[22] Further, these studies (whatever their strain of Marxian analysis) usually wanted to trace the determinative effects of penetrant capitalism and the state on local society. Little attention was paid to the impact of local culture in mediating or structuring those global forces of change.

A second stream of political economy was more historical in approach, although it engaged many of the same theoretical concerns as the emerging scholarship on contemporary agrarian-class issues, particularly the historical problematic of agrarian transition and transformation.[23] The central debate focused on the nature of European mercantile exploitation of native peasant and slave populations and its capacity to subordinate the Andean (and more broadly, Latin American) hinterlands to the expanding world market of Europe. As we shall see shortly, much of the new Andean historiography that was nurtured by these earlier debates in political economy only came of age in the decade of the 1980s. But already by the mid-1970s, a small number of scholars began to study the insertion of Andean regions into a global political economy. The most promising area was the new historical research on the "first transition" to commercial capitalism and colonialism, following the European invasion in the sixteenth century.[24] While many historians still studied the colonial Andes primarily in terms of its subordinate relation to Europe, a new generation of social and economic historians in the 1970s was beginning to crack the Eurocentric mold and investigate economic, demographic, and social processes internal to Andean colonial society.

Among those historians, Carlos Sempat Assadourian's research on the early colonial economy of the Andes dramatically shifted in perspective.[25] In the tradition of political economy, Assadourian studied the formation of the "mercantile colonial economy" of the southern Andes in the broader global context of European expansion and colonial domination, but he focused primarily on the internal dynamics of the early colonial political economy. His work approached the silver mining economy of Potosí as the principal motor force of structural change that affected all facets of economic life and social relations throughout the Andes, and he situated that mining town in the larger field of force to explore the complex nature of Andean colonialism. In Assadourian's view, the locus of colonial exploitation was to be discovered at the intersection of commercial capitalism and the coercive power of a tributary state. The imperatives of the state to raise monetary tribute, together with its dependence on tax revenues from silver mining, created the need to engineer the partial integration of peasants into the monetary economy. Historically, he argued, the enforcement of Andean peasant participation in mine labor and markets created an enormous economic subsidy for European enterprises, at the cost of the progressive impoverishment of peasant villages. And yet here—in Assadourian's analysis—was strong evidence of brisk overland traffic in indigenous labor and goods and of vigorous Andean efforts of commercial adaptation during the late sixteenth and early seventeenth centuries. Assadourian showed that the trade arteries feeding the Potosí market were lubricated by Andean surplus agricultural production, transport, and trade. His empirical findings were striking: native peoples supplied the overwhelming bulk of foodcrops and other staples to Potosí during the late sixteenth century. They were the primary producers, traders, and consumers in the expanding product market that began to interweave far-flung regions into commercial networks strung across the Andes.

While Assadourian's essays on the early colonial political economy had broad and exciting implications for the ethno and social history of Andean involvement in the early colonial economy, he did not pursue critical issues related to peasant strategies of livelihood or resistance.[26] Fundamentally concerned with the systemic inner workings of colonial exploitation, Assadourian's early work drew on the broader conceptual debates over imperial expansion and agrarian transition. His work marked a clear advance beyond the rigid dichotomies (feudalism versus capitalism; world market versus local economy; production versus exchange) and, for both its theoretical and empirical rigor, did much to stimulate new thinking in Andean historiography in the late 1970s and 1980s.[27] Assadourian's research on interregional markets, for example, opened analytic space for studying the ways that subordinated peasantries participated in, and shaped, the evolving colonial economy. Thus, while Assadourian's research priorities and premises came out of the creative tensions of political economy, the implications of his empirical findings opened new possibilities for studying Andean peasants as social and economic actors in the early colonial economy. He has continued to explore the ethnohistorical ramifications of his early pathbreaking work (see, for example, Chapter 4 in this volume).[28]

By the end of the 1970s, then, Murra and Assadourian were charting parallel new directions in Andean anthropology and history. Although they focused on different problems, their work fundamentally broke with earlier Eurocentric concerns and preconceptions to investigate Andean political and economic structures on their own terms. Both engaged in painstaking historical reconstruction, in search of the internal logic of political and ideological structures that governed the production and distribution of Andean surpluses and the means of subsistence. Both focused their attention on the political and economic relations between local ethnic groups, or peasant communities, and a centralizing (Inca or Spanish colonial) state. For the most part, both Murra and Assadourian placed their analytic stress on political economy and social structure, rather than on social agency.

And yet, unwittingly, their influences on the emerging fields of Andean social and ethnohistory contributed to somewhat of a bipolar, Janus-like, view of the colonial and postcolonial Andean world. Inspired by Murra's work, many ethnologists set out to map the unique structural properties of an Andean social and mental world that seemed impervious to change and far removed from the messy, dynamic context of power relations and struggle. In the meantime, Assadourian's work made a compelling case for the transformative power of mercantile colonialism that battered Andean communities, while channeling peasant labor toward accumulative European ends. Juxtaposed, their work seemed to reinforce the notion of two coexisting and fundamentally antagonistic economic orders: one governed by the ideals of communal self-sufficiency and reciprocity, the other by mercantile precepts and the norms of competitive individualism. Certainly, many anthropologists and political economists took this conceptual duality as their point of departure and assumed an inherent cultural incompatibility between Andean and European strategies of subsistence and accumulation. The striking contrast between the economic organization of the late Inca empire and the expansive economy of imperial Spain provided a powerful historical contrast. Where they parted company, of course, was in their fundamentally different approaches to post-Conquest Andean history. While anthropologists documented the capacity of Andean non-market institutions and norms to shield ethnic groups from penetrant capitalism, political economists and historians pointed to the destructive impact of the colonial and modern market economies.

This implicit paradox in the maturing field of Andean studies presented a fundamental challenge to cultural anthropologists and Marxist historians who came of intellectual age in the late 1970s and 1980s. Many anthropologists and historians were beginning to push against the frontiers of their own disciplines. The developing field of ethnohistory, which originated within the anthropological camp, offered a conceptual meeting ground for both historians and anthropologists seeking to quicken interdisciplinary dialogues. Their interests converged, as Frank Salomon noted in 1985, as they "looked for ways to handle culture and history as complementary notions, integral to one another."[29] Murra's earlier ethnohistorical work with colonial documents was an inspiration to many scholars, who began to experiment with combinations of ethnographic-historical methods to explore a variety of social and historical themes. While anthropologists and historians did not necessarily share the same research agenda, methodologies, or central premises about the relationship between material and cultural processes, they moved the dialogue and debate well beyond earlier formulations about the relative determinism of base and superstructure.

This they did in two fundamental ways. First, they became more attentive to the possibilities of social agency, while keeping in mind the constraints of structure. Andean social actors, particularly subordinated ethnic groups and classes, were placed center stage in order to understand the ways in which they mediated or structured the impact of structural forces (Inca rule, the Spanish invasion, market expansion, state-building, acculturation, liberal and populist agrarian reforms, and so on).[30] More analytic space was opened for the study of everyday pursuits of livelihood and social amelioration.[31] New research on Indian involvement in the early colonial economy, for example, revealed the active role that Indians played in shaping the emerging commodity markets—without fully assimilating themselves into the dominant society.[32] Further, social historians who worked on local or regional agrarian histories began to reconsider the shifting power balances between European and native institutions and forces. Regional studies of long-term agrarian change began to explore the historical possibilities of Andean strategies of survival and struggle as a shaping force, one that sometimes imposed sharp limits on the extractive institutions of the colonial or republican state and on regional elites. This particular theme informed several important regional and sectoral studies of the 1980s, which together cast serious doubt on the historical determinism of commercial capitalism and the colonial state to effectively harness the labor power of indigenous economies to the mining export sector or to the colonial Exchequer.[33] Historians working on nineteenth-century Peru and Bolivia, in turn, focused sharply on indigenous forms of resistance and social mobilization to stall or block the advent of liberal reforms and modern methods of labor control on haciendas in several regions of the Andes.[34]

Second, the poststructuralist turn toward social agency and experience compelled social and ethnohistorians to historicize the concepts of culture, community, and *mentalité*. Although poststructuralist approaches to culture vary widely, they give the concept of culture a "kinetic, mutable, nonconsensual character."[35] This critical effort to inject politics, power, and historical agency into conversations about Andean culture and community has punctured some of the myths surrounding *lo andino*. Instead, ethnohistorians have sought to understand the open-ended, dynamic political culture of local communities, inextricably linked to diverse historical experiences of struggle and survival, accommodation and collusion, and grounded in the politics of memory, hope, and identity.[36] This cross-disciplinary effort to look at local rural communities as historical constructions, and as the locus of cultural struggle and change, has launched something of a revisionist movement in nineteenth- and twentieth-century Andean historiography by casting ethnohistorical light on once-familiar processes of market and nation-state formation, as well as on the politics of ethnic identity and alterity in diverse regional/historical contexts (see Chapters 8 and 12 in this volume).[37]

No less important is the recent revisionism swirling around the theme of Andean market participation and cultural change. Recent work in history and anthropology sheds light on the manifold ways that Andean peasantries redirected agriculture toward commercial ends; engaged in trade and commerce; pursued artisanry and wage labor; mortgaged, sold, and purchased lands; and sometimes even invested in the material and ideological trappings of European prestige.[38] But while scholars now recognize that local Andean communities (*ayllus*) simultaneously engaged in kin-based and barter reciprocities, as well as market relations, they are only beginning to explore the broader historical and cultural implications of this insight. Further, these findings raise important methodological issues about ways to approach the study of Andean communities, local political cultures, and markets, which transcend the conceptual antinomies that guided earlier approaches (see Chapter 3 in this volume).

New Approaches to the Study of Andean Market Interventions

This book gathers perspectives on Indian communities, political cultures, and market participation under varied and changing social and historical conditions. Its geographic scope encompasses the central and southern Andean highlands, a region stretching roughly from Cuzco to southern Bolivia, once the heartlands of Tawantinsuyu, where a diversity of Quechua- and Aymara-speaking ethnic groups continued to cluster in "Indian communities" during colonial and republican rule. Historically, the high plateau, sierra, and high, intermontane valleys of the southern Andes encompassed a complex of productive activities—mining, agriculture, raising livestock, and rustic industry—that circulated throughout the Andean interior and connected the Andes to the world economy during export booms. This region provides a fascinating social laboratory for exploring our collective concerns about the historical and cultural significances of Andean involvement in markets and mercantile enterprises. The contrasting variety of Andean social ecology and ethnic subcultures, however, cautions against generalizing from particular case studies, and most authors shy away from broad generalization. Indeed, we invited Susan Ramírez to contribute a chapter (Chapter 5) on northern patterns of pre- and post-Conquest exchange in order to bring some comparative perspective to the book's southern highland focus. But the book does not pretend to offer balanced coverage of Andean regions or historical periods; rather, our aim has been to balance a diversity of ethnographic and regional historical studies against the synthetic interpretations offered in the introduction (Chapter 1) and the conclusion (Chapter 12). As a whole, these studies challenge lingering assumptions about the destructive or assimilative powers of global market forces in Andean history, without falling into the trap of naive voluntarism—implicitly celebrating Andean commercial ingenuity (the *homo economicus* of the mountains!) or reifying peasant resistance. Further, these essays break loose of narrow-gauged analyses of economic and ecological problem-solving or market rationality to implicate the cultural and political dimensions of Andean insertions into particular product, labor, and land markets. More precisely, our concern is with the complex interaction between the historical conditions and experiences of Indian market involvement, on the one hand, and the changing contours of local political cultures that both shaped, and were shaped by, Andean modes of livelihood, on the other. Besides their individual empirical contributions, then, the articles raise a variety of substantive and methodological issues that point the way toward richer social and ethnohistories of local Andean communities and their participation in the making, and unmaking, of regional and national market economies at particular historical times.

Andeans at the Intersection of Kinship, Tributary, and Market Economies

First, these studies explore the regional variety and historical contingency of Andean subsistence strategies. They provide a kaleidoscopic view of diverse Andean social groups struggling to preserve or develop kin-based reciprocities, while improvising tributary and mercantile strategies in colonial and postcolonial local and regional markets. In Chapter 3, Steve Stern poses the issue vividly. He argues that Andeans actively intervened in marketplaces, while adapting their kin-based institutions and norms to changing circumstances. Working from evidence of financial speculation among the Parinacocha ayllus of the Cuzco region in the late sixteenth century, Stern shows how ethnic groups turned short-term mercantile tactics toward long-term strategies of social reproduction. By the late sixteenth century, ethnic groups across the southern and central highlands suffered deteriorating tributary terms and conditions, as well as cyclical drought that sapped their communities of life and vitality. As Stern makes clear, Andean hybrid strategies did not reverse colonial mercantile penetration, but they often allowed Andeans "to resist . . . abject surrender to market forces and demands on terms they could not control."[39]

Stern's argument finds ample empirical support. The studies by Sempat Assadourian (Chapter 4), Susan Ramírez (Chapter 5), and Thierry Saignes (Chapter 6) show Andeans struggling to hold together an ensemble of social reproductive strategies that allowed them to meet their multiple obligations to the state and their kinsmen, as well as to the church and the local deities, while providing for their immediate and future subsistence needs. Some strategies involved interethnic exchange that etched new patterns of circuitry and alliance across the Andean landscape, quite apart from the flow of commodities between the Andean and Spanish sectors. Assadourian, for example, explores interecological exchanges among the Lupaqa peoples during the 1560s. As many historians have shown, it was a critical decade of turbulence and transformation, when Andean archipelago patterns were still visible to the discerning European eye. Assadourian uses the visitas of Huánuco and Chucuito to document growing mercantile incursion, territorial/political shrinkage, and new mercantile and tribute demands. But what is striking is that ethnic and ecological fragmentation was accompanied by intensifying barter and trade among distinctive ethnic groups inhabiting the altiplano. The Lupaqa peoples, for example, negotiated barter arrangements with other highland ethnic groups living along the shores of Lake Titicaca to secure their supplies of *chuño* and *quinoa* in years of frost or drought. Such glimpses of "horizontal" exchanges raise a variety of cultural and political issues concerning intra-Andean diplomacy and trade under early colonial rule.

Other Andean strategies required ethnic lords to reorganize and reorient communal labor on the *chacras de comunidad* in order to meet tribute demands of the *encomenderos.* According to Ramírez, in the northern highlands of Peru and Ecuador, caciques were forced into entrepreneurial roles to meet their communal tributary quotas. Not infrequently, they marketed surplus crops and accumulated monies—presumably to cover future tribute debts. But Ramírez argues that such practices did not signal economic assimilation. Compared to the southern zones where silver mining and commercial overland traffic were already changing the economic landscape by the 1560s, the north remained off the beaten track, at least for a while. Although Spanish commerce was introduced early on, along with multiple royal regulations designed to enforce tributary relations, trade and markets were confined mainly to coastal ports and to a few central highland towns in Ecuador. The "enclave" nature of the northern markets was a far cry from the wholesale reorientation of the southern highlands around the pulsating markets of the mining towns. As a result, Ramírez shows, the early experiences of trade and commerce were limited primarily to ethnic lords. This situation was to change gradually, under the impact of massive Indian migration, divestiture of communal lands, and decay of ethnic authority structures during the seventeenth and eighteenth centuries. In much of the Ecuadorian sierra, for example, a resilient Spanish hacienda/manufactory complex changed the rural landscape of power by the mid-seventeenth century. By contrast, in southern Peru and Bolivia, where Andeans trafficked in mining town markets since early colonial times, most highland Indians nevertheless continued to inhabit freeholding communities until well into the nineteenth century. These divergent paths of north-south colonial development plead for broad comparative approaches rooted in the subsoil of precolonial ethnic formations north and south of the *páramo*. The Ramírez study of the northern Andes is a call to arms.[40]

With Saignes's chapter on indigenous society in seventeenth-century Charcas (Bolivia), the book again shifts its regional focus to the south and moves onto a broader temporal plane. Saignes sketches a fluid and intricate picture of Andean peoples' improvising economic and political strategies to offset the pressures of tribute, *mita,* and population decline. A central concern is the apparent dispersion and decline of Indian villages due to the outmigration of Indian male tributaries (*hatun runas*)—those responsible for paying tributary and labor dues to the colonial state. Saignes shows, for example, that tributaries used a variety of tactics to avoid their colonial obligations, often by abandoning their ayllus of origin and passing into the fiscal ranks of *yanacona* or mestizo. Women often played a vital role in this process, by "disappearing" their sons or husbands at the time royal inspections were taken or at baptism. Official demographic statistics tell part of the story, for while the tributary population dwindled, sex ratios became sharply imbalanced in many Indian villages of Charcas. As Saignes makes clear, however, that is only part—and perhaps the most familiar part—of the story. Migratory routes also circled back to the original community, and caciques themselves often sent colonists to forge new vertical trading relations with maize cultivators on the eastern slopes. Thus, Saignes tries to dispel lingering assumptions that Andean migration and resettlement signaled the abrupt rupture of kin ties or the meltdown of highly differentiated subcultures into one seamless category of "Indian" peasantry. He seeks to understand how slowly disintegrating ethnic groups struggled to achieve social reintegration and how, in the process, they reordered the social and ideological bases of ethnic community, hierarchy, and identity.[41]

Methodologically, several authors argue for conceptual approaches that explore the entanglements between Indians' commercial initiatives and traditional Andean relations (see especially chapter 3). How did ayllus accommodate tributary and commodity pressures and needs? How, and with what longer-term consequences, did specific ethnic groups simultaneously manipulate fiscal and tributary categories, move in and out of commodity relations, and reinvent "traditional" forms of barter and trade with long-term vertical trading partners in response to evolving market pressures and colonial policies? With a critical eye on the problems of historical sources and interpretations, Stern's provocative essay provides a methodological road map into the ambiguities of colonial life. He argues that those very ambiguities underlay a "Colonial Andean logic" that made calculated use of both kinship and commercial strategies.

While most case studies in this book do not encompass such general questions, they draw attention to the particular ways that Andean peoples struggled to preserve, or reconstitute, their access to diverse ecological regions through changing relations of transhumance, barter and trade, and migration. Such noncommodity forms of circulation continued to provide varying degrees of social insurance—and alternative commitments—against the vagaries of the market, uncertainties of climate, and extractive pressures of the state. On varying scales and through differing modalities, many Andean communities burst the bounds of the imposed nuclear village (*reducción*)—the strategic hamlet of Spanish colonialism—and reconstructed microvariations of the ancient vertical archipelago. These fragile, east-west vertical webs represented small, but significant, victories in the face of Viceroy Toledo's draconian efforts to redraw Andean cultural geography. While they were fragile and vulnerable to the punishing cycles of epidemic and drought in the highlands, they also served as defensive measures against the most threatening European-colonial incursions during the late sixteenth and seventeenth centuries.

Andeans as Commodity Producers, Traders, and Entrepreneurs in Colonial and Postcolonial Markets

Second, these cases speak to the enduring presence of Andeans in local and regional markets. Several articles give glimpses of Andean mercantile initiatives that put the lie to myths of Andean marginality or market resistance. As tributaries and *mitayos,* Indians spilled their sweat and blood into Spanish coffers, helping to build the world's richest and most powerful empire in the sixteenth century. Understandably, the historical spotlight has been on Indian labor in the silver and mercury mines, but in the shadows of Potosí, Indians also worked in artisanry, commerce, and trade; other Andean people colonized lands to promote cash-crop agriculture. It is this hidden side of Indian market participation that excites the historical imagination. If we peer beneath the iron arm of Toledo, we can begin to apprehend a mountainous land swarming with indigenous commodity producers, traders, and pack drivers. This is a promising vein of research: to trace the pathways to market traveled by those Aymara- and Quechua-speaking entrepreneurs who used their "comparative advantages" in the early colonial economy for their own individual and collective ends.

To be sure, then, Andean people controlled much of the overland trade and transport industry throughout the southern Andes in the early colonial decades, but our field of vision clouds up and fragments for the late colonial period. Some of the historical literature on the eighteenth century has tended to imply the gradual withdrawal of Indian traders and pack drivers from the center to the margins of the maturing colonial economy. This line of reasoning runs along the axis of regional specialization, hacienda growth, and creole merchant monopolies, which gradually assumed control over most overland trade in colonial products. In the meantime, petty commerce and the carriage trade nurtured a growing plebian subculture of mestizo ruffians, those who rose up in scattered, urban riots against Bourbon efforts to raise commercial taxes in the 1770s and early 1780s. According to this trajectory, Indians were slowly and silently dislodged from colonial overland trade and commerce.[42]

Other historical studies, more directly focused on the deteriorating economic conditions and political climate predating the massive Indian uprisings of 1781, have examined the coercive machinery of the internal market that enforced the distribution of commodities (*el repartamiento de mercancías*) among peasant households in Indian villages. Few historians argue that this distribution functioned as the primary "motor force" of the internal market of eighteenth-century Peru and Bolivia,[43] but most agree that the shifting global and local conditions conspired to create a political climate of coerced commerce in many parts of the rural Andes.[44] The use of political threat and violence to squeeze mercantile profit from unwilling peasant consumers required local interethnic alliances to be forged, however precariously, between the Spanish purveyors of compulsory goods and local intermediaries. Inevitably, ethnic authorities were plunged into situations of potential conflict and strife—more often than not among their own kinsmen and tributaries, as the case of Tapacarí shows (see Chapter 8).

What we clearly lack, however, is a sense of the global parameters of indigenous participation in, and even control over, interregional trade circuits and transport in the second half of the eighteenth century. Although several regional studies have unearthed evidence of robust local peasant economies engaged in commodity production and trade,[45] our stereotype of the period invokes images of the Indian-as-victim, enduring the intensifying pressures of coerced commerce, Bourbon tax hikes, and hacienda encroachment until the lid blew off in the Indian uprisings of 1781. In an initial effort to move beyond such stereotypes, Enrique Tandeter and his coauthors (Chapter 7) sketch a picture of the relative importance of Indian involvement in long-distance trade and commerce in the late eighteenth century. Through painstaking analysis of various quantitative records, Tandeter et al. "deconstruct" the product market at Potosí in order to gauge the magnitude, character, and origins of imported goods, and their traders, in 1793. While it is clear that commerce at Potosí had diminished since the decades of peak silver production in the early colonial period, the study makes a strong case for reconsidering the status of Potosí as a great mining center and market in the interior of the Andes at the end of the colonial era. By then, the Atlantic port of Buenos Aires had virtually replaced the Pacific port of Arica as the gateway for 80 percent of overseas trade. But the authors find that, in spite of the aggressive Bourbon trade reforms, European goods composed only a quarter of the registered value of trade imported to Potosí in the sample year of 1793. The bulk of Potosí's imported goods still came from regional Andean economies, including the traditional provisioning regions of lower Peru. Further, the authors show that a considerable sector of that trade was handled by small-scale and occasional traders. In fact, merchant capital exercised only limited control over colonial imports to Potosí. While precise global estimates are not possible on the basis of the available evidence, the study makes ingenious use of a historical anomaly—the fact that for a certain time period Potosí authorities did not allow Indian traders to claim the customary exemption from sales taxes (*alcabalas*) on native goods—to argue that a multitude of Indian and mestizo traders supplied the city with a wide range of commodities.

As a piece, the case studies on the colonial period take us a long way from earlier notions of colonialism as a system that reduced Indians to rural autarky. Gone are the images of the colonial Andean state as an iron arm of conquest, erecting caste barriers to create stable, nucleated villages of impoverished Indians out of the surviving native population. For while the colonial state imposed strict limits on indigenous engagement in Spanish markets, the changing imperatives of the colonial economy weakened state policies regulating indigenous commerce, land sales, and labor, as well as, simultaneously, opened spaces for indigenous commercial initiatives. Thus, most of these studies raise questions about the social consequences of Indian subsistence strategies for local and supralocal power relations and balances. Whether the focus is on the growing circuitry of interethnic trade in the mid-sixteenth century (Chapter 4), Andean flight and dissimulation before colonial authorities in the seventeenth century (Chapter 6), the massive involvement of Indian and mestizo traders at Potosí in the eighteenth century (Chapter 7), or the fierce intravillage struggles between peasants and caciques over communal rights and responsibilities under pressures of coerced commerce (Chapter 8), these cases argue for reconsidering the multifaceted ways that Andean kinship, market, and migratory strategies affected the evolution of colonial norms and institutions at different historical moments.

Further, they make an implicit case for broader, comparative analyses of Andean economic and cultural adaptations to mercantile colonialism. In general terms, the ethnic communities of the southern Andes probably enjoyed a greater degree of subsistence autonomy and flexibility than did native peasantries in northern Peru and Ecuador, or for that matter, throughout much of central Mexico. Why was that the case? This question feeds into a variety of demographic, cultural, and economic issues beyond the scope of this book. But it is clear that in the southern highlands many Andean communities participated in commodity markets within the parameters of kin-based economies, and they sometimes did so to considerable advantage, particularly during early colonial times. The camelid-based societies of the altiplano are a case in point.[46] From the 1560s,

Aymara herding peoples moved the bulk of the silver and other commodities across the vast interior of the Andes and down to the coastal ports, linking up far-flung indigenous communities to the evolving global economic order. The llama caravan trades created possibilities for indigenous investment in specialized branches of trade (coca, salt, and livestock products, for example) and for controlling crucial triangular trade routes in the southern and central Andes, at least until the eighteenth century. Even during the eighteenth century, when overseas trade and overland transport was reoriented to the port of Buenos Aires (and Argentine livestock ranches sprang up to serve the commercial traffic between the port and Alto Perú), Indian traders still provisioned the colonial cities of the Andes. Further, the existence of large herds of alpaca and llama on high steppes and the upper reaches of the sierra effectively shielded highland communities from the spread of Spanish ranches and haciendas. As market conditions changed, many highland Indian communities gradually shifted from llama and alpaca herding to sheep and cattle. This adaptation of the pastoral/agricultural matrix allowed them to hold onto their pastures and herds and to accumulate marketable stock as a form of social insurance. Overall, highland pastoralists maintained communal control over pastures and cropland, such that, as Nils Jacobsen has noted elsewhere, even by the late eighteenth century, "the extension of the *mancha india* was practically identical with what may be called the *mancha cameloida* both stretching from Huancavelica southward through High Peru."[47] Without trying to collapse the issues into a formulaic explanation (camelid pastoralism = communal landholding = Indian community survival), this observation suggests the importance of reconsidering the long-term, strategic advantages and adaptive vitality of indigenous pastoral-based economies.

It also raises implications about Andean adaptation to postcolonial regional and export markets. In a recent essay Paul Gootenberg argued that in the postindependence years, "many early economic developments positively enhanced Indian circuits and cultures, inversely to the decay of core Hispanic mining, market, and urban pursuits."[48] Particularly interesting is the emerging picture of resurgent Indian trade and commerce during the 1830s, 1840s, and 1850s as silver and wool exports revived, but before British mercantile capital reorganized the wool export trade around the turn of the twentieth century. In the early republican economies of Peru and Bolivia, Andean pastoral-agricultural communities played a critical role in supplying llamas, foodcrops, fuel, and wool to the fledgling export sectors. They also organized inland economic space around several great annual fairs that flourished at the crossroads of Indian trade, migration, and pilgrimage. During the de facto protectionism of the early republican decades, mestizo and creole merchant/middlemen remained fairly marginal to the fairs, as Andean traders themselves set the cultural terms of market etiquette.[49] Tristan Platt's chapter (Chapter 9) on the Lipes of Bolivia's southern puna suggests the relative power of Andean communities to set the terms of their own involvement in regional labor and product markets around the mid-nineteenth century.

If the Andean presence remained central to the scope, rhythms, and ethics of rural market exchange until well into the nineteenth century, when was the historical break—the moment of Polanyi's "great transformation," when regional markets no longer served as sites of "material-means provisioning" for most Andean peasants, but came to represent instead the onslaught of economic and political forces? When did the balance and terms of commodity exchange shift sharply, perhaps irreversibly, against most Andean peasants? Most historians chart this sea change in the period between the War of the Pacific and the Great Depression—that is, between 1880 and 1930. It was a time when modernizing export markets and nation-states began to clamp down on Andean juridical, economic, and cultural autonomies, by redefining the terms under which Indians would be integrated into the nation-state and the market. While none of the authors focus directly on the transformative impact of liberalism and market penetration on Andean material and cultural lifeways, these issues are taken up in the book's concluding essay on ethnic identity and market relations (Chapter 12).

Olivia Harris identifies the late nineteenth and early twentieth centuries as a key historical moment in the transformation of caste categories (with their ascribed ethnic obligations, rights, and jurisdictions) into a complicated bundle of class relationships. In the emerging liberal-positivist discourses, the "Indian" was reconfigured into an impoverished, hapless, illiterate, and uncivilized subject (a far cry from their illustrious Inca ancestors), who remained on the margins of the market economy, neither interested in nor capable of mercantile initiative or productive enterprise. Of course, the naturalization of the Indian as an immiserated creature living beyond the pale of civilization both reflected, and legitimated, erosive economic changes unleashed around the turn of the twentieth century. Liberal land and tax reforms that divested native Andeans of their traditional rights to communal lands, tax exemptions, and judicial privileges; free-trade policies and ideologies that opened the interior highlands to cheap foreign wheat and other products which, in turn, dislodged traditional Andean suppliers and traders from regional markets; and the spread of scientific racism (in all its variants) that converted Indians into biological subjects incapable of promoting, or sharing in, Order and Progress—all converged to undercut earlier Andean modes of adaptation and struggle, livelihood and resistance. In the various schemes of nation-builders, Indians were to be converted from landholding tributaries into low-cost laborers for the nations' mines and plantations, or into precarious rural laborers on modernizing haciendas. But whatever economic niche they might occupy, Indians were now destined to take their place as their nations' underclasses. This ideological and economic shift toward modern capitalist market-building radically altered the terms under which Andean peoples struggled to negotiate their own economic integration into regional and export economies.

Contested Meanings and Moralities of Commodity Exchange

If this book tries to integrate Indians into the broader history of market and state formation in different historical periods, it also burrows deep into particular Andean communities as they negotiated the meanings and moralities of mercantile exchange and accumulation. Rooting the study of Andean market strategies in dynamic local cultural contexts, most authors place more analytic weight on local institutions, values, and identities than on individual motivations or enterprise. On the other hand, these studies go some distance toward analyzing the cultural and social dynamics at work within Andean communities and households, as Andeans devised migratory and market strategies under diverse regional/historical circumstances. Because commodity production had the potential power to transform the labor process, property rights, and power relations, the Andean community and household often became nested terrains of cultural conflict. For, as David Lehmann has pointed out, it is one thing to examine "the use of kinship as a language to formulate social obligations, that is, as ideology," it is quite another to take for granted "its effectiveness as a principle of organization."[50]

In the pieces by Thierry Saignes (Chapter 6) and Marisol de la Cadena (Chapter 11), we can see the eruption of power struggles within local Andean households and communities, triggered in part by the outmigration of Indian men in two different historical contexts. In seventeenth-century highland Bolivia, indigenous households and communities were often at odds over tributary strategies—with hatun runa fleeing to distant eastern valleys to evade communal obligations (tribute, mita, etc.), and their caciques plotting various ways to contain the human hemorrhaging of their highland ayllus and reduce the tribute quotas they owed the colonial state. By the early seventeenth century, such intra-ayllu conflicts often escalated into major jurisdictional disputes between highland and valley caciques over tributaries and lands in the eastern maize valleys. At base, these conflicts had to do with the politics of ethnic identity and communal loyalty, which sharpened as tributary burdens grew heavier and as ethnic and colonial lords tried to contain Andean mobility. At the other end of the historical spectrum in contemporary Cuzco, de la Cadena examines the micropolitics of gender, ethnic, and class relations in the peasant village of Chitapampa, located a short distance from the city of Cuzco. She shows how men and women's differential access to the urban economy and dominant culture has reinforced the social basis of gender inequality in this community. Chitapampas's migratory, wage-earning men acquire many of the material and cultural accoutrements of social mobility (cash, a modicum of Spanish literacy, urban contacts, commodities, experience, and so on). In many ways, they have begun to challenge ethnic and class relations of domination by moving into the urban orbit of Cuzco. Indeed, they frame their experiences of social and geographic mobility and empowerment in ethnic terms: they say they are becoming "mestizo." But de la Cadena also explores the ramifications for peasant women left behind in the village, toiling on family plots of land. This narrative is enriched by multiple layers of irony, a central one that, as inheritance customs and the diversifying peasant economy thrust more agricultural work into the hands of women, in effect liberating peasant men to migrate cityward, the cultural value of women's work has declined. Their deteriorating status in Chitapampa is no better expressed by the commonplace that peasant women are "more Indian" than their menfolk.

Several of these studies, then, puncture the smooth analytical surfaces of communal, peasant, household economy to capture some sense of intra-Andean power struggles and cultural conflicts surrounding peasant strategies of livelihood and resistance. As Saignes hints, one route into the intimate interior of local Andean political culture is through the rifts opened by litigious struggles over lands, taxes, and—perhaps most enlightening—the legitimacy of caciques claiming the labor and loyalty of the community. Since the early pathbreaking work of Karen Spalding, historians of the colonial Andes have tried to track caciques in their myriad pursuits and as the pointmen in the colonial economy—empowered by the state to enforce extractive policies and yet entrusted by the community to meet or contest those imposed obligations.[51] The enormous legal apparatus, and the codification of Indian rights under colonial rule, provided room for political manuever and contestation, so that Andean lords were often thrust into judicial politics that may or may not have implicated their own moral standings in their communities. In any case, the long, rich tradition of Andean litigation under colonial rule provides one window (albeit an opaque one) on Andean discursive struggles in the distant past. In the ethnographic present, of course, oral testimony and participant observation supplement legal (or other forms of documentary) evidence of intra-Andean conflicts, allowing the observer ample opportunity to shift the locus of analysis to different social or discursive domains. While colonial historians are usually confined in their studies of intra-Andean conflicts to what got thrashed out (and recorded) in the courts or in rare moments of insurgent violence, ethnohistorians of the recent past can use oral history and participant observation to reconstruct implicit cultural understandings at the level of everyday practice and popular discourse.

Here the case of Tapacarí comes to light. Rosario León and I (Chapter 8) bring together our research in history and ethnography to draw sharp contrasts between the social character and consequences of market relations in the mountainous region of Tapacarí, situated to the west of the Cochabamba valleys, in the eighteenth and twentieth centuries. Where eighteenth-century historical sources, particularly the long-term legal cases, open perspectives on the contested legitimacy of caciques and the immorality of extractive institutions in Tapacarí, twentieth-century ethnographic analysis zeroes in on the microscopic politics of exchange in Tapacarí's outlying peasant markets. These contrasting perspectives do not intend to "trace" the long-term evolution of market relations in Tapacarí. But, juxtaposed, they suggest that postcolonial political transformations—specifically, the deinstitutionalization of the royal Indian village of Tapacarí and the fragmentation of power—have relaxed municipal control over the outlying highland *estancias* and allowed them freer access to mercantile exchange. From the perspective of bilingual (Spanish-Quechua) "mestizo" merchants, transporters, and landowners of the river valley town, twentieth-century Tapacarí is a rural backwater whose golden age passed with the colonial period. Indeed, the entire river valley (once a trade corridor to the altiplano) has lost its commercial and political vitality. But the "break-away" mountain hamlets have gained more autonomy and, in recent decades, reconfigured a system of rotative, weekly markets where Aymara and Quechua-speaking traders predominate. This sharp contrast between the extractive economy of eighteenth-century Tapacarí and the decentralization of peasant markets in recent times cautions against broad teleological notions of progressive market penetration and dislocation in the southern highlands.

If we shift the ethnogeographic focus slightly southward toward the ayllus in the Department of Northern Potosí, we can appreciate the active, creative force of local cultural norms that mediated, and often blunted, the raw edges of market incursion and class differentiation. The complex hierarchies of these ayllus dramatically defy prevailing notions about "traditional peasant economies" poised on the margins of the market. For while they still circulate goods between valley and puna through kinship networks, they have moved in and out of mining-based regional markets since early colonial times. In the early nineteenth century, the ayllus of Northern Potosí "were considered among the richest Indians of Bolivia . . . those most able to support the burden of tribute on which state finances depended." [52] They supplied wheat and other goods to distant urban markets, to coca plantations in the yungas, and to towns along the Pacific coast. Andean commerce complemented, but never displaced, traditional trading alliances that moved crops, salt, and livestock between valley and puna, however.

In this volume, Platt (Chapter 9) shifts his site of study from the punas and valleys of northern Potosí to the arid western province of Lipes. His aim is to make cultural sense of the Lipes's calculated ambivalence toward regional market activity. He shows us how commodity production was strictly adjusted to the seasonal rhythms and demands of ayllu agriculture, transhumance, and tribute collections. Yet the ayllus also supplied pack drivers and llama caravans, wheat, and seasonal wage work to the nearby mining towns, and cash-earning opportunities expanded in the mid-nineteenth century. But Platt shows that the ayllus' economic decision-making was governed less by fluctuating price incentives than by their commitment to their annual trading journeys into the eastern maize valleys. To break it would jeopardize their privileged access to temperate valley resources at relatively constant rates of exchange. Accumulative strategies made collective sense only in certain moments of the community's ceremonial and agricultural year. This inquiry into the "ethnic value of labor time" flatly contradicts premises about Andean market resistance, but it also probes the complex cultural logic of ambivalent market relations among the Lipes communities.[53]

Olivia Harris (Chapter 10) charts a different route into local cultural meanings in her study of the contemporary Laymis of northern Potosí. Building on an earlier generation of anthropologists who studied folk notions of money and wage work, Harris explores the multiple symbolic functions that money serves in the economic and ritual life of the Laymis. Like other ayllus in the region, the Laymis continue to practice transhumance and barter. Yet they have also engaged in cash-based markets since colonial times. At the intersection of kinship, tributary, and market economies, the Laymis inscribe ambivalent values and meanings in money—it is an artifact and a metaphor, but as a medium of exchange, money has limited use. The Laymis use cash to purchase livestock and ritual materials, make symbolic payments of tribute to state authorities, and facilitate exchange between close kin in remote rural sites. In fact, the Laymis accept cash reluctantly, usually as a favor to a close relative or friend. In the countryside, they prefer to conduct barter transactions, measured by bulk at relatively constant rates of exchange. Not only do monetary values fluctuate, but Laymis traders have to travel long distances to spend cash. The value of coin in Laymi ritual practices is much less ambivalent, however. Rich in ontological, political, and historical meanings, coins are associated with the fertility of lands, herds, and mines, and they symbolize the Laymis' mythic tributary pact with the Bolivian state. In this striking example of Andean cultural assimilation of the most Western of all symbols, money itself, Harris shows how its protean nature goes to the heart of Laymi cosmology and historical memory.

Ethnic Identity and Market Participation

As its title suggests, this collection explores the dynamic interaction between ethnic identity (and self-identity) and market relations in colonial and postcolonial regional economies. By "ethnicity," we mean a social construction that is rooted in concrete historical experiences and struggles at the intersection of material conditions, social practice, and consciousness. Put simply, "it is one way (among others) in which people define themselves and are defined by others who [may] stand in opposition to them."[54] Ethnicity, of course, may serve both hegemonic or popular functions: it may subjugate or empower, or it may simply set the ideological parameters of power-laden negotiations or conflicts among different classes or power blocs.

This book approaches interlocking issues of ethnic identity and market relations from various vantage points. In the concluding synthesis, Harris (Chapter 12) examines the changing hegemonic functions of colonial-ethnic categories of "Indian" and "mestizo" to structure, constrain, and subordinate Andean peoples to the political economy dictates of the state. She shows how these ontological European inventions were designed to circumscribe the economic, social, and political freedom of indigenous peoples, to set them apart from the emerging civil society under the tutelage of the Crown and church, and to maintain a reserve labor force for the patrimony of the state.

As cultural *mestizaje* became commonplace in the late colonial period, Indians and mestizos came to mean different things in the mental schema of colonial elites. Until the mid-nineteenth century, Indianness was still predominantly a juridical and fiscal category inscribed in colonial (or neo-colonial) policy, law, and ideology; it did not fully crystallize into a biological or class category until around the turn of the twentieth century. By then, racialist ideologies—the rigid bipolarization of non-Europeans into Indians and mestizos—had invested the Indian with biological and class attributes, suitable for rationalizing Andean disenfranchisement. The

Indian became the immiserated victim of feudal exploitation (according to *indigenistas*), and simultaneously the obstacle to development (according to liberal-positivists). As imposed ethnic difference became synonymous with class hierarchy, the mestizo emerged as the preeminent rural predator, commercial agent, and source of national shame. To this day, Indian and mestizo are labels attached, respectively, to rural, subsistent peasant and semiurban, commercial middlemen. To be "Indian" today is to be rural, poor, and antimarket.

In Andean rural society, negotiations over ethnic self-representations have been the stuff of everyday peasant politics since colonial times. Historians have long recognized that resurgent "Indianness" (that is, the juridical and discursive struggle to reclaim one's communal or indigenous identity in order to recover lost colonial rights) was a weapon of the weak in the postindependence period.[55] Less understood, however, are the changing social bases and politics of popular self-other distinctions in everyday social practice—in the quotidian battlefields of rural markets, city streets, government chambers, and peasant communities. In rural Andean society, class relations and economic status continue to be inscribed in ethnic and racial differences, but everyday understandings and discourses of self, other, and society vary by region, situation, and interlocutor, and they rarely collapse into rigid racial bipolarities (Indian versus mestizo, or Indian versus white).[56]

Rural Andeans often use more subtle forms of discrimination that combine ethnic, gender, class, and regional criteria to sort out and evaluate power relations in the marketplace, village, city, and elsewhere. In many parts of Peru and Bolivia, for example, Quechua-speaking women traders who frequent rural markets encode their own identities (and that of others) by their hats, woven *aguayos,* and seed bags. These ethnic and village markers are crucial for establishing their position and legitimacy in the rural marketplace, which is a highly ritualized space in Andean rural society in which commodities, kinship, and power relations are played out. Ethnic, village, and class identities intersect in ways to map boundaries and (de)legitimate hierarchies within which peasant traders negotiate and bargain over the terms of exchange (see Chapter 8). Under the threat of aggressive market (and/or state) pressures, a shared sense of ethnic identity can serve as a weapon in the everyday struggle for control over lands and fair market exchange. But rural Andeans, of course, do not always nurture ethnic identity to reinforce class or communal solidarity against outside threats. As de la Cadena shows (Chapter 11), ethnic-racial issues also surface within peasant communities, and even households, to advance individual interests or legitimate patriarchal power. Alternatively, local gender ideologies mediate different forms of market integration by peasant men and women. Peasant families may have collective "livelihood strategies," but Andean women and men do not necessarily move into the market at the same pace, in the same ways, or with the same social or cultural consequences. In some parts of the Bolivian altiplano, for example, peasant women have moved into prominent economic positions within their communities and households as itinerant traders, urban market women, and creditors. In the eyes of their own rural kinsmen, they have become "*cholas*" (part Indian, part mestizo), empowered by their mercantile savvy and far-flung kinship and mercantile networks. But if we look closely at the dynamics of ethnic and gender identity in rural Andean villages, the picture is much bleaker for the women "left behind." In the Cuzco village of Chitapampa, for example, peasant men regularly migrate to the city, while their women stay home to till the soil, becoming ever more rustic and "Indian" in the process. Much more research is needed in this area—particularly on the engendering of ethnic identity in specific regional and sectoral economies[57] and the historically and regionally specific meanings and processes of *mestizaje* and *cholaje*.[58] We still have much to study about the social sinews of Andean regional economies: the swollen, overlapping sectors of intermediaries who emanated from, and tenuously connected, the disparate cultural and economic fragments of Andean society.

If this book offers a rich tapestry of Andean case studies, it also tries to locate them in broader historical contexts of colonial and postcolonial domination. But it does not argue away the central historiographical paradox discussed at the beginning of this chapter: namely, the reproduction and transformation of Andean ayllus and lifeways in the midst of vigorous, fluctuating regional and mining markets. Rather, it inverts the paradox, by exploring the adaptive vitality of Andean livelihood strategies and their wide-ranging impact on the formation and transformation of interior regional markets, states, and agrarian ethnic/class relations. The authors pay particular attention to the diverse histories of local Andean political cultures, as they improvised and partially accommodated a changing, often hostile, world. Our effort to counterbalance historical synthesis and case study sets a methodological agenda for studying ethnicity markets and migration in the Andes across disciplinary boundaries. It charts the way toward capturing local Andean perspectives on markets and money, tribute and labor, property and patriarchy. If we now recognize that rural Andean peoples fundamentally shaped historical processes of market expansion and state formation, we have only begun to explore how local peasantries and their lords continually reconstructed cultural meanings and identities, as they moved into (or sometimes, out of) the orbit of regional and world markets.

Notes

1. The initiative was taken by Olivia Harris and Enrique Tandeter, following a lively seminar at the Institute of Latin American Studies, where Tandeter presented a paper on eighteenth-century trends in agricultural production, prices, and tithes in Alto Perú. The paper was subsequently published: Enrique Tandeter and Nathan Wachtel, *Precios y producción agraria: Potosí y Charcas en el siglo XVIII* (Buenos Aires, 1983); published in English as "Prices and Agricultural Production: Potosí and Charcas in the Eighteenth Century," in Lyman J. Johnson and Enrique Tandeter, eds., *Essays on the Price History of Eighteenth-Century Latin America* (Albuquerque, 1990), 201–276.

The term "Indian" is, of course, a social construction of the Spanish conquerors and colonizers. A generic category imposed by the Europeans on all native peoples of the Americas, it was eventually inscribed with jural, political, social, historical, and biological meanings—although those meanings were historically contingent, contested, and often contradictory. In recent years, anthropologists and historians (including many of the contributors to this volume) have explored specific political and discursive struggles over the definition and significance of "Indian" and, more broadly, the duality between "Indian" and "mestizo" (see Chapter 12). Increasingly, scholars are interested in local Andean strategies of representation, particularly popular understandings and self-conscious uses of racial and ethnic identities for purposes of collective action.

2. The Joint Committee on Latin American Studies sent a circular in 1980 to many leading Latin Americanists, asking for their assessment of exciting recent developments in different areas of the field. Andean studies was identified as a promising field, just beginning to come of age. It was decided then to organize a research planning committee to prepare a proposal for a collaborative research

project in Andean history and anthropology. The document was drafted by Steve Stern and Brooke Larson, then discussed and revised by the research planning committee, which met at the Social Science Research Council in October 1981. The tripartite project, calling for three interrelated conferences, was entitled "Markets, Coercion, and Responses in the Andean World." We continue to be grateful to the Joint Committee and staff of the SSRC for its generous intellectual and financial support for this project.

3. See Steve J. Stern, ed., *Resistance, Rebellion, and Consciousness in the Andean Peasant World, 18th to 20th centuries* (Madison, 1987), and the Spanish-language edition, *Resistencia, rebelión y conciencia campesina en los Andes, siglos XVIII al XIX* (Lima, 1990). The second conference volume was published in Ecuador: Segundo Moreno Yañez and Frank Salomon, eds., *La reproducción y transformación de las sociedades andinas, siglos XVI–XX* (Quito, 1991), 2 vols.

4. Olivia Harris, Brooke Larson, and Enrique Tandeter, eds., *La participación indígena en los mercados surandinos: Estrategias y reproducción social, siglos XVI–XX* (La Paz, 1987). We are grateful to the Centro de Estudios de la Realidad Económica y Social (CERES) for their support and collaboration in this endeavor, and to our many colleagues in Bolivia who helped in the organization of the conference and publication of the collected essays.

5. This synoptic description of the "culminating achievement" of Andean societies is drawn from John V. Murra, "'El Archipiélago Vertical' Revisited," in Shozo Masuda, Izumi Shimada, and Craig Morris, eds., *Andean Ecology and Civilization: An Interdisciplinary Perspective on Andean Ecological Complementarity* (Tokyo, 1985), 3–13.

6. Marxist historiography turned against the earlier tide of cultural history to explain the enduring features of agrarian poverty and feudal-like relations of domination on haciendas. This scholarship rejected earlier explanations based on the putative historical legacy of Hispanic cultural traditions, ethos, or mentality to focus attention instead on the driving historical forces of mercantile exploitation introduced by the Europeans beginning in the sixteenth century. The first influential current of Marxist historical scholarship dates to the 1930s and 1940s. The pioneering work of Latin American scholars, such as Sergio Bagú, Caio Prado Jr., and Alexander Marchant, set the colonial economies of Latin America in the broader global context of mercantile colonialism and the expanding world market of Europe undergoing the transition to commercial capitalism. These perspectives were enriched and deepened in the 1960s by a new generation of Marxist historians. Deeply influenced by the social science critique of neoclassical economics and modernization theory, many historians and historically minded social scientists gave new emphasis to the external forces that constrained and distorted the internal processes of economic development in Latin America. These critical debates

came to be known generally as "dependency theory." For a painstaking and careful analysis of these historiographical traditions, see Steve Stern's article, "Feudalism, Capitalism, and the World-System in the Perspective of Latin America and the Caribbean," *American Historical Review* 93.4 (October 1988): 829–872; see also the subsequent interchanges between Immanuel Wallerstein and Stern, ibid., 873–897. Stern's article is reprinted in Frederick Cooper et al., *Confronting Historical Paradigms: Peasants, Labor, and the Capitalist World System in Africa and Latin America* (Madison, 1993), 23–83.

7. Following World War II, the scholarly community of anthropologists working in the Andean field became more international and diversified. In Peru, there was an abrupt shift toward field study of contemporary Andean peoples. Luís Valcarcel was responsible for much of this boost to ethnological research, but the pioneer of postwar Peruvian ethnological insight was José María Arguedas. The son of an itinerant highland lawyer, he grew up in a rural community and spent his life producing a rich literary opus in both Quechua and Spanish, as well as several monographs based on ethnographic methods of field research. In the United States, the postwar period in Andean studies was ushered in by the Smithsonian Institute's publication of the *Handbook of South American Indians* (1946). Much of the postwar ethnology was harnessed to policy goals or ideals of integrating indigenous peoples and fostering "development." But the most exciting developments in the field explored pre-Hispanic Andean societies on their own terms and took pains to divorce ethnographic and ethnohistorical study from the implicit developmentalist agenda of the day.

This assessment of field developments draws heavily on Frank Salomon's valuable review articles on Andean ethnology. For a synthetic overview of the field of Andean ethnology since colonial times, see Frank Salomon, "The Historical Development of Andean Ethnology," *Mountain Research and Development* 5.1 (1985): 79–98.

8. Ibid. See also Salomon, "Andean Ethnology in the 1970s: A Retrospective," *Latin American Research Review* 17.2 (1982): 75–128.

9. John V. Murra, "The Economic Organization of the Inca State," Ph.D. dissertation (University of Chicago, 1955). It was published in Spanish as *La organización económica del estado inca* (Mexico, 1978) and in English as Supplement 1 to *Research in Economic Anthropology* (Greenwich, Conn., 1979). See also his article "On Inca Political Structure," in Ronald Cohen and John Middleton, eds., *Comparative Political Systems: Studies in the Politics of Pre-industrial Societies* (New York, 1967), 339–353.

10. Many of these articles were collected and published in Murra, *Formaciones*

económicas y políticas del mundo andino (Lima, 1975). But see also his article, "La guerre et les rebellions dans l'expansion de l'état inka," *Annales ESC* 33 (1978): 927–935, reprinted as "The Expansion of the Inka State: Armies, War and Rebellions," in John V. Murra, Nathan Wachtel, and Jacques Revel, eds., *Anthropological History of Andean Polities* (Cambridge, 1986), 49–58. This volume is the English-language version of the important 1978 *Annales* issue devoted to recent, innovative studies in Andean ethnohistory.

11. See Murra, "An Aymara Kingdom in 1567," *Ethnohistory* 15.2 (1968): 115–151, republished in revised form in Murra, *Formaciones económicas y políticas*; Murra, "Aymara Lords and Their European Agents at Potosí," *Nova Americana* (Turin) 1 (1978): 231–244; and Murra, " 'Nos Hazen Mucha Ventaja': The Early European Perception of Andean Achievement," in Kenneth J. Adrien and Rolena Adorno, eds., *Transatlantic Encounters: Europeans and Andeans in the Sixteenth Century* (Berkeley, 1991), 73–89.

12. Felipe Guaman Poma de Ayala, *El primer nueva corónica y buen gobierno*, ed., John Murra and Rolena Adorno (Mexico, 1980), 3 vols.

13. One of the most fruitful areas of recent research in Andean studies is the crossing of literary and ethnohistorical perspectives on Andean thought and writing in the colonial period. See especially, Rolena Adorno, *Guaman Poma: Writing and Resistance* (Austin, 1986); Adorno, ed., *From Oral to Written Expression: Native Andean Chroniclers of the Early Colonial Period* (Syracuse, N.Y., 1982); and Frank Salomon and George L. Urioste, eds., *The Huarochirí Manuscript: A Testament of Ancient and Colonial Andean Religion* (Austin, 1991).

14. Murra, "El 'control vertical' de un máximo de pisos ecológicos en las economías de las sociedades andinas," in Iñigo Ortíz de Zúñiga, *Visita a la provincia de León de Huánuco* [1562] (Huánuco, 1972), 2:429–476; reprinted in Murra, *Formaciones económicas y políticas*.

15. See Frank Salomon's critical review articles on Andean ethnology and ethnohistory, cited above in notes 7 and 8. Also, his annotated bibliography of South American ethnohistory in the *Handbook of Latin American Studies* (Gainesville, 1986), 48:87–356.

16. Salomon, "Andean Ethnology in the 1970s," 91. Some of this ethnological work exploring modern analogues of "vertical archipelago" appeared in two anthologies, published in the 1980s: David Lehmann, ed., *Ecology and Exchange in the Andes* (Cambridge, 1982), and Shozo Masuda, Izumi Shimada, and Craig Morris, eds., *Andean Ecology and Civilization: An Interdisciplinary Perspective on Andean Ecological Complementarity* (Tokyo, 1985). An important, recent collection of essays that explores the interaction between values and market transactions

is Jonathan Parry and Maurice Bloch, eds., *Money and the Morality of Exchange* (Cambridge, 1989).

17. See the essays by Roderick Burchard, Glynn Custred, and Benjamin S. Orlove in Giorgio Alberti and Enrique Mayer, eds., *Reciprocidad e intercambio en los Andes peruanos* (Lima, 1974); Antoinette Fioravanti-Moliniè, "Reciprocidad y economía de mercado en la comunidad campesina andina: El ejemplo de Yucay," *Allpanchis Phuturinqa* (Cuzco) 5 (1973): 121–130; Frank Salomon, "Weavers of Otavalo," in Norman E. Whitten, Jr., ed., *Cultural Transformations and Ethnicity in Modern Ecuador* (Urbana, 1981): 162–210; Benjamin S. Orlove, *Alpacas, Sheep and Men: The Wool Export Economy and Regional Society in Southern Peru* (New York, 1977); Norman Long and Bryan Roberts, eds., *Peasant Cooperation and Capitalist Expansion in Central Peru* (Austin, 1978); and Judith-Maria Buechler, "Las negociantes-contratistas en los mercados bolivianos," *Estudios Andinos* 5.1 (1976): 57–76. Particularly interesting were the combined anthropological and historical studies of Jürgen Golte: *La racionalidad de la organización andina* (Lima, 1980) and *Repartos y rebeliones: Túpac Amaru y las contradicciones de la economía colonial* (Lima, 1980).

18. Salomon, "Andean Ethnology in the 1970s," 80. Salomon cites Leslie Brownrigg's 1973 preface to her bibliographic essay on South American ethnology for the *Handbook of Latin American Studies.* She argued that the thrust of recent ethnological work was toward the conceptual convergence of John Murra's work on vertical archipelago patterns and R. Tom Zuidema's structuralist analysis of Inca organization and thought in the search for unique social properties and cultural logics intrinsic to the Andean world.

19. For a brief overview of earlier Marxist historiography, see note 6. In the late 1960s, much of the hard-driving theoretical debate over agrarian change in Latin American gave a New World cast to an Old World Leninist/Chayanovian dialogue about the nature of the contemporary agrarian class structure and, more particularly, the peasant economy. Behind much of this research lurked the familiar ideological and political issues concerning the historical fate of the peasant class and its revolutionary potential in third world contexts of dependent capitalist development. The works of Mexican scholars, such as Roger Bartra, Arturo Warman, and Rodolfo Stavenhagen, defined much of the debate about Latin American peasant classes and agrarian transformations. But see also Alain de Janvry, *The Agrarian Question and Reformism in Latin America* (Baltimore, 1981). Other, more "mainstream" social science studies of peasant movements raised similar questions—for example, Henry Landberger, ed., *Latin American Peasant Movements* (New York, 1969).

20. For a first-rate review article on these intersecting debates, see Klaus Hey-

nig, "The Principal Schools of Thought on the Peasant Economy," *CEPAL Review* (April 1982): 113–139. Also helpful is Peter F. Klaren and Thomas Bossert, eds., *Promise of Development: Theories of Change in Latin America* (Boulder, Colo., 1976). For a helpful critical review of literature on peasant rebellion in the Andes and in Latin America, see Steve J. Stern, "New Approaches to the Study of Peasant Rebellion and Consciousness: Implications of the Andean Experience," in Stern *Resistance, Rebellion, and Consciousness,* 3–28, and William Roseberry, "Beyond the Agrarian Question in Latin America," in Cooper et al., *Confronting Historical Paradigms,* 318–368.

21. For example, José María Caballero, *Economía agraria de la sierra peruana antes de la Reforma Agraria de 1969* (Lima, 1981); Javier Iguinez, ed., *La cuestión rural en el Perú* (Lima, 1983); and Antonio Figueroa, *Capitalist Development and the Peasant Economy in Peru* (Cambridge, 1984).

22. This point is forcefully made in Stern's essay, "New Approaches to the Study of Peasant Rebellion and Consciousness," 15–17; see also Roseberry, "Beyond the Agrarian Question." There were important exceptions, as always. For example: Pierre Van Den Berghe and George Primov, *Inequality in the Peruvian Andes: Class and Ethnicity in Cuzco* (Columbia, Mo., 1977), and Aníbal Quijano, *Dominación y cultura: Lo cholo y el conflicto* (Lima, 1980).

23. The European roots of the debate over the transition from feudalism to capitalism in early modern Europe (c. 1450–1650) go back to the 1950s, with the publication in *Science and Society* of the Sweezey/Dobb debate over the nature of early capitalist development in England. (This series was reprinted in Rodney Hilton et al., *The Transition from Feudalism to Capitalism* [London, 1976].) A new generation of scholars reinvigorated the debate, on a broader scale with more attention to the "peripheral" regions of the third world. Keystone works included Immanuel Wallerstein's first volume of his global history of capitalism, *The Modern World-System: Capitalist Agriculture and the Origins of the European World-Economy in the Sixteenth Century* (New York, 1974), and T. H. C. Aston and C. H. E. Philpin, eds., *The Brenner Debates: Agrarian Class and Economic Development in Pre-Industrial Europe* (New York, 1985). Debates already flourished in Latin America, however. Several critical works circulated in the early and mid-1970s, among them Ernesto Laclau, "Feudalism and Capitalism in Latin America," *New Left Review* 67 (1971): 19–38; Carlos Sempat Assadourian et al., *Modos de producción en América Latina* (Mexico, 1973); and Marcello Carmagnani, *Formación y crisis de un sistema feudal* (Mexico, 1976). This literature framed many of the questions that Andean colonial historians posed to their own areas of research. See the stimulating discussion in Stern, "Feudalism, Capitalism, and the World-System."

24. Although these studies were resolutely empirical, they embraced issues of colonial domination and exploitation. The works of Carlos Sempat Assadourian stand out and will be discussed below. But also worth mentioning are the pioneering studies by Nathan Wachtel, *La visión des vaincus: Les Indiens du Pérou devant la conquête espagnol, 1530–1570* (Paris, 1971); Karen Spalding, *De indio a campesino: Cambios en la structura social del Perú colonial* (Lima, 1974); Robert G. Keith, *Conquest and Agrarian Change: The Emergence of the Hacienda System on the Peruvian Coast* (Cambridge, Mass., 1976); Nicolás Sánchez Albornoz, *Indios y tributos en el Alto Perú* (Lima, 1978); and Noble David Cook, *Demographic Collapse: Indian Peru, 1520–1620* (Cambridge, 1981).

25. See Assadourian's intervention in the Marxian debates over the nature of capitalism and exploitation in Latin America, in his article, "Modos de producción y subdesarrollo en América Latina," in Assadourian et al., *Modos de producción*, 47–81. His more empirical work on mining and mercantile exploitation, published in various journals in Latin America during the late 1960s and 1970s, is brought together in *El sistema de la economía colonial: Mercado interno, regiones y espacio económico* (Lima, 1982); see also the important article, "La producción de la mercancía dinero en la formación del mercado interno colonial: El caso del espacio peruano, siglo XVI," in Enrique Florescano, ed., *Ensayos sobre el desarrollo económico de México y América Latina (1500–1975)* (Mexico City, 1979), 223–292.

26. See the critique by Steve J. Stern, "New Directions in Andean Economic History: A Critical Dialogue with Carlos Sempat Assadourian," *Latin American Perspectives* 12.1 (1985): 133–148.

27. For example, Assadourian's model of internal "economic space," structured by the mining economy, was the basis for a collective research project in 1980, under the auspices of the Instituto de Estudios Peruanos. The project's aim was to study the articulation of diverse productive sectors and regions to the exigencies of the mining economy. Carlos Sempat Assadourian et al., *Minería y espacio económico en los Andes, siglos XVI–XX* (Lima, 1981). Many of the conceptual issues addressed by Assadourian also had resonance in other studies of the mining economy, such as Antonio Mitre, *Los patriarcas de la plata: Estructura socioeconómica de la minería boliviana en el siglo XIX* (Lima, 1981); Enrique Tandeter, *Coercion and Market: Silver Mining in Colonial Potosí, 1692–1826* (Albuquerque, 1993); José Deustua, *La minería peruana y la iniciación de la república, 1820–1840* (Lima, 1986). (However, two recent studies on Potosí mining diverge sharply from Assadourian's theoretical approach: see Peter J. Bakewell, *Miners of the Red Mountain: Indian Labor in Potosí, 1545–1650* (Albuquerque, 1984), and Jeffrey Cole, *The Potosí Mita, 1573–1700: Compulsory Indian Labor in the Andes* (Stanford, 1985). Assadourian's framework also influenced my own approach to regional agrarian change: see

Brooke Larson, *Colonialism and Agrarian Transformation in Bolivia: Cochabamba, 1550–1900* (Princeton, 1988), chs. 1–3; also the recent work on nineteenth-century trade circuits by Erick D. Langer: "Espacios coloniales y economías nacionales: Bolivia y el norte argentino," *Siglo XIX* 2 (1987): 135–160.

Assadourian's emphasis on the coercive nature of the early colonial economy was reinforced by Karen Spalding's important article, "Exploitation as an Economic System: The State and the Extraction of Surplus in Colonial Peru," in George A. Collier, Renato I. Rosaldo, and John D. Wirth, eds., *The Inca and Aztec States, 1400–1800* (New York, 1982), 321–342. Cf. Juan Carlos Garavaglia, *Mercado interno y economía colonial* (Mexico City, 1983).

28. See also Assadourian, "Dominio colonial y señores étnicos en el espacio andino," *HISLA: Revista Latinoamericana de Historia Económica y Social* (Lima) 1 (1983): 7–20, and Assadourian, "La crisis demográfica del siglo XVI y la transición del Tahuantinsuyo al sistema mercantil colonial," in Nicolás Sánchez Albornoz, ed., *Población y mano de obra en América Latina* (Madrid, 1985), 69–93.

29. Salomon, "Historical Development of Andean Ethnology," 87–88.

30. For example, the central theme of the important collection of articles in Lehmann, ed., *Ecology and Exchange* was formulated as follows: "In what ways has the impact of market penetration and capitalist development on peasant economy and haciendas in Andean countries been shaped by a heritage of political culture and the characteristics of ecology and climate?" (1). The introductory essay, however, then goes on to emphasize the cultural and ecological diversity of the Andean world.

31. This focus on "everyday forms" of subsistence/resistance became a dominant theme of study in many corners of the emerging, international field of peasant studies during the 1980s. Inspired largely by the work of James Scott on the theme, the *Journal of Peasant Studies* devoted a special issue on "Everyday Forms of Peasant Resistance in South-East Asia," 13 (January 1986). See also James C. Scott, *Weapons of the Weak: Everyday Forms of Peasant Resistance* (New Haven, 1985). Several other currents of scholarship fed the new interest in subaltern politics and resistance, particularly the new social history on European popular culture, moral economy, and community that sprang from the British Marxian scholarship of E. P. Thompson and others, and from the later *Annales* and post-*Annales* scholarship on peasant culture, religion and ritual, mentality, and everyday life. See Lynn Hunt, ed., *The New Cultural History* (Berkeley, 1989). New interest in Gramscian concepts of cultural hegemony and counterhegemony animated historical work in the Subaltern School of Indian scholarship, and Africanists also turned toward issues of peasant politics, culture, and consciousness during the 1980s. See David Arnold, "Gramsci and Peasant Subalternity in India," *Journal of Peasant Studies*

11.4 (1984): 155–177, and Allen Isaacman, "Peasants and Rural Social Protest in Africa," *Journal of African Studies* 33.2 (1990): 1–120, reprinted in Cooper et al., *Confronting Historical Paradigms*, 205–317.

32. See the pioneering essays of Karen Spalding, especially "Social Climbers: Changing Patterns of Mobility among the Indians of Peru," *Hispanic American Historical Review* 50 (1970): 645–664, and Spalding, "Kurakas and Commerce: A Chapter in the Evolution of Andean Society," *Hispanic American Historical Review* 53 (1973): 581–599. More recent studies include Luís Miguel Glave, "Trajines: Un capítulo en la formación del mercado interno colonial," *Revista Andina* (Cuzco) 1.1 (1983): 9–67, and Glave, *Trajinantes: Caminos indígenas en la sociedad colonial, siglos XVI–XVII* (Lima, 1989); Murra, "Aymara Lords and Their European Agents at Potosí"; Roberto Choque Canqui, "Los caciques aymaras y el comercio en el Alto Perú," in Harris et al., *Participación indígena*, 357–378; Silvia Rivera Cusicanqui, "El mallku y la sociedad colonial en el siglo XVII: El caso de Jesús de Machaca," *Avances* (La Paz) 1 (1978): 7–27; Tristan Platt, "Acerca del sistema tributario pre-toledano en el Alto Perú," ibid.: 33–44; Thierry Saignes, "Las etnías de Charcas frente al sistema colonial (siglo XVII), *Jahrbuch für Geschichte von Staat, Wirtschaft und Gesellschaft Lateinamerikas* (Cologne) 21 (1984): 27–75; and Steve J. Stern, "Paradigms of Conquest: History, Historiography, and Politics," *Journal of Latin American Studies* 24 (1992): 1–34.

33. For example, see Steve J. Stern, *Peru's Indian Peoples and the Challenge of the Spanish Conquest: Huamanga to 1640* (Madison, 1982); Karen Spalding, *Huarochirí: An Andean Society under Inca and Spanish Rule* (Stanford, 1984); Luís Miguel Glave and María Isabel Remy, *Estructura agraria y vida rural en una región andina: Ollantaytambo entre los siglos XVI y XIX* (Cuzco, 1983); Thierry Saignes, *Los Andes orientales: Historia de un olvido* (Cochabamba, 1985); Saignes, "Politique de recensement dans les Andes coloniales: Décroissance tributaire ou mobilité indigene?" *Histoire, Economie, Société* (Paris) 4 (1987): 435–468; Enrique Tandeter, "La producción como actividad popular: 'Ladrones de minas' en Potosí," *Nova Americana* (Turin) 4 (1981): 43–65; Tandeter, "Forced and Free Labor in Late Colonial Potosí," *Past and Present* 93 (1981): 98–136; Bakewell, *Miners of the Red Mountain;* Ann Zulawski, "Labor and Migration in Seventeenth-Century Alto Perú," Ph.D. dissertation (Columbia University, 1985); Nelson Manrique, *Colonialismo y pobreza campesina: Caylloma y el valle de Colca, siglos XVI–XX* (Lima, 1985); and Larson, *Colonialism and Agrarian Transformation in Bolivia*. Some of these studies served as empirical ammunition for Stern's critique of Wallerstein's thesis about the driving power of world capitalism to restructure economic life in the colonial hinterlands; see Stern, "Feudalism, Capitalism, and the World-System."

34. Landmark studies on Peru include Christine Hünefeldt, *Lucha por la tierra y*

protesta indígena: Las comunidades indígenas entre colonia y república (Bonn, 1982); Juan Martínez Alier, "Relations of Production in Andean Haciendas: Peru," in Kenneth Duncan and Ian Rutledge, eds., *Land and Labour in Latin America* (Cambridge, 1977), 141–164, and the earlier pioneering monograph by the same author, *Los huacchilleros del Perú* (Lima 1973); Florencia E. Mallon, *The Defense of Community in Peru's Central Highlands: Peasant Struggle and Capitalist Transition, 1860–1940* (Princeton, 1983); Alberto Flores Galindo, *Arequipa y el sur andino, siglos XVII–XIX* (Lima, 1977); Nelson Manrique, *Yawar Mayu: Sociedades terratenientes serranas, 1879–1910* (Lima, 1988); Manrique, *Mercado interno y región: La sierra central, 1820–1930* (Lima, 1987). On Bolivia, see Erwin P. Grieshaber, "Survival of Indian Communities in Nineteenth-Century Bolivia: A Regional Comparison," *Journal of Latin American Studies* 12.2 (1980): 223–269; Silvia Rivera Cusicanqui, *Oprimidos pero no vencidos: Luchas del campesinado aymara y quechwa* (La Paz, 1984); Rivera, "La expansión del latifundio en el altiplano boliviano," *Avances* (La Paz) 2 (1978): 95–118; Tristan Platt, *Estado boliviano y ayllu andino: Tierra y tributo en el norte de Potosí* (Lima, 1982); Platt, *Estado tributario y librecambio en Potosí durante el siglo XIX* (La Paz, 1986), and his articles, "Liberalism and Ethnocide in the Southern Andes," *History Workshop Journal* (London) 17 (1984): 3–18, and 'The Andean Experience of Bolivian Liberalism, 1825–1900: Roots of Rebellion in 19th-Century Chayanta (Potosí)," in Stern, *Resistance, Rebellion, and Consciousness,* 280–323; Xavier Albó, "From MNRistas to Kataristas to Katari," in ibid., 379–419; Victor Hugo Cárdenas, "La lucha de un pueblo," in Xavier Albó, ed., *Raíces de América: El mundo aymara* (Madrid, 1988), 495–532; and Erick D. Langer, *Economic Change and Rural Resistance in Southern Bolivia, 1880–1930* (Stanford, 1989). A fascinating synthesis of much of the historical literature on the nineteenth-century Andes and Mexico is Florencia E. Mallon's "Indian Communities, Political Cultures, and the State in Latin America," *Journal of Latin American Studies* 24 (1992): 35–53.

35. Salomon, "Ethnohistory: South America," 87. This effort to reconceptualize culture in Andean contexts parallels broader postmodernist concerns with putting "culture into motion," in the words of Renato Renaldo, and to emphasize different visions, voices, and vantage points of the historical actors themselves in the context of shifting power relations, historical experience, and consciousness of subordinated ethnic groups or classes in colonial or postcolonial societies. Such approaches to culture flow from several overlapping sources: ranging from symbolic and semiotic anthropology to neo-Marxist work on questions of cultural hegemony, popular culture, and subaltern consciousness. On the influence of poststructuralist approaches on the subdiscipline of ethnohistory (across culture zones), see Shepard Krech, "The State of Ethnohistory," *Annual Review of*

Anthropology 20 (1991): 345–375, and Emiko Ohnuki-Tierney, "Introduction: The Historicization of Anthropology," in E. Ohnuki-Tierney, ed., *Culture through Time: Anthropological Approaches* (Stanford, 1990). For a synoptic overview of poststructuralist research on popular culture and politics, see Terry Eagleton, *Ideology: An Introduction* (New York, 1991).

36. In particular, see Platt, *Estado boliviano y ayllu andino;* Joanne Rappaport, *The Politics of Memory: Native Historical Interpretation in the Columbian Andes* (Cambridge, 1990); Gavin A. Smith, *Livelihood and Resistance: Peasants and the Politics of Land in Peru* (Berkeley, 1989); Roger Rasnake, *Domination and Cultural Resistance: Authority and Power among an Andean People* (Durham, 1988); Nathan Wachtel, *Le retour des ancêtres: Les indiens urus de Bolivie, XXe–XVIe siècles* (Paris, 1990): María Lagos, *Autonomy and Power: The Dynamics of Class and Culture in Rural Bolivia* (Philadelphia, 1994); William Carter and Xavier Albó, "La comunidad aymara: Un mini-estado en conflicto," in Albó, *Raíces de América: El mundo aymara;* Heraclio Bonilla, ed., *Los Andes en la encrucijada: Indios, comunidades y estado en el siglo XIX* (Quito, 1991); and Moreno Yañez and Salomon, *Reproducción y transformación de las sociedades andinas.*

37. See the provocative article by Paul Gootenberg, "Population and Ethnicity in Early Republican Peru: Some Revisions," *Latin American Research Review* 26.3 (1991): 109–157. Also, Charles Walker, "La historiografía en inglés sobre los Andes: Balance de la decada del 80," *Revista Andina* 9.2 (1991): 513–528, and the various articles on the nineteenth and twentieth centuries in Stern, *Resistance, Rebellion, and Consciousness,* and in Alberto Flores Galindo, ed., *Comunidades campesinas: Cambios y permanencias* (Chiclayo, 1988).

38. See note 32. Worth mentioning here is the important 1982 article by Olivia Harris, where she first conceptualized the "ethnic economy." See her "Labour and Produce in an Ethnic Economy, Northern Potosí, Bolivia," in Lehmann, *Ecology and Exchange in the Andes.* Another early tribution toward the rethinking of Andean subsistence strategies is Frank Salomon, "The Dynamic Potential of the Complementarity Concept," in Masuda et al., *Andean Ecology and Civilization.* See also Manuel Chiriboga et al., *Estratégias de supervivencia en la comunidad andina* (Quito, 1984); Marisol de la Cadena, "Cooperación y mercado en la organización comunal andina," *Revista Andina* 4.1 (1986): 31–58; and Smith, *Livelihood and Resistance.*

39. Stern's essay goes on to explore the cultural dimensions of these fluid and flexible livelihood strategies and to raise pragmatic issues of historical methodology and sources for the study of Andean market initiatives and social reproduction in the early colonial period.

40. On northern colonial landscapes, see the early study of colonial Quito, John L. Phelan, *The Kingdom of Quito in the Seventeenth Century* (Madison, 1967); Robson Brynes Tyrer, "The Demographic and Economic History of the Audiencia of Quito: Indian Population and the Textile Industry, 1600–1800," Ph.D. dissertation (University of California at Berkeley, 1976); Karen Powers, "Indian Migrations in the Audiencia of Quito: Crown Manipulation and Local Cooptation," in David Robinson, ed., *Migration in Colonial Latin America* (Cambridge, 1990), 313–323; Powers, "Resilient Lords and Indian Vagabonds: Wealth, Migration, and the Reproductive Transformation of Quito's Chiefdoms, 1500–1700," *Ethnohistory* 38 (1991): 225–249; and the suggestive comparative sketches by Magnus Mörner, *The Andean Past: Land, Societies and Conflicts* (New York, 1985).

However, as Ramírez makes clear in her article (Chapter 5 in this volume) Andean north/south comparisons must be rooted in pre-Hispanic patterns of social organization and exchange. Although some evidence of modified archipelago patterns have been found for northern regions, the "classic models" drawn from the Lupaqa and Huanuco cases do not obtain for the regions north of the páramo. Frank Salomon's research, in particular, reveals a complex pattern of alliances among smaller, relatively decentralized chiefdoms in the north. See Salomon, *Native Lords of Quito in the Age of the Incas* (Cambridge, 1986). Rather than strive for vertical self-sufficiency, these northern polities used long-distance trade and diplomacy to maximize their outward reach and circulate goods from a wide variety of ecological zones. This fluid complex of entangling alliances among northern ethnic polities, the brisk maritime and overland traffic of people and goods, and the existence of a privileged corps of exchange specialists in some parts of Ecuador conspired to create false impressions among some European observers in the mid-sixteenth century. Hence, their confusion (and scholarly controversy) over whether markets and merchants predated the Conquest (see Chapters 2 and 5 in this volume).

41. Andean migration has attracted much recent attention among colonial historians. See especially, the work of Thierry Saignes, Noble David Cook, and Nicolás Sánchez Albornoz, cited above (notes 24 and 33), as well as Herbert S. Klein, "Hacienda and Free Community in Eighteenth-Century Alto Perú: A Demographic Study of the Aymara Population of the Districts of Chulumani and Pacajes in 1786," *Journal of Latin American Studies* 7.2 (1973): 193–220, and his book, *Bolivia: The Evolution of a Multi-Ethnic Society* (New York, 1982). More recent work includes Ann W. Wightman, *Indigenous Migration and Social Change: The Forasteros of Cuzco, 1570–1720* (Durham, 1990); Ann Zulawski, *"They Eat from Their Labor": Work and Social Change in Colonial Bolivia* (Pittsburgh, 1995);

the articles by Karen Powers on colonial Ecuador, cited above (note 39), and the collected volume, edited by David J. Robinson, *Migration in Colonial Spanish America* (Cambridge, 1990).

42. For example, historians have emphasized the central role that landowners and plantation owners (particularly the Jesuit estates of the Arequipa-coastal regions) played in supplying colonial cities with wines, *aguardiente,* and certain foodcrops; other Spanish haciendas, particularly in the Cuzco region and in the central highlands of Ecuador, specialized in commercial production of woolen cloth. See Nicolas P. Cushner, *Lords of the Land: Sugar, Wine and Jesuit Estates of Coastal Peru, 1600–1767* (New York, 1980); Glave and Remy, *Estructura agraria y vida rural en una región andina;* Magnus Mörner, *Perfil de la sociedad rural del Cuzco a fines de la colonia* (Lima, 1978); and Pablo Macera, "Feudalismo colonial americano: El caso de las haciendas peruanas," in Macera, *Trabajos de historia* (Lima, 1977), 3:139–227.

43. But see Golte, *Repartos y rebeliones.*

44. In a nutshell, several historians have argued that the long-standing practice of forcefully distributing goods (*repartos*) to Indian villages was legally instituted in the middle of the eighteenth century, in large part because of the deepening economic recession in the Peruvian viceroyalty and the inflated power and corruption of provincial colonial authorities. Suffering from the collapse of their overseas trade monopoly, Lima merchants increasingly sought investment/political alliances with the *corregidores* (and other colonial authorities), who would use their political power and authority to enforce the distribution of commodities among the Indian villages under their jurisdiction. This partnership benefited both parties: the merchant houses found an alternative mercantile outlet in the interior of Peru and Bolivia, while the corregidores could count on merchant loans in order to purchase their political office for a five-year term. In the meantime, the crown found the sale of *corregimientos* to be very lucrative. The system collapsed with the outbreak of the Túpac Amaru rebellion of 1781. For recent studies on the subject, see Golte, *Repartos y rebeliones;* Alfredo Moreno Cebrián, *El corregidor de indios y la economía peruana del siglo XVIII: Los repartos forzosos de mercaderías* (Madrid, 1977); Scarlett O'Phelan, *Un siglo de rebeliones anticoloniales: Perú y Bolivia, 1700–1783* (Cuzco, 1988); Spalding, *Huarochirí: Andean Society under Inca and Spanish Rule;* Larson, *Colonialism and Agrarian Transformation in Bolivia;* Stern, "The Age of Andean Insurrection, 1742–1782: A Reappraisal," in Stern, *Resistance, Rebellion, and Consciousness,* 34–93; Javier Tord, "El corregidor de indios del Perú: Comercio y tributos," *Historia y Cultura* (Lima) 8 (1974): 187–198; and Kenneth J. Adrien, *Crisis and Decline: The Viceroyalty of Peru in the Seventeenth Century* (Albuquerque, 1985).

45. See Platt, *Estado boliviano y ayllu andino;* María Cecilia Cangiano, *Curas, caciques y comunidades en el Alto Perú: Chayanta a fines del siglo XVIII* (Tilcara, 1987); Larson, *Colonialism and Agrarian Transformation in Bolivia;* Magdalena Chocano, *Comercio en Cerro de Pasco a fines de la época colonial* (Lima, 1982); Fernando Iasaki Cauti, "Ambulantes y comercio colonial: Iniciativas mercantiles en el virreynato peruano," *Jahrbuch für Geschichte von Staat, Wirtschaft und Gesellschaft Lateinamerikas* 24 (1987): 179–212; and Lyman L. Johnson and Enrique Tandeter, eds., *Essays on the Price History of Eighteenth-Century Latin America* (Albuquerque, 1990).

46. The camelid-based economies (and their gradual shift to sheep and cattle) provided many highland ethnic groups with strategic advantages in their interethnic trading relations (particularly with valley kinsmen and trading partners). Some ethnic groups managed to develop agricultural-pastoral modes of complementarity to reproduce, on a small scale, vertical ecological integration. More common in the southern highlands, however, was the articulation of high-altitude herding with tuber and maize zones at lower altitudes through bartering arrangements. For a synoptic discussion of the range of ethnographic studies on varieties of pastoral-agricultural complementarity in the Andes, see Frank Salomon, "Andean Ethnology in the 1970s," 78–79. In particular, see the key work, Jorge Flores Ochoa, ed., *Pastores de puna: Uywamichiq Punarunakuna* (Lima, 1977).

47. Nils Jacobsen, "Livestock Complexes in Late Colonial Peru and New Spain: An Attempt at Comparison," in Nils Jacobsen and Hans-Jürgen Puhle, eds., *The Economies of Mexico and Peru during the Late Colonial Period* (Berlin, 1986), 122.

48. Gootenberg, "Population and Ethnicity in Early Republican Peru," 146.

49. Some of the literature on nineteenth-century peasant fairs is discussed in Erick D. Langer, "Economic Geography and Ethnic Economies: Indian Trade in the Andes," in Lance H. Grahan, ed., *Indian Trade in the Americas: A Comparative Perspective* (Lincoln, forthcoming). See also Flores Galindo, *Arequipa y el sur andino;* Erick D. Langer and Viviana E. Conti, "Circuitos comerciales tradicionales y cambio económico en los Andes centromeridionales, 1830–1930," *Desarrollo Económico* (Buenos Aires) 31.121 (1991): 91–111; and for the Peruvian central sierra region, Manrique, *Mercado interno y región.*

50. Lehmann, "Introduction: Andean Societies and the Theory of Peasant Economy," in Lehmann, *Ecology and Exchange in the Andes,* 11.

51. See Spalding, *De indio a campesino,* and *Huarochirí: Andean Society under Inca and Spanish Rule;* Sánchez Albornoz, *Indios y tributos en el Alto Perú;* Stern, *Peru's Indian Peoples,* ch. 7; and Larson, *Colonialism and Agrarian Transformation in Bolivia,* ch. 4.

52. Tristan Platt, "The Role of the Andean *Ayllu* in the Reproduction of the

Petty Commodity Regime in Northern Potosí (Bolivia)," in Lehmann, *Ecology and Exchange in the Andes*, 28.

53. See also Tristan Platt, "Divine Protection and Liberal Damnation: Exchanging Metaphors in Nineteenth-Century Potosí," in Roy Dilley, ed., *Contesting Markets: Analyses of Ideology, Discourse, and Practice* (Edinburgh, 1992), 131–158.

54. See the insightful review essay, Carole Nagengast and Michael Kearney, "Mixtec Ethnicity: Social Identity, Political Consciousness, and Political Activism," *Latin American Historical Review* 25.2 (1990): 61–92, quotation on p. 62.

55. Tristan Platt's work on northern Potosí is central here, of course. But see also Ricardo Godoy, "State, Ayllu, and Ethnicity in Northern Potosí, Bolivia," *Anthropos* 80 (1985): 53–65; Rasnake, *Domination and Cultural Resistance;* Rappaport, *Politics of Memory;* Lagos, *Autonomy and Power;* Norman E. Whitten Jr., ed., *Cultural Transformations and Ethnicity in Modern Ecuador* (Urbana, 1981); Greg Urban and Joel Sherzer, eds., *Nation-States and Indians in Latin America* (Austin, 1991), particularly the article in that volume by Thomas Abercrombie, "To Be Indian, to Be Bolivian; 'Ethnic' and 'National' Discourses of Identity." See especially Olivia Harris's interpretive synthesis of much of this literature on ethnicity in the nineteenth-century Andes, in Chapter 12 in this volume.

56. Several older studies on ethnicity in the Andes deserve rereading: François Bourricaud, "Indian, Mestizo and Cholo as Symbols in the Peruvian System of Statification," in Nathan Glazer and Daniel P. Moynihan, eds., *Ethnicity: Theory and Experience* (Cambridge, Mass., 1975), 350–387; Enrique Mayer, "Mestizo e indio: El contexto social de las relaciones interétnicas," in Fernando Fuenzalida et al., *El indio y el poder en el Perú rural* (Lima, 1970), 87–152; and Jorge Flores Ochoa, "Mistis and Indians: Their Relations in a Micro-economic Region of Cuzco," *International Journal of Comparative Sociology* 15.3–4 (1974): 182–192. See also the recent studies by Rossana Barragán, *Espacio urbano y dinámica étnica: La Paz en el siglo XIX* (La Paz, 1990); Hiroyasu Tomoeda and Luis Millones, eds., *500 años de mestizaje en los Andes* (Osaka, 1992); and Guillermo Nugent, *El laberinto de la choledad*.

57. But see the recent studies by Rossana Barragán, "Aproximaciones al mundo 'chulu' y 'huayqui' " *Estado y Sociedad* (La Paz) 8 (1991): 68–88; Linda Seligmann, "To Be in between: The Cholas as Market Women," *Comparative Studies of Society and History* 31.4 (1989): 694–721; and Florence Babb, *Between Field and Cooking Pot: The Political Economy of Marketwomen in Peru* (Austin, 1989). Also relevant are the older studies by June Nash, *We Eat the Mines and the Mines Eat Us: Dependency and Exploitation in the Bolivian Tin Mines* (New York, 1979); Susan C. Bourque and Kay B. Warren, *Women of the Andes: Patriarchy and Social Change in Two Peruvian Towns* (Ann Arbor, 1981); and Carmen Diana Deere, "Peasant

Production, Proletarianization, and the Sexual Division of Labor in the Andes," *Signs* 7.2 (1981): 338–360.

58. See the recent debates in Bolivia: Thérèse Bouysse-Cassagne and Thierry Saignes, "El cholo: Actor olvidado de la historia," *Revista UNITAS* (La Paz) 5 (1992), and Rossana Barragán, "Identidades indias y mestizas: Una intervención al debate," *Autodeterminación* (La Paz) 10 (1992): 17–44. For fascinating studies of the *"indio ladino"* in colonial and postcolonial society, see Rolena Adorno, "Images of *Indios Ladinos* in Early Colonial Peru," in Kenneth J. Adrien and Rolena Adorno, eds., *Transatlantic Encounters: Europeans and Andeans in the Sixteenth Century* (Berkeley, 1991), 232–270; and Chantal Caillavet and Martin Minchom, "Le Métis imaginaire: Idéaux classificatoires et stratégies socio-raciales en Amérique latine (XVe–XXe siècle)," *L'Homme* (Paris) 122–124 (1992): 115–132.

II

From Inca to Spanish Rule:

The Making of Indians

and Markets

2

Did Tribute and Markets Prevail in

the Andes before the European Invasion?

JOHN V. MURRA

In many precapitalist societies, goods do move from region to region even if tribute and commerce are unknown or are not the significant exchange mechanisms. To confuse such movements of goods and services with institutions familiar in the contemporary West is for some reason more common today than it was sixty years ago when Marcel Mauss wrote his "Essai sur le don," inspired at least in part by his discovery of the Trobriands and of Malinowski's *kula* ring of exchanges (see Chapter 5 in this volume).[1]

Ethnic authorities, eventually the state, must find revenues. How these are raised differ from one civilization to another, but everywhere revenues are extracted from the incorporated ethnic groups if armies, courts, and bureaucrats of the priesthood are to perform their chores. The question before Andean studies is this: How did Tawantinsuyu, a latecomer in the history of Andean statecraft, skim off the productive capacity of the high-altitude or desert ethnic groups?

Since we still do not have access to Andean accounts or written sources, our understanding of Inca institutions is incomplete and most likely wrong: like Prescott or Cunow in the nineteenth century,[2] we rely on the impressions and guesses of the rare alien invader curious enough to record his early insights, the justifications he later offered for his actions or his deathbed regrets.

Among these well-informed European eyewitnesses, none compare with lawyer Juan Polo de Ondegardo.[3] No dissertation has considered his career exemplary enough to take it as its subject. Yet he reached the Andes in his early twenties, at the beginning of the second decade of European rule, and was widely known for his familiarity with and perception of those Andean matters that were relevant in the pursuit of European goals. He was frequently consulted by viceroys, and he died in 1575.

Ondegardo had arrived in the Andes as part of the retinue of his uncle, Agustín de Zárate, the emperor's treasurer, sent by Charles V to mind the Crown's interests in Peru. A few years earlier, the emperor had already communicated his dissatisfaction with the Crown's personal share of the loot;[4] this claim was now restated. The Pizarros had been promising at court a survey of the whole country, to determine the revenue potentials, and in 1540, just before Ondegardo's arrival, such a *visita* was undertaken. It was based on the *khipu* knot records still available at Cuzco.[5] The man in charge of the survey for Charcas, what today is Bolivia, was an old hand at "Indian" affairs in both Guatemala and the Andes: Gabriel de Rojas, who later moved his residence from Cuzco to the newly settled La Paz, closer to both the silver mines at Potosí and the coca-leaf terraces. He was to become Ondegardo's mentor.

The two men met during the "civil" wars of the 1540s; both fought on the side of the Crown, yet they also knew Gonzalo Pizarro intimately, since all three were aiming to settle in Charcas. Rojas and Ondegardo were not attracted by the "independence" designs of the Pizarros to set up a separate "Peruvian" kingdom. This was to be sanctioned not only by the original invasion but also by the birth of the young princes, sons of the Pizarros, born of their unions with royal Inca women.

As late as 1547, fifteen years after the invasion, lawyer Polo (as he took now to sign his name), was able to utilize Inca storehouses to feed some 2,000 European soldiers gathered at Xauxa for seven weeks, a miracle he was tempted to describe for the emperor. After the defeat of the Pizarros, both Rojas and Ondegardo settled in Charcas—the older man enjoying the revenues from a large coca-leaf *encomienda*[6] while in charge of a second census of what later became Bolivia. The younger one was ordered by the president of the Lima royal court, the *audiencia,* to take over administration of the newly discovered mining center at Potosí; his effective jurisdiction was even wider—he was expected to adjudicate various conflicting claims to south Andean ethnic groups formulated by local *encomenderos,* some of them his own kinsmen. All this led to early and intimate familiarity with Andean institutions and the ethnic groups' multiple claims to dispersed territories and energies. In the process, Ondegardo became an encomendero himself.

While lawyer Polo seems unique to us today because of the pertinent questions he asked of his informants and because of the hopes we still nurture that further memoranda from his pen will eventually be located, he was not the only one to be well informed. Pro-indigenous lawyers like Francisco Falcón; the widely experienced and well-connected judge Santillán; the philologist and future bishop of Charcas, Domingo de Santo Tomás; administrator Damián de la Bandera; the half-Andean Jesuit Blas Valera; the coastal informants Castro and Ortega Morejón—all these arrived in the Andes early enough to perceive the salient features of local organization. All had practical experience in administering, litigating, converting, and protecting or persecuting the heathen; unfortunately, they left us even sketchier accounts of Andean organization than we get from Polo de Ondegardo.

All of the above agree that there was no tribute in the Andes, in the sense that no household owed their ethnic or state authorities any goods that had come from the peasant's own larder or loom. Falcón, a lawyer well known at the royal tribunal in Lima for his indigenous clientele, informed the bishops gathered in conclave at Los Reyes that the only "tribute" in pre-European times had been the labor conscripted for cultivating, building roads, weaving, hauling, or mining. "They contributed only their personal work, the main tribute being the working of state and sun lands,"[7] claimed Blas Valera. Polo came back to this distinction in several memoranda: "All that they gave their king were personal services . . . no other obligations but work . . . to the point where [today] they resent it more if they must give a peck of potatoes than when they work for fifteen days at some task with the community." In a later report he elaborated: "No one contributed from his own things, nor from what he harvested—only the toil of his own person" and "the tributes were paid from whatever the Inca or the Sun had earmarked for themselves and not from what everyone raised."[8]

We have no evidence that Polo participated in the compilation of the second, "general" visita, or census (1548–1549): very few fragments of this inquiry have been located so far. But we do have a chapter from it, recorded further north, in the Huallaga valley.[9] I have analyzed elsewhere[10] the details of this census, first published by the French historian Marie

Helmer. The year 1549 was seventeen years after the invasion, but in the Huánuco and the Huallaga region it was an even shorter period. The local population had resisted the European takeover, and alien institutions had not reached it till 1542. The evidence from this extraordinary record was knotted into the khipu only six or seven years after the occupation.

The Huallaga valley witnesses interviewed as part of the *visita general* were still unbaptized but already aware of the differences between their own system and the tributes in kind imposed by the invaders. When asked about the obligations to the Inca, they read off twenty-five cords on their khipu: they had owed energy to the Crown—some of it delivered in Cuzco; some at the provincial Inca installations at Huánuco Pampa on the *qhapaq ñan,* the state highway; still other duties were performed in their own Huallaga valley. Of these twenty-five strings, twenty-three listed numbers of people owing building, farming, porterage, weaving, and other services. Only two cords listed commodities to be turned over in kind: honey and feathers, both uncultivated, "wild" goods, usually gathered by youths.[11] I have suggested elsewhere that such "raw" items (to use Lévi-Strauss's contrast) were governed by rules other than the "cooked" commodities processed by the adult citizenry.[12]

Although European rule was so recent in the Huallaga valley, the witnesses were already aware of the structural differences between what the Inca had expected and what the newcomers now demanded of them. Since cloth was a commodity of high value in both the Andean and the European systems,[13] it may be useful to compare what the witnesses said about it: the Inca had provided the fibers to be woven for him from state herds and cotton fields, while Gomez Arias, their recently named encomendero, expected the peasantry to contribute not only the labor but also their own threads. The khipu transcribed in 1549 expressed the wish that their new masters provide the wool.[14]

Such Andean labor revenues of the lords and the state inform our understanding of other exchanges. In a territory so broken up by altitude, aridity, and brusque alternations from diurnal tropical heat to as many as 275 nights of frost a year, we should expect wide differences between ecological or production zones. If we now add the dimension of a dense population, which we know from archaeology inhabited both the altiplano and the irrigated coast, from Moche to Chavín to Chuquisaca, access to the productivity of contrasting zones becomes indispensable. This could have been achieved by maintaining a series of markets at different altitudes, run by the ethnic groups inhabiting each separate ecological niche. However, this was not the Andean solution.

They opted for the simultaneous access of a given ethnic group to the productivity of many microclimates—from the coastal oases up to the puna and eastward, down to the wet *yunka*.[15] This was achieved by attempting to settle one's own people on as many tiers as circumstances (military, religious, and kinship ties) allowed. The caravan traffic between these several zones was continuous; while the complementary access to their products is well documented, the probability of pirate raids on the caravans must be contemplated. The variety and details of social and economic bonds that tied these dispersed geographic and production zones into single systems like the Lupaqa, Pakaqa, or Charka polities are still to be elucidated.

Polo de Ondegardo was one of the first observers of the Andean landscape to notice the existence of such complementarity.[16] After finishing his turn as *justicia mayor* at Potosí, he was assigned in the late 1550s to the same job at Cuzco, formerly the capital of the Inca. There he located the mummies of past Inca kings by tracing their lineages through their living custodians; he also influenced several of the Spanish viceroys, particularly the marquis of Cañete. Polo was probably the author of the *ordenanzas* signed by the marquis, regulating the growing, harvesting, and transport of coca-leaf from the lowlands of Paucartambo[17] to the silver mines, almost 1,000 kilometers southward. He also managed to attract the viceroy's attention to the fact that when encomiendas had been granted to the Europeans during the first two decades of alien rule, the complementary distribution of the lands and their inhabitants had been ignored. Thus the archipelago-like holdings of people inhabiting simultaneously a lowland coca-leaf garden, an oasis planted to hot peppers, maize terraces, and highland potato fields, plus a share of the pastures at 4,800 meters, would be dismembered. Each of these separate microclimates was turned over to a different European, to the great detriment of the food supply and of the traditional complementary linking this mosaic into one productive whole.

Polo argued that this was unfair to the Andean population but also to the privy purse of His Majesty, who had been awarded the Aymara-speaking kingdom of the Lupaqa in 1536. This polity had later lost their lowland outliers and the emperor part of his income because the administrators had not understood Andean complementarity.[18] The viceroy agreed with Polo. The encomendero in question, one Juan de San Juan, returned to the Crown the oases near the coast that had belonged to the Lupaqa; he was compensated elsewhere with a grant of people and lands.

It is a notable fact that the memoranda and litigation records flowing from Polo's pen never mention markets or traders.[19] I documented this impression in 1955 [1980] and will not review that evidence here; I do not pretend that the topic is closed. In 1968, Dr. Roswith Hartmann published a thorough critique of that position showing that in the north, what later became the audiencia of Quito, there is evidence of marketing. The matter was reexamined by Udo Oberem (1978) and Frank Salomon (1986); they documented the absence or the very late appearance in the northern reaches of Tawantinsuyu of the kind of "ecological archipelagos" described above for the central and southern Andes. They point to the presence in the north of *mindala* traffickers, linking several geographic tiers. There is even some evidence for a pre-Columbian market at Quito, with European informants using the Nahuatl term *tiangues* to describe it.[20]

The northern reaches of Tawantinsuyu bring us closer to the Pacific Ocean and to evidence of long-distance maritime traffic, apparently thousands of years old. The earliest European confrontation with the high civilization of the Andes was a raft met on the high seas by Bartolomé Ruyz, one of Pizarro's pilots. He was the first to venture to the open ocean, away from what today is the coast of Manabí, in Ecuador.[21] There he ran into a large raft (he estimated the crew at about twenty), made of balsa trunks and outfitted with sails and a keel. Ruyz calculated the raft's capacity at about thirty *toneles,* compared with the forty for his own vessel.[22] Ruyz offered a sketchy description of the cargo; he mentions textiles, metals, and a steelyard. What impressed him most was that "all this they carried to barter for some seashells of which they make beads, red as if coral and also white. The whole vessel was almost filled with them."[23]

Spondylous is a mollusk that does not live in the cold Pacific waters south of the gulf of Guayaquil, yet its shells were considered indispensable by the rainmakers of the central and southern Andes. There is ample archaeological evidence of its early and widespread use in the highlands as far south as Chile and Argentina.[24] Local deities at Huarochirí, in the mountains above Lima, are described in early oral traditions as cracking these shells between their teeth.[25] On the south Peruvian coast, at Atico, people are reported to have specialized in the carving of northern spondy-lous; they are said to have sent annually some artisans to Cuzco to work the shells at court.[26] We do not know what fleet brought the raw materials that far south of Lima and Chincha, but note that the artwork was not "sold" at the capital, nor was it owed by Atico as part of "tribute." The artists were imported to work off their traditional corvée duties. Move-ments of people carrying the shells by sea and by land covered thousands of kilometers. The question before us is: What kind of traffic was it that carried literally tons of shells southward, over many centuries, so far from their warm water habitat?

This seaborne traffic deserves careful scrutiny, separating the archaeo-logical and documentary evidence from plausible, Eurocentric construc-tions.[27] As early as 1930, Jacinto Jijón y Caamaño postulated a *liga de mercaderes*[28] operating along the Pacific coast, north of Ecuador, part of Uhle's and his own hypothesis of Maya influences in the northern Andes. In 1953, Olaf Holm returned to the topic and described the traffic in *mullu*, the Andean name for spondylous: "An item of commerce, in great de-mand. . . . There is agreement among all observers that the mullu were much appreciated, more than gold or precious stones. [The shells] can be reckoned, with some justification, to be a kind of pre-Columbian jew-el."[29] Archaeological and historic evidence for how spondylous was fished for and processed off the coast of Manabí has recently been located by Jorge Marcos and Presley Norton.[30]

The historical information to match the archaeological presence of mullu in the central Andes is limited. The most detailed text is offered by María Rostworowski in her *Costa peruana prehispánica*.[31] She starts from an *aviso*, a memorandum she located in a Madrid archive, prepared by an anony-mous hand some forty years after the invasion. Since by the 1570s the coastal population had virtually disappeared, the author had to rely on an earlier lowland account to which we have no access. At Chincha, this had recorded a large, prosperous population,[32] some 30,000 households.

Of these, 12,000 were said to have farmed the irrigated lands of the coastal valley; 10,000 more were "fishermen," settled along a stretch of five leagues (some twenty-five kilometers) facing the coast; and 6,000 more were described as *mercaderes* (merchants). Some of these merchants were said to have plied their trade in the southern highlands, *por todo el Collao*, while others traveled "to Quito," by sea:

These people of Chinca were very daring and well organized so that one can say they were the only ones in this kingdom to deal with coins [*moneda*] while among themselves they bought and sold with copper whatever they needed for food and clothing and they knew the value of each *marco*[33] of copper.[34]

This is the most specific, if extremely brief, reference to "trade" in our sources. Note that "they were the only ones" to engage in such exchanges; what did all other ethnic groups do to gain access to foreign goods? The author of the aviso is writing from hearsay; nowhere in the Andes is there independent confirmation of people trading for food or clothing "with copper." And yet there is ample archaeological evidence for intervalley movement of turquoise and emeralds; fish, seaweed, and wool; and silver, gold, and their alloys.[35] Some ethnic groups were widely known for their weaving; others for metal-working or spondylous-carving skills.

A hint to the power context in which people, if not goods, moved from coast to highlands: the earliest European settlers at Cuzco ran into and utilized resident silversmiths of coastal origin to shoe their horses or smelt down the loot from Inca temples. Testimony recording Charles's royal fifth of such transactions also lists the fact that the artisans had been brought to Cuzco within living memory. During the first decade of European rule, the silversmiths had lost their Inca patrons yet had not returned to their desert homes. Some assume that they were prevented from doing so by their new masters;[36] within a few years of the siege of Cuzco by Manco Inca, Fray Luis de Morales was informing Madrid of the artisans' unemployed, alienated condition.[37]

To understand the movement of goods in the Andes we need an awareness that such traffic was inseparable from the continuous physical mobility of households and populations. These *mitmaq*[38] performed fishing, cultivating, pottery making and metalworking, coca-leaf harvesting and tree felling, storing, or guano-gathering duties far from home; in return, they were guaranteed eventual access to highland mates and goods, to shrines, possibly even to a share of political power. There was continuous traffic to and fro.

How such enclaves were tolerated by the existing inhabitants of any given niche and how the caravans confronted potential pirates on their routes remain matters for investigation. One can visualize truces, temporary or long lasting, based on shared, complementary expectations. At times these broke down in what Waman Puma called *awqaruna* times, when wars prevailed, "of all against all." We know that artisans were also fitted into this pattern, though the details are still unclear.[39] It is plain that Inca rule involved modifications in earlier exchange arrangements; many state *mitmaq* now found themselves very far from home and assigned to garrison duties having no apparent reciprocal functions.[40] A notable feature of the changing system was that the fall of Tawantinsuyu did not encourage a massive return of the state *mitmaqkuna* to their places of origin.

Since archaeologists prefer to work on the coast and Ruyz's captured raft is our earliest Andean presence, research has focused attention on longitudinal movements by sea.[41] Let us return to coastwise traffic and exchange.

The scope of seaborne movements once studied by Jijón and Olaf Holm has since expanded to include early maritime travel in both directions. In 1971, Carlos Zevallos Menéndez called a conference to deal with this traffic;[42] the reports included Allison C. Paulsen's indication that Ecuadorean pottery of the Guangala period (100 B.C. to 600 A.D.) was found on the coast of Costa Rica. Donald Lathrap argued for an inverse flow during the later part of the same period;[43] so did José Alcina Franch and his students.[44] In 1986, Jorge Marcos brought together the data then available on such long-distance traffic with an explanation for its continuing flow: given the inexhaustible demand from the central Andes for exotic shells needed for rainmaking and for burial furniture, people had to go further and further afield, beyond the waters of Manabí, to fetch spondylous, some of it from the waters off Mexico.[45]

Recent laboratory analytic studies by Dorothy Hosler[46] of West Mexican and Andean copper alloy artifacts have indicated that some components of Andean metallurgical technology were introduced directly into western Mexico. Hosler can distinguish two periods of such transfers: an earlier one, from approximately A.D. 800–1200, when a series of artifact types appear in western Mexico made of copper. These are identical in fabrication technique, type of metal, and design to Andean objects.

During a subsequent period, 1200 A.D. to sometime before the European invasion, three typically Andean alloy systems were introduced: two of them bronzes (copper-tin and copper-arsenic) and one copper-silver alloy:

What moved from the Andes to Mesoamerica were neither finished objects (with a few exceptions) nor stock metal. Rather, the knowledge and technical know-how behind mining, smelting, and the manipulation of metal; an interest in producing certain classes of objects, such as needles, tweezers, open rings and "axe-monies"; [also] specific attitudes about the qualities of metal as a material—its color, for example— . . . important in channeling West Mexican investment in the new medium, were what West Mexicans took from their distant neighbors to the south.[47]

Hosler suggests that trade may be an explanation of such transfers, yet I wonder if this is a necessary conclusion. We note the long-distance transfer of rainmaking, high-status water mollusks, traveling south and of "fundamental similarities . . . in the purposes to which metal was put in all three metallurgical areas [the Andes, Central America, and western Mexico]: for objects that command status, power and hierarchy."[48] I feel no compelling need to place such exchanges in a commercial framework.

It so happens that spondylous necklaces are tokens of considerable interest elsewhere in tropical Pacific waters. In Melanesia such worked shells were and still are in great demand. Some of these necklaces were recognized by name; they moved repeatedly in a predictable pattern. Ever since Malinowski's recognition of a *kula* ring at the time of World War I, students have returned to reexamine these exchanges and the social structures involved. Some of the more revisionist efforts have tried to detect what *economic* dimensions coexisted with other considerations in the quest for shells.

The reevaluation of the Trobriand kula by nineteen scholars in the early 1980s is instructive; it reexamines the ethnographic and historic context of the traffic in spondylous covering hundreds of miles of open ocean.[49] It may be revealing to contemplate some of the salient features of kula traffic as listed by one of the editors, J. W. Leach:

> 1. The kula is a system of socioeconomic exchange of two kinds of valuables, armshells and necklaces, with other minor valuables of secondary use;
> 2. The two valuables must circulate against each other—armshells being exchanged for necklaces . . . , but never armshells for armshells or necklaces for necklaces; . . .

4. The valuables are system-communal property and cannot be owned privately or kept in one's possession for very long;

5. The valuables derive their principal social value and meaning from being the objects of kula exchange, having few other uses in the social lives of the transactors or in their pursuit of an economic livelihood; . . .

11. Kula exchanges occur between kula partners, individuals who are, unless serious breaches take place, in fixed life-long relationships with each other; . . .

13. A man is brought into the kula at adulthood by a kinsman, usually a father or a mother's brother; . . .

18. Transactors do not haggle with their partners over relative values in exchanges;

19. Men gain considerable prestige from participating; . . .

21. Kula partners do not trade or barter in a utilitarian sense with each other.[50]

As far back as Malinowski's own account, elements of an economic dimension have been noted in kula exchanges. In the Leach and Leach symposium, Raymond Firth, the anthropologist closest to Malinowski as a student of the Pacific, notes that the master had frequently taken into account "magnitude and value" in kula exchanges:

Getting people to realise the wider social implications of what they may first think of as simple material transfers is important. But material problems about the transfers are still crucial. . . . By what principle are the objects exchanged actually valued and matched?[51]

Firth reminds us that every spondylous necklace transferred, has its "price," if it be recognized by Trobrianders as matched in exchange.

Given as *vaga* or opening gift, [it] predicates an ultimate matching item in return. . . . Why is this necklace given in return for that armshell? . . . A most important criterion of price-making in the *kula* is that most transactions are not to be taken as a single on-off event but as part of a *flow* [emphasis in the original] which can go through the life-time of a participant and even be inherited.[52]

Sir Raymond has many other stimulating things to say to students of precapitalist economies. As early as 1957 he had noted that at the time of

World War I Malinowski had already recognized "the existence in primitive economic systems of what others have later referred to as different circuits or spheres of exchange."[53]

With Marcel Mauss, Karl Polanyi, Marshall Sahlins, and Paul Bohannon we have learned that all over the precapitalist world, exchanges did and do take place in a variety of noncommercial contexts. I suggest that in the Andean zones long-distance, maritime exchanges of precious goods (rain-making spondylous, unworn textiles that took literally years to weave and were then buried with the dead, and fancy metals that imitated gold) took place in contexts which it is our task to unravel, not to dismiss with Western labels such as "trade," "tribute," or "markets."

Notes

1. Marcel Mauss, "Essai sur le don: Forme et raison de l'échange dans les sociétés archaïques," *Année Sociologique* (Paris) 1 (1924).

2. William H. Prescott, *History of the Conquest of Peru* (New York, 1847); Heinrich Cunow, "Das peruanische Verwandschaftsistem und die Geschlechtsverbände der Inka," *Das Ausland* 64 (1891).

3. There is no good, recent edition of Juan Polo de Ondegardo's work. Of the dozens of memoranda and reports he prepared for a succession of viceroys, so far only two are accessible. One was prepared for the audiencia in Lima in 1561, immediately upon concluding the years as the corregidor of Cuzco—see his "Informe al licenciado Briviesca de Muñatones sobre la perpetuidad de las encomiendas en el Perú" [1561], *Revista Histórica* (Lima) 13 (1940): 125–96. The second was written, if probably unsolicited, for the eyes of Viceroy Toledo: "Relación de los fundamentos acerca del notable daño que resulta de no guardar a los indios sus fueros" [1571], in *Colección de libros y documentos referentes a la historia del Perú*, 4 vols. (Lima, 1916), 3:45–188.

4. Silvio Zavala, ed., *El servicio personal de los indios en el Perú*, 3 vols. (Mexico, 1978–1979), 1:3–5.

5. While still in Cuzco, before any of them had seen the territories in question, the inspectors and early encomenderos were in possession of lists naming ethnic groups, their lords, numbers in the population, and the location of towns, farms, and pastures. This information may have been recorded on maps, khipu, or other devices still unfamiliar to us. See Tristan Platt et al., *Qaraqara/Charka o*

el rojo y el blanco: Transformaciones históricas de una confederación andina (La Paz, forthcoming).

6. See a house-to-house description of the coca-leaf growers of Sonqo in John V. Murra, *Visita de los valles de Sonqo en los yunka de coca de La Paz (1568–70)* (Madrid, 1992).

7. As quoted by Garcilaso de la Vega, *Los comentarios reales* [1609], book 6, ch. 35 (Madrid, 1960), 242.

8. Ondegardo, "Informe al licenciado Briviesca de Muñatones," 165, 169; Ondegardo, "Relación de los fundamentos," 66, 88.

9. Iñigo Ortíz de Zúñiga, *Visita a la provincia de León de Huánuco* [1562], 2 vols. (Huánuco, 1967, 1972).

10. John V. Murra, "The *mit'a* obligations of ethnic groups to the Inka state," in George A. Collier, Renato I. Rosaldo, and John D. Wirth, eds., *The Inca and Aztec States, 1400–1800: Anthropology and History* (New York, 1982), 237–262.

11. See testimony of Huallaga valley inhabitants about what they had owed the Inca in Ortíz, *Visita de Huánuco*, 1:305–307.

12. John V. Murra, "Las etno-categorías de un *khipu* estatal," in Murra, *Formaciones económicas y políticas del mundo andino* (Lima, 1975), 243–254.

13. John V. Murra, "Cloth and Its Functions in the Inka State," in Annette B. Wiener and Jane Schneider, eds., *Cloth and Human Experience* (Washington, D.C., 1989).

14. In testimony from the Huallaga valley, in Ortíz, *Visita de Huánuco*, 1:307–308.

15. John V. Murra, "El 'control vertical' de un máximo de pisos ecológicos en las economías de las sociedades andinas" [originally in Ortíz, Visita de Huánuco, 1972, 2:429–476], reprinted in Murra, *Formaciones económicas y políticas*. Detailed, later commentaries are found in Shozo Masuda, Izumi Shimada, and Craig Morris, eds., *Andean Ecology and Civilization: An Interdisciplinary Perspective on Andean Ecological Complementarity* (Tokyo, 1985).

16. Ondegardo, "Relación de los fundamentos."

17. An *ordenanza de la coca*, issued by Viceroy Cañete while Polo de Ondegardo was *corregidor* of Cuzco, still unpublished, is filed in the Biblioteca Nacional (Madrid).

18. This *provisión* of the viceroy is in the Archivo de Indias, *Justicia* 405. Polo refers to it in "Relación de los fundamentos," 81.

19. John V. Murra, "Barter and Trade," *The Economic Organization of the Inka State* (1980). Compare this with the M.A. thesis by Darrel LaLone, "Historical Contexts of Trade and Markets in the Peruvian Andes" (Ann Arbor, 1978).

20. See, for example, Roswith Hartmann, *Märkte im alten Peru* (Bonn, 1968). See also Udo Oberem, "El acceso a recursos naturales de diferentes ecologías en la sierra ecuatoriana (siglo 16)," in *Actes*, 42nd Congrès International des Américanistes (Paris, 1978), 4:51–64. Also Frank Salomon, *Native Lords of Quito in the Age of the Incas* (Cambridge, 1986).

21. Adam Szászdi, "Dos fuentes para la historia de la empresa de Pizarro y Almagro: La relación Sámano," in *Historiografía y Bibliografía Americanistas* (Seville) 25 (1981): 80–146. See also Presley Norton, "El señorío de Salangone y la liga de mercaderes," *Miscelánea Antropológica Ecuatoriana* (Guayaquil) 6 (1986): 131–143.

22. *Tonel*—the measure used by Ruyz—is translated in Sebastián de Covarrubias's *Tesoro de la lengua castellana o española* [1611] (Madrid, 1943) as deriving from a barrel used for packing salt fish. A later dictionary, compiled by the Real Academia Española in 1737, rejects this derivation and relates *tonel* to the German *Tonne*, a vessel holding wine; see the Gredos edition of 1969 (Madrid).

23. Szászdi, "Dos fuentes para la historia," plate 3, following p. 146.

24. Pablo J. Arriaga, *La extirpación de la idolatría en el Perú* (Madrid, 1968), 209, 211. See also Richard Burger, *The Prehistoric Occupation of Chavín de Huantar, Perú* (Berkeley, 1984).

25. G. L. Urioste, *Hijos de Paria Qaqa* (Syracuse, 1983), ch. 23, par. 299, 184–185.

26. Guillermo Galdós Rodríguez, "Visita a Atico y Caravelí," [1549], *Revista del Archivo de la Nación* (Lima) 4–5 (1977).

27. Compare, for example, Carlos Zeballos Menéndez, *Simposio de correlaciones andino-mesoamericanas* (Guayaquil, [1971] 1982), with Robert MacCormick Adams, "Anthropological Perspectives on Ancient Trade," *Current Anthropology* 15 (1974): 239–258, or Max Gluckman, *Politics, Law and Ritual in Tribal Society* (Chicago, 1965).

28. Jacinto Jijón y Caamaño, "Una gran marea cultural en el noroeste de Suramérica," *Journal de la Société des Américanistes* (Paris) 22 (1930): 107–197.

29. Olaf Holm, "El tatuaje entre los aborígenes pre-pizarrianos de la costa ecuatoriana," *Cuadernos de Historia y Arqueología* (Guayaquil, 1953): 7–8.

30. Jorge C. Marcos and Presley Norton, "Interpretación sobre la arqueología de la isla de La Plata," *Miscelánea Antropológica Ecuatoriana* (Guayaquil) 1 (1986): 136–154. See also Marcos, *Arqueología de la costa ecuatoriana: Nuevos enfoques* (Guayaquil, 1986).

31. Published first as María Rostworowski de Diez Canseco, *Etnía y sociedad: Costa peruana prehispánica* (Lima, 1977). A second edition called more accurately *Costa peruana prehispánica*, appeared in Lima in 1989.

32. In his reminiscences, Pedro Pizarro, an eyewitness of the invasion, recalled that forty years earlier he had noted that only one of the ethnic lords accompanying King Atahualpa was carried in a litter. At the time he had inquired about the identity of the personage and was told that he was the lord of Chincha, master of 100,000 rafts on the sea [in *Biblioteca de autores españoles*, 168 (Madrid), 159–242].

33. *Marco*—"a silver peso worth 65 *reales*," in Covarrubias, *Tesoro de la lengua castellana*, 2:789.

34. Rostworowski, *Costa peruana prehispánica*, 224–228.

35. Walter Alva, "Discovering the New World's Richest Unlooted Tomb," *National Geographic* 174 (1988): 4.

36. A notable fact: after the military collapse of Tawantinsuyu, one could expect massive repatriation of the many ethnic groups resettled by Cuzco. Early colonial records indicate that few of the displaced populations made the effort to return "home." An unusually alert invader, Francisco de Carvajal (Gonzalo Pizarro's ideologue) did attempt to claim "his Indians" deported to Pocona, but few such "repatriations" can be found in the record. Two distinct groups, originally from the Cuzco area and deported to Huánuco, did abandon their garrison duties at the Inca frontier but made no effort to return to Cuzco.

37. Luis de Morales, "Relación sobre las cosas que convenían proveerse," in Emilio Lissón Chavez, *La iglesia de España en el Perú* (Madrid, 1943), 1:41–98.

38. *Mitmaq* in Quechua; plural, *mitmaqkuna*—people resettled away from their original ethnic group, either on their own initiative or by order. The verb *mitiy* means "to leave; to be sent."

39. See Murra, "Etho-categorías de un *khipu* estatal," 109–114, and Murra, "The Expansion of the Inka State: Armies, War and Rebellions," in John V. Murra, Nathan Wachtel, and Jacques Revel, eds., *Anthropological History of Andean Polities* (Cambridge, 1986), 49–58.

40. See details in Ortíz, *Visita de Huánuco*, vol. 2, paragraph in sixteenth-century script, on cover.

41. Izumi Shimada, "Perception, Procurement and Management of Resources: Archaeological Perspective," in Masuda et al., *Andean Ecology and Civilization*, 357–399.

42. Menéndez, *Simposio de correlaciones andino-mesoamericanas*.

43. Donald Lathrap, "Complex Iconographic Features Shared by Olmec and Chavín and Some Speculations Concerning Significance," in Zeballos, *Simposio*, 301–327.

44. José Alcina Franch, "La vasija trípode como rasgo diagnóstico de influencias mesoamericanas en el area andino," in Zeballos, *Simposio*, 349–358. Also Franch, "Navegación precolombina: El caso del litoral pacífico ecuatorial—evidencias e

hipótesis," in *Revista Española de Antropología Americana* (Madrid) 143 (1987): 35–73.

45. Jorge Marcos, *Arqueología de la costa ecuatoriana: Nuevos enfoques* (Guayaquil, 1986).

46. Dorothy Hosler, "Ancient West Mexican Metallurgy: South and Central American Origins," in *American Anthropologist* 90.4 (1988): 832–855.

47. Dorothy Hosler, Heather Lechtman, and Olaf Holm, *Axe-Monies and Their Relatives, Studies in Pre-Columbian Art and Archaeology* (Washington, D.C., 1990), 2.

48. Hosler, "Ancient West Mexican Metallurgy," 849.

49. See Sir Edmund R. Leach and Jerry W. Leach, eds., *The Kula: New Perspectives on Massim Exchange* (Cambridge, 1983).

50. Ibid., 2–4.

51. In ibid., 89.

52. In ibid., 90.

53. Here Firth is thinking of such studies of non-European economic institutions as discussed by Paul Bohannon and George Dalton, *Markets in Africa*, or *Primitive, Archaic and Modern Economies: Essays of Karl Polanyi*, edited by George Dalton.

3

The Variety and Ambiguity of Native Andean

Intervention in European Colonial Markets

STEVE J. STERN

European Mercantile Expansion in the Andean World

"Please God, take me to Peru," went the refrain.[1] To sixteenth-century dreamers, Peru evoked visions of treasure. In Andean America, the legendary mines created dazzling markets that drew commodities from afar. Deep in the high altiplano of modern Bolivia, the great silver city of Potosí—by the late 1500s the home of well over 100,000 people[2]—drew china and silk from the Philippines; luxury cloth from Spain; coarser textiles from Mexico, Quito, Huánuco, and Tucumán; salted fish from Peru's Pacific coast; slaves from Brazil; wheat from Chile and Peru; and food and pack animals from Argentina and Peru.[3] The volume and market value of such commodity flows were no trifling matter. In 1597, the Cuzco region suffered a severe meat shortage because high prices diverted an estimated 600,000 head of sheep to Potosí. In Potosí, the city's Indian population alone annually drank some 1 million large jugs of *chicha* (corn beer). Each year, according to an estimate written in 1603, Potosí spent nearly 9 million pesos ensayados on labor and supplies—five or six times the Inca Atahualpa's famous ransom treasure.[4]

Spanish colonization, in other words, brought frenetic mercantile expansion to the Andean highlands. Potosí and Lima, although key "magnets" of commercial dynamism, constituted anything but isolated enclaves. From the beginning, in the Andes as in Mesoamerica, colonizers eager to gain fortune and status aggressively sought out opportunities for private commercial gain (even if the ultimate goal of many was to establish high noble status for their families and lineages). Except perhaps in the most isolated backwater regions, *encomenderos* incorporated the territorial spaces they dominated into an expanding mercantile structure. They marketed their Indian tributes; identified key commodities for sale on American or European markets; and invested in mining, agriculture, and ranching, textiles (the *obraje* workshops as well as putting-out systems), trading companies, or other commercial enterprises.[5] In Peru and Bolivia, the spectacular mining boom boosted the prospects of commercial reward dramatically.

Over the long run, several forces guaranteed the permanence of such mercantile penetration. The discovery of gold, silver, and mercury mines in scattered Andean regions; the growing population of colonials, Indians, and mixed-bloods (*castas*) living in or near cities and mining camps, or devoted to petty commodity production for cities and mining camps; the growing poverty, long-distance migrations, and changing tastes of the Indian population; the development of a political apparatus enabling colonizers to expand markets artificially through forced sales of goods and expropriation of needed subsistence resources—all contributed to enduring and complex internal markets for products, land, and labor.[6] The colonial marketplace had rules that mixed outright coercion with mercantile incentive; its hired laborers never developed into an expanding and stable wage-labor proletariat; its scale, logic, and cycles of growth and decay contrasted sharply with those we associate with modern capitalist economies. Often, the colonial marketplace harnessed noncapitalist relations of production to more modern goals of profit accumulation through investment and market sale.[7] These features distinguish the colonial economy from modern capitalism (and also from classical images of precapitalist economies). They impart a modest quality to the colonial marketplace when compared to the ever-expanding internal markets of capitalism and its industrial revolutions. But as Carlos Sempat Assadourian has brilliantly demonstrated, the particularities of colonial markets and mercantile incentives made them no less real, expansive, or decisive in the political economy of colonial society.[8]

One can speak fairly, in the Andes and elsewhere, of a "European colonial" model of economic behavior closely associated with the incorporation of the Americas into an expansive commercial system. (This "European" model, as we shall see later, refers more to a cultural logic associated with early modern Europe than it does to the biological ancestry of its practitioners.) To simplify, European colonizers sought to exploit commercial opportunities for private gain. More precisely, entrepreneurs aggressively made use of economic resources and market realities, political privilege and extraeconomic controls, and the emergence of a diverse ensemble of colonial labor relations to try to accumulate the liquid profits (in the form of precious metals or readily exchangeable commodities) available in a commercialized setting. Entrepreneurial reliance on political influence, and the importance of honor and social display in acquiring or maintaining such influence, meant, in practice, that those who sought private commercial gain often acted as "aristocrat-entrepreneurs." In varying degrees, they invested both their stature as "aristocrats" and their resources as "entrepreneurs" to build, defend, and expand their fortunes. In its petty and grander forms, this brand of economic entrepreneurship flourished in the diverse markets that sprang up in colonial Peru—markets for products such as precious metals, raw materials, pack animals, food and drink, cloth, craft goods, and ritual and prestige goods; markets for lands and waters purchased for commercial agriculture and ranching, and for purposes of prestige or political and social domination; markets for labor in such forms as slaves, servile tenants attached to landed estates, and limited service sales by individual laborers or by their overlords; markets for political standing in the form of titles, administrative or judicial position, and marriage alliances.[9]

Yet Europeans did not act on a "blank slate" when they colonized the Andes. How did Andean highland peoples respond to European market penetration and expansion? It might appear reasonable, for two reasons, to assume that Andean peoples rejected the colonial market economy and resisted involvement in it. One might note, first, the unquestionable disaster the commercial boom wrought on Andean societies in the early colonial period. The lust for fortune and profit, the discovery of fabulous mines, the rise of numerous secondary arenas of profit making—all imposed intense pressures on native peoples for goods, labor, and lands, and all contributed greatly to the story of Andean pauperization under colonial rule.

One might add, second, that market expansion penetrated a culture region whose preexisting social relations had left little room for market activity. To be sure, one can speak of significant trade or markets in selected Andean regions: the ethnic groups of the northern Andean highlands (the *"páramo* Andes" of Ecuador), and the societies along Peru's Pacific coast.[10] Even in these cases, it would be important to distinguish between the material and cultural matrix that governed and constrained commodity production and exchange in pre-Columbian Andean societies and the more unbridled logic of private commercial gain associated with European colonial ventures.[11] Most important for our purposes, however, is the comparative unimportance of market experience in the heartland of the Inca Empire, the highlands of modern Peru and Bolivia. Here, goods were produced and circulated according to ethnic and political criteria that placed high value on the self-sufficiency of the relevant kin, ethnic, or political group and on the distributive "generosity" of Andean leaders and conquerors. In general, Andean rules of reciprocity and redistribution served—in lieu of market exchange, barter, or other principles—to govern the exchanges and prestations of labor that produced goods; the exercise of rights in lands, waters, and other means of production; and the circulation flows that collected goods and redistributed them among the population. One may speak fairly, in this culture region, of a "traditional Andean" model of economic behavior rooted in pre-Columbian history. Andean peoples sought self-sufficiency, as members of *ayllus* (kin groupings or lineages claiming descent from a common ancestor) who themselves belonged to larger "ethnic families," by engaging in reciprocities enabling the collective kin or ethnic group to directly produce diverse goods in scattered ecological zones; they sought individual or group prestige by engaging in unequal reciprocities whereby the "generous" redistributed goods to ayllu or ethnic "relatives" and to politically subordinate groups. This pattern of economy consigned market exchange and private commercial gain to a rather anomalous and exceptional status.[12]

One might reasonably infer, therefore, that Andean peoples resisted the colonial market economy as an imposition both cruelly exploitative and culturally alien. In the abstract, the inference seems reasonable. In historical reality, it proves utterly false.

Notwithstanding the ruthless pressures imposed by the commercial economy, and notwithstanding the vast gulf between "colonial European" and "traditional Andean" patterns of political economy, Andean peoples intervened in the colonial market economy from its very beginnings. I cannot pretend to undertake the ambitious task of synthesizing and assessing the rather extensive literature now emerging on Andean market initiatives; nor do I wish merely to restate my own findings for the Huamanga region. Suffice it to say that recent ethnohistorical research and the essays in this volume demonstrate that Andean peoples, as individuals and as corporate groups, intervened in all kinds of product, land, and labor markets; that they did so throughout the colonial period; that such interventions cast them in diverse roles—as collaborative allies, as junior and senior partners, and as competitive rivals—in their relations with European economic actors; and that Andean initiatives played a major role in determining the specific character and workings of the colonial market economy. In 1919, Rómulo Cúneo Vidal gave us a spectacular example of Andean market initiative. Don Diego Caqui, son of a Tacna *kuraka* (ethnic lord), by 1588 owned four vineyards and a winery, a llama train to transport wine to Potosí, and two frigates and a small sloop for commerce between Tacna, Arica, and Callao (Lima's port).[13] We now know that Cúneo Vidal's early research on Tacna pointed not to an isolated coastal example, but to a broad social pattern encompassing highlands and coast. Ethnic groups, led by their chiefs, sold and occasionally bought labor services; rented, bought, and sold lands; produced, marketed, and bought commodities of Andean and European origins; and invested in mines, obrajes, and trading companies. Andean individuals and families, acting more independently of ayllu and ethnic groupings, participated in and sometimes dominated various labor, land, and product markets.[14] And in the great center of Potosí itself, the efforts of Indian men and women to intervene directly in silver ore and product markets sparked serious struggles for leverage over the conditions of labor and marketing.[15]

We ignore a vast array of evidence, therefore, if we speak of Andean resistance to the market *as such*. One might say with greater truth that Andean peoples frequently *initiated* marketplace participation, on their own terms if possible, in order to resist market participation under less favorable circumstances. A commercial economy run by and for European colonizers imposed severe exploitative pressures, but it also created markets that Andean groups or individuals might use to alleviate pressures, accumulate funds, or recapture lost subsistence resources. Aside from forced participation, almost always on highly unfavorable terms, native Andean relations with the market included a subtle and diverse range of responses. On one end of the range one finds outright rejection of commercially inspired demands. This might include, for example, resistance to labor drafts for the mines, refusal to sell goods to merchants sponsored by local *corregidores,* or riots against forced distribution of goods at inflated prices.[16] Another set of responses relied on market initiatives to defend well-being, as defined in Andean culture—to protect subsistence rights, preserve a measure of ethnic independence, or defend the corporate integrity of a kin or ethnic group. Such initiatives might include, for example, growing a cash crop to gain a supplementary income that might, in turn, be used to protect or reclaim ayllu lands by purchase or litigation; "renting" laborers to replace relatives otherwise liable to a dangerous labor draft for the mines; or engaging in collective sales of ayllu labor to prevent a dispersal of individual laborers that weakened ethnic control.[17] Finally, on the opposite end of the spectrum of Andean responses, one finds more opportunistic ventures that advanced the private well-being of individuals or households at the expense of traditional Andean responsibilities. These might include, for example, an Indian building a "private" economic domain by investing heavily in ethnically alien rural areas or in cities; or Indians merging into multiracial "power cliques" by using colonial tactics of coercion and economic domination against ethnic and ayllu "relatives."[18]

The diversity of Andean responses to mercantile expansion requires us, in each region, time period, or set of case studies, to discern the "cultural logic" governing Andean market interventions. When Andean actors surface in the colonial records as buyers and sellers of lands, goods, and services, as speculators and potential beneficiaries in commercial transactions, how are we to assess the motives and consequences (unintended or intended) of their economic actions? When are they acting in accord with a "colonial European" model of private commercial gain? This kind of behavior, if widespread, would have accelerated the destruction and transformation of traditional Andean social relations, cultural principles, and subsistence capacity *from within* native Andean societies. When, on the other hand, are Andean actors intervening in accord with a modified "traditional Andean" model granting primacy to responsibilities to ayllu-ethnic self-sufficiency and well-being, but relying on market initiatives to advance these goals in a colonial setting? This kind of behavior, if widespread and successful, would have laid the groundwork for enduring continuities in the internal organization of Andean societies despite the destructive pressures of colonial rule. Do the two categories mentioned constitute a sufficient heuristic framework, or do we need to speak of yet a third "cultural logic" arising from colonial conditions?

These questions of interpretation are crucial for serious study of economic, social, or cultural history. But they are methodologically troublesome because, as we shall see, our records often "mask" the cultural logic and social function of Andean market interventions.

The "Masks" of Andean Market Intervention

Let us turn, then, to false appearances. In the late sixteenth century, the Crown assumed greater control over various *encomiendas* by collecting tributes on the Crown account, and reducing encomendero heirs and Crown clients to the status of pensioners with partial claims on encomienda revenue. In practice, this meant that royal treasurers sold tributes in kind (more precisely, the right to collect them) at public auction to generate revenue for the Crown and its pensioners. We have records of tribute auctions in the city of Cuzco for the years 1575–1582, for example, and they include sales of tributes from the Parinacochas *repartimiento* districts on the western fringes of the Cuzco region.[19] If one reads the lists of merchants and other speculators who bought rights to the maize, wheat, and *chuño* (freeze-dried potatoes) tributes of Parinacochas, occasionally one finds Indians among the purchasers. This should not surprise us, since at least a sprinkling of Indian entrepreneurs, merchants, and commodity producers competed with Europeans and castas even in the most "Hispanic" sectors of the commercial economy.[20] As mentioned earlier, the "colonial European" model of economic behavior describes not just Europeans and their descendants; Indians could also engage in European-style market transactions for private commercial gain.

When we look more closely, however, the significance of occasional Indian buyers in the Cuzco auctions appears more problematic and ambiguous. First, in each case, the Indian purchasers of tributes were chiefs or notables from the ayllu-ethnic groupings that owed the grain and potato tributes in the first place.[21] Second, independent documentation from the Parinacochas region strongly suggests that at least from the early 1570s until the late 1590s, Parinacochas ayllus organized their colonial tribute

Table 3.1. Tribute Auctions of Foodstuffs, Parinacochas "Upper" Moiety, 1576–1582

Date	Indian Buyer?	Price (tomines/fanega)	Comment
Nov. 1576	No	4	
July 1577	No	3	
June 1578	No	4	
June 1579	Yes[a]	5	
June 1580			No tributes sold or collected.
June 1581	Yes/No[b]	5–5.5	Two years of tribute.
July 1582	No	5	

[a] Don Francisco Suni and Don Diego Guamansuri.
[b] Don Francisco Suni (purchased one-half of a double tribute).
Source: Yale University Latin American Collection, Sterling Library, Department of Manuscripts and Archives, vol. 3, "Libro de los remates de los tributos de los repartimientos que se cobran en esta caja . . . [Cuzco] 1575–1582."

responsibilities by applying the "traditional" rules well known by students of Andean culture. The chiefs and notables of the various ayllus met in council to divide the labor burden, in accord with local reciprocities among the various ayllu and kin groupings; each of the smaller kin groupings relied on its own internal reciprocities to divide the labor burden among the various tributary households.[22] Third, a close look at timing and prices hints that elites may have purchased the tributes to alleviate the subsistence distress of their tribute-paying groups. The records are most complete for the "upper" moiety of Parinacochas peoples. Here chiefs intervened twice to purchase tribute foods. They paid a premium price to purchase grains and chuño in 1579; the price relative to earlier years probably indicates poor or at best moderate harvests in the Parinacochas area. In 1580, no grain or chuño tributes were collected at all—a further indicator of probable subsistence difficulties. In 1581, the ayllus paid a double tribute to make good on tributes in arrears since 1580, and Don Francisco Suni intervened to buy back half the tributes at a premium price (see Table 3.1). For the "lower" moiety of Parinacochas, the evidence covers only four years but points in a similar direction. Here Andean notables intervened first in 1580 (when the "upper" group paid no grain or chuño tributes) and paid

Table 3.2. Tribute Auctions of Foodstuffs, Parinacochas "Lower"
Moiety, 1579–1582

Date	Indian Buyer?	Price (tomines/fanega)	Comment
June 1579	No	5	
June 1580	Yes[a]	6.5	
June 1581			No tribute sold or collected.
Nov. 1582	Yes[b]	6	Two years of tribute.

[a] Don Alonso Curiñaupa.
[b] Don Rodrigo Guayqui Cabana.
Source: Yale University Latin American Collection, Sterling Library, Department of Manuscripts and Archives, vol. 3, "Libro de los remates de los tributos de los repartimientos que se cobran en esta caja . . . [Cuzco] 1575–1582."

a steep price. In 1581, no food tributes were collected, and a year later, an Indian chief intervened to buy back the double-tribute due in 1582 (see Table 3.2).

These details acquire greater meaning once we consider Andean practices and norms regarding tribute. We know that within the terms of Andean cultures, the ayllus viewed tributes in kind as a violation of time-honored rights. A shrewd colonial observer commented that Indians would rather work fifteen days as a community on other fields than give up for tribute a few potatoes grown by the family for its own use.[23] This stubbornness was rooted in practical experience. When enforced, it shielded ayllus from the possibility that the well-known irregularity of sierra harvests, combined with a steady demand for tribute in goods to higher authorities, would force ayllus to turn over goods produced for subsistence precisely in the years of bad harvests. In pre-Columbian times, ayllus had given their authorities a tribute in labor only, rather than in finished products. The Inca state demanded labor on fields set aside for its use, but if a crop failed on state lands, the state had to absorb the loss. It could not demand a tribute in goods from harvests on fields set aside for ayllu subsistence production.[24] After Spanish conquest, Andean groups defended the integrity of ayllu subsistence by adapting earlier practice to colonial circumstances. Ignoring the formal definition of tribute by the colonial state, Andean peoples set aside lands specifically designated to pay colonial tax obligations. They thereby preserved—by their own rules, at least—the inviolate character of ayllu subsistence lands.[25]

We can now suggest an alternative hypothesis interpreting Indian participation in the Cuzco grain and potato auctions. What appeared, at first sight, as simple transactions including Indians among the commercial speculators may actually have "masked" the defense of economic rights defined with the terms of a "traditional Andean" logic. The particular ayllu-moiety identities of the Indian buyers, the evidence of continued adherence to Andean forms of tribute management in Parinacochas, the indicators of duress in the years of market intervention, the culturally sacrosanct character of subsistence production on ayllu lands—taken together, these features suggest that our apparent speculators, in reality, may well have acted to enhance the welfare of their "kin" by enforcing an ancient Andean right. Suppose that poor harvests, in some years, meant that to pay their tributes in kind, at least some ayllus would have had to turn over goods produced on lands expressly reserved for local community or family use. If this were the case, the logic of Andean political economy would have *required* that responsible chiefs and notables of affected ayllus try to prevent the loss of "tribute" goods, if necessary by intervening in the auctions that sold colonial tribute rights.

We cannot definitively prove that this hypothesis is correct. But it explains more facets of the known evidence than a hypothesis assuming that the Indian buyers acted within a "colonial European" framework. And it warns us, as historians, to respect the anthropologists' insistence that surface changes appearing in the documentation may disguise underlying continuities. As John Murra has warned in a similar case: "One must beware of notarial or judicial records that phrase land transactions in European terms, thus masking enduring Andean relationships."[26]

But it would also be unwise to make the opposite mistake—that which *assumes* "enduring Andean relationships" and thereby concludes that market interventions by Andean leaders disguised a hidden logic rooted in Andean culture history. Appearances may deceive in many directions. In 1596, for example, Don Juan Uybua, a local lord in the village of Cancha,[27] agreed to save Sebastián Cabana, an ayllu Indian of the same village, from imprisonment. Cabana had allegedly lost four cows and three horses valued at 90 pesos—a huge debt for a poor ayllu peasant. Uybua prevented

Cabana's imprisonment by paying the debt.[28] At first sight, the transaction appears to document the continuity of Andean relationships. A local lord, bound by long-term reciprocities requiring, among other things, that he act "generously" on his kinfolk's behalf, appears to have intervened in the credit market to protect one of "his" households.

When we look more closely at the details, however, the transaction takes on a different flavor. We discover, first, that Uybua, like many European colonials, used the debt as a labor recruitment device. Cabana had to agree to serve Uybua continuously for nearly seven years to repay the debt he now owed Uybua. Second, the two Indians were identified with different (although perhaps loosely "related") ayllus; to keep Cabana in his service, Uybua agreed to pay Cabana's Andean lords the annual tribute owed by the indebted peon.[29] These particulars suggest an alternative hypothesis interpreting the transaction. In his misfortune, Sebastián Cabana proved unable to call on the generosity of the lords who, by Andean standards, held direct responsibility for his household's welfare. His only alternative to jail was servile obligation to a far less "intimate" patron, a patron less bound by Andean reciprocities and freer to shape the relationship in the terms of colonial debt peonage. Uybua's intervention in the regional credit and labor market does not necessarily document a persistent Andean tradition of "generosity" protecting kin from market burdens. It may well have served, instead, to advance a private economic domain. This interpretation, although not definitively provable, more fully accounts for the nuances of the transaction and of internal Andean social organization.

Our two examples, although anecdotal, illustrate a larger methodological issue. In our first case, economic intervention clothed in "colonial European" garb probably disguised a "traditional Andean" substance. The apparent pursuit of private commercial gain actually served, in my view, to enhance the well-being—as defined in Andean cultures—of native kin groups and polities in Parinacochas. In our second case, economic intervention seeming to reflect the strength of "traditional Andean" generosities probably disguised the rise of a "colonial European" logic *within* native Andean societies. Uybua's eager protection of a fellow Andean villager actually served, in my view, to advance private economic interest and to weaken the economic integrity of Cabana's ayllu. In both cases, the appearances in documentation recording economic transactions prove a rather treacherous guide to the content of social relations.

In addition, we have no assurance that the "traditional Andean" and "colonial European" models by themselves constitute an adequate guide to the multiple logics of Andean market interventions. My own research experience suggests that we need to add a "colonial Andean" model reflecting the genuine ambiguities and ambivalences of colonial life.[30] This pattern involved an attempt to hedge bets, or more precisely, to protect one's well-being by developing diverse and sometimes deliberately ambiguous socioeconomic relations that might later be used, as needed, in either a "traditional Andean" or "colonial European" direction. Let us return to our first example for a hypothetical illustration. Suppose that Don Francisco Suni, a Parinacochas lord who bought wheat, maize, and chuño tributes, revitalized local reciprocities by redistributing the maize and chuño to ayllu storage, but sold the wheat to Europeans in Cuzco or Potosí. Suppose, further, that the wheat sales funded not community work, tribute payments, or cash reserves, but a personal hacienda near Cuzco and a small trading site in Potosí. This "colonial Andean" economic trajectory had its contradictory aspects. Ayllu Indians might resent Suni's diversion of resources to alien arenas and people effectively beyond their claims and influence; alternatively, a drop in hacienda revenues or Potosí prices might sorely tempt Suni to hold back on the costly local reciprocities that made him a credible Andean patron in Parinacochas. But the inherent contradictions of "colonial Andean" adaptations might be kept latent, or at least manageable, over a considerable length of time. And keeping the door open to alternate economic logics might provide the best insurance against the pressures of colonial society. If Suni cultivated and enjoyed a reputation as a generous and exceptionally responsible chief amidst trying colonial conditions, he might rescue his hacienda's profitability by "begging" kin to reciprocate in a new way—by laboring on his Cuzco hacienda. (The idiom of Andean reciprocity was such that chiefs often "begged" kin to serve their lords.[31]) In this example, "traditional Andean" relations would assist faltering "colonial European" enterprise. If, on the other hand, a ruthless corregidor plundered the ayllus and lords of Parinacochas and destroyed Suni's local reputation, he might flee and rely on his Cuzco and Potosí investments for a fresh start. Or he might use his "private" revenues to relieve pressure in Parinacochas and restore his Andean reputation. In these examples, "colonial European" relations

made it possible to compensate for—even abandon—increasingly unten-
able "traditional Andean" relations.

The "colonial Andean" logic enhanced long-term well-being by *avoiding*
clear-cut commitments to either a "traditional Andean" or "colonial European" pattern of political economy. In the current state of research, it is
difficult to specify whether the "colonial Andean" logic is best understood
as a third "model" of economic behavior, with internally coherent and
verifiable "laws" of its own, or whether it simply represents contradictory
and at times confusing management of two coexisting, yet in certain respects antithetical models ("traditional Andean" and "colonial European")
by Andean actors simultaneously oriented to both. My own suspicion is
that as research develops, we should be able to specify a formal economic
model that represents more than eclectic and Janus-like adaptation to two
poles or economic models.[32] In either case, however, the "colonial Andean"
logic describes behavior that adds to the ambiguities of documentation the
ambiguities of colonial life itself.[33]

We face, then, a methodological quandary: when appearances are so
deceiving, the available documentation limited, and the reality of social
relations ambiguous and contradictory, how are we to assess the "true"
social significance of economic transaction records documenting Andean
intervention in European colonial markets? How do we pierce the various disguises of Andean market participation? And once we pierce the
disguises, what might we learn about a central theme of this book—the
relationship between Andean market participation and ayllu subsistence
defenses?

The Significance of Andean Market Initiatives:
Methodological Probes

A neat package of powerful tools that will break our methodological ter-
rain does not exist. Such tools might in any event require a quality and
quantity of documentation and research findings that outstrip what we
can realistically expect in the near future. I doubt, therefore, that we can
soon develop definitive findings on the relative frequency, regional and
ethnic variation, periodization, and social causes of various "models" of

Andean intervention in colonial markets. These tasks await development of "thicker" and more coordinated sets of Andean research data. What we can do in the meantime is to refine the methods by which we probe for *clues* to the underlying significance of Andean market transactions.

The ongoing boom in Andean ethnohistory and economic history may well lengthen and refine the list of probing devices, but let me begin by mentioning four. First, we need to use "noneconomic" sources as much as possible to "track" specific Andean economic actors, over considerable lengths of time, in their social and ethnic milieus. Documentation recording economic transactions will usually offer too one-dimensional a view to allow us to distinguish between "traditional Andean," "colonial European," and "colonial Andean" patterns of economic intervention. The most desirable complementary sources would provide insight into the social motivations and imperatives of Andean actors in the colonial marketplace, and into the way such actors were viewed or subjected to claims by their Andean clienteles, collaborators, or enemies.

For these purposes, two sorts of noneconomic sources could provide exceedingly useful information. On the one hand, sources on local religion and symbolic behavior would clarify the "self-presentation" of Andean economic actors and the methods by which they sought acceptance, successfully or unsuccessfully, in their social environments. Such sources might tell us, for example, that Indians accumulating personal wealth in European fashion in the mercantile economy also risked their gains in symbolic gestures of "idolatrous" loyalty to Andean gods. They might add, further, that such Indians spent their "personal" fortunes to finance local community celebrations (whether Catholic, Andean, or a syncretic blend). In other cases, these sources might pinpoint economically successful leaders who *refused* to support popular—and expensive—religious celebrations. A second type of complementary source would lay bare internal Andean political rivalries and conflicts. Such sources might enable us to discover, for example, when particular ayllus or polities turned against an Andean lord after supporting or tolerating him for, say, twenty years. This kind of information, when combined with research on the economic transactions of the lord and those of his political rivals, could provide a much clearer view of the social content and imperatives of economic transactions.[34]

A second probing device would systematically compare relationships that crossed Andean "fault lines" with those that did not. These "fault lines" would include ayllu and ethnic divisions reaching back into the pre-Columbian past, as well as new sorts of Andean divisions arising under colonial rule. Probably the most important new type of "fault line" distinguished between *forasteros* (immigrant Indians no longer living with their original kin and ethnic groups) and *originarios* (ayllu Indians still living among original kin groups descended from common ancestor-gods).[35] The kind of comparison suggested here might show, for example, that an Indian operating in a "colonial European" style in relations with ethnically alien forasteros in one region nonetheless used mercantile adaptations for "traditional Andean" purposes in relations with ethnic kin in another region. But we might also find that the same Indian channeled only a small portion of his or her personal income into originario relations, and that, upon facing death, the Indian willed a good deal of personal wealth to friends, patrons, and clients in the forastero world. A perceptive social interpretation of this Indian's market participation would hinge on an inclusive approach analyzing the totality of social relations our economic actor pursued with various Andean and non-Andean groups and individuals. Since Andean peoples traveled across broad and far-flung territories, this sort of methodological probe might require that we build a collective data bank through the cooperation of researchers in various national, regional, and local archives. A practical step of this kind could make a tangible contribution to future research methodology.

A third method that might illuminate the deeper significance of market transactions would deliberately study regions and time periods that include known moments of internal crisis among Andean peoples. The assumption here is that moments of crisis are most likely to bring latent tensions out into the open and to generate the complementary noneconomic sources and information discussed earlier. Such moments may therefore provide exceptionally valuable research opportunities. The *katarista* wing of the Andean insurrection of the 1780s led to major political shake-ups, under pressure from below, among native Andean authorities in the Bolivian altiplano.[36] Would it not make sense to target specific peoples, deposed leaders, and elected successors for systematic social and economic study over a significant time period? To take a less dramatic example, we know that the eighteenth century saw a surge of legal disputes between Andean chiefs and their peoples. This surge may well have signaled that the contradictions of "colonial Andean" market intervention sharpened enormously in the late colonial period.[37] Could we not take specific instances of local conflicts between kurakas and their peoples as a point of departure for systematic study in "economic" and "noneconomic" sources? The danger of such an approach is that an exceptional and extreme moment generating high-quality sources might dominate and distort our vision of an entire era. But conscious of this danger, we can strive to minimize it, in part by inserting such moments in longer periods of study encompassing time both before and after the crisis points.[38]

A fourth probing device, more indirect but nonetheless promising, would sharpen our ability to *notice* clues through comparative readings. The specialization and pace of publication in contemporary academic life impede serious analytical dialogue—not only across disciplinary lines, but also across lines of area specialization. But the issues under discussion here—patterns of indigenous participation in European colonial markets, and the methods we might use to interpret their social significance— arise in research on Mesoamerican, African, Asian, and other colonized peoples. In our eagerness, as "Andeanists," to emphasize the particular stamp that Andean peoples placed on European mercantile expansion,[39] we perhaps make of professional vice a virtue and thereby justify isolating ourselves from valuable comparative findings and perspectives. We would surely err if we simply transferred findings from one culture, colonial experience, and historical era to another; more intensive comparative thinking would surely heighten our sensitivites to nuances in the evidence and enlarge the reservoir of pertinent questions and possibilities we bring to our research. Historians of Africa, like Andeanists, place a high premium on cross-fertilization of history and anthropology. This occurs in part because they grapple with similar historical, theoretical, and methodological issues. Surely we can learn from their efforts and take advantage of their access to the oral history of relatively recent colonial experiences. Reading comparatively will not provide us foolproof tools to liberate us from our methodological difficulties, but it will enable us to add further probing devices as we search for clues to the underlying content of Andean market initiatives. Systematic comparative readings and seminars may yield as many clues as further archival research.[40]

These and other methodological probes really have two purposes. On the one hand, they will bring to bear new sorts of information with which to interpret Andean market intervention. Less obvious, but equally promising, they will also enrich our research intuition—the "radar" that enables researchers to sense and take notice of "clues" in the first place. The irony, I suspect, is that as new experience, questions, possibilities, and comparisons sensitize our radar, we may well notice a sprinkling of once neglected clues hidden in the economic transactions documents themselves.[41] Read qualitatively and quantitatively, the records of Andean market participation may yet provide more than one-dimensional glimpses.

Andean Market Participation and Subsistence: Three Hypotheses

A methodological and speculative essay such as this one lends itself to hypotheses rather than definitive conclusions. The hypotheses proposed here concern matters of both method and historical substance. They cast the relationship between Andean market participation and internal subsistence organization in terms that are sometimes conflictual, sometimes complementary, sometimes deliberately ambiguous.

My first hypothesis is that under most circumstances, thinking in terms of Andean resistance or accommodation to "the" market will prove useless. The rise of a colonial mercantile economy certainly imposed severe pressures on Andean peoples. The prospect of colonial profit in regional and international marketplaces heightened demands for *particularly destructive* tributes and labor drafts,[42] and it encouraged an interpenetration of "commercial" and "subsistence" economic sectors that altered and partly "monetized" Andean needs and obligations. This interpenetration occurred while colonial expropriation of native resources made it impossible for ayllus to meet their altered and "monetized" needs and obligations consistently on the basis of their own ethnic Andean economies.[43] Colonial mercantile penetration thus battered native self-sufficiency, a traditionally high priority in highland Andean cultures, and, in some regions and time periods, left native peoples vulnerable to "market incentive" as well as extraeconomic coercion. At the same time, Andean peoples responded, often shrewdly and creatively, to the forces around them and resisted colonial expropriations.[44]

Yet none of this shows that Andean peoples responded to "the" market or to "mercantile forces" as a *general* phenomenon. Responses were more specific and varied. Andean peoples responded to particular product, land, and labor markets and to the particular demands and opportunities arising from such markets. Often, they responded to market-inspired demands and pressures not by resisting the market as such. Instead, Andean peoples voluntarily "engaged" certain market sectors and opportunities in order to alleviate or avoid other market-linked oppressions and in order to resist more abject surrender to market forces and demands on terms they could not control. To state the matter more empirically, if an Indian group met its cash needs by selling coca leaf to colonial merchants, it might better resist pressure to work on a nearby sugar hacienda's harvests for paltry wages.[45] This pattern—initiating engagement with parts of the colonial-sponsored economic structure to avoid more abject surrender—strikingly resembles native responses to the political-judicial structure of the colonial state.[46]

Once we recognize Andean initiatives in European colonial markets, we must of course confront the motivations, social imperatives and functions, and socioeconomic consequences that defined the "logic" of such initiatives. It is in this context that I propose a second hypothesis: a degree of accommodation and adaptation to market forces was, for many Andean peoples, a *precondition* for the continuity of subsistence and for the ongoing corporate integrity of ethnic-ayllu groups.[47] Andean peoples, under conditions of colonial rule, did not enjoy the luxury of viewing "commercial" and "subsistence" sectors as necessarily antithetical. The key issues concerned the specific relationships and power balances that shaped the consequences of colonial market penetration on the one hand and Andean market interventions on the other. Andean market participation could serve to defend native subsistence as long as the following conditions prevailed:

> 1. Andean peoples retained the ability to enter buoyant markets on somewhat independent terms and to integrate such participation into a broader cycle of socioeconomic activities whose logic did not correspond to a market-investment logic;
>
> 2. Andean peoples could protect their mercantile accumulations from external colonial raiders such as corregidores and could limit the use of such wealth internally, within ayllu-ethnic society, to the collective and overlapping claims emphasized in "traditional Andean" culture; and

3. Andean peoples enjoyed a sufficiently diverse base of lands, waters, and human energy to revitalize and expand "subsistence" activities when faced with market stagnation or collapse.[48]

Few colonized Andean peoples could hope to meet these conditions in such pristine form. Too many colonial relations undermined independent market participation, subjected Andean cash and commodity accumulations to purposes of private gain, and robbed native peoples of a healthy land-water-labor base. But one can envision approximations that, with varying degrees of success, incorporated market initiatives into the broader subsistence strategies of internally modified Andean economies. I suspect that many colonial conflicts that appeared to pit "subsistence" or "natural economy" imperatives against mercantile or "market economy" imperatives actually involved a more subtle struggle to control the conditions of Andean participation in colonial markets.[49]

Such struggles not only pitted the colonizer and the colonized against one another, but also internally divided Andean peoples. As we have seen, it mattered a great deal if Andean economic actors directed their market interventions to "traditional Andean" ends, to "colonial European" accumulation, or to the diversification of "colonial Andean" eclecticism. We cannot probe the character and significance of Andean market participation unless our tools and sensitivities enable us to distinguish between these various logics, despite the false appearances so prevalent in our documentation.

The gap between documentary appearance and historical substance leads, finally, to a third hypothesis: we will learn very little even about the economic character of Andean market interventions unless we "imbed" the documentation recording economic transactions in a broader study of social relations. The search for clues to the social logic, functions, contradictions, and consequences of Andean market participation will rarely yield definitive proofs, but it provides the only alternative to a rather one-dimensional analysis based on untested assumptions and models purporting to "explain" the logic of economic behavior. Even the economic historian of Andean peoples, therefore, will need to resort to methodological probes in "noneconomic" sources of the sort described in this paper. One can safely rely on records of economic transactions only if the relationships among the economic, political, social, and cultural dimensions of life are sufficiently clear and consistent to inspire confidence in a model explaining the "logic" or laws of economic activity.[50] But it is precisely these relationships that are at stake during moments of great social transformation, and in colonial situations more generally. Like the Andean peoples whose history and contemporary condition we study, we will need to sort out the various "logics" of market intervention by Andean actors. And like the ayllu natives who may have wondered about the trajectory of leading Andean figures, we must learn to identify the clues that enable us to pierce outer appearances and to distinguish one "economic logic" from another.

Notes

1. R. C. Padden, ed., in Bartolomé Arazáns de Orsúa y Vela, *Tales of Potosí,* trans. Frances M. López-Morillas (Providence, 1975), xiii.

2. This is a conservative calculation. On Potosí's population, see ibid., xxiv, 204 n. 25; Carlos Sempat Assadourian, "La producción de la mercancía dinero en la formación del mercado interno colonial: El caso del espacio peruano, siglo XVI," in Enrique Florescano, ed., *Ensayos sobre el desarrollo económico de México y América Latina (1500–1975)* (Mexico City, 1979), 229–230.

3. See Gwendoline B. Cobb, "Supply and Transportation for the Potosí Mines, 1545–1640," *Hispanic American Historical Review* [hereafter *HAHR*], 29.1 (February 1949): 25–45; "Descripción de la villa y minas de Potosí" [1603], in Marcos Jiménez de la Espada, ed., *Relaciones geográficas de Indias—Perú*, vol. 2, as reprinted in *Biblioteca de autores españoles*, vol. 183 (Madrid, 1965), 372–385.

4. Gwendoline B. Cobb, "Potosí and Huancavelica: Economic Bases of Colonial Peru, 1545 to 1640," Ph.D. dissertation (University of California, Berkeley, 1947), 224; "Descripción de Potosí," 380. On the value of Atahualpa's ransom-treasure, see James Jockhart, *The Men of Cajamarca: A Social and Biographical Portrait of the First Conquerors of Peru* (Austin, 1972), 13.

5. For examples from a variety of areas, see José Miranda, "La función económica del encomendero en los orígenes del régimen colonial de Nueva España (1525–1531)," *Anales del Instituto Nacional de Antropología e Historia*, 2 (1941–46): 421–462; G. Michael Riley, *Fernando Cortés and the Marquesado in Morelos, 1522–1547* (Albuquerque, 1973); James Lockhart, *Spanish Peru, 1532–1560: A Colonial Society* (Madison, 1968); Steve J. Stern, *Peru's Indian Peoples and the Challenge of the Spanish Conquest: Huamanga to 1640* (Madison, 1982); and Murdo J. MacLeod,

Spanish Central America: A Socioeconomic History, 1520–1720 (Berkeley, 1973).

6. For cogent studies of internal markets in the Andes, see Assadourian, "Producción de la mercancía dinero," 223–292; Assadourian, *El sistema de la economía colonial: Mercado interno, regiones y espacio económico* (Lima, 1982), esp. chs. 1, 3, 4, and 6. On the specific points mentioned regarding mines and markets, population and petty commodity production, Indian economy and migration, and economic uses of the colonial political apparatus, consult the following sources: Carlos Sempat Assadourian et al., *Minería y espacio económico en los Andes, siglos XVI–XX* (Lima, 1981); Peter J. Bakewell, *Miners of the Red Mountain: Indian Labor in Potosí, 1545–1650* (Albuquerque, 1984); Bakewell, *Silver and Entrepreneurship in Seventeenth-Century Potosí: The Life and Times of Antonio López de Quiroga* (Albuquerque, 1988); Jürgen Golte, *Repartos y rebeliones: Túpac Amaru y las contradicciones de la economía colonial* (Lima, 1980); Alvaro Jara, *Tres ensayos sobre economía minera hispano-americana* (Santiago, 1966); Robert G. Keith, *Conquest and Agrarian Change: The Emergence of the Hacienda System on the Peruvian Coast* (Cambridge, Mass., 1976); Brooke Larson, "Caciques, Class Structure and the Colonial State in Bolivia," *Nova Americana* (Turin) 2 (1979): 197–235; Larson, "Rural Rhythms of Class Conflict in Eighteenth-Century Cochabamba," *HAHR* 60.3 (1980): 407–430; Nicolás Sánchez Albornoz, *Indios y tributos en el Alto Perú* (Lima, 1978); Karen Spalding, *De indio a campesino: Cambios en la estructura social del Perú colonial* (Lima, 1974); Stern, *Peru's Indian Peoples;* Enrique Tandeter and Nathan Wachtel, *Precios y producción agraria: Potosí y Charcas en el siglo XVIII* (Buenos Aires, 1983).

7. On the logic of the mature colonial marketplace and labor system in the Andes, see Larson, "Rural Rhythms," 407–430; Brooke Larson, *Colonialism and Agrarian Transformation in Bolivia: Cochabamba, 1550–1900* (Princeton, 1988); Stern, *Peru's Indian Peoples,* 106–108, 138–157, 189–193; Enrique Tandeter, "Trabajo forzado y trabajo libre en el Potosí colonial tardío," *Desarrollo Económico* 20 (January–March 1980): 511–548; Tandeter, "La producción como actividad popular: 'Ladrones de minas' en Potosí," *Nova Americana* (Turin), 4 (1981): 43–65. For a comparative and theoretical perspective on markets and labor in the Andes, see Steve J. Stern, "Feudalism, Capitalism, and the World-System in the Perspective of Latin America and the Caribbean," *American Historical Review* 93.4 (October 1988): 829–872, reprinted in Frederick Cooper et al., *Confronting Historical Paradigms* (Madison, 1993), 23–83.

8. Assadourian, "Producción de la mercancía dinero," 223–292; Assadourian, *Sistema de la economía colonial.* For the continuing importance of market-related forces in the eighteenth century, see Golte, *Repartos y rebeliones.*

9. On European "aristocrat-entrepreneurs" in the Andes, see Stern, *Peru's*

Indian Peoples, esp. pp. 36–37, 80–113, 138–157. For similar patterns in Mexico, see Miranda, "Función económica del encomendero," 421–462; David A. Brading, *Miners and Merchants in Bourbon Mexico, 1780–1810* (London, 1971); Doris M. Ladd, *The Mexican Nobility at Independence, 1780–1826* (Austin, 1976). Elsewhere, I have focused more precisely on the labor dimension of this economic logic and on the specificities of a colonial "law of diversity," an economic logic premised on combining a variegated ensemble of labor relations and strategies. See Stern, "Feudalism, Capitalism, and the World-System," 870–871.

10. Frank Salomon, *Los señores étnicos de Quito en la época de los Incas* (Otavalo, 1980); María Rostworowski de Diez Canseco, *Etnía y sociedad: Costa peruana prehispánica* (Lima, 1977). Cp. Chapter 2.

11. Penetrating studies showing the distinction between the matrices shaping market activity in capitalist and precapitalist settings are Karl Polanyi, *The Great Transformation: The Political and Economic Origins of Our Time* (Boston, [1944] 1957); Polanyi et al., eds., *Trade and Market in the Early Empires: Economies in History and Theory* (Chicago, 1957). For application of Polanyi's concepts to the Aztec and Inca states, see Pedro Carrasco, "The Political Economy of the Aztec and Inca States," in George A. Collier, Renato I. Rosaldo, and John D. Wirth, eds., *The Inca and Aztec States, 1400–1800: Anthropology and History* (New York, 1982), 23–40, esp. p. 39. The Marxian tradition has contributed important debates on the analytical distinction between commercial activity in precapitalist and capitalist settings. For a sampling, see the well-known debate originally published in *Science and Society* in the 1950s and reprinted in Paul Sweezy et al., *The Transition from Feudalism to Capitalism* (London, 1978); cf. more recent historical discussion in T. H. C. Aston and C. H. E. Philpin, eds., *The Brenner Debate: Agrarian Class Structure and Economic Development in Pre-Industrial Europe* (New York, 1985); Peter Kriedte, *Peasants, Landlords, and Merchant Capitalists: Europe and the World-Economy, 1500–1800* (Leamington Spa, 1983).

12. See Sally Falk Moore, *Power and Property in Inca Peru* (New York, 1958), 86–89, 132; John V. Murra, *Formaciones económicas y políticas del mundo andino* (Lima, 1975), 42, 265–267; Rostworowski, *Etnía y sociedad,* 16–19, 260–262. I refer to a "traditional Andean" model not to imply a fixed or unchanging "tradition," but to identify, for heuristic purposes, an economic "logic" historically constructed and flexible, yet rooted in pre-Columbian cultural history and sharply contrasted with a "European colonial" logic. Although the model of Andean economic organization pioneered by John V. Murra in the 1950s to 1970s, upon which I have heavily relied, has been subjected to significant critical reevaluation and some modification, I consider its main outlines still quite sound. For recent discussion and Murra's own retrospective assessment, see Shozo Masuda,

Izumi Shimada, and Craig Morris, eds., *Andean Ecology and Civilization: An Interdisciplinary Perspective on Andean Ecological Complementarity* (Tokyo, 1985).

13. Cúneo Vidal, cited in Franklin Pease G. Y., *Del Tawantinsuyu a la historia del Perú* (Lima, 1978), 198–199 n. 8. See also John V. Murra, "Aymara Lords and Their European Agents at Potosí," *Nova Americana* (Turin), 1 (1978): 231–233.

14. For examples of the findings mentioned in this paragraph, consult the following sources: Assadourian, "Producción de la mercancía dinero," 223–292; Elinor C. Burkett, "Indian Women and White Society: The Case of Sixteenth-Century Peru," in Asunción Lavrin, ed., *Latin American Women: Historical Perspectives* (Westport, Conn., 1978), 101–128; Ricardo Cappa, *Industria fabril que los españoles fomentaron y arruinaron en América* (Madrid, 1891), 33, 64–65, 69–70; Roberto Choque, "Pedro Chipana: Cacique comerciante de Calamarca," *Avances* (La Paz) 1 (1978): 28–32; Emilio Hart-Terré, *Negros e indios: Un estamento social ignorado del Perú colonial* (Lima, 1973); Larson, "Rural Rhythms," 407–430; Murra, "Aymara Lords and Their European Agents," 231–243; Silvia Rivera Cusicanqui, "El mallku y la sociedad colonial en el siglo XVII: El caso de Jesús de Machaca," *Avances* (La Paz) 1 (1978): 7–27; Spalding, *De indio a campesino;* Spalding, "Hacienda-Village Relations in Andean Society to 1830," *Latin American Perspectives* 2:1 (1975): 107–121; Stern, *Peru's Indian Peoples;* Tandeter, "Producción como actividad popular," 43–65; Ann M. Wightman, *Indigenous Migration and Social Change: The Forasteros of Cuzco, 1570–1720* (Durham, 1990).

15. For a review of struggles and conditions of labor and marketing in Potosí, and a guide to bibliography, see Stern, "Feudalism, Capitalism, and the World-System," 849–855.

16. For historical examples, see Stern, *Peru's Indian Peoples,* 103–104, 130; Golte, *Repartos y rebeliones,* passim.

17. For historical examples, see Luis J. Basto Girón, *Las mitas de Huamanga y Huancavelica* (Lima, 1954), 10–11; Murra, "Aymara Lords and Their European Agents," 235, 238–240; and Stern, *Peru's Indian Peoples,* 30–34, 38, 40–44, 90–91, 149–150.

18. For historical examples, see Larson, "Caciques," 202–205; Sánchez Albornoz, *Indios y tributos en el Alto Perú,* 99–107; Spalding, *De indio a campesino,* 47, 52–55, 61–87; Stern, *Peru's Indian Peoples,* 158–175.

19. Yale University Latin American Collection, Sterling Library, Department of Manuscripts and Archives [hereafter YULAC], vol. 3, "Libro de los remates de los tributos de los repartimientos que se cobran en esta caja . . . [Cuzco] 1575–1582." For the Parinacochas accounts, see ff. 90–94, 146–149, 185.

20. Mining—the nerve center of the colonial economy—constitutes a conspicuous example. See Assadourian, "Producción de la mercancía dinero," 223–292, for

the case of early colonial Potosí; see Biblioteca Municipal de Ayacucho, book 1.31, ff. 48–71v, for the case of early colonial Huancavelica. For further examples, see the sources in notes 15 and 19.

21. YULAC, vol. 3, "Libro de los remates," ff. 93r, 94r, 147v, 149r, 185r for specific Indian interventions in the auctions.

22. See YULAC, vol. 5, "Libro común de sumas . . . por el tesorero Miguel Sánchez. Cuzco, 1572–1573," ff. 62v, 63r; Biblioteca Nacional del Perú, Sala de Investigaciones [hereafter BNP], A236, 1597, "En la residencia secreta que se le tomó a Dn. Francisco de Cepeda, Corregidor . . . de Parinacochas," ff. 20r, 22r.

23. See Juan Polo de Ondegardo, "Informe al Licenciado Briviesca de Muñatones sobre la perpetuidad de las encomiendas en el Peru" [1561], *Revista Histórica* (Lima) 13 (1940): 169.

24. See Juan Polo de Ondegardo, "Relación de los fundamentos acerca del notable daño que resulta de no guardar a los indios sus fueros" [1571], in *Colección de libros y documentos referentes a la historia del Perú*, 4 vols. (Lima, 1916), 3:60, 66–67, 70–73; Murra, *Formaciones económicas y políticas*, 30–34, 146, 154–157, 251.

25. For Andean assumptions that one set aside fields specifically for colonial obligations, see Basto Girón, *Mitas de Huamanga y Huancavelica*, 10–11; Archivo General de Indias, Sevilla, V, Lima 308, "Relación de la visita del Obispo [Verdugo de Huamanga] . . . 1625," p. 10 (of microfilm copy). See also Stern, *Peru's Indian Peoples*, 40–41, 35.

26. Murra, "Aymara Lords and Their European Agents," 240.

27. This probably refers to Cancha-Cancha, near Chuschi in the contemporary Department of Ayacucho.

28. Archivo Departamental de Ayacucho [hereafter ADA], Protocolos Notariales, Peña 1596, f. 266.

29. Ibid., f. 266v.

30. For more extensive discussion of some of these ambiguities, see Frank Salomon, "Ancestor Cults and Resistance to the State in Arequipa, ca. 1748–1754," in Steve J. Stern, ed., *Resistance, Rebellion, and Consciousness in the Andean Peasant World, 18th to 20th Centuries* (Madison, 1987), 148–165; Spalding, *De indio a campesino*, 50–60, 79–81, 84–86; Steve J. Stern, "The Struggle for Solidarity: Class, Culture and Community in Highland Indian America," *Radical History Review* 27 (1983): 21–45, esp. 35–39; cf. the discussions of *kuraka* ambivalence and contradiction in Manuel Burga, *Nacimiento de una utopía: Muerte y resurrección de los incas* (Lima, 1988); Karen Spalding, *Huarochirí: An Andean Society under Inca and Spanish Rule* (Stanford, 1984). The larger issue that gives rise to many such ambiguities and ambivalences, in peasant and colonial settings, is what I have elsewhere called "resistant adaptation." For a conceptual discussion, see Stern, "New

Approaches to the Study of Peasant Rebellion and Consciousness: Implications of the Andean Experience," in Stern, *Resistance, Rebellion, and Consciousness*, esp. 8–11.

31. Murra, *Formaciones económicas y polítas*, table 2, 216 (between 212–213); Spalding, *De indio a campesino*, 51.

32. For a pertinent discussion of a "law of diversity" and its economic logic in colonial political economy, see Stern, "Feudalism, Capitalism, and the World-System," 870–871.

33. A further complication that would take us beyond the scope of this article is that we ought probably to refer to more than one "European" entrepreneurial logic. I suspect that we can distinguish between a more stagnant *rentier* logic, apt to dominate under certain kinds of colonial conditions, and a more aggressive logic driving for investment-accumulation-reinvestment on an expanding scale. For a penetrating study of a *rentier* logic among owners of export-oriented feudal estates in Eastern Europe, during the early modern period, see Witold Kula, *Teoría económica del sistema feudal*, trans. Estanislow J. Zembrzuski (Mexico, 1974). A full treatment of economic "logics" would also have to consider the subsistence-oriented marketing logics of independent smallholders of various racial backgrounds. On smallholders in the Andean region, see Keith, *Conquest and Agrarian Change*, 81–84, 91–92; Larson, "Rural Rhythms," 407–430. Ultimately, a holistic analysis encompassing all significant economic actors of colonial society may need to study four or five distinct "logics" and the interrelations between them.

34. These hypothetical examples are not arbitrary. For Indians who risked their fortunes and success, see Salomon, "Ancestor Cults," 148–165; Spalding, *De indio a campesino*, 48–49, 79–81; and Stern, *Peru's Indian Peoples*, 164, 181–182. On leaders refusing to support popular and expensive celebrations, I am indebted to discussion of Tom Abercrombie's doctoral dissertation research at a seminar I gave at the University of Chicago in January 1983 on "Historical Fallacies about the Age of Andean Insurrection." See also Stern, *Peru's Indian Peoples*, 179. Finally, for Andean peoples turning against a lord they had earlier tolerated, see Larson, "Caciques"; the discussion of the 1780s in Roger Rasnake, *Domination and Cultural Resistance: Authority and Power among an Andean People* (Durham, 1988); Karen Spalding, "Resistencia y adaptatación: El gobierno local y las élites nativas," *Allpanchis* (Cuzco) 17–18 (1981): 17–19. The volatile and shifting political relations of lords and Andean peasants will be greatly illuminated in Sinclair Thomson's forthcoming dissertation (University of Wisconsin) on eighteenth-century Aymara politics and insurrection in the La Paz altiplano.

35. The "fault line" term is borrowed from Karen Spalding's study of the Huarochirí revolt of 1750 in *Huarochirí: An Andean Society under Inca and Span-*

ish Rule. On the complexity of forastero-originario relations, and evidence that such distinctions could be bridged, see Larson, "Caciques," 201–202; Stern, *Peru's Indian Peoples,* 126–127, 174; and Wightman, *Indigenous Migration and Social Change,* passim.

36. For broad overviews, see Scarlett O'Phelan Godoy, *Rebellions and Revolts in Eighteenth-Century Peru and Upper Peru* (Cologne, 1985); Stern, *Resistance, Rebellion, and Consciousness,* parts I and II. For more specific discussions of politics in the Bolivian altiplano, see the references to publications and dissertations by Abercrombie, Larson, Rasnake, and Thomson in note 34 above.

37. Larson, "Caciques," 202–203; Sánchez Albornoz, *Indios y tributos en el Alto Perú,* 99–107; Chapter 8 in this volume.

38. For methodological discussion of the advantages of multiple time scales incorporating long-term frames of reference in the study of crisis points, see Stern, "New Approaches to the Study of Peasant Rebellion and Consciousness," 11–13.

39. This desire comes through in the planning document for the Social Science Research Council project on "Market Penetration and Expansion in the Andes, 16th–20th Centuries," which served as a basis for the 1983 conference in Sucre, Bolivia, that led to this volume. The planning document points out emphatically that "anthropologists have insisted that the Andean region and its peoples imposed specific conditions on the process of European market penetration and expansion. They insist that mercantile development in the Andes did not necessarily follow the same laws as those established for European history, or other parts of the 'underdeveloped' world, and that precapitalist economies are neither all alike, nor subordinated to the world economic system in an identical and therefore predictable way" (p. 4).

40. A recent impressive effort to write a global history of European expansion and indigenous responses is Eric R. Wolf, *Europe and the People without History* (Berkeley, 1982). Wolf's tour de force demonstrates, I believe, that systematic comparative work blending the perspectives of the historian and the anthropologist is indeed a practical possibility. A good starting point might be organization of comparative seminars whose members will have agreed to do a common set of background readings in advance, and who would then meet to discuss research papers on a specific issue of broad comparative interest. On the resonance of issues and scholarship in Africa and Latin America, see Frederick Cooper et al., *Confronting Historical Paradigms: Peasants, Labor, and the Capitalist World-System in Africa and Latin America* (Madison, 1993).

41. It is worth noting that in both the Parinacochas and Uybua-Cabana transactions discussed here, some (but not all) clues to the underlying significance of the transactions were drawn from a close reading of the transaction records them-

selves. But reliance on transaction records alone would have hindered my ability to notice clues buried in such records.

42. By this I mean that one can envision tribute and labor draft systems whose particular features and dynamics might have been much more compatible with the needs of Andean subsistence economies, but less desirable from the point of view of colonial profits. Comparison of Inca and colonial Spanish tribute and labor draft systems makes this point especially evident. See Stern, *Peru's Indian Peoples*, 82–89.

43. See ibid., 148–157, 186; Spalding, *De indio a campesino*, 52–60; Spalding, "Hacienda-Village Relations," 111–113.

44. That such responses began early, well before the famous eighteenth-century rebellions, and that they took subtle and sometimes nonviolent form, is documented for Huamanga in Stern, *Peru's Indian Peoples*. Of special comparative interest are the following studies of Oaxaca in colonial Mexico: Woodrow Borah, *Silk Raising in Colonial Mexico* (Berkeley, 1943); María de los Angeles Romero Frizzi, "Economía y vida de los españoles en la Mixteca Alta: 1519–1720," Ph.D. dissertation (Universidad Iberoamericana, 1985); William B. Taylor, *Landlord and Peasant in Colonial Oaxaca* (Stanford, 1972); Taylor, *Drinking, Homicide and Rebellion in Colonial Mexican Villages* (Stanford, 1979).

45. This is not an arbitrary example. In 1607–1608, the Indians of Ongoy, in western Andahuaylas, sought to save lucrative coca fields in the montaña of La Mar, in eastern Ayacucho. The income from the coca fields was used, among other things, to pay colonial tributes. The Ongoy Indians faced an uphill struggle to retain their holdings in the lucrative coca zone of Mayomarca, and in the 1630s we find Ongoy's Indians earning their tributes not by selling coca, but by working on an Andahuaylas sugar hacienda. ADA, Cabildo, Causas Civiles, Leg. 2, C. 16, 1699, Untitled document on Mayomarca lands, f. 6; Biblioteca Nacional del Perú, Sala de Manuscritos, Z1124, 1631, "Expediente . . . en nombre de los hijos legítimos y herederos de Dña. Bernardina de Romaní . . . ," ff. 495v–496r, 498v.

46. See the articles by Borah and Stern in Collier et al., *Inca and Aztec States*, 265–320; and Taylor, *Drinking*, passim. On the sheer volume of Indian litigation, and its institutional implications in Mexico, see Woodrow Borah, *Justice by Insurance* (Berkeley, 1983).

47. Market participation as a precondition for defense of subsistence and corporate integrity is a response that outlived the colonial period proper. For post-colonial examples, see Henri Favre, "The Dynamics of Indian Peasant Society and Migration to Coastal Plantations in Central Peru," in Kenneth Duncan and Ian Rutledge, eds., *Land and Labour in Latin America: Essays on the Development of Agrarian Capitalism in the Nineteenth and Twentieth Centuries* (Cambridge,

1977), 253–268; Florencia E. Mallon, *The Defense of Community in Peru's Central Highlands: Peasant Struggle and Capitalist Transition, 1860–1940* (Princeton, 1983). For a profoundly important study that sets the issues in a long-term perspective that spans the colonial/postcolonial divide, see Larson, *Colonialism and Agrarian Transformation in Bolivia,* esp. the conclusion.

48. Mallon, *Defense of Community,* 268–307, 337, shows that it is precisely the inability to channel a diverse communal resource base into revitalized "subsistence" activity, under conditions of market collapse, that constitutes a watershed in the history of peasant proletarianization. Her discussion centers on the Mantaro Valley central sierra region during the 1930s.

49. An early example involves the resistance of the Lucanas peoples of southern Huamanga to labor drafts for newly discovered mines in the 1560s and their subsequent leadership of an anti-Christian millenarian movement. In truth, the Lucanas peoples had earlier taken the initiative in participating in the colonial commercial economy by exploiting local mines on their own terms and by collaborating with colonials if such cooperation allowed them to defend their own perceived interests. See Stern, *Peru's Indian Peoples,* 30, 35, 38–39, 48–49, 55. Cf. the research on Potosí and Oruro discussed in Stern, "Feudalism, Capitalism, and the World-System," 849–855; Ann Zulawski, "Wages, Ore Sharing, and Peasant Agriculture: Labor in Oruro's Silver Mines, 1607–1720," *HAHR* 67.3 (August 1987): 405–430.

50. This is a basic point made long ago by "substantivists" in their debates with "formalists" in economic anthropology and by Marxian historians emphasizing the material and ideological characteristics that distinguish the capitalist mode of production from other economic types. For examples, see George Dalton, ed., *Studies in Economic Anthropology* (Washington, D.C., 1971); Eugene D. Genovese, *The World the Slaveholders Made: Two Essays in Interpretation* (New York, 1971), esp. part 2; Genovese, *The Political Economy of Slavery: Studies in the Economy and Society of the Slave South* (New York, 1965); Kula, *Teoría económica;* Polanyi, *Great Transformation;* Marshall Sahlins, *Stone Age Economics* (Chicago, 1972).

4

Exchange in the Ethnic Territories between 1530 and 1567: The *Visitas* of Huánuco and Chucuito

CARLOS SEMPAT ASSADOURIAN

Writing in a time of transition, Juan Polo de Ondegardo observed the flow of exchange between different altitudes: "In very few lands, or none in the sierra, can the Indians survive without going to another for their necessities." Polo also collected profiles of the past from indigenous oral sources: Inca rule restrained the coastal-sierra trade that used to include gold and silver, so that in Tawantinsuyu "there was little trade . . . and what existed was petty exchange, such as cotton clothing for wool clothing or fish for other foodstuffs. The former was between leaders, because the common people only exchanged food items, and this in small amounts, although these customs varied from region to region" (*RH* 145).[1] Polo did not see fit to elaborate his perception of "varied customs" that regulated exchange, and he generalized: "Under the old order the community sent a few people to bring for all," because "if each one had to go themselves for what they needed, the villages would be deserted each year with no one to care for their own concerns" (*RH* 176). Polo probably generalized from the example of the peoples of the Collao, where "a few go for all," and neglected the customs of other ethnic groups, in which it was possible for "each one to go for what they needed." Even so, a basic implication of his generalization is valid for both cases: under "the old order," exchange between different altitudes had not led to the development of specialized merchants.

The Huánuco Visita

Circulation among Direct Producers

The *visitas* (inspections) of Huánuco and Chucuito are sources that allow for deeper explorations into the question of indigenous exchange. Two chapters of the instructions charged the *visitador* to Huánuco with investigating this issue. One chapter, which alluded to the question of tributary inequalities in Tawantinsuyu, mentioned merchants as a possible stratified group; the other one called for inquiry into the productive possibilities of the ethnic groups and the contemporary "trade agreements, flow of goods, and petty bartering that the said Indians have" (*VH*).[2]

The visitador received the following typical responses about merchants from ethnic leaders:

There are no merchants that live from that activity. Instead, each one goes when he needs to and others likewise come to them. (*VH* 1:219)

Among them there are no people who do trading as a way of life; instead, one does it according to particular needs, and in the same way, others come to them and in this way they interchange and make deals. (*VH* 1:179)

In the time of the Inca there were no merchants as a group as there are among the Spanish. Instead, in the *tiangues* Indians sold only food to each other, and nobody bought clothing because everybody had what they needed; and there were few other things, and there were none who traded great amounts of merchandise. (*VH* 2:29)

[There were no] merchants, but in the tiangues there were those who sold trifles and these were very modest exchanges of chili and wool and little things, trading one for the other. (*VH* 2:58)

The first two testimonies belong to Chupachu and Quero leaders (*principales*), who pointed out the absence of sites reserved exclusively for trading activities. The last two statements from a principal of the Cuzco *mitimaes* and the Yacha *curaca* referred to Tawantinsuyu and pointed to the existence of tiangues. It is unclear whether these tiangues actually corresponded to the meaning of the term in Spanish (market, commercial activity) or "appeared" when the visitador transcribed the statements into his own language and discourse, but the contexts in which the tiangues are mentioned seem to imply internal movements of goods among households of a single ethnic group (see Chapter 9 in this volume).

The information collected by the inspector concerning trade and commerce among the Indians, both in Tawantinsuyu and after the arrival of the Spanish, indicated a circulation of goods without apparent centralized organization, without merchants, and without meeting places established by custom or by ethnic alliances as permanent trading centers or rotating markets.

This inspection confirms Polo's generalization on a general level: in Tawantinsuyu there were exchanges of "food for food in small amounts" among producers themselves, without these relations creating the specialized function of the merchant. But it seems to contradict one aspect of Polo's account in that the natives of the region of Huánuco undertook exchanges individually: "According to their needs each one goes and others come to them."

The same inspection illustrates the nature of multiethnic exchange. The Chupachus, for example, directed the flow of their goods toward the Yaros, Guamalís, Yachas, Chinchacochas, Guanucos, and mitimaes. These other ethnic groups appeared as "neighboring Indians," located at distances of from three to five or six days. In the statement of Señor Diego Xagua we find the composition of Chupachu exchange:

> In their land they have cotton, coca, and maize and those who come to trade, the Yaro and the Guamalís and other Indians from the *xalcas* [high slopes of the cordillera], bring with them dried meat and wool and sheep, for which they take away coca and cotton and chili and maize, and they also bring salt for the same trade. . . . Likewise, the Indians of this area go to the xalca with the things they have to trade with the Indians there for livestock and dried meat and the other things they have. (*VH* 1:29)

A Quero leader detailed the composition of the flow of goods in each direction:

> They carry chili and trade with the Guamalís for wool, and they also take chili and potato and maize to the Yachas and they trade it for wool and livestock; and to Chinchacocha they take maize and potato and chili

and sometimes coca when they have it, and for this they bring back salt and wool and fish. (*VH* 1:179)

The inspection contains information about the material resources that gave rise to these multiethnic contacts. The Chupachus controlled three ecological zones with abundant land: (1) the cold, high sierra, to cultivate *oca*, potatoes, *maxua,* and *ollucos;* (2) the temperate lower sierra for maize and *quinoa;* and (3) the hot lowlands for coca, cotton, "and also wheat, maize, chilies, peanuts, squashes, sweet potatoes, *cachcoa,* and beans" (*VH*). However, as they had insufficient livestock for wool and dried meat, the Chupachus used the surplus from the temperate and hot zones to obtain goods from the xalca through exchange with other groups.

European Domination and the Expansion of Interethnic Exchange

The inspection by Ortíz shows clearly how European dominion enlarged the sphere of indigenous exchange. Let us take the case of tribute in cotton clothing. As in the time of the Inca, all Chupachu members had direct access to the lands of Cayra, which were suitable for cultivating cotton; the visita even suggests that they had more land than they could work. Inquiring among the leaders and *hatun runas*, the inspector received a mass of similar responses:

> They have lands in Cayra where they can harvest cotton, but they acquire what they spin for the tribute by exchanging their potatoes. They do not sow cotton because they cannot, because they are very busy working for the tribute and working in the city and they do not have time for it. (*VH* 1:159)

> They have land for cotton and it is not sown; with all the time they are occupied with the tribute they have no time for tending to it, and they lose it, so they obtain it by trading maize and potatoes and *cavi* and *cochies.* (*VH* 1:182)

In other words, although they maintained their access to the lowlands, the Chupachus could no longer cultivate all of it, both because of the amount of time required to cultivate cotton itself, and the production of surplus destined for the *encomendero,* and also because of the crisis of human energy that the group suffered with population loss (in relation to the time of the Inca, the number of Chupachu tributaries had declined by 80 percent). Therefore, the tribute in cloth led the Chupachus to a new and suggestive use of their trade relations. Even with access to adequate land, they acquired the cotton "that they needed to produce tribute in cloth by trading in the *yungas,*" and "they [came] to trade for it in the lowlands," offering the surplus produce from their temperate and cold zones.

Their tribute obligations had another consequence. According to Lord Diego Xagua, "they often lack the cloth they have to deliver, and they buy it with money in the stores of this city" (*VH* 1:29). Another European tribute item, *alpargates* (leather shoes), could produce the same effect; the Inca mitimaes, for example, "buy the shoes that they send as tribute because they don't know how to make them and they cost sometimes a tomin and a tomin and a half and even sometimes 2 tomines, and the only way they have to pay for those shoes is with the work and the wages earned by the Indians who work in this city" (*VH* 2:42).[3]

The Case of Salt

The case of salt is very interesting. All the groups visited—Chupachus, Queros, Yachas, mitimaes—traded for salt with the Yaros and Chinchacochas, taking maize, potatoes, and chilies. In Huánuco and probably in all of Tawantinsuyu, the ethnic groups had access to this basic good even though the salt pans fell outside their territories.[4] How then did salt become an object of exchange?

The Cuzco mitimaes, asking to be exempted from tribute in salt, said that they had a salt man "who worked within the territory of the Yaros and for this reason the Yaros harassed him. Since he was there to provide the Cuzco mitimaes with salt, they requested that the Yaros stop harassing him and let him fulfill his task" (*VH* 2:29), but this conflict does not fully explain the extent of trade in salt. For example, the Chupachus and Queros also traded for salt although they had salt pans in the territory of the Yaros. Moreover, the Chupachu leaders reported to some inspectors that in the time of the Inca they were 4,000 strong, and they sent sometimes sixty and other times forty-five men, in other words from 1.1

percent to 1.5 percent of their married male population, to collect salt. In 1562 the Chupachus had approximately 800 male members, and they sent "ten Indians to collect salt . . . some elderly among them," in other words the same percentage of 1.1 percent to 1.5 percent of adult males, depending on whether or not the elderly were counted (*VH* 1:306).

The Chucuito Visita

"Horizontal" Trade and the "Vertical Archipelago" of the Lupaqa

The case of Collasuyo offers new frameworks for analyzing flows of exchange. Pedro Sancho summarized the information given to Francisco Pizarro by the first two "Christians that were sent to see the province of Collao": traveling through that "very high . . . and extremely cold sierra," they observed that the inhabitants of the altiplano had to drive their sheep to "trade for goods with those who live close to the sea . . . and also with those living in the lowlands near the rivers."[5] This traffic in livestock for goods of the lowlands must have been impressive for the two Europeans to record it as one of the notable features of the territory and for Juan de Matienzo, decades later, to characterize the people of the Collao as "people rich in livestock and big merchants and dealers. They seem Jews in their trading and dealing."[6]

The 1567 visita to Chucuito by Garci Diez de San Miguel represents the best information we have for a group from the Collao, the Lupaqa Kingdom, whose 20,000 households were nearly all located in the highlands. Their control of the highland puna steppes made the Lupaqa a "people rich in livestock" (*VC* 208).[7] However, the altitude limited their agricultural production to quinoa and tubers such as potatoes, oca, and *luki*. Given this insufficiency, the Lupaqa used their abundant livestock to obtain products cultivated in temperate and warm zones.

The statements of Señor Martín Cari and the Spaniard Bernaldino Fasato summarize the information collected in the highlands concerning the spatial parameters of the flow of Lupaqa goods: "The Indians of this province go most years to acquire maize in Arequipa and to the coast and to Moquegua. . . . They also trade for the same throughout the Collao, as far as Cuzco and Chuquiabo" (*VC* 17); "They go to trade and barter in Larecaja and in other parts of the yungas" (*VC* 61). Particular points here suggest various forms of exchange. One of the destinations mentioned by Lord Cari, "as far as Cuzco," must refer strictly to those Indians who were rich in livestock and derive from the demand for coca. Cari himself asserts that the Indians of this province "also trade . . . throughout the Collao" (*VC* 21). Given that the debate has tended to focus on the factors that determined access to different resources located in multiple ecological planes, this allusion to "horizontal" exchange in the highlands is surprising at first. However, the text of the inspection contains information that explains the causes for this circuit of exchange.

Ten months into the visita, the Lupaqa leadership brought forward information about the "infertility of this province." In the fifth section of the questionnaire (*VC* 146–150), the chiefs claim that in addition to the infertility "more often than not they obtain very little food and it is not uncommon to have blight, and they do not have enough water or else it rains too much and so their fields and farms suffer; and other years it freezes, and this is more common in this province than in any other part of these kingdoms." In the following sections the chiefs make a link between these problems in highland agriculture and the recurring crisis to which it is subject, with the fact that they have substantial livestock resources and caravans that go to acquire basic supplies in the temperate and warm zones.

The witnesses presented by the ethnic lords confirmed the fragility of Lupaqa agriculture and the extent of their exchange relations with the cultivators of the lower zones and emphasized that, if it were not for that exchange, "its infertility would make the province uninhabitable" (*VC* 156). Furthermore, the leaders noted that the Lupaqa "also go to other regions to get *chuño* and quinoa since what they can produce on their land is not enough to sustain them and in order to get these things they bring livestock to trade" (*VC* 156).

> In most years there is a freeze that makes the crops fail, and the same happens for lack of water; and other times there is a lot of rain, which causes damage because, according to the Indians, the water breeds worms in the potatoes. And it seems that this province is much more infertile than any other of the Collao because its people go to buy food from the other peoples of the Collao, and this witness has never seen that these other Indians come here to obtain food. (*VC* 163)

Even before this Lupaqa information appeared, the inspector recorded very similar testimony: "They have enough land, although some years it freezes, and when it freezes they sometimes fall short of what they need although they compensate for it with livestock" (*VC* 55). They would go to trade for food "in [other parts of] the Collao because they suffer shortages because in comparison with other lands in this area this province is more sterile than the others" (*VC* 143).[8]

While we must remember this practice of "horizontal" exchange, it is clear that the bulk of Lupaqa trade was directed toward the temperate and warm lands. Garci Diez reiterated that the goods going down from the puna were llamas, wool, and dried meat. Up to this point, the goods exchanged were the same as under the Inca. However, in 1567 the Lupaqa informed the visitador that their goods also included clothing and silver (*VC* 80, 112). Assuming that the silver is a new item, it remains unclear whether the offering of cloth to lowland cultivators was rooted in the traditions of Tawantinsuyu or if it was a new development since the European invasion.

The Chucuito visita of 1567 reveals the nature of demand for exchange goods among the inhabitants of the puna: maize was a high priority and then chilies. The visitador grouped together other goods of less importance as "other things," "things they do not have" (*VC*). An important aspect of this demand, its ethnospatial dimension, was not the subject of detailed investigation by Garci Diez. He noted the statement of Lord Martín Cari to the effect that he used to send his Indian servants to Cuzco with llamas to exchange for coca and that other Indians also took sheep, wool, and dried meat to Cuzco for the same trade. As regards maize, Garci Diez only notes that they went to the coast—to Larecaja, Arequipa, and Chuquiabo—that is, to areas where the Lupaqas had direct access to lands with high yields of maize. The details noted by Garci Diez in the puna do not reveal whether the Lupaqa caravans made centralized exchanges only with their kin who cultivated those zones of their archipelago or whether they traded freely with cultivators of other ethnic groups.

The Chucuito inspection illustrates the social differences embedded in such flows of goods. The established theory of pastoral societies is valid for the Lupaqa case: animals, more than land, are the real productive capital, and this resource is unevenly distributed. According to the Spanish, the Lupaqa "generally have some livestock, whether a lot or little;" "generally even the poor have animals" (*VC* 50, 59). However, the statements of ethnic lords reveal clear inequalities. The upper and lower moiety leaders of Acora maintained that "some Indians have no livestock at all" (*VC* 92), "that some Indians have no livestock, although these are few" (*VC* 98), while a lower moiety leader of Ilave said that in his village "those with livestock might be half of the Aymara Indians and the other half are poor, some so poor they do not even have blankets for their beds" (*VC* 112). Indian leaders in Juli repeated the same proportion: among their people "half would have livestock and the other half would not" (*VC* 116). Among owners, wealth in animals was quite unevenly distributed, ranging from three to 300 head according to the chiefs: "Some Indians have three sheep and others six and ten and 100 and 200 and others have more or less" (*VC* 80); "they have 300 head and 200 and 100 and eighty and fifty and twenty and so forth, up to the aforementioned flock of 300" (*VC* 116).[9] The inequality affected the flow of goods to temperate and warm regions. A Spaniard observed, "those who have enough sell alpaca wool, and those who do not use it to dress themselves" (*VC* 139), while Martín Cusi noted differences among his people: "Those who have livestock go to trade in the yungas, and those who do not go to work in the yungas and in other parts" in order to get foodstuffs from those ecological zones (*VC* 29).

The Lupaqa Economy and the Effects of European Pressure

USE OF CREDIT   Let us look at the effects of trade with the Europeans. In the judgment of Lord Cari, "about thirty Spaniards" resided in Chucuito, "engaging in trade and petty barter with Indians and selling them coca and wine" (*VC* 49). Such a large number of merchants shows the crucial importance of native livestock during this first phase of colonial rule. According to the data of the visita, between the large market for coca and the more restricted demand for wine, shawls, and Spanish clothing for affluent natives and chiefs, merchants acquired from 5,000 to 8,000 head of livestock annually (*VC* 251). Such a serious drain on local resources was facilitated by selling on credit. One Spaniard very familiar with the area, Pedro de Entrena, stated that the Indians "fall easily into the habit of accepting everything that is offered them on credit without considering the price and without having need of the merchandise, and if they had to pay in advance they would go without buying a tenth of it, for they could easily do without" (*VC* 59).

The ethnic lords considered these transactions unjust: "The Spanish cheat the Indians by giving them coca on credit and, to the caciques, wine and Spanish clothing; and since it is on credit they charge more than the true value. They quote a price in small livestock and afterward they take big animals" (*VC* 83–84). Here too there is evidence of social stratification among the Lupaqa. According to statements of Spaniards familiar with the area, when the chiefs were in debt, they settled their accounts by lending out Indian laborers "even when they could pay in silver and still have money left over" (*VC* 59). "Recently in this province there has been much upheaval caused by lending to Indians and more than 500 Indians are missing, because they are afraid of being pressured for what they owe" (*VC* 48).

CORREGIDORES AND FORCED PRODUCTION OF CLOTH   Following instructions from Lima, the inspector Garci Diez paid close attention to transactions between Spaniards and native authorities for the manufacture of *abasca* cloth and the rental of Indians for caravans between Arica, Ilo, Arequipa, Cuzco, and Potosí. His report states that "compelling the Indians to make cloth against their will" is a new phenomenon (*VC*). Given that he left the post of *corregidor* of Chucuito in 1560, Garci Diez seems to suggest that the introduction of this practice occurred after that date.[10] The text of the inspection registers some data about the extent of this forced insertion into the sphere of mercantile activity. According to the corregidor Estrada, since he had taken office twenty months earlier the Lupaqa chiefs had received 6,000 pesos for the rental of Indians and 10,000 pesos more for 5,000 pieces of clothing woven by their Indians. Another Spaniard said that during the same period the ethnic lords had organized the production of more than 4,000 pieces of clothing and had rented out more than 300 Indians for the Cuzco–Potosí trade circuit, at a rate of 14–15 pesos for each trip (*VC* 49, 58).

The transactions in clothing combine Andean and European features. Garci Diez specifies that all the contracts were formalized before the notary of Chucuito in the presence of the corregidor and with Lord Cusi and Lord Cari assuming responsibility for the agreements.[11] The process of allocating work followed Andean patterns. After making the contracts, declared Martín Cusi, "the leading caciques of this town divide the work among the entire province" (VC 76). A Spanish witness confirmed this: the deals were made with Cari and Cusi, and "they have the other caciques of the province divide the work among their *ayllus*" (VC 58). Although the numerical data of the inspection are flawed, they show that the distribution of clothing manufacture among the Lupaqa towns adhered to the Andean form of allocating surplus labor—that is, proportionate to the amount of surplus labor the group had available, or had available according to the last Inca *quipu*. Undoubtedly, authorities allocated labor within villages and households according to the same formula. Furthermore, it is very likely that, during the time dedicated to spinning and weaving, households had to rely on their own subsistence resources.[12] When they delivered the clothing, each cacique of the seven towns would receive the agreed price in silver bars from the Spanish.

To be sure, these transactions responded to market pressures, but their implementation depended on mechanisms of power. In his final report, Garci Diez complained that a part of the cloth made "in the name of others" was actually destined for the corregidores, in direct violation of a specific prohibition issued by the *audiencia* of Charcas (VC 217–218). The Lupaqa lords also argued that if they went beyond their traditional rights to command native labor, it was because of the corregidores' coercion. Vilcacutipa, who was more than 100 years old, referred to the greater coercive power of the Spanish when he said, "the speaker has no wish to order Indians to make this clothing for the Spanish, because they do it unwillingly; rather, the corregidores order him to do it and he complies under force" (VC 109). The Acora principales also gave the impression that, although they were in positions of authority, they were also subordinates. The Indians would not work "unless the corregidores force them to because sometimes the corregidores pressure the caciques to provide the labor" (VC 91).

DEMANDS OF THE CHURCH The ethnic lords' versions are misleading because they do not mention the Dominican friars as another crucial element. They admitted that they received payment in silver bars for deliveries of cloth and Indian labor, but they also claimed that they "receive no personal gain from Indian labor" and "have not charged more than they have spent" (VC 73, 78). The silver bars, they emphasized, were destined to cover two expenses: the tribute owed to the king when the number of tributaries sent to Potosí fell short of the quota and that to the churches established in the seven main towns.[13]

To document the last expense, the chiefs presented quipus that tallied the monetary requirements of the new religious observances: wages of the masons and carpenters who built the churches and the friars' quarters; organs and flutes; clothing for the altar boys; ornaments; wine and oil; celebrations and dances for Corpus Cristi; masses "to prevent lightning and thunder," and so on. They explained, furthermore, that "they as caciques give the money that the friars ask for," but "everything spent in works of the church and ornaments and all the rest" goes through the hands of the Dominicans. The visita makes another discovery: when the quipu keepers presented the accounts of revenues in silver for the manufacture of cloth and the leasing of Indian labor and the expenses—that is, the money given to the friars—Garci Diez noted that the last figure was higher than the first. He received a vague explanation from the chiefs: "Sometimes they pay it from their own estate and then charge the Indians for it." Recognizing that "estate" means "livestock" among the Lupaqa, another observation clarifies the chiefs' response. Checking the quipus of the town of Pomata, Garci Diez discovered that the sale of community livestock constituted another source of money with which to pay the expenses of the church (VC 231).

INDIAN RESENTMENT TOWARD THE NEW OBLIGATIONS The private interests of the corregidor and the spiritual ones of the Dominicans pressured the curacas to use their power to harness the energy of their Indians in the sphere of commercial transactions. Certainly the response at the highest levels of Lupaqa government provoked resentment among the hatun runas and those in intermediate positions of power. The statements made by principales to the visitador revealed the source of tension: "Their only complaints concern the clothing that the caciques have them make and the wages they collect from leasing out Indian labor" (VC 94). They indicate the resentment felt by tribute-paying Indians at the amount of time they were forced to give to making cloth and caring for livestock, which took away from weaving for their families and tending their own crops. Charged with making sure that the contracts made by the ethnic lords were scrupulously fulfilled, the leaders felt the conflict directly. "They, as principales of the ayllus, suffer when they are called to send Indians, because the Indians do not want to go" (VC 116); "they, as principales, have a hard time distributing clothing among the Indians because they accept it against their will" (VC 118). Frequently, the Indians' indignation was turned against their principales: "Many times the principales cannot deliver the Indians as they are required to because they do not want to go and if they do not deliver the Indians then some principales must go and work." We can understand why the old chief Vilcacutipa wanted to be free of these duties: "He has no wish to ask the Indians to make the cloth . . . because they do it unwillingly" (VC 120).

Garci Diez's inquiry about the manufacture of cloth and the leasing of Indians for caravans touches a theme of great interest. As is known, there were Spaniards whose projects for hastening socioeconomic transformation called for native cooperation. If colonial rule could eliminate the intermediary function of the ethnic lords, they reasoned, the hatun runas would voluntarily offer their services as workers in order to profit directly by daily wages. But even in the region of Chucuito, with its intense trading activity, we can see the weakness of such models based on the idea that indigenous people would voluntarily fill the labor force.

During the inspection, Garci Diez repeatedly asked whether "if the Indians were to receive themselves the 2 pesos for each piece of clothing that the caciques have them make, they would do it willingly" (VC 54). The negative responses he received touch on various dimensions of the problem. One Spaniard repeated the commonplace about Indian lethargy—"They are lazy people and only work when forced" (VC 61)—but another with more insight noted how the mechanisms of tribute functioned: "They do not do it, since they pay their quota from the wages of the 500 that go to Potosí every year from all the province, and so they have no need to do other jobs here nor work for wages" (VC 58). Ten years a resident in Chucuito, Pedro de Entrena showed once again his sensitivity to Andean culture when he observed, "if the caciques did not order the Indians out to work and collect their wages, even if the Indians kept all of their wages, they would not go to work, because, as far as this witness understands, they really have no need to work for wages" (VC 58).

The native demurrals, as far as they can be gleaned from the text of the inspection, are persuasive. The upper moiety leaders of Juli stated that "even if the Indians were offered 2 pesos for each piece of clothing or for a trip to Cuzco or Potosí, they would not do it because they lose so much time from their own fields and livestock, and when they dedicate time to making cloth for the Spanish they cannot make it for themselves and their wives and children" (*VC* 118). The lower moiety leaders of Acora gave a more elaborate explanation for the reluctance of the Indians: they spent much time in the manufacture of cloth and neglected their own necessities, and "even if they were offered 2 pesos per piece they would not accept because they cannot eat with those 2 pesos, and the time that they spend making clothing would be better spent in their fields and other things" (*VC* 91). The response of the upper moiety leaders of Juli is equally suggestive: "If they were offered 2 pesos per piece they would not do it willingly because to receive 2 pesos would be like doing it for nothing" (*VC* 121). This observation expresses the result of a real conflict between the Andean value of energy expended in labor and the price with which the Spanish rewarded indigenous labor. If Andean peoples agreed to transform their capacity to work into the sale of their labor power, they would have to produce "a shawl and a shirt for the Spanish for 2 pesos." The energy thus spent would lose value in Andean terms, given that

> the Indians who cannot make their own cloth pay, for only a shawl without a shirt (which is half of what the Spanish get for 2 pesos), two skeins of wool which are worth 2 pesos, to whomever makes it and they also give food and coca and they also provide the spun wool to make the shawl—this is what they pay only to have it woven. (*VC* 121)

Murra's Model of the "Vertical Control of Multiple Ecological Tiers"
Kinship and Economic Networks

The work of John V. Murra has made all the substantive contributions to our understanding of the interethnic circulation of goods in Tawantinsuyu. In chapter 7 of his 1955 thesis, the model that years later he would call "vertical control of multiple ecological tiers" is described as "ethnic colonies" of mitimaes, whose production was shared with kinspeople in the distant nuclear community through mechanisms of exchange. With a critical approach unique among historians of the time, Murra challenged the chroniclers' version of this system, arguing that while the Incas promoted these colonies, the model itself was pre-Incaic.[14]

Although he addressed the issue on various occasions, it was only in 1972 that Murra published his model, entitled "Vertical Control of Multiple Ecological Zones in the Economy of Andean Societies," which has had such enormous influence on Andean research.[15] In 1983, he further developed two aspects of his model (see Chapter 2 in this volume). First, while noting the results of research in the Ecuadorean highlands, he confirmed the absence of merchants and marketplaces in the central Andean puna region. Furthermore, he rejected the possibility that there was extensive exchange between the ethnic groups situated south of Cajamarca. Since ancient times, he argued, Andean societies of the puna regions had rejected trade as a method of complementing their resources and instead followed another route, that of ecological archipelagos. Second, he reflected that in order to gain access to the productivity of others they had to establish bonds of mutuality, activating mechanisms that gave them access and rights to the labor of others, obligating them to a particular social organization based on an ideology of kinship ties.

Based on an analysis of the sources, let us first look at the possibility of studying the economic networks activated by political and kinship relations in the early colonial period. For political reasons, Europeans analyzing the Andean system of circulation and redistribution tended to focus on the flow of labor and goods from hatun runas to their leaders, neglecting the inverse flow of goods that reflected the "generosity" of the leaders. Quite possibly, the latter may have engaged in far more acts of reciprocity and generosity beyond the distribution of food for labor provided and the funding of collective ceremonies and hospitality to outsiders, which are recorded in the documents.[16]

For the same reason, our information about reciprocity based on kinship ties is very poor. Even the conflict between the Andean organization of work and the new tribute obligations, about which we might expect to find abundant data, barely appears in the documents. Our knowledge is confined to a few references, for example: "While the [Lupaqa] Indians are away from their home their fields might suffer, but they are never so alone that they have neither kin nor in-laws to help, although there are some Indians without family and they could suffer, but in the end they too manage every year to plant and harvest" (*VC* 141–142). Or, some time later, from Waman Puma:

> Government and marriage laws and public order: They called brother-in-laws *masa* and sister-in-laws *caca* in the old days. The godfather was called *uayno;* male family members were called *uauquicona,* and female members were *panicona.* . . . These relatives helped each other with work and other necessities, and if they were sick, and with food and drink, and in making celebrations and during planting time, and when there was a death they would come to cry and after death and always, while they still lived. And after, their sons and descendants, grandchildren and great-grandchildren observed and respected the law of their former God.[17]

Aside from their scarcity, I find other limitations in the data. I believe that reciprocity between related households involved exchange of goods, as well as labor exchange, but I am not optimistic about the possibility of finding data to confirm this. As with the silences of the sources, we must be on guard against "tricks" the documents can play on us. In a society like the Lupaqa, with such inequality in access to wealth in livestock, we would expect a greater showing of generosity on the part of the leaders and generalized reciprocity at all levels of the kinship network. However, in the text of the 1567 inspection, inequality takes only the form of a crude exploitation of "the poor." Perhaps this accurately reflects the social structure, but it is not difficult to imagine that details of that structure remained hidden to the eyes of outside European inspectors or that it fell outside their interests, especially since the official questionnaire did not ask for data on forms of reciprocity.

The "Vertical Archipelago" under Spanish Rule

By contrast, the sources allow us to consider in more detail the question of "vertical archipelagos." In 1542, the priest Luis de Morales described the lack of sufficient resources of the Collas in the highlands ("the natives of this area can grow no maize and survive on nothing but potatoes, quinoa, and chuño") and how the inhabitants had overcome the local scarcity through their access to produce of other ecological zones. Predictably,

Morales attributed this access enjoyed by highlanders to policies of the Inca ("Guaynacava . . . took from each village a number of natives that were called mitimaes") and connected it with the whole structure of power. The vertical archipelagos were linked to ethnic hierarchies; the Inca established them so that the colonists "would plant maize and thereby pay respect to their native lord."[18]

Morales protested that the Spanish, when drawing the Indians of Collasuyo into *encomiendas* "had divided them, with their lords in one part and with one overseer and the mitimaes in another" and asked the king for a revision so that the mitimaes, "vassals and subjects of that lord and cacique, might come to serve him as before and offer him those things that they offered in the past." Morales denounced the economic effects of these new divisions, "owing to which natives and lords suffer in misery from the lack of corn and coca and everything else the vassals used to give them," but his complaint was principally motivated by considerations that the Europeans ought to respect indigenous hierarchies of power.[19] In his defense of the Indians, Morales is contrasting two policies: the Inca system that provided the highlands with access to other ecological planes and benefited the ethnic lords; and that of the Spanish which, only seven years after their arrival in Cuzco, threatened to unravel the entire system.

In his letter to the Council of the Indies in July 1550,[20] Fray Domingo de Santo Tomás also complained in more precise and accurate terms about the same policy. The distribution of Indians had "reduced and dismembered" the ethnic groups, reducing the status of the native lords and depriving them of many of their vassals. There is more than a difference in tone in the new complaint. While in 1542 the priest Morales only lamented the separation of the mitimaes, in 1550 Domingo de Santo Tomás protested because the Spanish had disrupted Indian society at a more serious level. They had dismembered the ethnic groups by dividing villages subject to "a cacique principal, and those of two or three or four lesser-ranking chiefs who were subjects of the cacique, between different encomiendas."[21] The extent of these disruptions changed the very perspectives employed to understand Andean social space. While in 1542 Morales was only concerned to maintain the vertical archipelago, in 1550 Fray Domingo saw the risk to the integrity of nuclear territories themselves. These he described as a steep continuum that ran from the lower, warm regions to the cold highlands of potatoes and livestock "since the land in these parts is generally very uneven, some parts very cold because of their altitude, others at two or three leagues distance very hot, because they are low and alongside rivers."

According to Santo Tomás, households only had direct access to the resources of the zones in which their villages were located, and "because of this, the people of the warm lands cannot grow the produce of the cold country, and vice versa, in the cold provinces they want for that which abounds in the hot places." The gap between households' direct production and their consumption needs was bridged by the circulation of goods between villages of different altitudes. "Since they were all subjects of a single high lord, although they might also be immediate subjects of other, lesser caciques, they treated each other as brothers in exchanges of food and other things." Thus Santo Tomás argues that by breaking up the ethnic groups among several different encomiendas, the Spanish broke this structure of circulation and damaged "the common good, so that those who have one type of food lack another, as they are divided and they cannot communicate or share as before when they were a single body."

ETHNIC LORDS AND CONTROL OVER THE ARCHIPELAGO In 1561, Polo de Ondegardo also briefly addressed the question of vertical archipelagos. Although he confined his comments to the people of the cold highlands, he indicated that the model applied extensively, derived from the Inca policy that each province "would have what it needed and could sustain its existence" (*RH* 177). Polo also makes a confusing reference to the form of distribution of the produce of ecological zones. The Inca distributed lands "although they might be very distant, and placed Indians there from each province so that they could reap the fruits of the land. The Inca ordered that each community go to collect the harvest with their own llamas, and without this they could not easily survive" (*RH* 177).

Let us look more closely at these early versions. The statement of the priest Morales in 1542 has to be compared with Polo's report of 1561, which recognized losses but suggested that most of the ethnic groups maintained their archipelagos. His comments on the persistence of control ("all the Indians of the Omasuyo, that for this purpose have people in Calavaya, those of Urcosuyo who have people down on the coast, those of Cotabanba who have people in Tayapaya, and those of Pocona who are in the coca fields and in general most of those in this land") suggested a greater permanence of the system than when he commented on the process of loss—for example, "those who, because of this arrangement have been broken up, suffer want. They only sustain themselves with difficulty, for example the Carangas lost their mitimaes, who through ignorance were included in the encomienda of Arequipa and the same happened in the case of Chucuito until the marquis [Cañete], following my advice, returned them" (*RH* 177) (see Chapter 2 in this volume).

Morales and Polo, like most Spaniards of their time, attributed the formation of archipelagos to the policies of the Inca. As we have seen, Murra challenged this assumption by suggesting that the networks of access reflected a pre-Incaic model. While accepting his argument, we should nevertheless reflect on the logic of the European version. It was developed on the basis of the testimony of native informants. An obvious but plausible explanation for a possible discrepancy between the actual process and the oral testimony is that the Inca legitimized this constellation of access routes and was in the last instance the guarantor of the rights of each ethnic group to archipelago land. This hypothesis is flexible enough to include the possibility that the Spanish (or indigenous?) version applied literally to the ethnic groups located away from the altiplano, for whom the Inca extended the preexisting model, providing access for them to specific resources such as salt or coca. The hypothesis also allows for the possibility that the Inca incorporated and extended the ancient system of archipelagos, but modified its character by assigning full control to the lords.

According to Morales, the mitimaes that cultivated the archipelagos of the highland groups were "vassals and subjects" of the ethnic lords. The 1567 visita to Chucuito confirms this aspect.[22] The Chucuito Lord Cari informed the visitador that in zones of the Lupaqa archipelago situated thirty, forty, or fifty leagues from Chucuito "there are Indians from throughout the province." He adds that "the caciques and principales have maize fields there," as did another group: "And other Indians also have . . . some plots for maize" (*VC* 17). Given that only a restricted group of highland people had direct access to the lands of the archipelago, I would like to look closely at the status of the inhabitants of the warm zones.

In the inspection, the Spanish informants called the cultivators of the archipelago "mitimaes," a term which surely indicates their status, although it seems to refer generically to their geographical position.[23]

Other categories that appear in the inspection are more precise. Following the inspector's distinction between tribute and services rendered, Cari declared the labor he received as tribute and then enumerated the individuals who gave service: "This town of Chucuito and its subjects give sixty Indians in service, who perform the following tasks: ten Indians tend to the livestock that he has and twenty-five Indians that he has in Moquegua work in his maize fields." To this group he added thirty-six individuals sent by five other villages of the province, among them twelve "that the town of Juli gave to this area as their ancestors had done since before the Incas ruled this land," who care for the livestock of the highlands and who "have multiplied so that at the present they include fifty-nine or sixty women and children" (*VC* 20–22). In the same way, Cusi gave the number and origin of the individuals that gave him labor as service Indians: "This town of Chucuito and its subjects give him thirty Indians," fifty-three are sent from six other villages of the province, while Moquegua, Sama, Larecaja, and Chicanoma send respectively fourteen, three, three, and two Indians who plant maize and coca in his fields (*VC* 33).

In the visita, then, these 200 people appear as a single group. If we combine the testimonies of the two lords with those of the upper and lower moiety lords of the four towns surveyed by the main inspection, forty individuals are clearly distinguished as *yanas* ("*yanaconas*"). However, the manner in which the lords distinguish their service Indians, and two other points that I develop below, suggest that the group was composed entirely of "yanaconas." First, whether or not they appear explicitly in the visita as yanas, these service Indians all receive the same level of generosity from the lords, whereas, for the Indians who give labor collectively or by turns, the lords display another, lesser type of generosity.[24] Second, the final report of Garci Diez includes a revealing section on the condition of these service Indians as yanas:

The caciques and principales of ayllus and other individual Indians of this province have many such Indians working in their fields and caring for their livestock and other things, with the justification that their fathers and grandfathers had received service Indians from the ayllus and others they had taken by their own authority. And not only did these Indians serve them all their lives, but also their children and descendants as if they were slaves. This led to disorder because there were caciques, and even some who were not caciques, who had 100 Indians or more in service. (*VC* 221)[25]

The Chucuito visita includes a joint statement from the Lupaqa lords, which also indicates the presence of "service Indians" working in the warm zones of the archipelago:

The servants that the chiefs have in the areas where they grow maize give the maize to the caciques to make *chicha* since the fields belong to the chiefs. They were asked who gave the leaders the servants who serve them all their lives, and they said that the Inca had given servants to some of the caciques principales, and these had given servants to their own subordinate chiefs. (*VC* 197)

This statement from the inspector raises interesting questions. Garci Diez denounces those "ordinary Indians" who, along with the ethnic lords, hold Indians in personal service. This seems to me a situation in accord with Andean tradition. The ordinary Indians must have been those rich in livestock, and relatives of the caciques principales. We know that the yanas did not hold the status of personal retainers to particular individuals of high rank but rather belonged to the entire family line that they served.[26] In this same section, Garcia Diez also informs the government in Lima that among the Lupaqa there were both yanas of ancient standing and others whom the caciques "had taken themselves and on their own authority" (*VC*).

To what era do the service Indians belong who cultivated the lords' lands in the archipelagos of the Collao? In 1542, Morales got a partial explanation from his native informants that they were from the time of the Inca. Wayna Qhapaq put them there as mitimaes "so that they would grow maize and provide for their lord" (*VC*), but this seems doubtful in the light of existing evidence, considering that the archipelagos are very old and that according to Lord Martín Cari his ancestors had yanas "before the Incas ruled this land" (*VC* 125). On the other hand, demographic data from the Chucuito inspection show that a high percentage of the service Indians located in the Lupaqa archipelago in 1567 had assumed this status in more recent times. According to Lord Cari's reading of the last quipu, "done in the time of the Inca," there were "200 *yungas naturales* in Sama that came from both moieties" (*VC*). However, inspector Garci Diez found 382 married individuals in Sama, and Spaniard Juan de Matute informed Garci Diez that six years earlier in the valley "he had visited said Indians and found that there were more or less 540 tributaries" (*VC* 125). After the European onslaught, the entire coast suffered terrible depopulation, but in Sama the number of Indians doubled. This suggests that in 1567 more than 50 percent of those farming this zone were recent arrivals, sent by their leaders as *criados*, or service Indians, after the European invasion. Let us return to Matute, who linked the process of repopulation taking place in Sama with Indians arriving from the puna: "Among the 540 tributaries were all the natives that they call yungas and mitimaes sent by the Inca and Indians from outside, some of whom came many years ago" (*VC* 125).[27]

Another question remains. Murra considered whether the condition of yanas was inherited, examining the statement of Chief Vilcacutipa: "When one of these Indians dies, one of his grown sons takes his place; and if this son proves incapable, then another one will come; and if the servant leaves no sons, then the ayllu sends no one to replace him, and his position ends there."[28] In relation to the service Indians sent by native authorities to produce coca in Chicanoma, the inspector noted that the climate led to frequent deaths and, "so that these deaths would not multiply and so that the Indians would not disappear in a short time," the caciques "arrange that when one Indian dies his ayllu must send another member to the coca field" (*VC* 243). Vilcacutipa's version of the form of yanas' succession contradicts the inspector's impressions of the replacement of service Indians, but the inspector's version does coincide with another statement by Vilcacutipa: when the Inca "asked for mitimaes to be sent to a certain area, they gave them and if among these some die, then others were given" (*VC* 106).

DISTRIBUTION OF ARCHIPELAGO PRODUCTS Having identified the producers of the warm zones (or some of them) as retainers to ruling families, we must consider two other issues: (1) how the produce of these zones was divided between the direct producers and the leaders and (2) how each group used its respective surplus.

Garci Diez did not address the first problem. An inspection of Quito, a very different region, indicates that "the political authorities divided the production of the 'archipelago' equally with the *kamayujkuna*, that is, those who had come from other areas to work, and that this was the system followed during Inca times."[29] The visita of Chucuito confirms this, in a certain sense. Lord Cusi stated that in the yunga of Chicanoma "they give him another two Indians who harvest three or four baskets of coca and he feeds them as he does the rest, and the Indians keep half of the said coca for themselves" (*VC* 33). Salomon presents his Quito example as "surprising information" and it is, since it suggests there were sharecropper peasants in Tawantinsuyu, but the information from Chucuito is a second, independent indigenous testimony that helps confirm it. Nevertheless, we may still have our doubts that the investigators reduced the explanations of the native informants to their own European system of measurement. If that proves to be so, what might the original system have been? A coherent hypothesis would be that the service Indians of the archipelago cultivated land for themselves and gave labor to cultivate the land of the ruling families. It might be objected that this form functioned in the case of the work for their chiefs done by hatun runas, whose rights to the land they cultivated were firmly established. By contrast, in the archipelago, the ruling families seem to have taken over (or been accorded) rights to the cultivated lands. However, we can relate our hypothesis to the process of formation of state domains worked by the mitimaes of different ethnic groups. In these cases, for example Cochabamba, mitimaes cultivated lands of the Inca in return for *suyus*, plots of land for subsistence agriculture.[30]

Let us pass from these unconfirmed speculations on the question of how appropriation of produce in the warm zones was regulated to consider how surpluses were used. Data from the inspection establish certain guidelines. With respect to the members of ruling families with access to lands and service Indians in the archipelago, the inspector noted that in Sama "nobody planted [wheat] except the caciques, who do so in small amounts to supply the friars" (*VC* 124).[31] According to Lord Pedro Cotinbo, coca from Chicanoma "is only for the caciques and a few Indians to consume and not to be sold because what they harvest there is very little" (*VC* 39). A joint statement by the Lupaqa rulers explains this information: they distributed coca "to the Indians who go to Potosí to earn for the tribute . . . , to some of the leaders of the ayllus and to the Indians who do building work for the church" (*VC* 197). In addition, the chiefs gave coca to their retainers and to those tributaries who had contributed collective labor or who fulfilled the *mita*. Showing ritual generosity, the chiefs distributed part of the archipelago's maize supply among the hatun runas on the same occasions. Such use of coca and maize reappear in other situations. As Cotinbo said, they collected very little coca. The obligations of reciprocity induced the leaders, therefore, to obtain more coca by trade in Cuzco or through Spanish middlemen of Chucuito. The maize that they received from the archipelago, on the other hand, appeared sufficient for their household consumption and for their demonstrations of elite generosity.[32]

The cultivators of the archipelago circulated the surplus that they retained in various ways. The joint statement of the Lupaqa leaders affirms the following: "The retainers that the caciques have in the area where they get maize give the said caciques maize for chicha because the lands belong to the caciques." The paragraph is difficult to interpret: the chiefs might be referring to the part of the crop that belonged to them or indicating that they received an additional amount of the crops that the retainers harvest for themselves. In Sama the visitador notes that the Indians of the valley "provide rations for the church officials, which is good," while in Chucuito the chiefs testify that the maize "given in tribute by the Indians of Moquegua, Sulcavi, Vilcacopio, and Larecaja goes toward the rations of the priests; sometimes it is not enough, and it is paid by the rest of the Indians of the province" (*VC* 197). The visitador does not record the exact amount of maize given over in this way. Through related figures, we know that the rations for the Dominican friars totaled 384 *fanegas* annually, but it is possible that the cultivators were sending a greater amount to the highlands. On the other hand, they also contributed approximately 1,000 pesos in silver tribute.[33] Since they sent no Indians to Potosí, the money could have come from renting out Indians, from sales of maize and chili, or from additional amounts of grain paid to the puna leaders.[34]

Beyond these "institutional" obligations, a certain amount of agricultural surplus entered the sphere of exchange. It would be nice to be able to confirm this exchange with testimony from the cultivators themselves, but the only available data in the visita comes from three Spaniards in Sama. Let us combine their versions:

[The cultivators have] llamas in abundance . . . because they have arrangements with the Pacaxe and Lupaqa Indians in the sierra, . . . and
others, . . . who bring clothing and wool and livestock to barter . . . to
this valley for maize and wheat and chili and for the cotton that they harvest to make clothing for themselves and even to sell . . . to the Spanish
for their anaconas. (*VC* 124–30)

The quotations imply that vertical exchanges of Lupaqas in the valley
included those between non-kin. We cannot say whether this was an ancient pattern or a new one; only that the Pacaxes, the non-Lupaqa highland
group mentioned in the visita, also extended their archipelago to the same
coastal valley.[35] The visitador noted a further horizontal exchange: "Because they produce very little food, the Indians of Moquegua go to barter
for it with meat and coca and other things among the neighboring Indians,
which some encomenderos try to prevent, it being very common throughout this region since the time of the Inca for some Indians to trade with
others here" (*VC* 247).

The statements recorded in Sama about exchange with kin in the highlands offer no new evidence. Like the testimony collected by the visitador in the highlands, they only confirm the statement of Garcilaso de
la Vega that Murra quoted in 1955: "The Collas load their animals with
huge amounts of quinoa and chuño to exchange with their distant kin . . .
and dried meat that they call *charqui* and they return carrying maize and
chilies and fruits that do not exist in their lands."[36] Actually, the only new
data that we find in the visita is the passing mention by Juli's lower moiety
authorities of how meteorological factors influenced exchange between the
different zones. The people of Juli would go to the coast to exchange with
their kin and "when there is much hunger, the people in the coastal valleys
give no more than one and a half fanegas of maize for a sheep that is worth
6 or 7 pesos and when it is a good year they give three fanegas" (*VC* 120).

Finally, let us return to Polo's vague suggestion that all the puna inhabitants had the right to enjoy the produce of the archipelago. The most
precise information in the Chucuito inspection seems to suggest to the
contrary that rights to the maize and chili of the warm zones were enjoyed
only by the ruling families and by those Indians who possessed livestock
herds of a certain size. A statement by Martín Cusi may clear up this confusion: "The Indians of this province have llamas and alpacas, and those

who have them use them to trade in the yungas, and those who do not go to work in the yungas and in other areas." Instead of supplying goods from the puna, it seems that those with very little livestock or none at all were able to gain access to the produce of the archipelagos by offering labor in exchange.

Domingo de Santo Tomás and the Defense of Andean Society

I have left until this final section an examination of the protest submitted by Fray Domingo de Santo Tomás in 1550 which was the direct antecedent of the Huánuco visita of 1562. We have already noted that Santo Tomás described the ethnic territories as a continuum without mentioning the archipelagos. This would be a very serious omission if it were part of a generalized vision of the altiplano ethnic groups, but he was clearly referring to other areas. The visita of Huánuco is of central importance to Murra's model of ethnic control over multiple ecological zones, since it forms the basis of his first case, the Chupachus. My reading of the visita diverges from that of Murra. I have focused my interest along the lines of Domingo de Santo Tomás's observations, namely that the Chupachus exercised multiecological control over a continuum of ecological levels since the land "in these parts is very uneven, some parts of it very cold, since they are very high, and others, at two or three leagues, are very warm, since they are low and alongside rivers."[37] It should also be emphasized, given the terms of the debate in recent years, that whatever the altitude of their village, all households had direct access to the range of ecological levels located from hot lowlands to the cold highlands.[38]

The Huánuco visita also includes one of the three encomiendas into which the Yacha people were divided. This case allows us to test Fray Domingo's claim that such fragmentation harmed ethnic groups by breaking the easy flow "of food and goods as between brothers" that existed between the people of the sierra and the hot lands.

The curaca of this encomienda noted that his people "have lands for planting and for grazing their livestock and in their land they harvest maize and potatoes and quinoa and *taures* and ulluco and maxua and oca and beans and *maca* and other things, and they plant these in terraces because it is steep" (*VH* 2:58).[39] That is to say, this Yacha settlement, made up of

190 tributaries, productively controlled ecological tiers from the *quishwa* valleys up to 4,000 meters. The curaca makes no mention of hot lands, the lack of which was explicitly confirmed a little later by the leader of Caure: "They have no tropical slopes for wood, nor coca"; "they have no land for cotton" (*VH* 2:160). Neither curaca is inaccurate, as evidenced by two apparent contradictions recorded in the visita, one side being the testimony of an old hatun runa from the village of Guapia who stated, "they have lands below on the banks of the river that runs through this valley, and they do not plant them because they cannot" (*VH* 2:101), and the other from Chief Gonzalo Tapia, who said that "they have a coca field which produces a great sack at each harvest because the field is new" (*VH* 2:135).

A comment from the curaca might cause confusion: "There is a difference among the lands of these people in that in some of them they do not produce maize and in others they do produce maize and other things as they have said." This requires us to locate the twelve villages visited and the access of each household to arable land. Eight villages are located in the quishwa zone; Tancor was at a lower altitude, in the temperate land, at "one and a half leagues from the river" and Chacapampa possibly was located "on a temperate slope," while the other six villages were, according to the visitador, located on a cool slope ("more cold than warm"), but all had terracing to plant maize. The other peoples (Quiu, Nati, Caure, and Xacxa) were located above 3,000 or 3,500 meters. Quiu was "in the xalca where it is very cold," and the others were "in very harsh and cold land."

Although these villages were situated at different altitudes, households in each of them had access to arable land, both cold and temperate. Going from house to house, the visitador received from the hatun runas the same important statement, that "they have fields for all kinds of foods" and "they have their own fields, where they sow all kinds of foods." As the curaca Antonio Guaynacapcha said, "from their lands they get maize from temperate regions, and maize and potatoes and in those lands as well, potatoes and oca and quinoa and taures and ulluco and maxua." The visita allows us to see some specific variations, due to the settlement pattern. For example, the people of very high, cold settlements had at their door the produce of high altitudes, but they had to go varying distances to cultivate their maize fields. The people of Xacxa "have lands in Cochas which is half a league's distance away, and there they harvest maize." The people of Quiu went the same distance, but the hatun runas of Nati "have their maize fields in the neighboring lands in Chuccho, because in this village they cannot plant maize, and they have to carry it more than five leagues from there to here" (*VH*). The people of Caure, whose maize fields were located in Chacapampa, had to go even farther to reach them.

The curaca Juan Chuchuyaure presented the inspector with one complaint in particular: "The Yachas' *guaranga* was divided among three encomenderos . . . and they want to be all together under one encomendero because they are deprived by this situation, and together they would help each other, and they are also burdened by the tribute which is very varied" (*VH* 2:58). The phrase suggests that the effect of dividing the guaranga operated on various levels,[40] but I do not believe that it directly implies a breakdown of redistributive relations in the sharing among them "of food and work as between brothers" that Fray Domingo protested had happened to groups divided between cold and hot regions.

Chuchuyaure referred to his small group's exchange relations:

They are neighbors of the Chinchacocha and the Yaros and the Yungas, and they bring maize and beans to the Chinchacocha and the Yaros and exchange them for wool and fish and dried meat and sheep and llamas, and to those in the coca fields they bring dried venison and dried potatoes and cavi to exchange for coca, and they exchange the coca for salt and chilies and cotton. (*VH* 2:58)

The demand for highland wool, dried meat and livestock need not be attributed to the division of the Yacha guaranga among three encomiendas; the Chupachus remained united under a single encomienda and they too had to compensate for insufficient livestock supplies through mechanisms of exchange.

The curaca's reference to exchange with the Yungas people is surprising. The Yachas traded for more coca than they needed for their own consumption and used the surplus to obtain salt, chilies, and cotton. Another feature is also interesting: Chuchuyaure described the Yungas with whom they maintained trade as "neighbors," that is to say, not kin. The possibility exists that the Yachas of the other two encomiendas controlled the hot lands and, as Fray Domingo argued, they had lost their relation "of brothers" with the subjects of Chuchuyaure. However, I am inclined to think that the entire guaranga of the Yachas lacked direct access to the yunga resources. On the other hand, I doubt that the division of the Yacha guaranga in three encomiendas caused a shift to trade within the group. The direct access of their households to the quishwa and to the cold lands, which has already been mentioned, effectively negates this possibility.

Given the negative result of this comparison, let us approach Fray Domingo's protest from another perspective. In 1550 he had been in the region for ten years. Although at that moment his personal concern was to understand the ethnic groups of the coast, he nevertheless possessed enviable knowledge about the sierra, owing to his work on the general assessment ordered by La Gasca. Furthermore, he was nearly as dedicated a student of Andean social structures as Polo de Ondegardo. This being the case, it seems wrong to disregard his complaint simply because it does not fit the only case that we can analyze in depth. I am not, therefore, questioning the quality of Friar Domingo's studies. On the contrary, it is precisely his well-known insight into the Andean system that leads me to wonder if he deliberately misrepresented the situation. That is, in order to argue against those in the government who were dividing the ethnic groups between different encomenderos,[41] he inaccurately generalized the effects of the division that separated the mitimaes of archipelagos into various encomiendas. In these cases, the people in the cold lands and those of the hot lands actually did suffer a fracturing of their exchange "of food and work as between brothers."

Domingo de Santo Tomás made this error because he was committed to a moral stand with respect to the Indians, a stand that protected the traditional role of the native lords.[42] In his protest of 1550 he alleged that to dismember the ethnic groups into two or three encomiendas was a "great injustice against all human and divine laws and rights by depriving the lord of his vassals and peoples, and it results in there being as many lords as there are Spaniards between whom they are divided."[43] It is possible that, when addressing the political authorities, Fray Domingo found it convenient to underrepresent his own knowledge of the region. If his protest concerned only the humiliation of the native lords, it risked going unheard in the Council of the Indies. Instead, he increased the likelihood of receiving a positive response by linking his remarks to the sufferings of the "miserable Indians."[44]

Notes

All translations from the original Spanish sources in this chapter are by Julie Franks, José Gordillo, and Olivia Harris.

1. Juan Polo de Ondegardo, "Informe al licenciado Briviesca de Muñatones sobre la perpetuidad de las encomiendas en el Perú" [1561], *Revista Histórica* (Lima) 13 (1940): 125–196. Cited in text parentheses as *RH*.

2. Iñigo Ortíz de Zúñiga, *Visita a la provincia de León de Huánuco* [1562], 2 vols. (Huánuco, 1967, 1972). Cited in text parentheses as *VH*.

3. This was not the case of the Chupachus and Yachas, who had shoemakers and divided the work among members of the community.

4. In Marcos Jiménez de la Espada, comp., *Relaciones geográficas de Indias: Perú* [1881–1885] (Madrid, 1965), there is evidence of this multiethnic participation, but we should analyze this aspect considering, for example, that leaders of the Chupachus, Yachas, and Quichua mitimaes recognized that the salt pans were outside their lands, in another ethnic territory. This distinction had effects in indigenous history on conflicts, alliances, and Inca policy and is not restricted to the colonial period.

5. Pedro Sancho, "Relación para SM de lo sucedido en la conquista y pacificación de estas provincias de la Nueva Castilla y de la calidad de la tierra," in *Los cronistas de la conquista*, comp. Horacio Urteaga (Paris, 1938), 180–182.

6. Juan de Matienzo, *Gobierno del Perú* [1567] (Paris and Lima, 1967), 275.

7. With access, at the same time, to abundant fishing resources: "All those of said province of Chucuito have lakes from which they obtain fish close to their house, because there is a large lake of more than sixty leagues." Garci Diez de San Miguel, *Visita hecha a la provincia de Chucuito* [1567] (Lima, 1964), 208. Cited in text parentheses as *VC*.

8. In the altiplano there are microclimates because of the influence of Lake Titicaca.

9. The Spanish exaggerated when they stated that "there are caciques who have 10,000 sheep" and that "one Don Juan Alanoca de Chucuito . . . has more than 50,000 head of livestock."

10. However, in 1557 the agent Romani complained to the *Consejo de Indias* that Viceroy Cañete had named a member of his own court as corregidor of Chucuito and "that people say that in two years he will make 20,000 pesos because the office is so well suited for it that he could do it easily." Roberto Levillier, *Gobernantes del Perú* (Madrid, 1921), 2:495.

11. See Karen Spalding, *De indio a campesino: Cambios en la estructura social del Perú colonial* (Lima, 1974), 38–42.

12. However, the norms of "generosity" operated when people wove for the chiefs themselves. For example, according to Bernaldino Fasato, "old Indian women had come to complain to him as judge of this province that they had been made to spin wool for clothing and had been paid nothing for it, and this witness was angry with the curacas and principales about it; they said that they had given the women food, and later he was made to understand that they gave nothing in terms of money but rather food for the women to eat while they did the spinning and weaving that had been asked of them" (*VC* 62).

13. I agree with the assertion of Karen Spalding that the curacas "did not retain for themselves the income obtained from the work contracts in which they were involved."

14. John V. Murra, *La organización económica del estado inca* [1955] (Mexico, 1978).

15. John V. Murra, "El 'control vertical' de un máximo de pisos ecológicos en la economía de las sociedades andinas." In Iñigo Ortíz de Zúñiga, *Visita a la provincia de Huánuco* (1972) 2:429–476.

16. In the case of the Lupaqa, the hospitality of the chiefs was based in production of the fields and livestock of the community. See *VC* 23, 86, 92, 198, 212. On this point the declaration of Señor Martín Cari is illustrative: in Tawantinsuyu the chiefs showed hospitality with livestock, maize, coca, and chuño, which the Inca gave them for this purpose (*VC* 22).

17. Felipe Waman Puma de Ayala, *Nueva corónica y buen gobierno* [1615], 3 vols., ed. John V. Murra and Rolena Adorno (Mexico, 1980), 792–794.

18. Cited in Emilio Lisson Chávez, *La iglesia de España en el Perú* (Seville, 1943), I/3:78.

19. Ibid.

20. The letter has been published in J. M. Vargas, *Fr. Domingo de Santo Tomás* (Quito, 1937), 1–32, and in Lisson, *Iglesia de España en el Peru,* I/4:190–206.

21. This policy had been decided on much earlier; in 1540 instructions, F. Pizarro ordered a visitador to inquire "which ethnic groups corresponded to the territory of each cacique . . . and record in writing how many groups are in each, and how many Indians they have so that, if the position of the cacique is to be divided between two people, we will know how it should be done" (Levillier, *Gobernantes del Perú,* 1:21). In 1542, the lawyer Santoyo of Lima proposed that the ethnic groups should be kept united and that their collective tribute was to be divided among two or three encomenderos. See Lisson, *Iglesia de España en el Perú,* I/3:109.

22. When Murra studies the incomes of the Lupaqa lords—that is, the three categories of human resources to which they had rights—he situates these cultiva-

tors as hatun runas who act as *mit'ani*. See "Un reino aymara en 1567," especially table 2 (Ingresos de los reyes lupaqas) and "Nueva información sobre la población yana," in John V. Murra, *Formaciones económicas y políticas del mundo andino* (Lima, 1975), 193–223, 225–242.

23. Murra observes that in the sixteenth century the term mitimaes came to be used to designate many people who in pre-European times had been captives or *yana* (*Formaciones económicas y políticas*, 232–233).

24. In addition to the declarations of the lords, there is the testimony of Galamaquera, who offers further evidence on the issue we are considering by saying to the visitador "when my Indians come from the yungas" (*VC* 111).

25. Following the instructions of Governor Castro, the visitador Garci Diez issued an order that "declared free all the male and female servants" of the senior lords. Furthermore, he "ordered that all said servants contribute in their ayllus to the quotas of His Majesty and to what was owed the caciques and to the other expenses of the community and to the care of *tambos* that they contribute, as other Indians of this province are obliged to do" (*VC* 200–202). The same measures had been taken a little earlier by the *oidor* Cuenca during his visit to the North Coast.

26. Murra, *Formaciones económicas y políticas*, 241.

27. Our calculation may be incorrect if, in fact, the Inca quipu only recorded the yungas naturales and did not include mitimaes sent by the Inca.

28. Murra, *Formaciones económicas y políticas*, 240.

29. Frank Salomon, *Los señores étnicos de Quito en la época de los Incas* (Otavalo, 1980), 289.

30. See Waldemar Espinoza Soriano, "Las colonias mitmas múltiples en Abancay, siglos XV y XVI," *Revista del Museo Nacional* (Lima) 39 (1973): 283–294, and Nathan Wachtel, "Los mitimas del valle de Cochabamba: La política de colonización de Wayna Capac," *Historia Boliviana* (Cochabamba) 1.1 (1981): 21–57.

31. The chief Vilcacutipa denounced a situation that was apparently recent: "The priests who are there now do not want their share in wheat or in flour, but in money and so they [the chiefs] pay 8 pesos for each fanega of the priests' share of wheat, and they would prefer to give wheat or flour as they have done until now . . . because they have it from their harvest and the mitimaes they have on the coast bring it to them" (*VC* 108). The visitador summarized the conflict by saying that the chiefs want to give the priests' share "in flour and not in money, nor to go look for someone to buy the flour" (*VC* 231).

32. It may have been an infrequent occurrence, but it is striking that a Dominican friar directed Pedro Cotinbo to use that maize in the sense of Spanish

restitución. See "Documentos de Chucuito," *Historia y Cultura* (Lima) 4 (1970): 25.

33. The visita gives two figures for the amount of this money tribute: 1,140 and 900 pesos (*VC* 69, 248).

34. In his final statement, the visitador confirmed that "the caciques of said province try to give what they can of the tribute in wheat and maize" (*VC* 245). Visiting Sama, Garci Diez received suggestions that the Indians in the valley plant community fields in wheat, maize, and chili and pay tribute from their sales.

35. Jiménez de la Espada, *Relaciones geográficas de Indias*, 334.

36. Murra, *Organización económica del estado inca*, 206.

37. See note 20 for this source.

38. See Udo Oberem, "El acceso a recursos naturales en differentes ecologías en la sierra ecuatoriana (siglo XVI)," in Segundo Moreno Yañez and Udo Oberem, eds., *Contribución a la etnohistoria ecuatoriana* (Otavalo, 1981), 45–63. Around 1841, E. W. Middendorf wrote about Huaylas: "Most of the land is divided in very small plots, and the peasants possess pieces of land in different zones, as also occurs in certain regions of Germany." See E. W. Middendorf, *Perú* (Lima, 1973), 3:45.

39. The curaca explained: "the Inca gave part of the lands that they have and part they inherited from very long ago."

40. For example, as Fray Domingo himself observed, "it happens that some are married and live together in families, and when they are divided, the father falls under the domain of one encomendero and the son under that of another; the wife goes to one side and the husband to another. . . . [The encomendero] who has 200 Indians wants to maintain his house as if he had 1,000" (Vargas, *Fr. Domingo de Santo Tomás*, 13).

41. Undoubtedly, the attack was aimed directly at Viceroy La Gasca, who in 1554 confessed that, given the necessity to "satisfy" many Spaniards, some ethnic groups were divided between two or three or more encomenderos and that "many Indians have been displaced from the dominions of almost all the caciques, which seems to me to have been a grave affront to the ethnic lords, and I confess that I too sinned in doing it and I have become and today am conscious of it."

42. But at this time the Dominican still showed some ambiguity. In a report written to Bartolomé de las Casas about 1551 or 1552, arguing that "there must be corregidores in the Indian villages to administer justice," Fray Domingo seemed to want the imposition of a European bureaucratic apparatus that would subordinate ethnic power to the emergent colonial state.

43. Vargas, *Fr. Domingo de Santo Tomás*, 12–13.

44. For example, he obtained a royal order for the redress of injuries inflicted upon the ethnic lords. Likewise, in the margin of Friar Domingo's letter appears an agreement by the Council of the Indies to expedite another order that the Indians "should become united as they were before" and that their collective tribute should be divided among the encomenderos, as Santoyo requested in 1542. See Lisson, *Iglesia de España en el Perú,* I/4:195–196.

5

Exchange and Markets in the Sixteenth Century:

A View from the North

SUSAN E. RAMÍREZ

The economic history of the southern Andes in the sixteenth century seems to represent, in its starkest form, the story of the dramatic impact of the European mercantile economy upon peoples organized according to very different principles. In the south before 1532, the reciprocal and redistributive aspects of the vertical economy ensured circulation on a large scale without merchants (like the Mexican *pochteca*[1]), institutionalized market-places, or a consistent medium of exchange or currency. The economic history of the region reveals how the Spanish market economy initially coexisted with and began to articulate with nonmarket native modes of exchange (see Chapters 2, 3, and 4 in this volume).

The characterization of the economic history of the north in the six-teenth century—both immediately before the Spanish Conquest and there-after—is still being debated. In contrast to the south, it is complicated by Spanish reports of "merchants,"[2] who, in some cases, are purported to have existed before the Europeans arrived; of hoards of metal slugs (*hachuelos, naipes,* or *tejuelos*), which some think represent a type of currency; and of evidence of long-distance transport and exchange of such luxury goods as the ritually important spondylous shell. Ethnohistorians and archaeologists differ in their interpretation of these written and material records (see Chapter 2). Do they indicate that the north had a commercially based economy before the Spanish arrived? Until this question is resolved, it is hard to make any firm statement about the impact of the Spanish market system on the indigenous political economy.

Accordingly, the first part of the discussion that follows is an attempt to summarize the state of the debate on the pre-Columbian situation and to speculate on its market or nonmarket nature. It shows that there is considerable evidence for the existence of northern exchange specialists, perhaps wrongly described by the Spanish, which is not found in the early documents relating to the southern Andes. In the second section, the impact of the Spanish market economy on the north is assessed to the end of the sixteenth century. After 1532, an enclave-based market economy developed in the major cities and ports. It significantly affected the relatively small group of natives who had prolonged contact with it. The bulk of the rural population, still living in the indigenous communities, infrequently engaged, as far as we can tell, directly in mercantile activities, despite the colonial government's sometimes energetic efforts to promote them and suppress nonmarket mechanisms of circulation. They participated indirectly, however, to the extent that they became producers of goods—like cloth—that the Spanish sold to obtain the imported goods they needed to recreate a European society in their midst.

My discussion is limited to the north: the coastal region that extends from south-central Peru (Chincha) to northern Ecuador, as well as its mountain hinterland. The coast is an increasingly narrow strip of desert as one moves north to south, cut by rivers that originate in the Andean highlands. These rivers form valleys as they flow toward the Pacific Ocean. The local people built irrigation ditches from these rivers, enabling them to increase greatly the area of cultivation. The mass of rural population lived in small homesteads or hamlets scattered across the land near their fields. Coastal fisherfolk usually lived concentrated in one or more villages near the sea. The *curaca,* or paramount lord, of the various communities resided in a ceremonial center with his retainers, including widows who cooked and made maize beer (*chicha*), pages, and artisans who fashioned the luxury goods he used in rituals and for feasting and redistributive ends.

Pre-Hispanic Exchange Specialists

Historians, archaeologists, and anthropologists became excited in the late 1970s and early 1980s by the publication of a report about indigenous "merchants."[3] This report suggested that the north developed an economic system different from that found in the south.[4] Ethnohistorical evidence of "merchants" (see note 2), or exchange specialists, comes from four separate areas of the Inca empire: the south-central and northern coasts of what is today modern Peru, and the highlands and coast of modern Ecuador. The first example on the south-central coast, or Chincha, rests on a copy of a manuscript that exists in the library of the Royal Palace in Madrid. First published by María Rostworowski de Diez Canseco,[5] this undated copy of an unknown original, hereafter referred to as the "Aviso," mentions the existence of "merchants":

> There used to be in this great Valley of Chincha 6,000 merchants and each one of them had a reasonable amount of capital, because the one with the least worked with 500 pesos of gold and many of them traded [*trataban*] with 2,000 and 3,000 ducats; and with their purchases and sales they traveled from Chincha to Cuzco and throughout the Collao district, and others went to Quito and to Puerto Viejo, from where they brought a lot of gold beads and many rich emeralds and they sold them to the Indian lords of Ica, who liked jewels and were their nearest neighbors. . . . The people of Chincha were daring and intelligent and orderly, because we could say only they in this kingdom traded with money, because among themselves they bought and sold with copper food and clothes, and they had established the value of each unit of copper; and besides this they had valued each gold peso as more than ten times a silver peso and they had weights and scales with which they weighed the gold and silver and their touchstones and points with which they assayed the gold from 10 to 21.5 carats, because until now, no one has seen said worked gold of more carats.[6]

These "merchants" made up 20 percent of the population of Chincha. According to the quote, these merchants were rich, each having a minimum capital worth 500 gold pesos and as much as 2,000–3,000 ducados.[7] They engaged in long-distance transport and exchange, some traveling overland to Cuzco and throughout the Collao, others going north to Quito and Puerto Viejo, presumably at least part of the way by sea. They carried such products as gold beads and emeralds—that is, luxury goods of high value and low volume. The quote also indicates that they characteristically used standard mediums of exchange: copper, gold, and silver. They used copper to "buy" and "sell" the subsistence items they needed. They valued gold at ten times what silver was worth. They also had the technology to weigh the ores and determine the fineness of the gold. Thus, they had the hallmarks of merchants elsewhere: capital, a standard medium of exchange, specialization, and an implied profit motive.

The second example comes from the geographical area on the north coast of modern Peru, called Lambayeque.[8] Pre-Toledan era documents contain innumerable mentions of "merchants." Most are found in the records of the 1566 *visita* (inspections) and the 1572 *residencia* (judicial reviews of an officeholder) of Dr. Gregorio González de Cuenca.[9] Many petitions from these specialists ask for permission to travel outside their community[10] to trade. Yet, there seems to be no truly long-distance traders, like those of Chincha or Mexico, among them. Their petitions indicate that they did not specialize in luxury or subsistence products. Of five cases that listed what they sold, only one mentioned a single item, cloth. Three others mentioned food items, among other things. The last one mentioned cloth, wool, and shell beads and other items that may or may not have been subsistence goods. Finally, there is no mention of either capital or currency. Furthermore, none of the presumed "merchants"—whether individual or lord—were considered to be rich or to enjoy a privileged status.

A third example comes from farther north in what is today Ecuador and southern Colombia. Frank Salomon reports on the existence of a group of exchange specialists, called *mindaláes*. According to a document dated from 1559, these formed an elite specialist corps, who lived outside their home community in a privileged district of the city of Quito. They constituted a separate subsector without a recognized lord. Mindaláes existed elsewhere, especially north toward Pasto and the northern periphery and frontier of the Inca empire. Evidence on the existence of an analogous group south of Quito is scarce. Mindaláes enjoyed political protection to engage in long-distance trade for, usually, luxury goods, and were, under the Spanish, exempt from ordinary tribute. In some places, like Otavalo, they seem to have coexisted with artisan specialists who traveled to trade their own goods and others.[11]

We have another example of long-distance exchange in the way of an eyewitness account from 1525. A navigator named Bartolomé Ruyz sailing along the coast of Ecuador or southern Colombia observed a raft containing many pieces of silver and gold to adorn themselves . . . crowns and belts and bracelets and leg armor and breastplates and small tweezers and bells and strings and bundles of beads and red silver [*rosecleres*] and mirrors adorned with said silver and cups and other drinking vessels[;] they brought wool and cotton blankets and shirts and overcoats [*aljulas*, Moorish overcoats with narrow, short sleeves] and *alcaceres* [short, bleached or silken shirts?] and baggy trousers [*alaremes*] and many other clothes, most of which were richly worked and the colors of scarlet and purple and blue and yellow and of various types of multicolored embroidery and figures of birds and animals and fish and groves of trees, and they carried some small scales to weigh gold made like a balance and many other things[;] on some strings of beads were little emeralds and quartz [*caçedonias*] and other stones and pieces of crystal and resin [resembling myrrh].[12]

The quote indicates that most of the items were luxury goods, including elaborate metal objects, rich cloth and clothing, and jewelry. The native sailors brought these goods to exchange (*hazer rescate, contratar*) for beads made of spondylous shell: "All this they brought to barter [*rescatar*] for some seashells from which they make beads, red or coral and also white. They had filled almost the whole vessel with them."[13] This is the earliest written evidence of long-distance transport and exchange and the only one in which the specialists accompanying the goods are not specifically called "merchants."

Archaeologists have also found evidence in the material record that could be interpreted as an indication of systematic and standardized exchange. Axe blade–shaped copper slugs have been unearthed in archaeological excavations from Lambayeque to Ecuador. Bundles of these in various sizes have been found in tombs. Many believe these to be an indication of a standard measure of exchange—that is, a form of currency—or of wealth.[14] Also, at least one scale, and its weights, has been found in an archaeological context.[15] Hoards of spondylous shell fragments, ornaments, and beads are common, too. Because spondylous shell only comes from the warm waters off the coast of Ecuador, archaeologists interpret such finds as evidence for long-distance trade (see Chapter 2 in this volume).

This body of ethnohistorical and archaeological evidence is not irrefutable evidence of pre-Hispanic commercial exchange, implied by calling the specialists who transported the goods "merchants." The long-distance exchange specialists of Chincha, for example, are described in an undated, but apparently late copy of a "lost" original.[16] What makes the contents of this manuscript even more suspect is the existence of another well-known document about Chincha, written in 1558 by Fray Cristoval de Castro, vicar of the Dominican Monastery of Chincha, and Diego de Ortega Morejón, *corregidor* of the same valley.[17] Known as the "Relación," this complete and dated document (February 22, 1558) makes no mention of merchants, commerce, or exchange of any kind, except through the familiar mechanisms of redistribution and reciprocity. Curacas, other minor lords, and commoners are mentioned, but no specialized group of exchange specialists appears, raising doubts about the true identity and historical development of the "merchant" group mentioned in the "Aviso." This earlier "Relación" and the fact that archaeologists have found little evidence to document pre-Hispanic trade and related specialization in Chincha,[18] then, suggest that the "merchants" mentioned in the "Aviso" and their identification as such must not be taken literally. The long-distant "merchants" who have accumulated capital and a recognized currency and who travel by raft and overland, but who have no recognized and institutionalized markets that the "Aviso" mentions may, therefore, represent a group of natives who became merchants (in the Western, commercial sense) during colonial times as a result of their interaction with the Spanish.[19]

The same could be said about the "merchants" on the north coast, who appear in the written record in the 1560s, bartering locally without a recognized medium of exchange,[20] and who are nowhere described as rich. Since archaeologists have not found remains of pre-Hispanic marketplaces, commercial exchange, as Europeans understood it, was probably not a tradition there, either.

This evidence could be explained by other mechanisms of exchange that are known to be pre-Hispanic. Local sources describe one type of exchange as gifts or "presents." The best known case of this gift-giving exchange tradition is the practice of certain north coast lords, the curaca of Jayanca, for one, giving gifts (*presentes*) of cotton, chili peppers, and salt to the highland lord, Penachí (in this case), who controlled the headwaters of the river (specifically, the ravine of Canchachalá) that the former depended on to irrigate the lands on the coast.[21] Without such presents, the highland lord might divert the river water, thereby making most coastal agriculture an impossibility.[22]

A second mechanism was "resource sharing," whereby one lord allowed subjects of other lords to have access to resources used by his own people and, therefore, under his administrative jurisdiction in return for part of the produce of the guests' labor. This was the way coastal inhabitants gained access to the silver of the mines of Chilete (controlled by the highland curaca of Cajamarca) before 1540. Coastal Indians mined the ore and gave part of the take to the host lord of Cajamarca. Both highland and coastal peoples benefited—the former by getting the produce from additional units of labor, and the latter by gaining access to a commodity that they lacked in their own homeland district.[23] Resource sharing, the wide and dispersed geographical distribution of coastal peoples subject to one paramount lord,[24] and their continuing nonmonetarized exchange and cooperation into the 1560s may represent what appears to be the exploitation of multiple ecological niches, the archipelago model, although each site or "island" may not necessarily have been at as widely varying altitudes as in the southern Andes.[25]

Given that all the manuscripts were written in Spanish and that the Spanish interpreted what they saw in their own ethnocentric fashion, could not the reports of "merchants" have described retainers of the lords carrying goods (gifts, or the product of shared resources) from one site to another? I have suggested elsewhere that this was the case for the north coast.[26]

The resolution of the debate may hinge on the purpose of the long-distance transport and exchange of goods—whether they were destined for political or economic ends. What the Spanish probably saw was state-sponsored exchange, meant not for the accumulation of riches or individual gain in the Western sense, but for political purposes. Lords needed exotic luxury goods for ceremonial and redistributive ends. They could use such goods to cement alliances and build goodwill. After all, their conception of wealth was control of people, not an accumulation of material goods.

Frank Salomon and John Murra recognize that mindaláes sometimes acted as political agents, charged with collecting coca leaves, shell beads (*chaquira*), and other things to swell the cacical sector of their home polities and with redistributing these items in a manner that would strengthen their sponsor or his chosen beneficiary.[27] Salomon characterizes them less as entrepreneurs than as political agents, since the object of their expeditions was less the accumulation of luxury than the procurement of goods to benefit the political chiefs who protected them.[28]

Much of the debate and ambiguity concerning northern interethnic exchange relations may be attributed, then, to the fact that the Spanish were recording what they saw in their own language, often without the benefit of study and facility in the indigenous languages. They interpreted native reality according to their own cultural categories, employing familiar terms to describe nonmercantile exchange arrangements: for example, ascribing "merchant" status to persons who might have been more accurately described as retainers of the lords, political agents, or ambassadors, trading to obtain goods that would be used to buttress and fortify the generous reputation of their lord.[29]

This intercultural, terminological inconsistency is to be found in Roswith Hartmann's catalog of the Andean markets or fairs reported by chroniclers in the sixteenth and seventeenth centuries. Her earliest reference to markets is one by Miguel de Estete from 1534 in Jauja (a community in the Andes just inland from Lima and north of Huancayo): "According to the Spanish, 100,000 persons gathered each day in the main plaza, and the markets and streets of the town were so filled with people, that it appeared that no person was absent."[30] This is just one of Hartmann's collection of references which she offers as evidence of the existence of markets in Jauja and other places in the Andes. Yet Hartmann mentions in a footnote (number 8) an earlier letter from Hernando Pizarro to the *Real Audiencia* (Supreme Court) of Santo Domingo, dated November 23, 1533, that made no mention of markets. However, Pizarro's letter did describe the large plaza in Jauja, where more than 100,000 *indios de servicio* (tributary Indians; persons on duty or performing service) congregated. What did Estete mean by using the word "markets"? Did he observe Indians delivering products that they had grown on lands dedicated to the upkeep of the Inca and government or natives receiving rations or gifts that were expected while they were on duty or serving the state?[31] Elsewhere, in the same report, Estete suggested that the people gathered in Jauja were there *para hacer fiestas* (for a festival):

> There were men who were in charge of counting all these people, to know those who came to serve the soldiers; others were in charge of watch-

ing what [goods?] came into the town. Chilicuchima had lesser officials [*mayordomos*, overseers] who were in charge of supplying subsistence to the soldiers [*gente* (de guerra?)].[32]

In other words, designated men kept track of people who came into Jauja to serve the army and of the goods they brought into the center. Other lesser officials were in charge of supplying subsistence goods to the soldiers. This describes a redistributive mechanism, exchange, without the profit motive. It implies gain, but the item to be gained is intangible goodwill. It is exchange for political ends. The people who engage in it are government officials and ordinary citizens, not "merchants." There is, therefore, no reliable evidence in this instance of commercial exchange or exchange specialists in the places Estete called "markets." The so-called *ferias* were tied to redistributive ends or to ritual and ceremonial observance. "Merchants" were probably retainers of the lords, who supplied the sumptuary goods that lords needed to fulfill their redistributive duties, retain allegiance and goodwill, and meet the norms of hospitality expected by their subjects.[33] Furthermore, one must wonder if marketplaces were even necessary. Salomon writes that nobles had advantageous ways of procuring goods, that certain goods were commanded by lords more frequently than by commoners, and that sumptuary goods (portable, highly processed, valuable goods with exotic associations) were procured and redistributed by nobles.[34] If the products were being procured for a lord and he used them to enhance his power through securing his subjects' loyalty and support through the redistributive system, plazas—not marketplaces—would have been needed before 1532.

In fact, Salomon looks for marketplaces in connection with his discussion of the mindaláes and finds that the earliest written evidence of a marketplace in Quito dates from 1535.[35] Would not a marketplace have been established when the city of Quito was founded and laid out? Or, might not one have formed on an ad hoc basis on the plaza in front of the church, as a logical place to interchange information and goods? Salomon himself states that the Quito market was located in front of the church in the plaza.[36] Later, Fernando de Santillán ordered the establishment of *tiangueces* (Nahuatl word for markets) in practically every colonial urban center,[37] proving that marketplaces were specifically created after the Spanish Conquest.

In sum, Andean chiefdoms of the North had evolved a complex tradition of long-distance circulation and exchange of both subsistence and luxury goods, which existed as early as 1525.[38] In highland Ecuador and Lambayeque, exchange appears to have been state-sponsored, protected, and administered, largely for political ends. This trade coexisted and intersected with other mechanisms of exchange: reciprocity, redistribution, gift giving, resource sharing, and localized, informal exchange carried on at the household or lineage level without state intervention.[39] But there is little evidence of independent merchants, markets, or commerce before the European arrival.

Introduction of the Spanish Commercial System

A major and traumatic shock for the cultures of the northern part of the Tawantinsuyu was, of course, the Spanish invasion. The immediate permanence of the invaders was guaranteed by Atahualpa's ransom. Instead of satiating their demand for gold and ensuring their prompt exit, the ransom actually motivated Pizarro's men, those who followed shortly thereafter with Almagro and those who arrived later, after word of the hoard spread, to continue their search for more riches in the south. These Europeans lived off the offerings of food of the peoples they encountered and off the enormous quantity of maize and other crops stored in the royal Inca warehouses of Jauja, Cochabamba, and elsewhere.[40] Those Spaniards who had been favored at the distribution of booty at Cajamarca, however, began using their gold and silver to buy coveted objects—most importantly horses, which sold in the first few years after the capture of the Inca Atahualpa at Cajamarca at truly princely prices.[41] Such activities marked the introduction of an European-style market economy to Peru.

The circumstances of colonial settlement reinforced this beginning. By 1534–1535, the suspicion grew among the first wave of conquerors and explorers that the booty of Cajamarca was atypical and probably not to be encountered elsewhere. By that time, too, coastal cities such as San Miguel de Piura, Trujillo, and Lima, had been founded—duly mapped out on a grid system, with sites reserved for the church and town hall. To reward the Spanish for their risks and to encourage them to stay in Peru and settle in the newly founded Spanish towns, Pizarro as early as 1534 began to

distribute the native population in the north in the form of *encomiendas.*
For various reasons, some indigenous polities were divided among several
Spaniards. The paramount lord of the Jequetepeque valley, for example,
was given to one *encomendero;* three of his subordinate lords were parceled out, along with their subjects, to three other Spaniards. This fourfold
division of what was once one community meant a drastic reduction of
the resources—both human and natural—that the lords once had at their
disposal to provide for the basic subsistence needs of the community. Evidence from Jequetepeque indicates that the paramount lord (perhaps not
conforming to European expectations) continued to assert his authority
over the three lesser lords, although the Europeans now considered these
lords to be equal in status under the new encomienda regime.[42] Under
these circumstances, Andean lords were impoverished by the loss of authority over their traditional subjects and resources, and they suffered a
consequent loss of respect.[43]

Concomitantly, the encomienda enabled a small number of Spaniards to
control and administer a large number of natives, and it proved an effective way for the Spanish to begin to assert control over a social geography
whose scope, dimensions, and profile had not yet been totally explored,
or perhaps even grasped. The encomenderos mobilized laborers to unload
their ships; plant their gardens with imported crops, such as olives and
grapes; build houses, the town hall, the church, and bridges; clean irrigation ditches; spin cotton and weave cloth; tend maize fields; and raise their
newly imported horses, sheep, goats, pigs, and other cattle. They considered this work to be obligatory service that their charges owed them.[44]
Encomenderos sold some of the goods that "their" Indians produced, as
well as rented the urban real estate built by them to the new European
immigrants, thus commodifying the labor of their charges in order to purchase the imported goods they craved.[45] And, precisely because the natives
did not provide many of the types of goods the Spanish preferred, or
not in sufficient quantity, before 1550, a growing number of merchants
from Mexico, Guatemala, Nicaragua, and Panama arrived, bringing wheat
flour, wine, soap, candles, live cattle, saffron, silk, satin, velvet, porcelain,
and other household articles, along with the paraphernalia of soldiering,
as well as wax, honey, tobacco, and tar.[46]

The impact of these early changes—the distribution of encomiendas,
the founding of towns, and the continuous arrival of new European im-

migrants and merchant ships—on the natives of the north can only be suggested here. The small percentage of natives who came into contact with the Spanish in and about the urban areas on a routine and regular basis were probably the first to grasp the differences in the economic systems. Curacas who organized and directed work crews on specific jobs spent varying lengths of time in the cities. Indigenous woodworkers who moved to the Spanish cities, usually on orders of their encomenderos and who had previously produced drinking mugs and the like, learned quickly to adapt their skills to build edifices and repair ships. Other artisans, like the indigenous metallurgists who before the Spanish arrival had made head-dresses, bracelets, burial masks, or other ritual paraphernalia as part of the curaca's court, soon were employed by their new masters to make horse-shoes of copper and silver; whole sets of cups, plates, and serving pieces; chains and other articles of adornment; and crosses and chalices for the church in gold or silver. Native fishermen used their knowledge and skills to transport goods on rafts to Spanish ships anchored in deep water ports such as Chérrepe and Huanchaco.[47]

These individuals probably noticed that one Spaniard sometimes worked for another, receiving subsistence or wages in return. They observed that two individuals who were previously unknown to each other could inter-act and exchange without much ritual negotiation or previous gift giving by using a medium of exchange that was measured in quantity and degree of fineness. Natives probably observed that when one person wanted to exchange, he met with others and did so on or near the plaza. Or, they might have been rudely introduced to Spanish-style exchanges, as were the natives of Quito within two years of the city's Spanish founding, by Spaniards who forced them to "sell" Europeans the items they coveted.[48] To the plaza, too, came the encomendero or his agent, when he wanted to dispose of the surplus tribute goods his charges had carried into the city from the hinterland. Natives undoubtedly noticed that some persons had more goods and ate, dressed, and lived better than others did. Before the middle of the sixteenth century when colonial authorities took the first steps to regulate tribute, those who observed and could take advan-tage of the growing Spanish market system appear to have been the native lords, who brought contingents of their followers into towns to work for the Spanish; the artisans who served the small, but growing Spanish sector; and the native fisherfolk who turned into sailors and stevedores in the ports.

Already by 1540, a developing commercial economy was beginning to affect native peasant communities in myriad ways. The encomenderos Melchoir Verdugo and Lorenzo de Ulloa sent encomienda Indians to mine silver and pan for gold.[49] The native lords of Jayanca in the same year showed a Spanish inspector a scale to weigh the ore they delivered, as tribute, to the encomendero.[50] The tribute regulations instituted at mid-century and periodically thereafter increasingly forced community inhabitants into the monetarized economy. In Pedro de la Gasca's 1549 tribute lists for the north (as well as elsewhere in Peru), native communities were responsible for providing a wide variety of goods and labor services to the encomendero. Moreover, communities—even those that were acknowledged not to have any mines nearby—were assessed tribute in silver.[51] Subsequently, in the revisions of the 1560s and 1570s, tribute lists were simplified and regulated according to local production possibilities. Tribute payments in the north usually consisted of maize, fowl, and cash in the highlands[52] and maize, wheat, fowl, cloth, and cash on the coast.[53] Communities had the option of commuting some of the commodities to cash.[54]

Contemporary local accounts, however, suggest that the native lords continued to take an inordinately large role and responsibility for accumulating the tribute that had to be delivered semiannually.[55] Caciques coordinated the labor needed to plow, sow, weed, and harvest the communal fields (the *chacras de comunidad*), dedicated to tribute production. Often, they sold the surplus crops, accumulating cash (and sometimes the wages of their subjects' labor) for the stated purpose of covering future tribute debts. Such practices often amounted to a reorganization and reorientation of communal labor of the rural population, but rarely did they signal the population's wholesale incorporation into a monetarized economy.

During the 1550s and 1560s, too, the European immigrant population continued to increase, at the same time that the native population continued to plummet. European demand for a variety of goods outstripped the encomienda's ability to produce. The effective demand of the Europeans, therefore, for a variety of goods, ranging from wheat, olives, sugar, wine, and live animals to swords and cloth was supplied more and more by overseas merchants, who imported such goods from Mexico and Europe, via Panama. This proved the impetus for enterprising Spaniards in the north to seize the opportunities of an expanding urban consumer market. They began to establish local farms to grow wheat, grapes, sugar, and olives, under the protective umbrella of the relatively high prices of the imported goods.[56]

One brake on such entrepreneurial pursuits, here in the north and later elsewhere in Peru, however, was a growing scarcity of labor. After the suppression of personal service by decree in 1549,[57] European settlers received a few *mitayos* (draft native laborers) to help develop their rural estates, but these generally were too few to suffice.[58] Some owners encouraged natives to become *yanaconas* (personal retainers), but these too proved insufficient to meet the growing demand.[59] To ease the situation, Dr. Cuenca ordered in 1566 that the natives who wanted to work as wage labor could do so freely, and he issued general ordinances regulating wages and working conditions.[60] He also increased the supply of potential wage laborers by assigning natives who had fled their communities to new caciques without land. They had to hire themselves out to survive.[61] Before black slaves became readily available in the seventeenth century, Spaniards often solved their labor needs, therefore, by entering into contractual arrangements with these migrant Indians, under a variety of wage or piecework stipulations.[62]

The royal edict to resettle natives into nucleated villages, or *reducciones*, that dated from the 1560s in the north also increased the number of Indians who entered the emerging labor market. The reducción policy deprived some native communities of some of their dispersed land holdings and thus diminished the variety of resources they once controlled.[63] Community members, therefore, increasingly had to resort to exchange—to barter and purchase—to fulfill their needs.[64] Without sufficient arable land, others fled. Thus, by about the mid-1560s, the combination of the newly imposed and subsequently revised tribute regulations, the growing urban market and the increased demand for labor, the reducción policy, and the incentives and pressures on natives to adapt—all conspired to impel Indians of the northern Andes to participate in the emerging mercantile system.

Local-level documents indicate the uneven process of native integration into the colonial market. Already by 1555, the tradition of indigenous hospitality was eroding. Inhabitants of Jayanca, delivering tribute goods to the city residence of their encomendero, reported using cotton thread to exchange for food along the route.[65] A few years later, Dr. Cuenca's ordinances mandated the use of native wage labor and ordered an end to reciprocal labor exchanges among the Indians. Henceforth, the Indians were expected to pay each other wages in return for work.[66] He also restricted the distribution and drinking of chicha, without which the lords' subjects would not gather and work.[67] Other provisions required travelers to pay for fodder (*yerba*) for their animals and firewood when they passed through towns. Lords had to pay women to weave and to make cloth for them. They were also directed to pay their litter bearers (*hamaqueros*) for "their daily work, according to the wage scale." Priests had to pay for labor services that previously had been provided as unpaid personal service by their native parishioners. Cuenca, as indicated above, also formulated a wage scale in 1566.[68]

The ordinances, of course, do not provide an indication of the extent to which Cuenca's rules and regulations were enforced. Among the most recalcitrant of employers were the encomenderos, who were used to receiving unpaid personal services.[69] Pedro de Barbarán, the encomendero of Lambayeque, was subsequently sued and fined for not promptly paying his workers their wages.[70] Alonso Carrasco, the encomendero of Jayanca, was able to stall paying his mitayos and yanaconas over 340 pesos until Juan de Hoçes, Toledo's visitor and a corregidor (district governor), enforced the ordinances in the 1570s.[71] Other provisions followed to ensure that natives were paid individually and in cash. In spite of these reforms, their wages were routinely transferred to their lords.[72] It was not until the end of the century that small numbers of individual rural villagers specialized in crafts and services, which they sold on a seasonal basis to Spanish landlords for cash.[73]

Cuenca's 1566 ordinances also mention that both Andean lords and peasants engaged in trade. Lords were accused of "selling" community lands to Spaniards without authority.[74] Commoners and lords alike raised imported cattle, and artisans crafted goods. Some Indians sold cloth to have the means to purchase wine and other European merchandise. To help centralize and regulate these activities, Cuenca declared that there be founded a market (*tiangues*) every Thursday in the plaza of Jayanca, which also would serve as a central place for public punishments and festivals.[75]

But the Spanish colonial authorities' decrees that aimed to protect the Indians and preserve public order created some measure of disincentive for the rural native population to participate directly in commercial transactions. Dr. Cuenca, for example, learned that itinerant peddlars sold community inhabitants wine and other imported goods for high prices and bought their cloth and cattle at low prices. To remedy this, he required that all such transactions take place only before the corregidor or priest (an obviously impractical order). Subsequently, he prosecuted and fined twenty-one peddlars who were found to have "traded" with community members unlawfully.[76] Furthermore, Indians were officially prohibited from wearing Spanish clothes and riding saddled horses. They could not own arms or buy Spanish wine or dice (which were considered corrupting).[77]

Documentary evidence indicates that for most of the century such exchanges occurred occasionally. But, the majority of the Indians living in the north were probably minimally affected directly by the evolving and burgeoning commercial markets in the coastal cities and ports. For the peasant, living in a rural community at a distance from one of the coastal cities where the Spanish congregated, life went on with only infrequent involvement in market trading or wage labor. When native males served the *mita,* it was the curaca and lords who visited the outlying homesteads and hamlets to recruit labor and who supervised the work, and who usually received the wages, despite decree after decree commanding employers to pay individual Indians "in their own hands."[78] Commoners continued to practice kin-based reciprocity and interact without the use of money. Community members still worked together to cultivate communal land, to support the curaca and other lords, or to produce tribute goods for the Spanish. Widows continued their custom of manufacturing chicha for the curaca to serve to his subjects, despite Cuenca's ordinances.[79] Young men still served the curacas as unpaid pages through the 1570s and probably later.[80] Curacas continued their redistributive practices. The fragmentary records of the Indian *cabildo* (town council) between 1586 and 1611 of Lambayeque, for example, shows that land continued to be reallocated within the community, following the principle that they possess and use as much as they could personally work.[81] In short, the evidence suggests that most rural Indians did not depend on the market for their basic subsistence needs.[82]

In contrast, many Andean lords participated actively in the market. The last wills and testaments of lords from various communities of the north provide an inventory of the quantities and types of European goods they acquired, indicating a greater direct involvement in the market than their subjects. A small sample suffices to illustrate these acquisitions. Don Diego Quispe, alias Diego Tecapa, a lord or curaca[83] of the community of Tecapa (in the valley of Pacasmayo), died in 1560. He left knives, scissors, clothes made from linen and silk, and Spanish beads.[84] Another curaca, Santiago Guaman of the town of the same name, near Trujillo, who spoke only his native Muchik or Yunga in 1573, left ceremonial drinking mugs imported from Mexico, three silk suits, and numerous iron tools and objects (e.g., *barretas*).[85] Another native, born, raised, and still living in the town of Mocchumí, prized his white porcelain among all his other locally produced possessions, such as his gold and silver dishes and spoons; silver "crowns" (*con que baylan*, for dancing), and 600 strings of shell beads. A few years later, the cacique or *governador*[86] of Moro, Don García Pilco Guaman, listed a safe imported from Spain, silk clothes, various tools, spurs, and an arquebuse or firearm.[87] Such luxury consumption was confined to a small indigenous elite, however. Wills and other documents show that commoners rarely possessed imported goods.[88]

Not unexpectedly, peasants who left their rural communities and made their life in the cities became more dependent on the market. Although their wills and testaments do not provide details on day-to-day subsistence transactions, or information on how any particular item was acquired (through barter, gift, or sale), these documents show that Indians who lived in the city of Trujillo had more European goods than did their rural counterparts. In 1570, Ysabel, a bilingual, nonliterate Indian woman from Conchucos, who was married to a cobbler, left silk stockings, imported cloth, and Spanish table linens among her goods that also included several suits of indigenous-style clothes and various strands of gold beads.[89] Joana, who was born in Chachapoyas and was the widow of an Indian tailor, left clothes fashioned in the traditional native manner, but made of taffeta and silk.[90] Francisco Cuxmango, a bilingual cobbler who migrated from the highland town of Cusmango, left clothes of taffeta and silk, as well as tools.[91]

The same documents also clearly indicate that these Indians engaged in commercial transactions among themselves and with other members of colonial society that extended beyond the narrow confines of the town or city where they resided. A few wills mention specific purchases, usually of urban real estate. Luís, an Indian *mitima* (before 1532, native colonists, living apart from their community of origin) of Chuspo (near Chiclayo) earning a living as a tailor in Trujillo, for example, specifically mentions a house that he purchased with his *compadre* (ritual co-godparent), a carpenter.[92] A court case revealed that Indians in Trujillo bought maize with which to make chicha to sell to other Indians. The profit enabled them to buy cloth to satisfy their tribute obligations.[93]

Debts seem to be the most common and clear-cut indication of widespread native involvement in market transactions. The same Luís of Chuspo, mentioned above, was owed money by one or two lords of that community.[94] Isabel played creditor to a black slave who belonged to the notary Juan López de Córdova for 1.25 pesos; and Francisco owed her almost 15 pesos.[95] Pedro Atapillos, a native of a town in the jurisdiction of Los Reyes to the south, listed all the people who owed him money, including a yanacona of the city of Trujillo, alderman (*regidor*) Hernando de Paz, who owed him over 13 pesos that he needed as bail to get out of jail; Martín Oco, who owed him 16.5 pesos for a cartload of wheat; Catalina, a subject of the encomendero of Cazma, Andrés Chacón, who owed him 8.25 pesos for a mare he sold her; and Don Bartolomé cacique, who owed him almost 5 pesos. He owed, in turn, only one person, Anton Quisuia, yanacona of the ex-*alcalde* (mayor) and encomendero of Huamachuco, Don Juan Sandoval, not quite 2 pesos.[96] Indians originally from Mocchumí and Reque had similar profiles.[97]

This material concerning debts suggests that the use of money served purposes other than buying European luxury items. Those whose wills are cited above were either lords, who were in direct contact with the Spanish and brokered or mediated the contact of their followers, or Indians who had moved to the cities to serve the Spanish. Most of the debt/creditor relations tied urban-dwelling Indians to the elite of indigenous society who still lived in the rural villages or, more often, to other urban dwellers, including friends, relatives, acquaintances, artisans, and merchants.

The indigenous population, which dwelled in widely scattered homesteads, hamlets, or small villages, had only sporadic and indirect contact with the growing Spanish market system in the cities. Despite the fact that under the early encomienda system, they produced the goods and services that fed the local and international markets, most Indians were only marginally involved in market relations themselves. Few commoners received steady wages, and those who did most often were mitayos, serving two months at a turn. But mita wages were most often entrusted to the lord who accumulated them to satisfy the cash portion of the community's tribute requirements.[98] Commoners continued to work for their lords without monetary consideration and to produce tribute goods such as maize, wheat, and cotton on communal land. They raised their own food and made their own clothing and did not depend on the market for their subsistence needs, either in their communities or on Spanish estates, where they received a ration of food and clothing besides their wages.[99] Even as late as the Toledan period (1570s–1580s), European observers commented on the marginality of most natives. In summing up Spanish frustration at not being able to entice Indians to work for them, one Spaniard complained that natives did not participate actively in the market "because they get from their harvest food and clothing and because they are not inclined to accumulate wealth [hacienda] or leave property to their children."[100] The relatively small percentage of the Indians who did become dependent on the Spanish commercial system were those who had left their rural communities and settled in the cities.

Conclusion

The story of Andean modes of exchange in the north, then, is one characterized by resource sharing, gift giving, reciprocity, and redistribution in the immediate pre-Hispanic era. Spanish reports of "merchants" should probably be more accurately interpreted as evidence of long-distance exchange mechanisms, probably involving barter, that were directed by the lords. They sent their retainers to exchange goods—not for commercial purposes, but to procure exotic goods for political, ritual, and redistributive purposes. Some of the controversy among historians over the existence or nonexistence of markets and merchants in the northern Andes before the European arrival derives from the cultural ambiguities and misrepresentations in certain early colonial documents on Andean exchange. The Spanish employed words like "merchants" and "markets" to describe what they believed they saw—terms that have naturally generated much scholarly skepticism and debate.

Following the Spanish intrusion in 1532, a European commercial, profit-oriented system gradually grew in the northern cities to provide the Spanish population with wheat, olive oil, wine, and other goods. For the most part, these northern market circuits involved Europeans who lived in the interior cities and coastal seaports. Encomenderos and professional Spanish merchants and ship captains became the first directors of this commercial sector. Native lords held pivotal positions, too, mobilizing labor to produce the goods that ultimately were exchanged in the urban marketplaces. Tributary pressures impelled Andean chiefs to engage in commerce and trade, but many also developed a taste for European clothes and other imported items of prestige, and they coveted metal tools and other implements. In addition to the trading activities of Andean lords, the growing Spanish demand for skilled artisans attracted native craft specialists who had once served the indigenous elite. Some artisans moved to the cities, loosening ties to their home communities and becoming increasingly dependent on the market for their everyday subsistence needs. But aside from the small minority of Andeans (such as the itinerant butchers on Spanish estates) who worked for cash on an individual basis, the bulk of the rural population continued to produce tributary goods and to participate in rotational, two-month labor turns on European-run rural estates. Even as late as the 1590s, most Andean peoples in the north continued to provide for their own subsistence and to honor mutual kin-based obligations in their communities, despite a plethora of royal decrees and ordinances to the contrary.

This picture of the northern Andes in the early colonial era suggests that the development of markets unfolded more gradually and unevenly than in the southern Andean highlands during the same period. Compared to the southern regions, a smaller percentage of the peasant population in the north participated in market transactions in the late sixteenth century (see Chapters 3 and 4 in this volume). Nor did a significant sector of the rural Andean population move into the commercial orbit as forced or free wage laborers before 1600. This is due, in part, to the absence of early colonial mining centers in the north. There was no northern equivalent of Huancavelica, Oruro, or Potosí, which created the pressures and incentives to draw Indians away from their fields and communities for long periods of time. Over the long term, the mines of the South provided Indian laborers with monied wages, thus reinforcing the rapid development of the internal market system in the southern Andean heartlands. And yet, paradoxically, it was in the northern interior highlands—far more than in the southern regions—where the Spanish hacienda gradually came to prevail during the seventeenth and eighteenth centuries.

Notes

All abbreviations for the archival material cited here are listed on the first page of the bibliography. All translations of quotations are mine.

1. Aztec exchange specialists who dealt in luxury goods carried over long distances. They also served as spies and ambassadors.

2. I will use "exchange specialists" to describe natives who engaged in transport of goods and/or exchange. I favor this phrase rather than "merchant(s)" because the latter term connotes a commercial, profit motive, which I question below. When the word "merchant" appears in quotation marks in this text, it designates the term used in the original Spanish manuscript or the word used by the scholar who interpreted the primary source.

3. María Rostworowski de Diez Canseco, *Etnía y sociedad: Costa peruana prehispánica* (Lima, 1977).

4. Rostworowski, "La estratificación social y el hatun curaca en el mundo andino," *Histórica* 1.2 (1977): 249–286, and Rostworowski, "Breves notas sobre la estructura socio-económica en la costa peruana precolombina," in Roswith Hartmann and Udo Oberem, *Estudios americanistas* (Lima, 1979), 2:207–211.

5. Rostworowski, *Costa peruana prehispánica*, esp. 97–140.

6. Biblioteca del Palacio (Madrid) [hereafter *BP*], ms. 2846, folios 261–273, especially 271–271v. See also Chapter 2 in this volume.

7. These sums are equivalent to 827 to 2,750–4,125 pesos of 8 reales each. They were enormous sums, considering that the group represented 6,000 merchants. All prices and wages in the paper are converted to pesos of 8 reales each. If the type of peso is not indicated in the original source, the pesos are assumed to be of 450 maravedís each and are converted on this basis.

8. Defined as Pacasmayo on the south to Motupe on the north and inland to between 1,000 and 2,000 meters above sea level.

9. AGI, J418, 1573, 306v; J457, 843v; J458, 1920v; J461, 1043, 1454v, 1457v, 1461, 1463, 1464; J462, 1871; and AL 133.

10. "Community" here refers to the remnants of the pre-Columbian rural Indian community, which included individuals and families living scattered over entire river valleys and as far as thirty leagues inland from the ocean. The jurisdiction of the lords of these communities was defined by his subjects and where they

resided and worked and, therefore, did not necessarily imply a coherent, unified, coterminous, and bounded piece of territory. After 1532, as a result of colonial policies such as the granting of *encomiendas* (defined below) and the concentration of natives into nucleated villages, the lords' subject-based jurisdiction became more synonymous with a regularly defined and bounded area of land.

11. Frank Salomon, *Native Lords of Quito in the Age of the Incas* (Cambridge, 1986), 102, 202–203.

12. Sámano-Xerez, "Relación" [1525], in Raul Porras Barrenechea, *Las relaciones primitivas de la conquista del Perú* (Lima, 1967), 66. See also Murra's discussion of this material in *The Economic Organization of the Inca State* (Greenwich, Conn., 1980), 140–141. *Caçedonia* refers to chalcedony, the name given to the microcrystalline varieties of quartz that form concretionary deposits (partially of organic origin in the case of jasper). The name chalcedony probably comes from Calcedon or Calchedon, an ancient port on the Sea of Marmara, in Asia Minor. Curzio Cipriani and Alessandro Borelli, *Guide to Gems and Precious Stones* (U.S. ed.: New York, 1986), 198.

13. Sámano-Xerez, "Relación," 66.

14. Olaf Holm, *Monedas primitivas del Ecuador prehistórico* (Guayaquil, 1975); Izumi Shimada, "Perception, Procurement, and Management of Resources: Archaeological Perspective," in Shozo Masuda, Izumi Shimada, and Craig Morris, eds., *Andean Ecology and Civilization: An Interdisciplinary Perspective on Andean Ecological Complementarity* (Tokyo, 1985), 389–92; Dorothy Hosler, Heather Lechtman, and Olaf Holm, *Axe-Monies and Their Relatives* (Washington, D.C., 1990), 3, 51–53, 67–68.

15. Erland Nordenskiöld, "The Ancient Peruvian System of Weights," *Man* 30.154–155 (December 1930): 215–221.

16. Hector Omar Noejovich, "La cuestión del comercio y los mercados en la América precolombina," n.d., 14–15, believes that the "Aviso" dates from after 1570. Rostworowski, *Costa peruana prehistórica*, claims that it dates to about 1575. My dating of the "Aviso" considered the following: (1) The watermark of the paper, a potential clue to the approximate date of the composition. Because it is a copy, the watermark proved to be typical of other eighteenth-century marks and, therefore, was of no help in determining the document's antiquity. (2) The spelling and abbreviations used in the manuscript. These were not characteristic of an early sixteenth-century hand. (3) Evidence internal to the manuscript that hints about the date of its composition. These textual clues include (a) the inquiry about the tribute given to the Inca; (b) the argument to found a new Spanish town in the Lurinchincha valley, and not in Pisco; (c) the notice of abundant areas of vacant lands; (d) the decline of the population from 30,000 to slightly over 600;

(e) the mention of the *Príncipe que govierna;* (f) an argument to commute the cloth tribute to cash; and (g) the fact that it was written after Hernando Pizarro was the encomendero of Chincha, after Fray Domingo de Santo Tomás was Bishop of Charcas, and after the monastery of Chincha was founded.

Only a few of these potential clues are helpful in verifying the date the Chincha document was written. First, we know that the Dominican convent was founded by Santo Tomás in the 1540s (Rostworowski, *Costa peruana prehispánica,* 102; Alberto Rossell Castro, *Historia regional de Ica* (Lima, 1964), 120; Cristobal de Castro and Diego de Ortega y Morejon, "Relación de Chincha" [1558], in *Biblioteca Peruana: El Perú a través de los siglos,* primera serie, vol. 3 (Lima, 1968), 465–489. Second, we know that Santo Tomás served as bishop of La Plata or Charcas until his death in early 1570. See Ruben Vargas Ugarte, *Historia general del Perú,* 2d ed. 10 vols. (Lima, 1971), 2:158–159; Ruben Vargas Ugarte, *Historia de la iglesia en el Perú,* 3 vols. (Lima and Burgos, 1956, 1959), 2:128; Monseñor Julio García Quintanilla, *Historia de la iglesia en La Plata* (Sucre, Bolivia, 1964), 1:70. Also, although commutation of tribute products to gold and silver pesos began in the north in the 1560s (see also Salomon, *Native Lords of Quito,* 202; Susan E. Ramírez, "Tribute," in *The World Upside Down: Cross Cultural Contact and Conflict in Sixteenth-Century Peru* [Stanford, 1995]), interest in and collecting information on Inca tribute and the commutation of tribute goods to gold and silver elsewhere occurred under Viceroy Francisco de Toledo in the 1570s. Finally, perhaps the best indication of a date is provided by Nobel David Cook's population figures that show 979 tribute payers living in Chincha in 1575 and 412 in 1591. Assuming a constant rate of decrease over the sixteen years between 1575 and 1591, the population of Chincha would have hit 600 sometime during the biennium of 1585–1586 (the population in 1585 was 624–625; population in 1586 was 589–1875). See Noble David Cook, "Population Data for Indian Peru: Sixteenth and Seventeenth Centuries," *Hispanic American Historical Review* 62.1 (1982): 85. Hence, I believe the date to have been in the mid-1580s.

17. Castro and Ortega y Morejón, "Relación de Chincha [1558]," 465–489.

18. Richard Schaedel, "Commerce in Ancient Peru," draft typescript, 1990, 4; and Daniel H. Sandweiss, personal communication, March 1, 1992.

19. Susan E. Ramírez, "Retainers of the Lords or Merchants: A Case of Mistaken Identity?" *Senri Ethnological Studies* 10 (1982): 123–136. See also Noejovich "Cuestión del Comercio," 14–15, who for other reasons also believes the "Aviso" to indicate *una "españolización" manifiesta* and does not accept the "merchants" as merchants.

20. Ramírez, "Retainers of the Lords or Merchants"; and Patricia Netherly, "Fish, Corn and Cloth: Intraregional Specialization on the North Coast of Peru,"

paper read at the Annual Meetings of the American Anthropology Association, San Francisco, December 2, 1975, 10. Salomon, *Native Lords of Quito,* 114, also notes the existence of nonspecialist traders who worked out of their homes and did not travel far.

21. ACMS, 1654–1765, 7–7v; ANP, RA, 27, c. 95, 1610, 141; and Enrique Brüning, *Estudios monográficos del Departamento de Lambayeque* (Chiclayo, 1922–1923), 3:59; AGI, J460, 483; AL 92; Waldemar Espinoza Soriano, "El Valle de Jayanca y el reino de los Mochica, siglo XV y XVI," *Bulletin de l'Institut Français d'Etudes Andines* 4.3–4 (1975): 271; Pedro Cieza de León, *Travels of Pedro Cieza de León, ad 1532–50* (New York, 1964), 236, 240. For a case in Colombia, see also Robert G. Keith, "The Encomienda and the Genesis of a Colonial Economy in Spanish America," *Research in Economic Anthropology* 3 (1980): 144.

22. Cieza de León, *Travels,* 236, 240. The Inca used this tactic in conquering the Chimu empire.

23. Susan E. Ramírez, "Dimensiones Ethnohistóricas de minería y metalurgia del siglo XVI en el norte del Perú" *Historia Cultura* 23 (forthcoming). María Rostworowski de Diez Canseco, "La tasa ordenada por el Licenciado Pedro de la Gasca" [1549], *Revista Histórica* 34 (1983–1984): 90–91. On the exchange of use rights to resources among communities or ethnic groups, see Terrence N. D'Altroy and Timothy E. Earle, "Staple Finance, Wealth Finance, and Storage in the Inka Political Economy," *Current Anthropology* 26.2 (April 1985): 189. Salomon, also, without specifically mentioning it by name or type of exchange, presents evidence that suggests that resource sharing was operative in Ecuador also. Those stationed away from home had tributary duties in the place they were sent; they had to help the chief who controlled the lands or resource. This sounds like the "resource sharing" arrangements first noted in the silver mines of Chilete. See Susan E. Ramírez, "Social Frontiers and the Territorial Base of Curacazgos," in Shozo Masuda, Izumi Shimada, and Craig Morris, eds., *Andean Ecology and Civilization: An Interdisciplinary Perspective on Andean Ecological Complementarity* (Tokyo, 1985), 423–442; Salomon, *Native Lords of Quito,* 90, 112, 200. For a case of resource sharing of salt, see Chapter 4 in this volume. The Chupachus and Queros had saltmakers (*salineros*) in lands (at the salt pans) controlled by the Yaros.

Salomon mentions other mechanisms of exchange, too: reciprocity between households or small units in communities; ceremonial prestations; redistribution (*Native Lords of Quito,* 115); and direct trade between highland and lowland farmers (106) and archipelago islands or outliers, some of which were multiethnic (111–112).

24. In 1540 the people of Jayanca lived in about 250 settlements scattered over a

two-league radius from the lord's administrative center. Another lord had subjects "in a district of over thirty leagues from the sea to [the highlands of] Cajamarca." Espinoza Soriano, "Valle de Jayanca"; AGI, J461, 866v; and J458, 1778v–1779 and 1829v; AL 92, 1566; CVU, 1–4, 1564.

25. Susan E. Ramírez, "The 'Dueño de Indios': Thoughts on the Consequences of the Shifting Bases of Power of the 'Curaca de los viejos antiguos' under the Spanish in Sixteenth-Century Peru," *Hispanic American Historical Review* 67.4 (1987): 575–610.

26. Ramírez, "Retainers of the Lords or Merchants." For another example from the Inca south, see the recently published edition of the chronicle of Juan de Betanzos, *Suma y narración de los Incas* (Madrid, 1987). The Inca Guayna Capac sent lords out from Cuzco to "buy" (Betanzos's word) coca and chili peppers in Chinchaysuyu for the funeral rites of his mother. The choice and use of specific Spanish words to describe the activities of the Indians, such as "buy," distorts what they were doing (probably exchanging or requisitioning) and leads to misinterpretation when not critically assessed. See Betanzos, ibid., 189; Ramírez, "Social Frontiers," 432.

27. Salomon, *Native Lords of Quito*, 210–211. See also Chapter 2 in this volume.

28. Frank Salomon, "Systemes politiques aux marchés de l'empire," *Annales ESC* 33.5–6 (1978): 975.

29. Ramírez, " 'Dueño de Indios.' "

30. As quoted by Roswith Hartmann, "Mercados y ferias prehispánicas en el área andina," *Boletín de la Academia Nacional de Historia* (Quito) 54. 118 (1971): 215; original in Francisco de Jerez, "Verdadera relación de la conquista del Perú y provincia del Cuzco. . ." [1534], in *Crónicas de la conquista del Perú* (Mexico, n.d.), 104.

31. See ibid., 217, especially n. 16, which says that John Murra favors this interpretation. Note that Murra, Chapter 2 in this volume, mentions Hartmann's findings only for the area north of Cajamarca. However, he does not accept her interpretation of Estete's remarks on Jauja.

32. Jerez, "Verdadera relación," 102, 104.

33. Susan E. Ramírez, "The Inca Conquest of the North Coast: A Historian's View," in Michael E. Moseley and Alana Cordy-Collins, eds., *Northern Dynasties: Kingship and Statecraft in Chimor* (Washington, D.C., 1990), 507–537. John Hyslop ties plazas to ceremonial purposes. See Hyslop, *Inka Settlement Patterns* (Austin, 1990), 77, 87, 99–100.

34. Salomon, *Native Lords of Quito*, 94–96.

35. Ibid., 98. Where I differ from Murra (Chapter 2 in this volume) and Salomon

is on whether or not there were marketplaces in the north before the arrival of the Spanish. I do not believe, from the evidence I have seen, that they existed before 1532. If the ends of exchange are political gain and exchange for control by the native authorities, there would be no need for a marketplace as a centralized locale for exchange and trade.

36. Ibid., 99.

37. Cited by ibid., 102.

38. Exchange also antedated the Inca conquest of the north. See Ramírez, "Inca Conquest," and Juan Polo de Ondegardo, "Informe al Licenciado Briviesca de Muñatones sobre la perpetuidad de las encomiendas en el Perú," *Revista Histórica* 13 (1940): 145.

39. Schaedel, who has not studied the provenance of the documentary history thoroughly or questioned the reliability of the written sources, believes that the Inca enfranchised the Chincha to continue their long-distance trade as a state monopoly. See his "El Comercio en el Perú," in Modesto Suárez, ed., *Historia Antropológica y Política: Homenaje a Angel Palerm*, vol. 1 (Mexico City, 1990): 163–189.

40. Hyslop, *Inka Settlement Patterns;* D'Altroy and Earle, "Staple Finance," 187–206; Terrence N. D'Altroy and Timothy E. Earle, "Storage Facilities and State Finance in the Upper Montaro Valley, Peru," Jonathan E. Ericson and Timothy K. Earle, eds., in *Contexts for Pre-historic Exchange* (New York, 1982), 265–290; and Craig Morris and Donald E. Thompson, *Huánuco Pampa: An Inca City and Its Hinterland* (London, 1985), 98–108.

41. Susan E. Ramírez, *Provincial Patriarchs: Land Tenure and the Economics of Power in Colonial Peru* (Albuquerque, 1986), 16; Rolando Mellafe, "Frontera agraria: El caso del virreinato peruano en el siglo XVI," in Alvaro Jara, ed., *Tierras nuevas* (Mexico, 1969), 23.

42. CVU, 1-1, 1-VII-1550; ART, CoP, 1. 280, exp. 3583, 9-VIII-1563; AGI, J457, 1144v–1145.

43. Ramírez, " '*Dueño de Indios.*' " Sempat Assadourian (Chapter 4 in this volume) discusses the consequences of the subdivision of indigenous communities in the south.

44. ART, Salinas, 8-VIII-1539; López de Córdova, 21-IV-1559; ACT, I, 38 (for 1-IX-1551), 98 (for 1555); and 258 (for 28-VI-1557); José Antonio del Busto, "El capitán Melchor Verdugo, encomendero de Cajamarca," *Revista Histórica* 24 (1959): 364.

45. A sense of the growth of a European market in the cities is seen in the population figures for Trujillo. That the *villa* attracted a flood of new European immigrants is evident from the following facts: From twenty-four householding

citizens and their families in 1555, Trujillo grew to 200 *casas de vecinos moradores* in 1568; to twenty-eight encomenderos and 300 Spaniards (and their households) in 1570; and to 1,017 "whites" in 1575 (ACT, I, 87 and 181); Marco A. Cabero, "El corregimiento de Saña y el problema histórico de la fundación de Trujillo," *Revista Histórica* 1.2–4 (1906): 340.

46. ANP, RA, I. 33, 1594; Woodrow W. Borah, *Early Colonial Trade and Navigation between Mexico and Peru* (Berkeley, 1954), 43–47, 57; Ramírez, *Provincial Patriarchs*, chaps. 3–4, esp. 41–43; Teodoro Hampe Martínez, "Actividad mercantil del puerto de Lima en la primera mitad del siglo XVI," *Revista Histórica* 35 (1985–1986): 119.

47. ACT, I, 61–62 (for 4-III-1552); Miguel de Estete, "Noticia del Perú," in *Historia de los Incas y conquista del Perú, Colección de libros y documentos referentes a la historia del Perú*, vol. 8, ser. 2 (Lima, 1924), 40; AGI, J457, 841 and 1550v; J461, 1581v; and P 188, R. 22, 1561, 22v; and BM, Add. 17588, 51v.

48. Hartmann, "Mercados y ferias," 217.

49. AGI, J415, 199, JLC33, No. 3, 1570, 5v–10; AL 568, 217v; ART, Vega, I. 71, 13-IX-1578, 5v; del Busto, "Capitán Verdugo," 330.

50. Espinoza Soriano, "Valle de Jaynaca," 226; Nordenskiöld, "Ancient Peruvian System," 215–221. My interpretation of the 1540 visita of the encomienda of Jayanca makes me believe that the natives had not panned for gold before the arrival of the Spanish (Espinoza Soriano, "Valle de Jaynaca," 226).

51. Rostworowski, "Tasa ordenada," 88–91. It has been argued elsewhere that natives were forced into the market as a consequence of La Gasca's 1549 tribute requirements as laborers and consumers because of their need to buy things that they could not produce in their own locality. This seems less true for the north, judging from the types of goods listed in the 1549 tribute lists of the area. See Alejandro Málaga Medina, "El Virrey Don Francisco de Toledo y la reglamentación del tributo en el Virreinato del Perú," *Anuario de Estudios Americanos* 29 (1972): 603–604; Rostworowski, "Tasa ordinada," 88–91. See also Chapter 4 in this volume.

52. AGI, J457, 1566, 1149v; J461, 930.

53. AGI, J461, 1121.

54. Ramírez, *The World Upside Down*, ch. 4.

55. Ibid.; Ramírez, *Provincial Patriarchs*, 109, 162; Francisco López de Gómara, *Historia general de las Indias* (Madrid, [1552] 1941), 2:188.

56. ACT, I, 285 (for 21-I-1558); Ramírez, *Provincial Patriarchs*, 82. See also note 45.

57. Personal services, officially ended in a decree of 1549, were curtailed in practice much later in the northern cities. In Trujillo, for example, obligatory en-

comienda services were suppressed in 1558 and a decade or two later than that in the rural areas. Thus, as late as the 1560s, rural peasants continued to work on a temporary basis for the encomenderos without remuneration and to live largely without depending for subsistence on the market. Yet, significantly, the Spanish institution of the encomienda provided the mechanism to redirect the labor of Andean peoples to the gradually developing local and international markets. ACT, I, 296–297 (for 21-III-1558); ART, CoAG, 13-II-1565; C. H. Haring, *The Spanish Empire in America* (New York, 1963), 53.

58. AGI, J455, 1684–1685. The labor shortage appeared in other parts of Peru as well. See Steve J. Stern, *Peru's Indian Peoples and the Challenge of the Spanish Conquest: Huamanga to 1640* (Madison, 1982), 128–132, 140; and Brooke Larson, *Colonialism and Agrarian Transformation in Bolivia: Cochabamba, 1550–1900* (Princeton, 1988), 54–55.

59. AGI, J455, 1566, 1685; ART, CoO, 4-IV-1573.

60. AGI, J455, 1684–1685; J457, 1156, 1550v; J461, 1260 and 1263. Assadourian (Chapter 4 in this volume) shows that this occurred later in the south.

61. AGI, J457, 1156; ART, CoR, 30-VI-1576. The Trujillo *cabildo* (town council) noted a migratory stream of natives who came to the coast to work for wages as early as 19-VII-1557 (ACT, I, 261).

62. ACT, I, 38 (for 1-IX-1551); I, 261 (for 19-VII-1557); I, 296–297 (for 21-III-1558); ART, Vega, 1567; CoR, 30-VI-1576; CoO, 7-I-1580. They received a combination of goods and cash, plus room and board for the time of their labor.

63. Susan E. Ramírez, "Chérrepe en 1572: Un análisis de la visita general del Virrey Francisco de Toledo," *Historia y Cultura* 11 (1978): 79–121 (see, especially, 92–94).

64. Ramírez, "'Dueño de Indios,'" 597–599.

65. ART, López de Cordova, 1558.

66. The ordinances are published in María Rostworowski de Diez Canseco, "Algunos comentarios hechos a las ordenanzas del Doctor Cuenca," *Historia y Cultura* 9 (1975): esp. 149–150. The original manuscript is AGI, P 189, r. 11, 1566.

67. AGI, J458, 1779 and 2550v; and J461, 1769–1771.

68. Rostworowski, "Algunos comentarios," 133, 143, 145, 151, 153. For a sampling of wages see ACT, I, 296–297; ART, CoO, I. 147, exp. 131, 3-IX-1563, 4-IV-1573; and 11-VIII-1582; CoAG, 11-X-1585; Mata, 1596; AGI, P 97, R. 4, 17; P 189, R. 11, 1566; J455, 1684–1685; J457, 742v, 831v, 841; J458, 2249; J460, 12; J461, 1444; AL 28, 1574, 4, 7v; Archivo del Monasterio de San Francisco de Lima (ASFL), Reg. 9, No. 2, Ms. 2, 1572; and ANP, R, I. 3, c. 7, 1582, 152.

69. It stands to reason that native lords, used to unpaid labor service, were

surely reluctant to pay wages to commoners, too. For one example see ART, CoR, 30-VI-1576, for a case when Don Diego Mocchomí had not paid his "widows" for weaving in 1574. For another see ART, CoO, 11-VIII-1582.

70. AGI, J459, 3030v; BNP, A157, 128v.

71. ART, CoO, 18-I-1574.

72. ART, CoAG, 11-X-1585; CoR, 30-VI-1576; ANP, R, 1. 3, c. 7, 1582, 63v and 92.

73. ART, Mata, 1596.

74. This may not have been a "sale" in the commercial sense, but permission to use resources within a lord's jurisdiction in exchange for gifts. See Susan E. Ramírez, "Indian and Spanish Conceptions of Land Tenure in Peru, 1500–1810," paper presented at the American Historical Association Annual Meeting, Cincinnati, Ohio, December 29, 1988.

75. Rostworowski, "Algunos comentarios," 131, 141, 148–150.

76. Ibid., 148; AGI, J461, 1252, 1258v–1259v.

77. Jorge Zevallos Quiñones, "La visita del Pueblo de Ferreñafe (Lambayeque) en 1568," *Historia y Cultura* 9 (1975): 157.

78. AGI, AL 28, 15; AL 28B, No. 2, 33v; P 97, R. 4, [1569], 17–17v; ART, CoR, 30-VI-1576; and ANP, R, 1. 3, c. 7, 1582, 63v; Zevallos Quiñones, "Visita del Pueblo," 162–163.

79. AGI, J458, 1779v–1780; and J461, 1469v–1470, 1481v; P 189, R. 11, 1566.

80. AGI, J461, 462, 854, 857, 1400v; J455, 1566, 1685.

81. ANCR, 1586–1611; Ramírez, "Conceptions of Land Tenure in Peru."

82. Zevallos Quiñones thinks that inhabitants of Ferreñafe, a coastal community north of Lambayeque, were a "good market" for the "trifles or pseudosumptuary trade" (*comercio baratijero o seudo-suntuario*), but he provides no concrete evidence for this. See "Visita del Pueblo," 159.

83. He was identified as both.

84. ART, CoO, 1. 1, 6-XII-1560. He also owned a scale, as did so many others, for weighing out pesos before the ready availability of coins.

85. ART, Notarial, 1. 31. 1-VI-1573, 263v–265v.

86. A *governador* (governor) was appointed to this position during the incapacity of the legitimate lord.

87. ART, CoO, 1. 13, 11-VIII-1582 for 20-VI-1582.

88. ART, López de Córdova, 1. 4, 29-III-1563, 191–192; CaO, 1. 5, 24-I-1587; AGI, J461, 868v.

89. ART, Mata, 1. 11, 23-I-1570, 5v–7.

90. ART, Notarial, 1. 31, 6-VII-1573, 336–336v. There is no way of knowing

if her scale and several other items were imported. Throughout this section, I am only listing items known not to have been produced in Peru (ART, Notarial, 1. 31, 6-VII-1573, 336–336v).

91. ART, Obregón, 1. 40, 9-VII-1593, 262. For examples of this phenomenon in the south, see Saignes, Chapter 6 in this volume.

92. ART, López de Córdova, 1. 4, 29-III-1563, 191–192.

93. AGI, J404, 516–518.

94. ART, López de Córdova, 1. 4, 29-III-1563, 191–192. This also indicates that he maintained ties to his community of origin.

95. ART, Mata, 1. 11, 23-I-1570.

96. ART, Notarial, 1. 31, 9-VI-1573, 279v–280; ACT, II, 39; BAH, Muñoz, A-92, 66v–67.

97. ART, CoR, 30-VI-1576; CaO, 1. 5, 24-I-1587.

98. Curacas sometimes abused their trust and power and siphoned off some of this money to acquire their material trappings, items of dress, silver service, etc.

99. Zevallos Quiñones, "Visita del Pueblo," 162.

100. "Por tener de su cosecha el comer y vestir y no tener ynclinación a adquerir hazienda ni a dejar heredades [a] sus hijos" (AGI, AL 28A, No. 2).

III

Andean Tribute, Migration, and Trade:

Remapping the Boundaries of

Ethnicity and Exchange

Map 3. South Andean Ethnic Groups.

Indian Migration and Social Change in

Seventeenth-Century Charcas

THIERRY SAIGNES

In this chapter I wish to show how, under the impact of Spanish colonization, the previous system of stratification gave way to a new form of social articulation in the central southern Andes. As social relationships were redefined, new opportunities opened up, making possible a wide range of strategies, manipulations of existing networks, and paths for social mobility for certain identifiable individuals and groups.

To understand this process of rupture and recomposition in indigenous society, we must go back to the situation on the eve of Viceroy Toledo's administrative reorganization between 1570 and 1580, which was a key moment in the history of the region from Cuzco to Chichas. Our appreciation of the dilemma that confronted Toledo owes much to the analysis of an exceptionally perceptive observer of that moment, Licenciado Juan Polo de Ondegardo. In the babble of "opinions without purpose" concerning what measures would help reactivate the export of precious metals and harness the indigenous labor force, his "Report on the Reasons for the Notable Damage Resulting from Failure to Protect the Indians' Customs" of 1571 stands out as an accurate guide.

Polo's first observation that "there are not two republics, but only one" has not been given the attention it deserves. In his view the Spanish Crown's ideal of keeping the Republic of Christians and the Republic of Indians separate was pure legal formalism. However, while he noted the necessary relative interdependence between the two republics, he also advocated maintaining the traditional organization of Indian tribute and predicted that if it is decided that the Indians be registered and taxed individually, and that so long as they fulfill their obligations they be discharged from the rule and authority of their lords and freely go where they wish, that day the restraints that ensure that they stay together in harmony will be removed, the restraints by which they are maintained today, and were so before the Christians took over these kingdoms. If this policy were to be tried out for one year, its destructive effects would be clear."[1]

Faced with two options for colonial government, that of indirect rule leaving indigenous society with its traditional rulers, or that of direct intervention through Spanish officials, Polo chose the former.

In practice Toledo adopted a compromise solution. He retained the lords (*caciques*), but he regrouped the Indians into settlement towns (*reducciones*) where they were under the control of the *cabildo* (town council), the priest, and the *corregidor,* or his representative. He fixed the tribute individually and mainly in money, but the responsibility for paying it was collective at the level of the settlement town. Criticisms were voiced immediately. Two of the most explicit were by the Jesuit José de Acosta and the miner Luís Capoche. Acosta in a letter to Toledo in 1577 pointed out that "since the Indians do not have silver in their lands, except only for those who have mines, they now have to earn money with hard labor and leave their homes in order to find waged employment."[2] Capoche argued that "the tribute should be set either collectively or according to the true number of tributary Indians, but not by a mixture of these two principles. . . . Since it was not so organized, the tribute is paid collectively, and the living pay the quotas of the dead."[3]

The result was predictable. A few years after Toledo's return to Spain, waves of epidemics swept over Indian society. The survivors were burdened with more and more tribute and labor obligations, and they fled their homes to join other groups and enterprises not under the caciques' control. By the end of the seventeenth century, the whole of indigenous society, both caciques and commoners, was in a state of upheaval. The central issue for the historian is how social relationships were reformulated and how new forms of social and symbolic legitimation were established. I can obviously not produce full answers to such major questions here, but I shall seek to outline the process of social change from the perspective of internal migrations. After mentioning the ways this process was discussed in fiscal and legal terms, I shall describe how the transforming pressures of the market and the relocation of the indigenous population led to reformulations of group identity.

The Seventeenth-Century Debate on Migration

The social and geographic reorganization of the south Andean world in the seventeenth century reveals the triumph of divisive market pressures and colonial policies. The abandonment by Indians of their settlement towns and the changes in fiscal categories would seem to indicate that pre-Columbian segmentary organization was dissolved and replaced by a social order based on market relations. The tributaries (*hatun runa*) of the large federations, such as Kanchi, Lupaqa, Sura, and Chicha, lost their ethnic affiliation at this level and were recategorized as "natives" (*naturales* or *originarios*), "strangers" (*forasteros* or *agregados*), or "dependants" (*yanaconas*) within different types of specifically colonial enterprise. These fiscal categories emerged as a result of massive internal migration within the vast quadrilateral formed by the urban districts of Cuzco, Arequipa, La Plata, and Tarija. The importance of the categories of strangers and dependants has led some researchers to interpret these sociojuridical changes as a "rupture" or process of "ethnic disaggregation" in Andean society. But beneath the apparent changes there is evidence for the maintenance of links between migrants and their original communities, leading one to suspect that widespread resettlement may also have represented a new social and political strategy by the Andean peasantry themselves.

In the course of a long debate over the effects of the Potosí *mita* originating in the seventeenth century itself, which had set the dominant estates of colonial society against one another as competitors for peasant labor, it was often suspected that the intermediary agents (the notorious caciques, corregidores, and clergy) misappropriated large numbers of Indians registered as "absent" or "fugitive" in the tribute and mita lists. At the heart of the matter was the issue of whether or not the caciques maintained control over the migrants.

Our assessment of Andean social and demographic processes throughout the seventeenth century depends on the answer to this question. It should be pointed out, of course, that there is no single answer—or, rather, that the answer depends on the informant. The caciques argued that they had lost control, and the Spanish colonial authorities argued that they had not. This is an important administrative and fiscal problem, whose economic and financial implications should not be underestimated. In some cases the caciques appear to be right, but in others they seem to be concealing the truth. A complex picture emerges in which the relationships of the migrants to their cacique and town of origin are subject to various degrees of pressure and change, but do not necessarily end in complete severance. I shall attempt to describe these relationships, although it must be admitted that the quality of the documents does not give a clear picture of the internal structure of the *ayllus*.

The Changing Relationship between Highlands and Valleys

The practice of migration is deeply rooted in Andean history. The cyclical displacements, or "pendular" migrations, between the different zones of the ecosystem, whose length varied according to the region and the type of activity (crop cultivation, harvest, pasture, or mining), assumed different forms and meanings according to whether the dominant political system was tribal, imperial, or colonial. Part of the legacy of Tawantinsuyu in the southern Andes was the presence of descendants of the Inca *mitmaq* colonists who had been settled in large numbers in the eastern valleys from Carabaya to Tarija through Cochabamba and Chuquisaca, in the mines of Chuquiabo and Porco, and in the religious centers around Copacabana. Although some, for example the frontier garrisons, returned to their places of origin, others began a process of "naturalization" in valleys such as Pocona or Larecaja, or in the Indian parishes of the first cities of La Plata and La Paz (see also Chapter 2 in this volume). The ethnic groups took advantage of the confusion that followed the Spanish Conquest to seize ownership of lands worked by their own colonists (*mitimaes*) for the Inca, and which were sometimes recognized by the Spanish Crown. For example, Toledo probably allowed the "sale" of lands in the Cochabamba valley to the Karanqa in return for their dispatch of mita workers to Potosí. The confusion was compounded during the colonial registration of the indigenous population. In the valleys, Spanish officials included in the local lists the mitimaes (called "settled folk," *gente de asiento*, by Polo) and sometimes even temporary migrants (*llactarunas*) from the highland centers.

During the general inspection (*visita*) and resettlement program (*reducción general*) carried out by Toledo between 1572 and 1575, the highland centers and the mitimaes adopted different tactics with regional variations to maintain their claims to lands. The mitimaes would be registered in highland or valley settlements as natives, or even simultaneously in both towns by virtue of their dual residence (*doble domicilio*). When the pressures of their respective obligations became critical, disputes flared up between the caciques of the puna and those of the valley, as well as between the mitimaes and their highland kin.

The different methods of paying the tribute fixed by Toledo also indicate variations in the relationship between the highland and valley members of an ethnic group and are a good index of the situation in each region. The highland towns of Collao in the basin of Lake Titicaca show a clear division between those of the eastern sector (*umasuyu*), whose tribute included contributions of maize provided presumably by their mitimaes in the nearby valleys of Larecaja and Carabaya, and those of the western sector (*urqusuyu*), which did not have to provide valley produce. The Lupaqa case is even clearer. The puna nuclei did not have to supply valley produce, and their mitimaes at lower altitudes on both flanks of the cordillera were registered and assessed separately for tribute in maize and coca, except for those of the valley of Inquisivi (Capinota), who continued to be registered in their highland centers, and whose tribute was used to pay the salary of the priest of Capinota. By contrast, all the towns of the southern ethnic groups—the Sura, Karanqa, Charka, Qaraqara, and Killaqa—which had their mitimaes in the valleys of Chayanta and Porco, or in those of Cochabamba and Chuquisaca, had their tribute converted into money, because of their proximity to Potosí, so that the nature of the relationship is not explicit.[4]

These regional variations in valley production and the effects of the mining market appear to be significant factors in determining internal migrations in the southern Andes. Polo reminds us that the puna towns could not live without the resources of the valleys and that the seasonal migrations mobilized large sections of the Andean population each year. The Indians of Macha (Qaraqara) "took their turn" in the valleys during the month of October, and the caciques of the Collao went down during the same period to round up their migrants. Polo also makes it clear that the rapid fortunes accumulated by the puna caciques in the sixteenth century were due to their control of llamas as transport animals and to the profits of interregional trade, which enabled a number of them to pay with ease the contributions of the tasa and mita (see Chapter 4 in this volume).[5] Therefore, another important indicator of local and regional differences between the puna towns is whether they maintained direct access to their lands in the valleys whether collective, individual, or through the cacique or whether they lost them.

The routes, the numbers, and the categories of migrants all depended on the type of relationship that linked the inhabitants of puna and valley, such as ethnic affiliation, mixed marriage alliances, preferential exchanges, or wage labor. Unfortunately, a large part of this vertical dynamic is hidden from us through lack of adequate documentation. Present-day surveys of rural areas have revealed the complexity of the process: each ayllu in competition with its neighbors must keep up the pressure in order either to conserve or expand or, alternatively, to abandon its access to a particular sector of valley land. These decisions and their motives were not registered in colonial reports, except in cases of litigation with Spanish *hacendados*, where the tribute obligations were the Indians' main argument. The resettlement by Toledo probably ended highland control over distant valley lands in many instances, and epidemics such as the serious outbreaks of the 1590s undoubtedly also had an impact. As a result, the ethnic mosaic in the valleys must have been considerably simplified.

On the other hand, it is difficult to distinguish complete disappearance from temporary nonoccupation. The vicissitudes of the Lupaqa mitimaes colonists in Larecaja demonstrate this. At the beginning of the seventeenth century, "they had shrivelled in size" (*se han consumido*); their representative was able to pay the tribute in money, but not the quota of maize. In 1617 the governor of Chucuito had the responsibility for tribute shifted to the local corregidor of Larecaja, but in 1650, Don Juan Cusipuru, the cacique governor of Sorata in Larecaja, claimed he was unable to pay the tribute in money and produce of the Lupaqa "because the said moiety of the Lupacas has for many years been dissipated and lacking Indians." By the middle of the seventeenth century, the mitimaes had sold their lands, but between 1656 and 1660 they requested their restoration from the appeal judge (*juez de desagravio*), and then re-sold them. In 1684 only twenty-five mitimaes and migrants (llactarunas) remained from the seventy registered in 1574. On the other hand, the valleys were overflowing with forasteros and yanaconas of the Lupaqa.[6] It is likely that there was a recurrent cycle of occupation and abandonment, the circumstances of which are unknown. Climatic crises (*esterilidad*), which periodically affect the Andean ecosystem, sometimes in conjunction with a sharp rise in mortality such as that of 1590–1594, must have further damaged the financial circumstances of those towns unable to fulfill their tribute or mita obligation. We know that there were serious difficulties in 1641 and 1661 for these reasons.

The Caciques' Dilemma

As a result of these cyclical crises, some ayllus had to sell or rent out some of their communal lands. For example in 1642, the leaders (*principales*) of the Arapa ayllu, which was composed of Qulla mitimaes from the province of Azángaro settled in Hilabaya (Larecaja), decided to sell the lands of Machacamarca "from the need to pay the tribute deficit owed by the absentee indians of their ayllu who went away in bad and sterile years." The abuses committed by those in charge of the land settlements (*jueces de composición de tierras*) provoked protests by the caciques of Omasuyos whose mitimaes were unable to provide their contribution of maize. They claimed that "the maize which should help feed us is sold off to pay the tribute and the mita of Potosí." The same caciques did not hesitate to "dispose of" 170 ranches (*estancias*) belonging to towns' ayllus, "which served the ayllus to help pay their tribute and mita," in order "to give them to Spaniards who enjoy their possession today."[7] Such acts would explain why Omasuyos showed the largest drop in the numbers of "natives" (*naturales*) and the largest population of forasteros among the provinces of the puna in the census of 1645.

The incomplete census of 1645 reveals an overall transfer of the puna population to the cities and the valleys. In the provinces that provided mita workers, the demographic decline is dramatic. The Lupaqa, Pakasa, or Karanqa natives lost between three-quarters and four-fifths of the tributary population they had at the time of Toledo, but regained only a small fraction of this number in forasteros and yanaconas. By contrast, Cochabamba lost two-thirds of its natives registered in 1575, but made up the numbers with the new categories. The ratio between naturales and those of the other categories is even more striking in other regions. In contrast to the situation among the Lupaqa, Pakasa, and Karanqa, the naturales were outnumbered by the forasteros and yanaconas—41 to 59 percent in the province of Omasuyos and 35.5 to 64.5 percent in Sica Sica. In the valleys, the increase in population is even more marked, particularly since there was some underregistration of yanaconas on the cereal- and wine-producing haciendas and in the coca plantations who did not automatically belong to the category of "yanaconas of His Majesty"—that is, they did not contribute to the royal funds. For example, the absence of yanaconas in the valleys of Mizque and Pocona as far as Santa Cruz and their small numbers in the valleys and yungas of Sica Sica is surprising.[8]

If we disregard the incompleteness of the 1645 census, the statistics it offers by region and fiscal category can help us examine the degree of control exercised by the "obligated towns" over their absentees to make them contribute to the mita and monetary tribute. The statistics serve as indices of the tactics adopted in different regions to meet these colonial obligations. The caciques of Paucarcolla who were regularly imprisoned for failure to pay their towns' tribute (e.g., in 1647 and 1648), alleged that "[their towns] were all depopulated and their Indians fled into remote parts and valleys where they know nothing of them," but they were nevertheless able to comply with the mita of Potosí. In the province of Sica Sica, the town of Ayo Ayo, which "had abandoned the mita of Potosí for 18 years," began to comply with its obligation again, sending its quota of tributaries as a result of the resettlement of absent Indians.[9]

In the same way, the priest of San Pedro de Curaguara in Pacajes "brought his Indians back from different places outside their town of origin [reducción]" and helped them "pay their tribute and deliver their mitas to Potosí." But in five towns of the same province, described as "finished and dispersed," the tribute amounting to 40,000 pesos annually could not be collected "except just enough to cover the priest's synod, and the rest is just an extra charge which His Majesty and the encomenderos see nothing of." However, the cacique of Machaca, Don Gabriel Fernandez Guarachi, had "in his own town all those who had fled to hide in different parts" in addition to 320 Indians from Caquingora, and resolved in 1652 to supply the tributes of the five towns and the mita of Potosí. It was his protest against the abuses of the mita, and the inability of the captains of Pacajes to comply with it, that encouraged the authorities to carry out a survey which revealed in passing the financial resource represented by the hiring out of service Indians for a year (*marahaques*) to the Spanish miners and ranchers (*estancieros*) in the province: "Each year without exception great numbers of Spaniards go to the mining camp [of Topoco where the mita workers gather before leaving for Potosí] to hire Indians as marahaques, who are Indians that serve for a year" for the sum of 150 pesos, and it was frequently difficult to recover those Indians who had been hired out.[10]

In many cases the most successful caciques were ambivalent figures: their wealth relieved the burden of the collective tribute, but it also derived from the exploitation of communal resources and peasant labor. Some caciques did not hesitate to sell off or rent out communal lands, transform valley enclaves into haciendas, convert mita workers into resident yanaconas, or sell the produce of the lands or flocks belonging to the community. This manipulation for personal gain also profited from the substantial income derived from interregional trade, but it must be seen in light of the caciques' overall responsibility for tribute payments.

We can be certain that throughout the seventeenth century the cacique-governors installed increasing numbers of forasteros on the land belonging to their towns, although not without complaint from the natives. Those of Pocoata denounced their governor for having "accepted more than twenty forasteros, hiding them from their caciques" on his own land, and "without demanding the royal tribute from them." In the survey of 1690, the denunciation of these abuses in the highland provinces was widespread, "for previous caciques disposed of all the land and pastures, renting them out to Spaniards and Indian forasteros."[11]

The caciques, caught amid the colonial pressures, appear in varied lights. Many were able to take advantage of the new economic opportunities through their role as recruiters of mita labor and tribute collectors. But their personal wealth did not automatically lead to the destruction of their ayllus (see Chapter 3 in this volume). Gabriel Fernandez Guarachi, as we have seen, spent his wealth in defense of collective territorial and social cohesion in his province of Pacajes, while others aided by the corregidores used their position to enrich themselves at the expense of their Indians. Yet others failed in their business efforts, exposing their ayllus to land sales and the infiltration of non-Indians. It may be significant that the successful caciques were located principally in Urqusuyu, the division most trodden by the great roads and commercial caravans that plied between the Pacific coast and the mining centers. The failures can be found mainly in the eastern division of Umasuyu bordering the emerging Amazonian frontier.

Ambiguities of Fiscal Recategorization

To assess the degree to which the structure of the ayllus of the southern Andes was undermined, we have outlined the fiscal pressures and demographic changes that both conditioned and reflected the response of the Indian towns to colonial demands. For the numerous eyewitnesses throughout the century that followed the Toledan resettlement, these towns often appeared empty, "with their Indians dispersed," and even in ruins. The internal dimensions of the resettlement program must now be considered. Given the increasing weight of the migrants, it is important to investigate their social circumstances. How can we distinguish between a mitima, a llactaruna, a forastero, or a yanacona, categories which in the seventeenth century were all relative to one another? In this period of intense social and economic mobility, fiscal categories were not fixed; they changed meaning from one region to another—even from one town to another—and over time. The sources are scarce, and it is very rare for the voices of the migrants themselves to be audible. One indirect solution is to clarify the rights and obligations of the different categories of migrants, in order to distinguish between their responsibilities toward their ayllu of origin and those toward the ayllu, town, or hacienda of residence.

Links between Puna and Valleys

One change concerns the link between mitimaes and their ethnic nuclei on the puna. While the mitimaes of the province of Chayanta continued to fulfill their mita obligations in Potosí, those of Collao installed in the eastern valleys of Carabaya and Larecaja were already exempt from the mita at the beginning of the seventeenth century. The Lupaqa mitimaes in Larecaja and Chicaloma paid their tribute after 1617 to the local corregidor and not to their highland lords, while the Pakasa mitimaes in the Quirua and Inquisivi valleys in the province of Sica Sica continued owing tribute in their nuclear towns on the puna. In 1654 the "lord and commoners" of the Pakasa town of Tiahuanaca denounced their encomendero's agent who

> on his own authority collects their tribute in kind and money . . . and also charges the absentees . . . and mitimaes in the [valley] towns of Cohoni and Collana in the province of Sica Sica, who provide most of the tribute and have their lands in that province. . . . He does not allow the caciques either to collect the tribute or deliver the mita to Potosí.

It is interesting to note that these mitimaes numbered twenty in 1616, and probably more forty years later in 1658, when the puna tributaries of Tiahuanaco had been reduced to nine. The population transfer is clear. For the puna towns of Calamarca, Ayo Ayo, and Sica Sica, the nearby Quirua and Inquisivi valleys seem to have played a similar role of "refuge," to which in certain circumstances a large part of the highland population could be transferred.[12]

From the puna point of view, how can we differentiate between the status of mitimaes and those of other migrants who were more or less permanent? Geographical proximity is sufficient to explain why most of the tribute obligations affecting the puna community were taken on by the whole of the migrant community established in the valleys. The question is whether the same obligations were imposed on the Lupaqa who had "fled" from Potosí, where they were residents or mitayos, to the valleys on the frontier with Tomina, or on the "Indian tributaries of the Lupaqa ayllu settled in Tarabuco" in the same province of Tomina. The distinction between mitimaes and forasteros here becomes very fluid. In fact, the highland caciques made periodic searches throughout the southern Andes for their absentee Indians in order to make them pay the tribute and mita. In spite of their claims that they were unable to find them, the vast majority of witnesses confirmed that "there is no cacique who does not know where all his Indians are located." The fact that many migrants continued to pay their contributions to their original lords (caciques de origen) demonstrates their recognition of their bond with the distant towns where their ancestors and relatives lived and were buried, and where the sacred wak'a of the community still guarded over them.[13]

However, other migrants sought to cut their links. For example, Pedro

Alaca Arussi, a Kana native, attempted to change his status, "substituting the surname of Guallpa, native of Oruro, and serving in the Convent of San Francisco at Potosí as a yanacona of His Majesty," but he was later reclaimed by the lord governor of Yanaoca, province of Canas and Canchis, for mita service. A witness testified that "his father is a native of the town of Yanaoca . . . who, many years ago, while traveling to serve the mita of Potosí, came to the valley of Alcantari where he rented some lands and did his service from there" and that "his three legitimate children" did the same, but Pedro was a "bastard son" and "paid his governor to escape two turns of service" before installing himself in Potosí. His cacique tried to reestablish his legal claim over him in 1643, but the *audiencia* ordered him to be released.[14] The maintenance of the mita link with their Kana town by the legitimate sons of the migrant, who was a tenant on a Spaniard's smallholding, contrasts with the illegitimate son's desire to sever his links.

To live "in distant places" as arrendire, yanacona, or marahaque on a Spanish hacienda, or as a yanacona of His Majesty, or as a forastero in another town, did not necessarily imply a complete break with the town of origin. Let us not forget that the groups of Collao, for example Tiahuanaco, "make use of their absentee Indians" in Potosí and its "valleys close by" and that in Potosí "the caciques . . . have innumerable Indians from their jurisdiction as yanaconas of the king, and they make use of them, hiring them out to the mineowners as well as to bakers, butchers, and merchants." Another indication of this relationship can be found in "the journeys made by the caciques to different provinces, such as Cochabamba, Lipes, Caranges, Chuquiago, Larecaja, Canas, and Canchis, to collect contributions from the absentee and naturalized Indians resident in those places' in order to pay the salaries of the priests in the Indian towns of Collao.[15]

Given that many subterfuges were adopted by migrants in order to escape from their original lords, the contribution to the payment of the tribute or the priest's salary undoubtedly meant the maintenance of all their rights in their ayllu of origin and of their full status as hatun runa. If this were so, the difference between mitimaes, yanaconas, and forasteros becomes irrelevant. In the valley of Timusi, province of Larecaja, in 1683 we find eighteen tributaries who were llactarunas of Jesús de Machaca and incorporated as mitimaes, and thirty forasteros and eighty yanaconas settled on land belonging to the cacique of Machaca. Of the total yanacona population of 180, eighteen adults were natives of Machaca, of whom seven out of eight men continued to pay their tribute to the highland town. The one who did not was twenty years old and married to an Uru woman from Machaca. More interesting, perhaps, were the five Chinchaysuyu married couples from the neighboring village of Ancoraymes in Omasuyos, where they continued to pay tribute, who appear to have become a new enclave of highland mitimaes in the valley of Timusi, where they were classi- fied as yanaconas. In the neighboring valleys of Hilabaya, out of the 135 yanaconas on the Spanish haciendas, twenty-six were natives of the seven Lupaqa townships on the shores of Lake Titicaca. Of these twenty-six, fifteen "pay their tribute in their town of origin" and nine do not. The maintenance or not of the tributary bonds by the different categories of outsiders listed in La Palata's census deserves careful scrutiny on both the local and regional level, since it appears to be an important indicator of the true circumstances of the migrants and allows substantial quantitative analysis.

A final variant that highlights the maintenance of control by original lords over the migrants is provided by the yanaconas who worked on ha- ciendas belonging to the caciques. The case of the yanaconas of Machaca on the estate (*chacra*) of their cacique in the valley of Timusi (next to the llac- taruna "enclave") has already been mentioned. In the neighboring valley of Combaya, sixty-two yanaconas (among whom "it seems that most of the Indians are from the town of Acora") were registered on the haciendas of Porobaya, which belonged to the caciques of Acora, one of the Lupaqa towns in the province of Chucuito. More information is needed to estab- lish the precise status of the workers on the puna and valley haciendas in the possession of caciques, although we can assume it was a means of establishing ethnic enclaves with a better chance of surviving the greed of neighboring Spaniards or the local chiefs.[16]

Local Integration of Migrants

So much for the "vertical" links connecting migrants with their towns of origin. However, they also integrated into the areas where they lived, forming local, "horizontal" links with their neighbors. These processes of integration often involved contribution to the local tribute and mita obligations in return for access to land.

Regional circumstances vary, but some migrants—probably those who had cut their links with their towns of origin—paid the tribute in the towns where they were resident: 5 pesos in current coinage for the forasteros and 2 pesos in assayed coinage for the yanaconas of the king, and both categories contributed 1 peso in assayed coinage toward the salary of the local priest. In the Mizque and Pocona valleys, the inspections uncovered an abundance of outsiders in various circumstances. In 1631, for example, in the valley of Totora one Cristóbal Hernández was registered, who was 22 years old and a native of the Oroncota valley (Yamparaes), and who had been taken to La Plata, then to Mizque ("kidnapped by a Portuguese") and then to the land of Parichari as a yanacona. In Omereque he married the niece of the lord of Totora and "wishes to be registered in this town as a forastero," which he was permitted to do provided that he "pay the tribute like the other Indians of the town and bear his share of the obligations." Juan Aymoro, native of Santiago de Moscari in Charcas, was the shepherd (ovejero) of the encomendero of Totora "who has given him clothing every year and has paid the tribute he owes as forastero to the kurakas of this town." Lázaro Paychuri, whose father was an Indian from Santa Cruz and presumably a Chiriguano, and his mother, a woman from Colpavilque in Yamparaes, "came to Mizque with a barefoot monk. . . . He is unmarried and wishes to be registered in Totora and not continue his wanderings." Whatever the origin of an individual may have been, registration as forasteros implied tribute and labor obligations. Ten years later, the forasteros of Pocona, "married to Indian women of this town . . . and obliged to pay ten pesos," fled "taking with them their wives and children . . . and the main cause of their disappearance is the high tribute they pay." If the price of admittance became excessive, the migrants moved on.[17]

On the altiplano in the province of Omasuyos, the Indians of the town of Guaqui worked lands bordering those of neighboring Laja, thus provoking a long-standing dispute: "Many Indians of Guaqui are newcomers and fugitives [cimarrones] and they help with services in the town and tambo of Laja, as well as taking turns to serve the priests and corregidores as forasteros, in return for which the Indians of Laja graciously allowed them to stay on their lands."[18] This "gracious" surrender of land by Laja was simply an exchange for personal services, and it can be interpreted as an example of the mutual exchange of tributaries between two towns. In Copacabana, the cacique-governor was accused of charging the forasteros an excessive tribute of 30 pesos annually. His defense was that "four of them, of their own accord, asked him for land to sow in, offering him 30 pesos, and Don Lope conscientiously gave them some of his own land, so that they should help him pay the tribute." We do not know to what extent this was the cacique's private land or whether it had been appropriated from communal land, but here the exchange was land for tribute-money.[19]

Much less is known about the contribution made by the forasteros to the mita of Potosí. In 1667 the caciques of Laja offered evidence that their town "is dispersed and without Indians," and the priest testified that "the aforementioned governors, in order to deliver the royal mita, make use of Indians called 'sons-in-law' [*yernos*] and 'nephews' [*sobrinos*], as well as the absentees in the city of Potosí and other places nearby." That is, they employed both the services of the forasteros in their towns who were classified as subordinate kin and their own "absent" residents in Potosí and the surrounding valleys. The apparent strength of these bonds between migrants and their towns of origin runs counter to one's expectation that they would be broken, given the legal status of absentees, whether forasteros or yanaconas. However, the complaints made by Pedro Mamani, a "poor Indian and son of a forastero," against the chief of his ayllu of residence in Puna, province of Porco, provides us with an insight into what a forastero might often expect: he had to pay tribute and contribute to the mita "before coming of age," first for a full year as a *guatacamayo* (constable), and then for half a year, and he requested that he "not be obliged to fulfill a year's mita, like the natives of this town, but only six months, which is what he is able to do as a forastero, and he requests land." Eleven years later he repeated his request:

> I am a self-declared Indian and have not been given lands or a garden in which to sow . . . and yet I have served four years' mita in Potosí, and today according to my memory I am some 40 years old. . . . My father was an Indian incorporated [*agregado*] into this ayllu, and we do not have a plot of land or a household garden in this town.

The audiencia judged that "he should be allowed to rest, and also be given lands to sow in, for he serves in the town and pays the tribute." We do not know whether he paid the tribute partially or in full, nor the extent of his integration within the town, although in 1684 he mentions a "male child." But his request to contribute one half of the mita perhaps indicates that he had rights to half the amount of land allotted to a "native."[20]

This precarious access to land can further be illustrated by the unstable position of the forasteros in the Hilabaya valley with regard to the "few lands available here, since the common lands have been sold . . . and there are barely enough remaining for the Indians, so that to sustain the tributaries they are allotted only half of the two topos assigned to each tributary by the regulations." The forasteros were obliged to seek out more suitable settlements as a result of the pressures on land. In the absence of more evidence, it is not possible to confirm the existence for the seventeenth century of the phenomenon analyzed by Tristan Platt for northern Potosí in the nineteenth century, where the tribute categories were based more on the size of each plot of land than on the genealogy of its occupant. For the present, we can only agree with him about the importance of examining the changes in fiscal category according to the relation between population and land in each locality.[21]

These different ways in which forasteros were integrated into the towns of the southern Andes raise the question of the nature of the ayllu. It was simultaneously a kinship group, a territorial group, and a ceremonial group, and it was extensively restructured by demographic crises and the influx of different categories of migrants. Its structure reflects the close link between collective identity and the cacique, for all the ambiguity of his role.

The Market and Changing Identity

The population movements of the seventeenth century bring into focus the varying degrees of flexibility of the ayllus in their ability, or inability, to adapt to the circumstances created by migration. Collective identity and ethnic classification are closely linked to the dynamic of the ayllu segmentary system which builds up to the ethnic groups through a hierarchy of lesser units—household, hamlet, and moieties. In the southern Andes, the identification with the great regional ayllus, or "nations," and the local ayllu, *marka*, or towns, in spite of the destruction of their political autonomy, was maintained throughout most of the colonial period and manifest in the great insurrection of 1777–1782. It continues to the present day in certain areas such as northern Potosí (see Chapter 10 in this volume).

The variation in ethnic identification is connected to internal tensions within the ayllu, which are themselves determined by the contradictory effects of two types of external pressures. On the one hand, the nature of demands from the colonial state tended to reduce all Indians of whatever ethnic origin to a homogeneous category of tribute payers, but this homogenizing tendency was resisted by caciques and local mestizos who sought to retain the distinctiveness of their own ethnic groups (as can be seen in the refunctionalization of Andean dual organization by the colonial government and the use of pre-Spanish regional divisions in the administration of the Potosí mita). On the other hand, the expansion of markets, with Potosí at the center of the process, had the effect of weakening the bonds of peasants with their community, isolating them as individuals when they entered into market relations as producers, consumers, or wage-laborers.

The Urban World

Potosí was from very early on the most extreme example of the social and ethnic mixing that threatened group identity. B. Ramírez declared in 1580 that "for every ten Indians that come to Potosí, only six return home," and A. de Ayanz, the author of an extensive report on the southern Andes in the last decade of the sixteenth century, deplored the consequences of the "mixture of Indians from so many nations."[22] These consequences were denounced again and again throughout the seventeenth century: "They stay in Potosí where they hire out their services or become street-sellers of vegetables"; "there are over 50,000 Indians in Potosí who because they receive double wages, voluntarily hire themselves out to Spaniards and caciques, thus paying their tribute and maintenance."[23] However, this does not mean that they had abandoned links with their homes. The survey of 1690 makes clear that both the population permanently residing in Potosí and the floating population continued to contribute to the tribute and above all to the mita labor in the mines owed by their towns of origin.

The most serious erosion of ethnic affiliation was by registration as a yanacona of the king. This practice was on the increase during the middle years of the seventeenth century, with a minimum of 10,000 registrations in 1645, and it was denounced by the captains of the mita gathered in Potosí:

The absentee Indians . . . finally lose their ethnic affiliation [*llegan a perder su pueblo*], changing their habit and style of dress, and adopting that of the yanacona: cloak, silk stocking, and shirt. To disguise this deceit they set themselves to learn a trade as tailors, cobblers, silversmiths, silkweavers, and others. They and their sons register themselves as yanaconas, and by paying a mere 8 pesos each year plus 5 pesos in different jurisdictions, they become exempt from the mita service.

The caciques proposed, among other solutions, that "those who are resident in this city should be obliged to take off the clothing of yanaconas and put on their old clothing, without being permitted to go without shoes." We do not know whether this authoritarian stance on the dress used for social differentiation was sufficient to halt the process of social transformation.[24]

It probably was not, if we are to believe Fernandez Guarachi's denunciation of the various stratagems employed in the Indian towns:

The Indian widows and unmarried women leave their towns and provinces with their children and resort to populous places, towns and cities, where they become fraternity members and ritual sponsors [*mayordomos*] . . . and their male children are given to the church and put to a trade, as silkdrapers, tailors, and cobblers and thus they are converted into free yanaconas.

He goes on at length to explain:

Equally devious are the married Indian women who, while living with their husbands, register their legitimate children in the baptism ceremony as though they were children of unknown fathers, hoping in this way that fifteen or sixteen years later, they may be exempted from the mita when they are of an age and strength for it. And their husbands agree to it, and through these deceits they have their children registered as yanaconas, saying they are sons of muleteers, or llama-drovers [*arrieros*] from Chachapoyas, Cuzco, or elsewhere not subject for the mita service, hoping thus to free them in advance from the mita. . . . And also they say that when they married they already had three or four illegitimate children by different fathers, or that they married when already far advanced in pregnancy, and that their children are not legitimate, but rather by yanaconas and drovers and strangers, well-worn terms, and to avoid a drawn-out suit their deceit wins the day to general applause.

Other deceits noticed by the captain of the yanaconas are that when they say they never knew their fathers or their place of origin, they are written down without further question as being of His Majesty's Crown, and this occurs all over the kingdom. . . . Almost all the yanaconas of this kingdom were mita Indians.[25]

Here we see the range of tactics used to withdraw part of the male population from future tributary lists and thus break their bonds with their ayllu of origin. The deputy (procurador) of La Plata confirmed this breakdown: "On the whole, if an Indian brings four or six children from his town, fewer than half return, and in some cases they all disappear or are "sold" to Spaniards, and so they lose touch with their origins and never return." As a consequence of the disappearance of the male population, the ratio of the sexes within the ayllu was completely changed. In Tiquipaya (Cochabamba) "there were more than 230 widows and more than 100 old spinsters, and only eleven male Indians and four church cantors." In the towns of the mita, there was evidence of "women obliged to occupy the posts of mayors [alcaldesas] and councillors [regidoras] and to take turns in serving the tambo."[26] Various complaints also demonstrate that the caciques enforced the tribute and even mita obligations on these women. These civil and economic responsibilities exercised by women to enable the community to reproduce can be seen as a return to pre-Hispanic practices where women performed similar duties. However women were also the agents of change. They played a vital role in the conversion of their sons to the status of yanaconas and, also importantly, accepted migrants as husbands, thus enabling them to integrate into the ayllu through marriage. The study of migration would be greatly enhanced by integrated research on parish registers together with La Palata's census, which included the geographical origins—both town and ayllu—of marriage partners.

Growth of Mestizaje

The evasion of collective fiscal obligations through *mestizaje* is also fundamental. For example in 1603 the Carrillo brothers, tailors born in La Plata
whose mother was mestizo and whose father was an "Indian chief of Tacobamba," requested exemption from the mita imposed by the caciques of
Tacobamba. The judge (*oidor*) declared that "they are Indians . . . for that
is how they consider themselves, and at present they wear their hair and
clothing like Indians." He also added that it was not possible to exempt
all Indians with mestizo mothers, since this would result in depopulation
of the Indian towns. Nevertheless, the court of the audiencia disagreed
with him: "They should not be registered like the other tributary Indians, nor should they be obliged to perform personal services, and their
duties are only to pay the tribute." In 1612, 1615, and 1638 the Carrillo
brothers were obliged to seek legal protection from the caciques.[27] It is
important to note, however, that their bonds were not completely sev-
ered, since their incorporation in the town was acknowledged through the
payment of tribute.

The nonregistration of mestizos in the fiscal registers and in the census
makes it difficult to clarify their significance, but their numbers increased
considerably, as B. de Cárdenas noted: "They continue multiplying so
much that I know of a mestizo in the valley of Larecaja who has sixty mestizo children by different Indian women, and the sons imitate their father's
example by multiplying their number yet further," and he counted "more
than a thousand mestizos in this valley of Cochabamba." For Ramírez del
Aguilar, the indigenous population "will end up disappearing" as a result of epidemics, alcoholism, and the fact that "there are many mestizos,
which means the Indian race diminishes, and the Spanish one increases as
it attracts and consumes the Indians."[28]

Forms of Local Integration

The overall result of the migratory process is well known. The forasteros who constituted one-third of the tributary population in the southern
Andes in 1645 had grown to one-half forty years later. Social differen-

tiation within the ayllus had grown. Alongside the wealthy Indians (*colquehaque*) who paid tribute and commuted mita services at a very high price, there were many Indians with different status, property, and degrees of integration. There were various tactics possible for the legitimation of settlement and long-distance alliances. It seems very likely that it was particularly the system of festive duties (*cargos*) organized in the ayllus according to the Catholic ritual that made possible the rapid integration of all its members, both native and migrant, with their mixed origins and categories.

We are almost entirely ignorant of the history of the religious fraternities (*cofradías*) in the southern Andes. There is proof of their existence in rural towns during the first half of the seventeenth century, both in the puna and in the valleys where the cofradías held their own land (although not without some resentment on the part of the local ayllus). In 1632 the Franciscan B. de Cárdenas, inspector of the Charcas parishes, wrote from Cochabamba:

> In this kingdom there are innumerable religious fraternities of Indians and Spaniards in their separate towns. There is not a hamlet without some four or five Indian cofradías, and in the larger towns some ten, twelve, or twenty; and each has its banner that it brings out on feast days, and an Indian is chosen each year to see to this as ritual sponsor [*alferez*].

The Andean cargo system, a scale of civil and religious posts, has been interpreted as an institution of "ritual impoverishment" within a "prestige economy" whose function was to balance and redistribute private savings and wealth accumulated through profits in the market economy, which threatened the internal homogeneity of the ayllu. The wealthiest members of the community were obliged, through competition for prestigious office, to pay for extravagant celebrations of the feast day for the fraternity's patron saint. Cárdenas confirms this: "And as there are so many fraternities, great numbers of Indians are ruined each year—let us suppose 2,000 each year in this archbishopric of Charcas; and so they continue to ruin and impoverish themselves, because any who have a little fortune will spend it all and more."[29] Without statistical information on household income, it is difficult to establish whether the cargo system equalized or exacerbated internal divisions within the ayllu. But equally important is the fact that the expansion of cofradías allowed the migrants to establish land rights and their integration within the ayllu or town through participation in the hierarchy of the cargo system.

Another tactic adopted by the migrants to integrate themselves into the communities where they were resident was the development of real or ritual kinship ties. Some examples have already been mentioned. The use of the terms *yerno* (son-in-law) and *sobrino* (nephew), which are found in many seventeenth-century surveys of the highlands, suggest a direct relationship as a relative or a collateral in a subordinate position, though until we know the exact significance of these statuses, we cannot draw any definite conclusion. There is evidence that in the Mizque valleys forasteros married local women, although this did not prevent their running away with them when their contributions became too onerous, according to the caciques. There is also some evidence in the Timusi valley of *compadrazgo* between migrants, still linked to their groups of origin, and neighbors in their new place of residence. By linking two adults, this new form of contractual, ritual kinship channeled material and symbolic exchanges between households. It proved very successful at compensating for the loss of networks of mutual aid that had operated within the traditional endogamous ayllu.

The pattern of Indian settlement towns was also substantially modified. The "Relación" of Canon Pedro Ramírez del Aguilar, concerning the new parishes of the archbishopric of Charcas, comments:

> Although there are not more than 130 parishes, each one has many groups of parishioners numbering 50 or 100, living away from the town itself with their own chapels and accompanying *cofradías* in what are called annexes. If we include all these, there must be more than 600 settlements in the puna and valleys in which many Indians reside, both natives and migrants from other places.[30]

In these annexes, which developed gradually into towns, new civic and religious institutions were promoted, town cabildos as well as the religious offices held in rotation by all members of the new communities to celebrate the festivals. At the same time, new elites were promoted at the expense of the caciques. From this perspective, the cabildos, the cofradías, and the compadrazgo—the three significant Cs of social change—became the key institutions around which a more contractual type of sociability between coresidents began to crystallize. The previous hierarchical basis of relationships was derived from vertical submission to the three Cs of colonial government: the clergy, the cacique, and the corregidor. This was partially replaced by a horizontal relationship of equal and rotating access to a cycle of civic and religious responsibilities which legitimated peoples' incorporation in their new place of residence. A task for future research will be to assess the extent of this capacity for innovation by the Indian population in all aspects of daily life.

Migration and the Reordering of Society

The migrants are key to our understanding of the social readjustments of the seventeenth century. The distortions in the fiscal documentation that was manipulated by the very government agents entrusted with its preparation cannot hide the prodigious mobility of the peasantry, nor the flexibility in their status, nor the opportunities the migrants had to enter into contracts with both caciques and Spaniards. Whether they were hidden, fugitives, or runaways; whether they paid their tribute in their towns of origin or where they were resident, or did not pay at all; whether they became integrated or not into their new settlement—the migrants cannot simply be understood in terms of a progressive dissolution of ethnic bonds, a breakdown of rural society in the terms implied by debate in the seventeenth century and by much recent historical analysis, but more as a symptom and a process of the profound reordering of social life.

Attempts by both men and women to abandon their status as "natives" through transfer to yanacona or mestizo (although neither process automatically implied the ending of previous fiscal responsibilities) can be explained by the desires for individual advancement and to escape from the control of the caciques. This latter point is debatable; as we have seen, by the middle of the seventeenth century the caciques and captains of the mita declared that they had lost control, but official opinion of the corregidores and judges, and the evidence supplied in the survey of 1690, appears to contradict them. The maintenance or breakdown of control is linked to the authority of the cacique and his treatment of his subjects. The evolution of this relationship in the sixteenth century has been interpreted by some as a development "from reciprocity to despotism," but the southern

Andes presents a more complex picture. While abuses, above all economic abuses, became more frequent, in other cases the caciques fought on behalf of the ayllu. An overall appraisal must take into account the caciques' public positions, in which two bases of legitimacy were counterposed: that inherited from Andean traditions and that which derived from their success in dealing with colonial demands. In practice, the caciques incorporated both the old and the new modes of hierarchical relationships to form new configurations (see Chapter 3 in this volume).

In other words, our travels in the punas and valleys of Charcas have indicated that the effects of the market and the tributary and mining obligations did not result automatically either in the dissolution of ethnic solidarity or in the reproduction of particular social groups. It is still difficult to offer an overall interpretation of the phenomenon of migration as a response to the colonial system. Information on local economies is lacking—for example on access to land, levels of forced labor obligations, and the degree of mercantilization. So too is information on aspects of collective identity, such as the ancestor cult, oral tradition, and weaving styles. However, while identity drew on such traditional forms, it also incorporated European novelties, such as hats which, as many commentators of the time noted, rapidly replaced or complemented the traditional Andean woolen bonnet. The Indians' use of money and their participation in markets is also of crucial importance. It is noteworthy that in the Andes today, some of the ayllus that have been able to maintain collective resources and group identity are to be found in the Departments of Potosí and Oruro, precisely in the region which in the seventeenth century was one of the centers of the world economy (see Chapters 9 and 10 in this volume). Undoubtedly the skill with which caciques and Indians used Potosí as an economic center contributed to the strength of the region's ayllus today.

There is still much to understand about the internal logic of the migratory movements across the southern Andes. The model I propose is based neither on an idea of simple reproduction of the Indian communities nor of brutal rupture: I see migration as a means to reconstitute social relationships on a new basis, drawing both on Andean traditions and on European inputs. Of the former, the long-established traditions of population movement and the assignation of land rights to migrants, and the pivotal role of the Indian lords, were all important. Of the latter, apart from the market itself, perhaps the most outstanding was the establishment of cabildos, cofradías, and compadrazgo, all of them institutions that both reflected and promoted a profound reordering of social relationships.

Conclusion

In this picture of enormous complexity and local and regional variation, I have limited myself to outlining particular tendencies that can be summarized as a contrast between two systems of social articulation. On the one hand, there is the integrated system of the ancient despotic state articulated around the supreme mediation embodied or personified in a "divine ruler," such as the *kuraka* or *mallku*. The crowning expression of this was the Inca himself, the communicating link who brought together the visible and invisible worlds, a sacred being endowed with generative powers (*camac*), who was at the summit of a hierarchical order that radiated the power of mediation throughout the social body through ties of vertical subordination. On the other hand there is the hybrid system of early modern Europe, which combined hierarchical principles derived from feudalism and territorial monarchies with mercantile humanistic values founded on initiative and personal qualities, whose success indicated divine or social approval.

The encounter between these two systems through the current of internal migrations in Charcas and the collective strategies that underlay them resulted in the gradual transition from a society founded on filiation, ascription, kinship, and estate to one based on residence, achievement, territoriality, and class. The motor of this transformation was clearly the market—not the market of abstract mercantilist theories, but rural and urban markets as real places where producers, consumers, and intermediaries encountered each other, fettered though they were by the interventions and abuses of colonial rule.

Recognition of this process of rupture and recomposition obliges us to discard ideological interpretations that see the Indians' flight and absenteeism as straightforward acts of "resistance" behind which a supposedly "Andean" culture continued to exist. It also obliges us to go beyond the vision of Andean ethnohistory that focuses on the dissolution of ethnic identities and their replacement by a generic "Indian" identity, a symbol of dependence and colonial exploitation.

In contrast to these reductionist approaches, I have sought to emphasize the importance of mobility and the undermining of traditional hierarchy. The caciques retained more knowledge, and also control, over the whereabouts of their migrant subjects than has often been assumed; at the same time, however, social and religious relationships were gradually reordered in a creative and multifaceted restructuring of southern Andean society. This allowed the formation of new identities linked to coresidence in both the rural and urban setting and the forging of a new, more universalist basis for social ties through an equal and rotating access to civic and religious offices, particularly in the annexes growing up around the settlement towns. The reproduction of society through periodic communication with the sacred autochthonous powers and those of the state was thus assured under changed conditions.[31]

In reality, beyond those tens of thousands of migratory journeys crisscrossing the vast expanse of the central southern Andes between coast and forest, between the Titicaca basin and the gorge of Humahuaca, what the Aymara-, Puquina-, and Quechua-speaking households were experiencing was a true social and cultural revolution. Like any process of real change, it occurred silently, unnoticed either by the actors themselves or by the observers of the colonial world, for all the concern over the phenomenon of migration itself. The classic concepts of acculturation and counteracculturation are not adequate to express the enormity of this social change between the time of Toledo and the great epidemic of 1719–1720. For lack of more precise terminology, we can call the new, profoundly mestizo social order "colonial Andean" (Chapter 3 in this volume). It was a revolution paid for with a high price of dislocation, violence, and disorder and with the accompanying symptoms of conflict between the generations and between women and men. But it resulted in the creation of a new society, fundamentally different from both the old hierarchical order and Spanish models.

Notes

An earlier version of part of this chapter was published as Occasional Paper no. 15 of the Institute of Latin American Studies, University of London, translated by

Paul Garner and revised by Tristan Platt. We acknowledge the institute's kind permission for republishing it, in this revised and expanded version translated by Olivia Harris. All translations from the original Spanish sources in this chapter are by Olivia Harris. All abbreviations for the archival material cited here are listed on the first page of the bibliography. [note that some of the source citations are incomplete, owing to the untimely death of the author–EDS]

1. Juan Polo de Ondegardo, "Relación de los fundamentos acerca del notable daño que resulta de no guardar a los indios sus fueros" [1571], *Colección de libros y documentos referentes a la historia del Perú*, ser. 1, vol. 3 (Lima, 1916).

2. Acosta to Toledo, 1577, AGI, Lima 376.

3. Luís Capoche, *Relación general de la Villa Imperial de Potosí* [1585] (Madrid, 1959).

4. Noble David Cook, ed., *Tasa de la visita general de Francisco de Toledo* (Lima, 1975).

5. Ondegardo, "Relación de los fundamentos," 157–168.

6. See Thierry Saignes, *Los Andes orientales: Historia de un olvido* (Cochabamba, 1985), ch. 5, and Saignes, "Notes on the Regional Contribution to the Mita in Potosí in the Early Seventeenth Century," *Bulletin of Latin American Research* 4.1 (1985): 65–76. See also Clara López Beltrán, *Estructura económica de una sociedad colonial: Charcas en el siglo XVII* (La Paz, 1988), 276–278.

7. Quotes in this paragraph from Saignes, "Las etnías de Charcas frente al sistema colonial (siglo XVII): Ausentismo y fugas en el debate sobre la mano de obra indígena (1595–1665)," *Jahrbuch für Geschichte von Staat, Wirtschaft und Gesellschaft Lateinamerikas* (Cologne) 21 (1984): 21–75, and Saignes, "The Ethnic Groups of the Valleys of Larecaja: From Descent to Residence," in John V. Murra, Nathan Wachtel, and Jacques Revel, eds., *Anthropological History of Andean Polities* (Cambridge, 1986), 311–341.

8. See Thierry Saignes, "Politique du recensement dans les Andes coloniales: Décroissance tributaire ou mobilité indigène?' *Histoire, Economie, Société* (Paris) 4 (1987): 435–468.

9. ANB, EC, 1649-20. Evidence of the priest (*cura*) of Ayo Ayo in 1658, Lic. V del Espinar S., in AGI, Charcas 97.

10. See Saignes, "Etnías de Charcas."

11. Nicolás Sánchez Albornoz, *Indios y tributos en el Alto Perú* (Lima, 1978).

12. ANB, EC 1674-32. According to a list of inhabitants of Collana and Cohoni, Biblioteca Central (Universidad Mayor de San Andrés, La Paz), Ms 39. Archive of the University of Texas, MB, Manuscripts of Bolivia, vol. 4. Published in *Documento etnohistórico: Tiwanaku 1657* (La Paz, 1974). See, for example, the petition of the Indians of Ayo Ayo for their absent relatives in the Sapahaqui valley

to be included in the service of the *tambo,* according to the evidence of 1643 in AHLP, legajo 920, f. 226.

13. See Saignes, *Los Andes orientales,* ch. 4; Saignes "Parcours forains: L'enjeu des migrations internes dans les andes coloniales," *Cahiers des Amériques Latines* (Paris) 6 (1987): 33–58.

14. ANB, Minas t. 125, no. XI.

15. According to the "Relación y advertimiento . . ." of the priest D. F. de Alcayaga, La Plata, 1612, Archivo del Duque del Infantado, t. 38, doc. 66. See the survey of Mollinedo, Bishop of Cuzco, in H. Villanueva, ed., *Documentos* (Cuzco, 1982).

16. On Timusi, Larecaja, and Lupaqa, see Saignes, *Andes orientales,* chs. 3, 4, 6.

17. ANB, Mizque 1631–8 and 1640–3.

18. Testimony from the *interrogatorio* of the corregidor, Huarina, December 5, 1630, ANB, EC 1630–2, f. 186v; 1662, ANB, EC 1674–28, f. 38.

19. 1667, ANB, EC 1689–31.

20. Puna, January 31, 1669, and August 14, 1680. ANB, Minas, t. 126, no. 1121, 1684.

21. Tristan Platt, *Estado boliviano y ayllu andino: Tierra y tributo en el norte de Potosí* (Lima, 1982).

22. V. M. Maurtua, ed., *Descripción general del Perú: Juicio de límites entre Perú y Bolivia* (Barcelona, 1906), Tomo 1, and R. Vargas Ugarte, *Pareceres jurídicos en asuntos de Indios (1601–1718)* (Lima, 1951), 39.

23. D. F. de Alcayaga, 1612. "Medios propuestos por D. Antonio de Barrasa y Cárdenas al Virrey para la reducción del los indios," Sica Sica, 2, V. 1632, Biblioteca Nacional (Madrid), Ms. 19282, f. 236.

24. ANB, EC 1661–16, f. 59. There were various proposals in favor of the use of ethnic costume: for example the proposal of S. Vigil de Quiñones "that in Potosí each Indian should be obliged to dress with the costume of his province" around 1625. Biblioteca Universitaria (Seville), V. 330/122, doc. 43.

25. *Memorial,* Potosí, September 1661; AGI, EC 868A, ff. 15, 16, 20.

26. "Relación de La Plata," 1609; *Archivo del Duque del Infantado,* vol. 32, doc. 100 (photocopy in ANB), 1617 in Francisco de Viedma, *Descripción geográfico de Santa Cruz de la Sierra* [1788] (Cochabamba, 1969), 280. Report of Lic. Luna Ybarra, 1623–1626, in AGI, Charcas 54.

27. ANB, November 2, 1603. ANB, Minas t. 125, no. 1100.

28. "Memorial y relación de las cosas tocantes al reino del Perú" [Cochabamba, 1632], BNE MS 3198. Ramírez del Aguilar, *Noticias políticas de Indias* [1639], ed. J. Urioste, (Sucre, n.d.), 123.

29. "Memorial y relación de las cosas."

30. del Aguilar, *Noticias políticas de Indias,* 111–112.

31. On the scope and structure of this "double articulation" to autochthony and the state, see Thomas Abercrombie, "The Politics of Sacrifice: An Aymara Cosmology in Action," Ph.D. dissertation (University of Chicago, 1986).

7

Indians in Late Colonial Markets:

Sources and Numbers

ENRIQUE TANDETER, VILMA MILLETICH,

MARÍA MATILDE OLLIER, AND BEATRÍZ RUIBAL

The study of the modes of Indian and mestizo participation in supplying goods for colonial markets faces enormous documentary problems, yet this issue is fundamental to reconciling dualist perspectives on the relationship between Andean communities and markets. Most recent studies have limited their investigation to particularly recognizable cases of indigenous participation, such as merchant *curacas*, who left records similar to those of the great Spanish and creole merchants (wills, notary transactions, correspondence, litigation, etc.).[1] Such is not the case for the rank and file of Indians and mestizos who engaged in commerce but who left few traces of evidence. This skewed documentation about Andean market participation is particularly unfortunate in the context of Andean colonial history. As Olivia Harris notes in Chapter 12, the conclusion to this volume, "while the 'Andean' [was] inextricably linked with the commercial, participation in markets on whatever scale [tended] to be the affair of individual households." The curacas, as part of their changing role in the organization and control of communal reproduction (which Tristan Platt postulated as the "cacical mercantile model"), were able to control the commercialization of some portions of the collective surplus.[2] But this participation did not prevent tributaries from gaining individual access to markets in order to obtain the money they needed to meet the demands of the state and colonial church.

An example will help demonstrate the problem. Exceptionally rich documentation permits us to determine that, at the end of the eighteenth century, among the Awkimarcas of Chayanta in northern Potosí, the curacas oversaw the cultivation of barley, potatoes, maize, and wheat on communal lands, some of which was destined for consumption, exchange, or sale. It has been estimated that 90 percent of commercial production and 36 percent of noncommercial production were used to satisfy colonial demands. With this, Indian communities guaranteed the tribute payments of the "runaways, sick, and deceased" kin members, compensated the chief tax collectors, and financed "communal lawsuits" and the official documents needed for those suits, provisioned the *mitayos* during their journeys to Potosí, and made great quantities of *chicha,* which was consumed during communal rituals of tribute collection and *mita* recruitment.[3] These explicit communal expenditures, based on surplus production on *ayllu* lands, demonstrates clearly that the other expenses that burdened individual Indian households (such as tributes, ecclesiastical tithes, the cost of fiestas, commutation of the mita, and forced distribution of goods to Indian communities) created specific monetary needs that each household had to satisfy. Thus, to meet their own short-term and long-term needs of social reproduction, individual tributaries had to find the "least disadvantageous" means of engaging in market exchange relations (see Chapters 1 and 3 in this volume).

Colonial sources make frequent qualitative reference to the various products that Indians, from diverse regions of the Andes, marketed in colonial cities. But the lack of quantitative documentation inhibits evaluation of the global, or aggregate, importance of Andean commercial activity. On one hand, we seek to understand the role of Andean market involvement in terms of communal strategies of reproduction; on the other, we lack a sense of the relative importance of Andean commerce in provisioning the urban markets.

To a certain point, the explanation for the inadequacy of colonial sources on Indian trade should be sought in the relationships among these Indian or mestizo actions in the market, the activities of Spanish or creole merchants, and the politics of the Crown. Although the dominant colonial discourse affirmed Indian rusticity, judging their "poor integration" into the market by standards of Western civilization, the Indians did in fact compete in the market—at times, with a great deal of success. In exceptional cases we can glimpse Indian commerce in colonial sources, which make mention of their mercantile competence and its significance to Spanish and creole merchants. An early example comes from Potosí in the

1560s, when an anonymous commentator proposed to permanently prohibit Indian access to the urban markets.[4] A later case, from the beginning of the nineteenth century, captures the significance of Andean commerce and trade when the most important Spanish merchants of Potosí were asked to prepare a private report for "the Five Guilds of Madrid" (a powerful peninsular corporation that sought to expand its commerce in South America), in order to identify the areas and products most appropriate for commercial expansion in the region. One of these reports commented on the coca trade:

> Many interested parties deal in the coca business of La Paz, and the most involved are the Indians. These [people] never make any effort to keep accounts, either of their personal expenses or of the freight charges on the goods they transport, normally on their own animals; whereas, according to good business practice, all the costs arising from the transaction should be added to the principal.

Thus, the report concluded: *The Spaniard never prospers in a trade in which the Indian takes part.*"[5]

From the initial moments after the Conquest, the Spaniards used both legal and extralegal mechanisms to restrict and impose conditions on Indian participation in the market. The early foundation of the *consulados* of Mexico (1592) and Lima (1593) gave a strong institutional framework for corporate defense, and the Crown excluded Indians and mestizos from commercial privileges.[6] Beyond legal distinctions, the consulados and their members used other means to defend their position. For example, they attempted to reserve the title of "merchant" exclusively for Spaniards and creoles. In the same manner, the consulado of Buenos Aires (founded in 1794) tried to establish in 1804 a complete register of merchants in the cities under its jurisdiction. Disputes over ethnic distinctions, however, made it difficult to reach a consensus on the details of the project. In responses received by viceregal representatives from all over the viceroyalty of Río de la Plata, one can see a clear differentiation between the "whites," who were considered the true merchants (and those who apparently merited counting), and the "others," who were anonymous and uncounted. The city of La Paz, for example, registered forty-one merchants and explicitly stated that *cholos* and mestizos who made their living as petty merchants in the city were neither included nor counted. In Oruro, before being obliged to count the "mestizos and Indians," they preferred not to comply with the census.[7]

Similarly, in another discursive practice of great consequence for the historian, large merchants consciously distorted their evaluations and estimations of the importance of different branches of commerce according to whether a specific trade was in the hands of Spaniards or Indians. Thus, in the reports on the commerce of the grand market of Potosí, Spanish merchants emphasized the value of the traffic in wines and brandies, which was their own monopoly, over the coca trade which, as mentioned above, was the preserve of the Indians at the end of the eighteenth century. Although, as will be shown below, the trade in each was practically equal in quantity and total value, the reports of the merchants, with apparent quantitative precision, multiplied more than four times the values of their own trade while reducing to less than half the amount of the coca trade, in which "mostly Indians are involved."[8]

Indians and mestizos not only sought to occupy market spaces but also appealed to the judicial system to defend their rights to participate in the merchant traffic without discrimination. Paradoxically, while Indians were denied the exemptions and privileges accruing to those of merchant status, they were frequently burdened with obligations specifically intended for "Indian merchants." Thus, issued forth the following protest in 1797:

> We, Pedro Gaspar Mamani, Nicolás Coca, Xavier Portugal, Basilio Iugra, Diego Anco, and Diego Ari, Indians who are natives of the Ayllo Chayantacas in the District of Chayanta, and now resident in this city [La Plata] . . . declare that, needing to maintain our growing families and to fulfill our obligations to the royal tributes, and contemplating at the same time the small return earned from our labors, have undertaken for years the ridiculous trade from the city of La Paz to this one with a little coca and *bayetas* [coarse woolen textiles], products—which because of their small quantity and the cost of their transportation—hardly yield enough for our subsistence; we also [need to fulfill] other obligations, such as paying for fiestas in this city, financing altars at Corpus Christi, and contributing other small but multiple taxes which burdened us in our village.[9]

The Indian residents in La Plata who made this declaration in February 1797 were protesting tax increases of from 1 to 3 pesos, which were to de-fray the cost of bullfights during carnival. They explained in detail how in their village they complied with their tax duties and in La Plata they contributed to the collective obligations of the whole commercial community, but they called into question the discriminatory tax that they, as Indian merchants, had to pay. The result of their petition was favorable, and the tax was maintained at 1 peso. Ten years later, in 1808, the issue resurfaced. The most well-to-do among the Indian merchants then asked for a total exemption from the charge. They argued that they were "true merchants" and as such took their turns among the other merchants in covering the cost of the Feast of Our Lady of Guadalupe. The *audiencia* asked the local *junta de comercio* its opinion; the deputy turned to the Buenos Aires consulado, which worried about the implications of this incident

> which, without a doubt, would constitute a general rule for all other districts of this viceroyalty and . . . all individuals of commerce would certainly be sorry to find themselves classed together with those who, whatever their merits in actively supplying the town, are, nevertheless, socially inferior.[10]

In Buenos Aires, Juan Larrea, member of the consulado, countered with the opinion that "the natives upon whom the petition falls are true merchants, by the type of contracts, by the extension of their money and the quality of the goods which circulate in their negotiations." The Indians finally saw themselves freed of the discriminatory charge.[11]

The Potosí Alcabala as Historical Source

The discriminatory and exclusionary practices of Spanish and creole merchants against Indians and mestizos (as much economic as legal and discursive) thus contributed to a bias in the colonial documentation that makes it difficult for contemporary historians to evaluate the real importance of the latter in the market. This work is further complicated by a particular type of colonial legislation, the exemption of the Indians from paying the *alcabala,* an ad valorem tax that burdened many of the internal commercial transactions of the Latin American colonies. By the end of the eighteenth century, however, the sales tax exemption of Indians did not appear to be functioning in the city of Potosí.

Traditionally, colonial legislation exonerated Indians from alcabalas when trading their own goods or goods that had been acquired from other natives. This exemption was based initially on the presumed "poverty" or "rusticity" of the natives and, as such, formed part of the vast colonial tutelary regime erected by the Crown during the late sixteenth century. In the eighteenth century, however, political and legal commentary emphasized the utility of the alcabala exemption in promoting agriculture, industry, and commerce among the Indians.[12] But on January 30, 1779, as part of the Bourbon drive to increase fiscal revenues, José Antonio de Areche, the general inspector (*visitador general*) of the viceroyalties of Peru and the Río de la Plata, decreed the end of this tax exemption. Areche noted that the original exemption included the clause "for now" and that, two centuries later, the moment had come to increase Crown revenues by means of abolishing the Indian tax privileges. However, the Council of the Indies rejected the initiative in its resolutions of June 22 and July 13, 1787.[13] At the Lima customs house, from which Areche performed his inspection, the decree of 1779 was never applied; in 1780 the Indians were still exempted from the alcabala, although the customs administrator forced them to declare their shipments in detail. This trade registered up to 3 percent of the annual total.[14] A quarter of a century later, in Cerro de Pasco, the exempted Indian trade was still controlled through "waybill pardons," which differed from the usual customs waybill in that they not only identified the merchandise and its carrier but also verified the merchandise as free from the alcabala.[15]

It is worth considering the possibility that Areche's decree suspending the exemption could have been applied in Potosí. In that year, 1779, Jorge Escobedo, governor of the Royal City and Areche's future successor as visitador general, put into effect a new institution—a customs house— which was to serve as a way of increasing fiscal revenues. Only four months after the promulgation of Areche's decree, he established the Royal Customs House of Potosí, which took charge of the collection of the alcabalas from June 1779 onward. The possibility that the exemption for Indians might be suspended as part of the initial measures included in establishing the customs house receives indirect support from other sources. In fact, Areche and Escobedo discussed lifting other exemptions to the alcabala in their correspondence of 1779 and 1780. Thus, the exemptions for livestock products such as jerked meat, cured meat, and suet were abolished.

They also discussed the possibility of abolishing the exemption enjoyed by three other products—coal, firewood, and salt—because of their use as mining inputs. These were very significant cases, as their eventual taxation could have represented an increase for the Royal Treasury of around 40 percent of collections made up to that point. This project was not put into practice because of the opposition of Escobedo, who was worried about possible protests in the city. It is noteworthy, however, that not only was there a search for means to trim the exemptions but also in 1780 there was no consideration of the legal obstacle represented by the fact, evident to contemporaries, that the trade and production in question was absolutely monopolized by Indians who came to Potosí.[16] The obvious hypothesis is that Areche's decree was applied in Potosí and that the later resolutions of the Council of the Indies did not reverse the situation.

This hypothesis is strengthened by the abundance of Indian patronymics (even without counting the dubious cases) among the more than 40,000 transactions subject to the payment of the alcabala in the Royal Customs of Potosí between 1779 and 1810.[17] Furthermore, the source systematically includes the reference to merchandise shipped for the personal consumption of the Indian traders and required to pay the alcabala. The most common case was that of coca traders who, in addition to the bulk of their cargo, declared an additional basket for "their own consumption," which was then included in the total subject to the tax payment.

We propose, therefore, to use the alcabala records to approach the issue of Indian and mestizo participation in the urban market of Potosí at the end of the eighteenth century. We will start by quantifying the information on alcabalas levied on goods entering the city of Potosí in 1793.[18]

The data from the alcabala permit us to focus only on a segment of the total trade destined for Potosí since certain goods and certain traders were exempt from payment of the tax. Livestock, seeds and tubers, vegetables, and mining inputs escaped the control of the Royal Customs. In addition, the church, its members, and its dependencies were not subject to the tax. Further, the families of the forced laborers who arrived every year as part of the mita (the system of forced labor applied in the Andean region) were also exempted.

Thus, the traffic controlled by the customs authority for the payment of the import tax was only 35 percent of the total movement, while that portion of 65 percent exempt from the alcabala was made up of approximately

Table 7.1. Total Imports to Potosí, 1793 (pesos)

	South American Goods	European Goods	Totals	
Goods paying alcabala	852,558 (55%)	685,646 (45%)	1,538,204	(35%)
Goods exempt from alcabala				
Potatoes, frozen dried potatoes (*ocas*)	375,000			
Corn	650,000			
Wheat	360,000			
Table salt	30,000			
Barley and other grains	200,000			
Cows	200,000			
Mining salt	300,000			
Firewood and coal	300,000			
Wood for mining	25,000			
Mercury		292,000		
Iron for mining		75,000	2,807,000	(65%)
Total	3,292,558 (76%)	1,052,646 (24%)	4,345,204	

Sources for Tables 7.1–7.8: AGN (Buenos Aires), XIII 7-1-2, lib. 2–3; *Telégrafo Mercantil* (Buenos Aires), September 19, 1801; Archivo General de la Nación, *Consulado de Buenos Aires: Antecedentes–Actas–Documentos,* vol. 1 (Buenos Aires, 1936), 522–525; AGN (Buenos Aires), Manuscritos de la Biblioteca Nacional, 307, 5024; Enrique Tandeter, *Coercion and Market: Silver Mining in Colonial Potosí, 1692–1826* (Albuquerque, 1993).

40 percent food products and 25 percent mining inputs (see Table 7.1). As such, the great majority of exempted products was of South American origin. The proportion between European and South American goods changed radically from taxed to exempt transactions. While European goods, plus some "mixed" shipments, represented some 45 percent of the traded value subject to the tax, the percentage in overall trade was only 24 percent (see Table 7.1).

These data confirm the general lines of the interpretation of Carlos Sempat Assadourian in regard to the high degree of self-sufficiency in the area of the colonial Peruvian economy. His conclusions were presented with reference to a table based on the year 1603 showing the traffic entering Potosí according to estimates from a contemporary document.[19] This table showed that only 9.5 percent of goods entering for that year came from outside America. Almost 200 years later the percentage had risen to only 24 percent, a very slim increase, given the great Spanish commercial offensive after the 1778 *Comercio Libre* decree.[20]

Origin of the Merchandise

By 1793 there was a clear resolution of the multisecular conflict between the Pacific and the Atlantic in supplying Alto Perú with imported goods. Nearly 80 percent now came from Buenos Aires.[21] In contrast, the supply of South American goods was dispersed among different regions in Peru and the Río de la Plata (see Table 7.2). Thus, Potosí confirmed its position as a great mining center whose production attracted traders from the whole of the Peruvian area who came to the market with the objective of exchanging their goods for money. The production of silver in Potosí doubled during the half-century before 1793, and in this evolution merchant capital, local as well as from other zones in the viceroyalty, played a very small part. As a result, silver circulated inside and outside the city without any form of monopoly.[22] This situation contrasts sharply with that of Cerro de Pasco in lower Peru during these same years. The control exercised by the Lima merchants in Cerro de Pasco explains why between 1782 and 1819 81.8 percent of the trade entering the city, European as well as South American goods, originated in the viceregal capital.[23]

Potosí, on the other hand, maintained in general outline the kinds of ties with the Peruvian economic area that had developed during the peak years of its production at the beginning of the seventeenth century. Its capacity to foster this converging commercial traffic appears to have diminished relative to silver output, however, probably because the eighteenth-century increase in silver production was obtained through intensification of forced labor without a growth of the overall labor force. Moreover, the division of the mining surplus between absentee owners and tenant entrepreneurs did not encourage either mining investment or trading activities.[24]

Nonetheless, it bears emphasizing that Potosí continued to attract a

Table 7.2. Imports of South American Goods, according to Alcabala
Waybills, at Potosí, 1793

	Total Value Pesos	%	No. of Transactions	% %	Average Value (pesos)
With waybills from					
Arequipa	277,721	32.5	215	14.6	1,292
La Paz	241,526	28.3	414	28.1	583
Cuzco	146,257	17.1	98	6.6	1,492
La Plata	43,078	5.0	136	9.2	317
Salta	22,030	2.6	61	4.1	361
Buenos Aires	21,589	2.5	5	0.3	4,318
Cochabamba	17,457	2.0	88	6.0	198
Lima	6,718	0.8	19	1.3	354
Potosí	5,394	0.6	16	1.1	337
Cordoba	1,132	0.1	2	0.1	566
Puno	180	0.0	1	0.1	180
Without waybills	69,476	8.1	420	28.5	165
Totals	852,558	(99.6)	1,475	(100)	

See Table 7.1 for source of data.

wide range of trade. The separation in 1776 of the viceroyalty of the Río
de la Plata, in whose territory Potosí was located, and the viceroyalty of
Peru in no way signified the institution of frontiers that discouraged commerce. The lower Peruvian intendancies of Arequipa, Cuzco, and Lima
accounted for more than 50 percent of the trade in South American goods
destined for Potosí in 1793 (see Table 7.2). Contemporary sources stress
the fundamental role of this articulation between the productive Peruvian
areas with the mining zones of upper Peru, which, in return, brought to
the viceroyalty in Lima specie that alleviated the acute commercial deficit
that the region had accrued with the Spanish metropolis.[25]

The remaining 50 percent of the trade in South American goods was
commercialized within the limits of the Río de la Plata, but it is necessary to distinguish here between the regions of upper Peru and those that
later formed part of Argentina. While the former (Puno, La Paz, La Plata,
Cochabamba, and Potosí), including the entries "without waybill" that we
assume originated in the areas surrounding the Imperial City, came close

to 45 percent of the total, the intendancies of Salta, Córdoba, and Buenos Aires barely account for 5 percent.

The trade between the regions of upper Peru and Potosí is of importance not only for its value, close to 45 percent of the total of South American goods, but also for its enormous volume, 79.5 percent of the number of transactions in those goods, which indicates a very fragmented participation in these categories (see Table 7.2).

The Merchants

In 1804, when, as already stated, the consulado of Buenos Aires tried to establish a merchant's roster for the whole of the viceroyalty of the Río de la Plata, the deputy of commerce of Potosí informed that although there were more than 400 stores (*pulperías*) within the city's jurisdiction, the city's commerce was in the hands of thirty-three merchants of European goods, seven owners of warehouses (*casas de bodega*), fifteen traders in South American goods, and some other "neighboring Indian traders in coca, etc., not to mention the transient, which are not few."[26] We encounter again the discursive practices intended to obscure the complexities and numbers of actual trading practices.

In contrast, the import tax records of 1793 reveal the extent of the deliberate distortion implied in that report (see Table 7.3). Our source presents for the single year 1793 a total of 743 individuals who brought in goods subject to payment of the alcabala. They can be grouped in regular intervals, according to the total amount registered for the year, where the included values in one class are triple those of the preceding one.[27] It is useful to distinguish four groups of traders. The first, the large merchants, includes the three upper levels—importers who during the year handled transactions of over 10,000 pesos each. The second group, the medium-sized merchants, comprise the next two tiers with total annual amounts of between 1,000 and 10,000 pesos each per year. The third, the small traders, includes the next two levels with monetary limits of between 100 and 1,000 pesos. Finally, the last two tiers, with amounts below 100 pesos for the year, are the occasional traders.

There is a remarkable asymmetry represented in the distribution by the twenty-six large merchants. This group, 3.5 percent of the individuals who

Table 7.3. Statistics on Merchants Who Paid Alcabala,
by Total Values, Potosí, 1793

					No. of Transactions		Value of Transactions (pesos)	
Range of Value (pesos)	No. of Merchants	Merchants w/o Total (%)	No. of Transactions w/o Total (%)	Value of Transactions w/o Total (%)	Avg. per Merchant	Coefficient of Variation[a]	Avg. per Transaction	Relative Variability
Large merchants								
100,000–316,228	1	0.13	1.77	8.84	28.00	—	4,854.69	—
31,622–99,999	6	0.81	6.07	22.75	16.00	0.88	3,645.39	2.22
10,000–31,621	19	2.56	6.40	23.56	5.30	0.81	3,590.79	0.94
Medium-sized merchants								
3,162–9,999	51	6.86	11.75	18.90	3.63	0.76	1,572.67	0.77
1,000–3,161	131	17.63	20.46	14.54	2.47	9.82	689.37	0.76
Small traders								
316–999	218	29.34	23.08	8.45	1.69	0.70	351.96	0.65
100–315	204	27.46	21.13	2.67	1.16	0.61	114.18	0.58
Occasional traders								
32–99	101	13.59	7.61	0.35	1.23	0.46	53.67	0.40
1–31	12	1.61	0.79	—	1.08	0.30	21.52	0.27
Totals	743	99.99	99.06	100.06				

See Table 7.1 for source of data.

[a] Coefficient of variation computed as standard deviation/mean. This measure allows for comparison of relative variability between different sets of data.

operated in the import market of Potosí, account for almost 15 percent of the transactions and about 55 percent of the value traded. Furthermore, this group is not principally identified with the commercialization of European goods. On the contrary, eight of the twenty-six dedicated themselves exclusively to importing South American goods, including two merchants who occupied fifth and seventh place in the general statistics.

Trading in European goods was the preserve of a small group of merchants, however; forty-three individuals from a total of 743 were responsible for almost 10 percent of the transactions and 49 percent of the total value of imports. In addition to the eighteen large merchants referred to above, this group included twenty-one medium-sized merchants and even four small traders. Commerce in European imports was generally separated from wholesale traffic in South American goods, as shown by the fact that only eighteen of the forty-three importers of European goods took part in any transactions that involved South American products, which, in any case, never weighed heavily in their total activities. The exception was Indalecio González de Socasa, the largest merchant in the market and the only one whose transactions totaled over 100,000 pesos during the year, trading in European and South American imports in similar proportions.

Medium-sized merchants took part in a smaller average number of transactions per merchant annually, and, more obviously, those transactions were of much smaller average value than those carried out by the larger merchants. It should be emphasized, however, that it is this group which is most obscured in the controversial statistics recorded by the deputy of commerce of Potosí, given that they account for a quarter of the traders for the year, responsible for one-third of the transactions and one-third of the total value of imports.

The small merchants, for their part, constitute almost 57 percent of the individuals with 44 percent of the transactions but with only 11 percent of the total value. Finally, those whom we refer to as occasional traders—15 percent of the individuals—account for 8 percent of the transactions with a total value of less than 0.5 percent. It seems probable that the great majority of the small merchants, as well as almost all the occasional traders, came only once with their goods to Potosí during the course of the year. The difference here is that the small merchants supplied the Potosí market with one or two products, while the occasional traders only brought a single product. Note in the case of the latter the low average value of the transactions and their relatively low variability.

Our source provides very few elements for a more precise identification of each merchant group. The waybills that correspond to the 1793 transactions suggest that the European imports, as well as the products of the haciendas and *obrajes* (textile workshops), were sent to Potosí in consignment to one or more merchants, one of whom accepted the shipment and declared it in customs, but was not always the person who paid the tax.

The majority of wholesale merchants did not need a commercial outlet or store open to the public. The tax roll of 1793 lists the forty-two proprietors of the city's forty-five shops.[28] Only fourteen of these also figure in the list of merchants bringing goods into the city: two imported only European goods, another two traded in European as well as South American imports, and the remaining ten dealt only with South American goods.

The Merchandise

Alcoholic beverages and coca accounted for almost 60 percent of the total value of South American goods, with textiles and food items a long way behind. In terms of frequency, coca occupied first place, in spite of a decline in its relative weight. The percentages of brandy and wine diminished by less than half and were superseded in number of transactions by foodstuffs and textiles.

It is necessary to look more closely at the twenty-five most important products or groups of products out of a total of sixty-five traded in Potosí in 1793 (see Table 7.4). The average value per transaction of each article can be related with the average value per transaction in the market for South American goods that year (see Table 7.4, column 7).[29]

Brandy heads the list for total value of its operations, followed very closely by coca, and further down by South American clothing. The downward trend in percentages from the fourth product, sugar, is surprising. The table's first three positions confirm, then, the fundamental information based on geographical origin that was presented above. The brandy-coca-clothing triad encompassed the geographical triangle Arequipa-La Paz-Cuzco, which accounted for the overwhelming majority of domestic

Table 7.4. Transactions in South American Goods, Potosí, 1793

Most Important Goods	Value (pesos) (1)	Percentage w/o Total Value American Goods (2)	Average Value (pesos) (3)	Coefficient of Variation[a] (4)	No. of Transactions (5)	Percentage w/o Total Transactions (6)	(2)/(6) (7)
Brandy	258,954	30.6	1,726	0.71	150	10.2	3.00
Coca	235,543	27.8	656	1.07	361	24.6	1.12
Woolen clothing	122,872	14.5	2,275	0.96	54	3.6	4.08
Sugar	31,105	3.6	819	0.81	38	2.5	1.46
Chili peppers	28,874	3.4	278	0.93	104	7.0	0.48
Herbs/Farrow	23,130	2.7	2,891	1.02	8	0.5	5.62
Fat and tallow	18,140	2.1	219	1.43	83	5.6	0.37
Copper	17,625	2.0	463	1.31	38	2.5	0.80
Wine	15,625	1.8	248	1.15	63	4.3	0.41
Crude cotton cloth	13,693	1.6	232	1.44	59	4.0	0.40
Cecina and charque	9,488	1.1	158	1.55	60	4.0	0.25
Flannel cloth	8,380	0.9	113	1.02	74	5.0	0.18
Mules	7,339	0.8	667	0.44	11	0.7	1.14
Anil	6,850	0.8	3,425	0.92	2	0.1	8.00
Honey	5,779	0.6	148	0.71	39	2.6	0.23
Oil	4,528	0.5	566	0.65	8	0.5	1.00
Various	4,404	0.5	294	0.75	15	1.0	0.50
Cotton	4,106	0.4	124	0.67	33	2.2	0.18
Skins	2,952	0.3	268	0.67	11	0.7	0.42
Fish	2,858	0.3	94	1.23	30	2.0	0.15
Tin	2,692	0.3	448	0.70	6	0.4	0.75
Soap	2,618	0.3	90	1.24	29	1.9	0.15
Leather soles	2,575	0.3	151	0.76	17	1.1	0.27
Seed	2,452	0.2	408	0.53	6	0.4	0.50
Chocolate	2,280	0.2	2,280	—	1	0.0	0.00
Totals	834,862	(97.6)			1,300	(87.4)	

See Table 7.1 for source of data.
[a]See note, Table 7.3.

trade converging on Potosí. There is a notable difference in the quotient values of the three products, which express the relation between their average transaction and the average transaction of the combined American goods. While coca from La Paz has a quotient of 1.12, that is, slightly above the average of the sixty-five American products, the transactions in brandy were three times this value, and those in woolen clothing more than four times the average quotient.

Brandy was a relative newcomer compared with the majority of other products in the marketplace of Potosí. It was only after 1701 that brandy, previously considered a medicinal beverage, began to be sent in quantity from the Peruvian coast to the altiplano. Peak production was reached toward the end of the eighteenth century, with 80 to 90 percent of Arequipa's wine being converted into brandy.[30] Potosí occupied a prominent place as a market for wines and brandies from the coast, but even more so for products from the Moquegua region, which supplied the Imperial City with 86 percent of its consumption.[31]

Trading in wine, the ninth most valuable commodity among South American products, was obviously associated with that of brandy. However, it should be pointed out that, together with the wine trade from Moquegua, which accounted for 59 percent of consumption with a price ranging from 7 to 9 pesos per jug (*botija*), an inferior wine produced in the neighboring valley of Cinti entered Potosí with a uniform price of 4 pesos per jug.[32]

The relatively low variability coefficient for the trade in brandy points to operations that were almost always of great value. Potosí's import of wines and brandies was, then, very concentrated. During the year, ninety-four merchants engaged in these transactions, but only seven large merchants sold 46.5 percent of the total, while forty-four medium-sized merchants sold over 48 percent. This was a specialized trade, from which those merchants seldom strayed. Five of the large merchants, who alone were responsible for 42.5 percent of the total trade, devoted 94.6 percent of their annual returns to this commerce, while the forty-four medium-sized traders had 95.2 percent of their merchandising activities accounted for by this product.

Trade was channeled from the regions of production toward the altiplano in three different ways: by the great landowners who owned mule trains and transported their own products (but these were an exception),

Table 7.5. Transactions in Coca, Ranked according to Merchant Group,
Potosí, 1793

Value of Trans-actions (pesos)	Merchants		Transaction		Avg. No. of Trans-actions	Avg. Value of Coca Traded (pesos)	(%)
	No.	(%)	No.	(%)			
Large merchants							
10,000–316,228	3	1.2	4	1.1	1.3	5,781	2.5
Medium-sized merchants							
1,000–9,999	77	29.7	148	41.0	1.9	150,667	63.9
Small traders							
100–999	173	66.8	203	56.2	1.1	78,677	33.4
Occasional traders							
1–99	6	2.3	6	1.7	1.0	417	0.2
Totals	259	(100)	361	(100)	1.4	235,542	(100)

See Table 7.1 for source of data.

by other landowners who rented the mule trains for transportation, and by still others who chose to sell their merchandise to owners of the trains that descended from the altiplano to the coast.[33] It would be useful to define precisely the participation of this last kind of transport and establish what, in particular, was the role of the caciques, who had been so prominent in this trade during the seventeenth century.[34]

The trade in brandy was closely followed in total values by that of coca (see Table 7.4). However, the frequency of their operations and their average value differed markedly. The Indian monopoly in the coca trade has already been mentioned, and the predominance of Indian names in this commerce is confirmed by the alcabala registers. This was the classic "triangular" trade of the Andean world in which Potosí, as one of the major centers of coca consumptions, as well as a place where access to cash was relatively easy, formed a vertex.[35] Ninety-five percent of the coca that entered Potosí originated in the intendancy of La Paz.

Avg. Value per Trans- action	Total Value Traded (pesos)	Value Coca/ Value Traded (%)	Baskets of Coca	(%)	Baskets per Trans- action	Avg. Price Asses. per Basket
1,445	198,389	2.9	906	2.4	226	6.38
1,018	180,019	83.7	23,728	63.3	160	6.35
387	82,999	94.8	12,759	34.0	63	6.16
70	476	87.8	73	0.2	12	5.72
652	461,883	51	37,466	(99.9)	104	6.28

Nevertheless, one must distinguish between the high-quality coca, or *gatera,* and that of inferior quality, called *mercadera.* While 86 percent of the former arrived with waybills issued in the city of La Paz, the latter shows a clear predominance of waybills issued by the tax collector's offices near the production zones in the district of Chulumani.[36] The high-quality coca was produced by the haciendas and marketed through large merchants, while the inferior coca was produced by Indian *yanaconas* on the parcels granted them by the *hacendados,* or by members of the region's Indian communities. The latter was traded by *piqueros,* medium-sized or small merchants.[37]

The 259 individuals involved in coca transactions were almost 35 percent of the total merchants trading in Potosí during the year (see Table 7.5). Of these, only three were large merchants who seldom entered into the coca market but did so with operations of high average value, which doubled the general average of coca transactions. These did not have a significant

Table 7.6. Transactions in Woolen Clothing, Ranked According
to Merchant Group, Potosí, 1793

Value of Trans-actions (pesos)	Merchants		Transaction		Avg. No. of Trans-actions	Value (pesos)	(%)
	No.	(%)	No.	(%)			
Large merchants 10,000–316,228	5	15.6	22	40.7	4.4	77,598	63.2
Medium-sized merchants 1,000–9,999	22	68.7	26	48.1	1.1	44,277	36.0
Small traders 100–999	4	12.5	5	9.3	1.2	913	0.7
Occasional traders 1–99	1	3.5	1	1.9	1.0	84	0.1
Totals	32	(100.3)	54	(100)	1.7	122,872	(100)

See Table 7.1 for source of data.

effect on the total of their commercial earnings—2.9 percent—or on the
total value of the coca traded on the market, 2.5 percent.

On the other hand, more than 40 percent of all the medium-sized merchants dealt in coca, which represented more than 80 percent of their
yearly earnings. This group, less than one-third of the coca traders, was
responsible for almost 65 percent of the shipments in this product. The
overwhelming majority within this group belonged to the level of traders
who dealt with more than 1,000 and less than 3,162 pesos a year, making
two shipments of coca per year on different dates (see Table 7.3). Their
average transaction, 160 baskets, implied a significant mobilization of men
and animals for transport. The small traders, two-thirds of the coca dealers
in Potosí, accounted for one-third of the values traded. Their dedication
to the coca trade was almost total—94.8 percent. It should be emphasized
that, according to the data, only six of the 113 merchants who qualified as
occasional traders made any coca shipments.

Avg. Value per Trans- action	Total Value Traded	Value of Woolen Clothing/ Value Traded (%)	Varas[a] of Woolen Clothing	(%)	Avg. No. Varas per Trans- action	Avg. Price Asses. per Vara
3,527	233,197	33.3	223,668	60.2	10,167	0.35
1,703	83,612	53.0	124,565	38.4	5,483	0.31
182	2,088	43.7	4,800	1.3	960	0.19
84	84	100	450	0.1	450	0.19
2,275	318,981	38.6	353,483	(100)	6,879	0.33

[a] Vara is a measure of length, equivalent to thirty-three inches.

In total value traded, the group that follows wine, brandy, and coca is that of textiles. The focus of these comments will be on three textile products—*ropas de la tierra* (woolen clothing), the *tocuyos* (crude cotton cloth), and *bayetas* (flannel cloth)—which include 187 of the 224 textile transactions, occupying 3rd, 10th, and 12th place in the general statistics of the South American imports (see Table 7.4).

While the definition of the coarse cotton cloths (the crude weaves of cotton supplied traditionally by Cochabamba to Potosí) is clear, the distinction between woolen and flannel cloth is much less satisfactory. Both these woolen weaves presented a great variety of qualities, distinguished sometimes by name and sometimes by price. The criteria used by the officials of the different customs houses did not always coincide, so that what was authorized to leave a city as flannel could be regarded as wool at another destination, or vice versa. However, the dominant criterion in the Royal Customs House of Potosí can be deduced from the data on the

Table 7.7. Transactions in Flannel Cloth, Ranked According
to Merchant Group, Potosí, 1793

Value of Trans- actions (pesos)	Merchants		Transaction		Avg. No. of Trans- actions	Value	(%)
	No.	(%)	No.	(%)			
Large merchants 10,000–316,228	1	2	1	1.3	1.0	156	1.9
Medium-size merchants 1,000–9,999	4	8	4	5.4	1.0	832	9.9
Small traders 100–999	34	68	58	78.4	1.7	6,856	81.8
Occasional traders 1–99	11	22	11	14.9	1.0	536	6.4
Totals	50	(100)	74	(100)	1.5	8,380	(100)

See Table 7.1 for source of data.

geographical origin, derived from the place of issue of the waybills. We can assume that the woolen cloth was, in general, a textile produced at the Cuzco workshops (*obrajes*), the region that shipped 92 percent of that category. The flannel, on the other hand, came directly from La Paz or by way of Oruro, accounting for a total of 87.9 percent, to which 9.6 percent that entered without waybills should, perhaps, be added. The crude cotton cloth came, without doubt, from the Cochabamba region. To the 90.5 percent that entered with waybills from that region, a further 8.3 percent, shipped without waybills, should be added.[38]

The average transaction in woolen cloth was more than four times the average market operation, although with a relative variability of around 1 (see Table 7.4). The degree of concentration of the trade was even greater than in wines and brandy (see Table 7.6). Five large merchants were re-

Avg. Value per Trans- action	Total Value Traded	Value Flannel/ Value Traded (%)	Varas[a] of Flannel	(%)	Avg. No. Varas per Trans- action	Avg. Price per Asses. per Vara
156	47,362	0.3	500	1.1	500	0.31
208	8,154	10.2	4,360	9.5	1,090	0.19
118	11,119	61.6	37,095	81.2	639	0.18
49	610	87.9	3,740	8.2	340	0.14
113	67,245	12.5	45,695	(100)	618	0.18

See Table 7.1 for source of data.

[a]Vara is a measure of length, equivalent to thirty-three inches.

sponsible for 63.2 percent of the total value traded, while twenty-two medium-sized merchants accounted for the other 36 percent, with minuscule percentages for small merchants and occasional traders. In contrast to wine and brandy, in which merchants were involved to the almost total exclusion of all other products, wool cloth represented only 33 percent of the trade of the large merchants and 53 percent of the medium-sized traders. For all of them, the product that most frequently was traded together with clothing was sugar produced in the same region of Cuzco.

The flannel trade offers the perfect reverse side of the coin to wool: its relationship to the average transaction of the market was 0.18, as opposed to a quotient of 4.08 for wool (see Table 7.4). Some 81.8 percent of the trade was in the hands of small merchants, whose degree of specialization—61.6 percent—suggests that it is among these that the recognized

Table 7.8. Transactions in Crude Cotton Cloth, Ranked according to
Merchant Group, Potosí, 1793

Value of Trans- actions (pesos)	Merchants		Transaction		Avg. No. of Trans- actions	Value	(%)
	No.	(%)	No.	(%)			
Large merchants							
10,000–316,228	1	2.8	2	3.4	2.0	3,081	22.5
Medium-size merchants							
1,000–9,999	4	11.1	10	16.9	2.5	4,204	30.7
Small traders							
100–999	18	50.0	34	57.6	1.9	5,670	41.4
Occasional traders							
1–99	13	36.1	13	22.1	1.0	738	5.4
Totals	36	(100)	59	(100)	1.6	13,693	(100)

See Table 7.1 for source of data.

association between coca and flannel becomes apparent (see Table 7.7).
The price of the flannel, it should be stressed, was 45 percent lower than
the average price for wool and, therefore, the difference in total negotiated
values of both products (8,380 and 122,872 pesos) is much smaller when
measured in quantity of cloth—45,695 and 353,483 *varas* respectively (see
Tables 7.6 and 7.7).

Potosí absorbed 28.7 percent of the crude cotton cloth shipped from
the intendancy of Cochabamba.[39] The average transaction in crude cotton cloth, with a quotient of 0.40 compared with the general average, was
much closer to that of the flannel than of woolen cloth (see Table 7.4). The
relative variability that affected the average was high—1.44—given that
large, medium, and small merchants participated heavily in this trade (see
Table 7.8). The single large merchant, González de Socasa, with only two
operations, shipped 22.5 percent of the total, while four medium-sized

Avg. Value per Trans- action	Total Value Traded	Value Cotton Cloth/ Value Traded (%)	Varas[a] of Cotton Cloth	(%)	Varas per Trans- action	Avg. Price Asses. per Vara
1,540	135,931	2.3	14,390	20.9	7,195	0.21
420	11,552	36.4	20,564	29.9	2,056	0.20
167	7,079	80.0	29,889	43.4	879	0.19
57	858	86.0	3,944	5.7	303	0.19
232	155,420	8.8	68,787	(99.9)	1,166	0.20

[a]Vara is a measure of length, equivalent to thirty-three inches.

merchants traded 30.7 percent. The control of more than 50 percent of the trade by five merchants tallies well with the findings of Brooke Larson concerning the shortage of pack animals after 1781 and the control that, as a result, some transport monopolists were able to exert on the Cocha-bamba trade.[40] Nonetheless, the data reveal that more than 40 percent of the commerce was in the hands of small merchants with a high degree of specialization in trading crude cotton cloth.

Conclusion

The documentary evidence that we possess concerning the colonial market is, primarily, the result of the actions and writings of the great merchants, who were primarily involved in overseas trade. Those texts make their transactions tantamount to all mercantile practices. Indians and mestizos were excluded and discriminated against in the market, and negated or ignored in the texts.

Thanks to the unusual situation at Potosí, where Indians were not exempt from paying the alcabala even though they were accorded exemption by law at the end of the eighteenth century, we have been able to analyze a universe of commercial transactions in which Indians participated. This analysis has permitted us to glimpse an ensemble of merchants, whose numbers were superior to those recognized by the consulado. Still more important is distinguishing the diverse social characteristics and practices of the 743 individuals who paid the alcabalas on goods imported to Potosí during 1793. In particular, by analyzing the commercial activities of those traders involved in the importation of coca, flannel, and crude cotton cloth, in contrast to those merchants who imported brandies, wines, sugar, and other textiles, we have caught a glimpse of the vital and motley world of the small-scale, itinerant, and occasional traders who frequented Potosí. While it seems to us that an ethnolinguistic analysis of family names of merchants is an unreliable method of determining the origins and identities of small-scale merchants at Potosí, this analysis in its entirety permits us to hypothesize that Indian and mestizo merchants had a strong presence in Potosí's urban market in the late eighteenth century.

Notes

A preliminary English language version of this paper was published as Tandeter et al., "The Market of Potosí at the End of the Eighteenth Century" *Occasional Paper* No. 16 (London, 1987). We are grateful to the Institute of Latin American Studies of the University of London for permission to publish this revised version. All translations from the original Spanish sources in this chapter are by Enrique Tandeter. All abbreviations for the archival material cited here are listed on the first page of the bibliography.

1. John V. Murra, "Aymara Lords and Their European Agents at Potosí," *Nova Americana* (Turin) 1 (1978): 231–244; Roberto Choque Canqui, "Los caciques aymaras y el comercio en el Alto Perú," in Olivia Harris, Brooke Larson, and Enrique Tandeter, eds., *La participación indígena en los mercados surandinos* (La Paz, 1987), 357–378; Silvia Rivera Cusicanqui, "El mallku y la sociedad colonial

en el siglo XVII: El caso de Jesús de Machaca," *Avances* (La Paz) 1 (1978): 7–27.

2. Tristan Platt, *Estado boliviano y ayllu andino: Tierra y tributo en el norte de Potosí* (Lima, 1982).

3. María Cecilia Cangiano, "Curas, caciques y comunidades en el Alto Perú: Chayanta a fines del siglo XVIII" (Tilcara, 1987).

4. Karen Spalding, *Huarochirí: An Andean Society under Inca and Spanish Rule* (Stanford, 1984), 152–153.

5. Our emphasis. Archivo General de la Nación [hereafter AGN] (Buenos Aires), Manuscritos de la Biblioteca Nacional, 307, 5024.

6. Louisa Schell Hoberman, *Mexico's Merchant Elite, 1590–1660: Silver, State, and Society* (Durham, 1991); Manuel Moreyra Paz-Soldán, *El tribunal del consulado de Lima: Sus antecedentes y fundación* (Lima, 1950).

7. G. Tjarks, "Panorama del comercio interno del virreinato del Río de la Plata en sus postrimerías," *Humanidades* (La Plata) 36 (1960): 48.

8. Examples of these "statistics" are found in *Telégrafo Mercantil* (Buenos Aires) September 19, 1801; Marie Helmer, "Documents pour l'histoire économique de l'Amérique du Sud: Commerce et industrie au Pérou à la fin du XVIIIe siècle," *Revista de Indias* 10.41 (July–September 1950): 519–526; María del Carmen Cortés Salinas, "Una polémica en torno a la mita de Potosí a fines del siglo XVIII," *Revista de Indias*, 30.119–122 (January–December 1970): 131–215; AGN, Consulado de Buenos Aires: *Antecedentes–Actas–Documentos*, vol. 1 (Buenos Aires, 1936), 522–552.

9. Archivo Nacional de Bolivia [hereafter ANB] (Sucre), Audiencia 1797, no. 37, f. 1.

10. AGN, 11. (Buenos Aires), IX 4-6-13, ff. 163–217.

11. *Ibid.*

12. *Recopilación de leyes de los reynos de las Indias*, Libro 8, Título 13; *Reglamento de la Aduana de Lima*, 1773, cap. 2; C. J. Díaz Rementería, "Aproximación al estudio de un privilegio del indio: La exención de la alcabala," *Historia, Instituciones, Documentos* (Seville, 1984).

13. Díaz Rementería, "Aproximación al estudio."

14. Our calculations are based on Archivo General de las Indias [hereafter AGI] (Seville) 1219; AGI (Lima), 1181; John Jay Tepaske and Herbert S. Klein, *The Royal Treasuries of the Spanish Empire in America: Peru* (Durham, 1982), 383–384.

15. Magdalena Chocano, *Comercio en Cerro de Pasco a fines de la época colonial* (Lima, 1982), 29–30.

16. For all of this paragraph, see British Library, Add. Mss., 13893, passim.

17. Xavier Albó (personal communication) has indicated the distinction between Andean patronymics and cases considered dubious for a variety of reasons.

The books of Royal Customs of Potosí are now held in the AGN (Buenos Aires), room 13.

18. The data on the alcabala in Potosí for 1793 were found in the AGN (Buenos Aires), XIII 7-1-3, Libros 2–3.

19. Carlos Sempat Assadourian, "La producción de la mercancía dinero en la formación del mercado interno colonial: El caso del espacio peruano, siglo XVI," in Enrique Florescano, ed., *Ensayos sobre el desarrollo económico de México y América Latina (1500–1975)* (Mexico City, 1979), 233.

20. John Fisher, "Imperial 'Free Trade' and the Hispanic Economy, 1778–1796," *Journal of Latin American Studies* 13 (May 1981): 21–56; Enrique Tandeter and Nathan Wachtel, "Prices and Agricultural Production: Potosí and Charcas in the Eighteenth Century," in Lyman J. Johnson and Enrique Tandeter, eds., *Essays on the Price History of Eighteenth-Century Latin America* (Albuquerque, 1990), 202–213.

21. Tandeter et al., "Market of Potosí," table 3.

22. Enrique Tandeter, *Coercion and Market: Silver Mining in Colonial Potosí, 1692–1826* (Albuquerque, 1993), ch. 4.

23. Chocano, *Comercio en Cerro de Pasco*, 18–19.

24. Tandeter, *Coercion and Market*, ch. 4.

25. "Idea del comercio del Perú," Egerton Mss., 771, British Library; *Mercurio Peruano* (Lima) I, March 24, 1791; José Baquíjano y Carrillo, "Disertación histórica y política sobre el comercio del Perú [1791]," in José Carlos Chiaramonte, ed., *Pensamiento de la Ilustración: Economía y sociedad iberoamericanas en el siglo XVIII* (Caracas, 1979), 11.

26. Tjarks, "Panorama del comercio interno," 48.

27. For the procedure employed, see Tandeter et al., "Market of Potosí," 9n.

28. AGN (Buenos Aires), XIII, 25-9-2.

29. The quotient between columns (2) and (6) in Table 7.4 expresses this relationship. See the corresponding equations in Tandeter et al., "Market of Potosí," 12n.

30. Kendall W. Brown, *Bourbons and Brandy: Imperial Reform in Eighteenth-Century Arequipa* (Albuquerque, 1986), 44.

31. Tandeter et al., "Market of Potosí," 38; J. F. Wibel, "The Evolution of a Regional Community within the Spanish Empire and the Peruvian Nation: Arequipa, 1780–1845," Ph.D. dissertation (Stanford University, 1975), 63; Brown, *Bourbons and Brandy*, 76–88.

32. Tandeter et al., "Market of Potosí," 47.

33. Brown, *Bourbons and Brandy*, 85.

34. Choque Canqui, "Caciques aymaras."

35. Daniel J. Santamaría, "La participación indígena en la producción y comercio de coca, Alto Perú 1780–1810," in Harris et al., *Participación indígena*, 425–444.

36. Tandeter et al., "Market of Potosí," 39–40.

37. Santamaría, "Participación indígena"; Herbert S. Klein, "Hacienda and Free Community in Eighteenth-Century Alto Perú: A Demographic Study of the Aymara Population of the Districts of Chulumani and Pacajes in 1786," *Journal of Latin American Studies* 7.2 (1973): 193–220; María Luisa Soux Muñoz Reyes, "Producción y circuitos mercantiles de la coca yungueña, 1900–1935," M.A. thesis (Universidad Mayor de San Andrés, La Paz, 1987).

38. Tandeter et al., "Market of Potosí," 41, 43–44.

39. Francisco de Viedma, "Descripción geográfica y estadística de la provincia de Santa Cruz de la Sierra," in Pedro de Angelis, ed., *Colección de obras y documentos relativos a la historia antigua y moderna de las provincias del Río de la Plata* (Buenos Aires, 1970), 6:642.

40. Brooke Larson, *Colonialism and Agrarian Transformation in Bolivia: Cochabamba, 1550–1900* (Princeton, 1988), 266–267.

8

Markets, Power, and the Politics of Exchange

in Tapacarí, c. 1780 and 1980

BROOKE LARSON AND ROSARIO LEÓN

The truck that bounces up the dry riverbed to San Augustín de Tapacarí follows the age-old route connecting the village to the densely populated central valleys that compose the heartland of the Cochabamba Department. During the eight-hour journey, the traveler passes through the southeastern edge of the Valle Bajo into the wide mouth of the Tapacarí River to begin the slow ascent into the western sierras. Along the lower reaches of the river, peasants wash carrots and other vegetables destined for the marketplaces of Quillacollo and other distant towns in the central valleys. But beyond the fertile shores of Las Ramadas, the landscape looks bleaker as mountains slope precipitously down to the riverbanks. It is the dry season, when trucks and pack animals can still cross the narrow ribbon of water that meanders along the wide, rocky riverbed. Seasonal rains will soon make passage impossible during the three-month rainy season, but the journey upriver to Tapacarí is relatively smooth, and upon arrival the traveler encounters a small town of thatched roof houses perched somewhat precariously on a hillside at the confluence of three rivers that feed into the Tapacarí river basin.

First impressions of San Augustín de Tapacarí are surely colored by the somber shadows and hues of twilight, after a long day's journey. But fleeting impressions of a forlorn, forgotten town are only confirmed the next morning in the harsh light of day. In casual conversation with townspeople, the outsider listens to the tales of a town slipping further into solitude, cut off from national political and economic life. Memories stretch back to Inca and early colonial times to try to make sense of their place in the historical process, but there is no consensus about the primary cause of the town's social death. Instead, people express their discontent by eliciting images of a golden age, when once an Inca *tampu* (roadside lodgings and storage area) existed before the floods washed it away, and later in colonial times, when agriculture flourished, the town bustled with traders and muleteers, and the Spanish and Indian townspeople enjoyed great wealth, power, and prestige. But this nostalgia for the distant past reflects an urban bias. It is rooted in the social experiences and historical memories of the town's "mestizo" families who live by brokering goods, services, information, and power: the shopkeepers, merchants, and truckers; the landlords; and the political authorities who have seen the commercial and political atrophy of their town over the course of the last century. Modern times have destroyed their strategic advantage over interregional commerce in grains, dismantled the structures of political authority over the royal Indian village (*pueblo real*) of Tapacarí, and (after 1953) jeopardized many of the haciendas that once quilted the river valleys that cut through the province and empty into the central valleys of the Cochabamba region.

Yet popular perceptions of a dying town do not invoke much nostalgia among most peasants who live beyond the reach of San Augustín in the western highlands of the Tapacarí region. In fact, the scene seems refreshingly buoyant to the outsider who travels through mountainous western stretches of the Tapacarí province. In apparent parallel to San Augustín's decline, the economic life of the province seems to be dispersed among the smaller, often even more geographically remote hamlets and villages scattered across the vast, broken landscape. Quechua- and Aymara-speaking peasants of the western highlands have woven intricate webs of exchange and communication across the countryside. The movement of people, goods, and ideas among the rural villages of western, highland Tapacarí is not a recent development: itinerant trading networks, seasonal transhumance, and reciprocal exchanges have historically interlaced Andean communities. But in recent decades, these communities have evolved a regional network of rotative markets of "horizontal exchange" where the values of personalized, reciprocal, long-term exchange relationships mediate peasant economic behavior. The emergence of subsistence markets has not shielded the highland peasants and pastoralists against the incursions of commercial capital, myriad political pressures, or the risks of highland subsistence agriculture. But we argue here that in the specific histori-

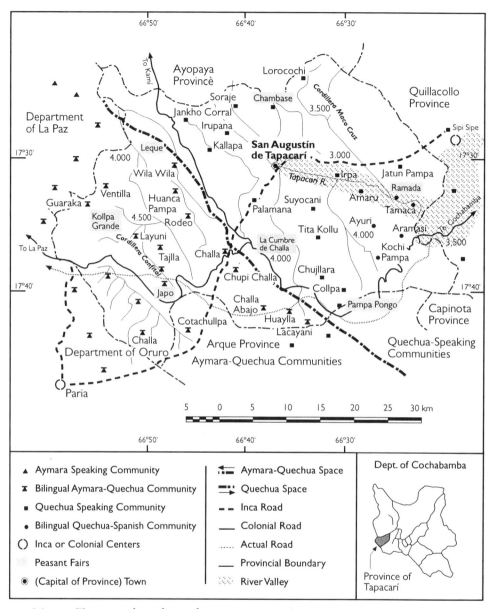

Map 4. Towns and markets of contemporary Tapacarí.

cal context of this region, the recent development of rural marketplaces throughout the western highlands of Tapacarí represents a significant shift over time in power balances and terms of exchange between the provincial capital (San Augustín) and central river valley of Tapacarí and the outlying mountainous villages and *estancias* of the southern and western highland districts (see Map 4). Not surprisingly, perhaps, the mythical past of San Augustín's colonial glory has little meaning in the historical consciousness of the outlying villagers.

This essay is a first and partial approximation to the social history of the Tapacarí region. We juxtapose historical and ethnographic research on Tapacarí to draw starkly different pictures of indigenous economic life, social relations, and ethnic/class identities in two moments in time: the late colonial period and the ethnographic present. In brief, we argue that in both the eighteenth and twentieth centuries, Tapacarí peasants simultaneously engaged in mercantile activities and nonmonetary, reciprocal forms of labor and product exchange as part of their manifold strategies of subsistence and reproduction. Furthermore, in each historical moment, different class and ethnic factions within Tapacarí communities made use of, or improvised, political institutions and ideologies to manipulate or contest unequal exchange relations. Yet the very different set of power relations and political culture of exchange in these two historical moments constrained and mediated the social patterns and ethics of local exchange relations. In the eighteenth century, the presence of local commercial capital buttressed by the dominance of colonial authorities—in particular, a powerful Indian elite—created the economic and ideological machinery of surplus extraction in the town of San Augustín to subordinate and drain the outlying highland villages. Further, tributary institutions and coercive practices subsidized (and masked) a bouyant interregional grain trade in the heartland of a "royal" colonial Indian community (the largest pueblo real in the colonial province of Cochabamba), where privileged indigenous elites advanced their emerging class interests. We examine how both indigenous peasantries, as well as rival caciques, manipulated colonial institutions and ideologies to challenge or defend the unequal terms of mercantile and reciprocal exchange that threatened the social peace within this colonial Andean region.

We then turn to look at structural conditions and political culture of exchange relations in contemporary Tapacarí. In the postcolonial period, the formal Indian community of Tapacarí has disintegrated into scattered rural hamlets, and the power of ethnic authorities has dispersed. Yet, the postcolonial atomization of Tapacarí has allowed Quechua- and Aymara-speaking peasants to reconfigure regional power relations around a network of rotative, subsistence *ferias* that interlace the highland hamlets and link them to national markets. In the microcosm of the rural market, women traders have improvised an etiquette of fair exchange among the suppliers of staple agricultural goods, while keeping the itinerant peddlars from the city and other outsiders at the margins. In this cultural process, ethnic and gender identities intertwine in complex ways to naturalize or censor marketplace behavior.

Let us turn to consider first the political economy and culture of paternal-commodity exchange relations in eighteenth-century Tapacarí.

Commerce, Coercion, and Political Strife in Eighteenth-Century Tapacarí

Throughout the colonial period, Potosí influenced the tempo and circuity of colonial trade in the southern Andes of Peru and Bolivia. Its spectacular growth as the primary source of Europe's silver in the late sixteenth century and the population explosion around the bleak mining camps of Potosí created, almost overnight, a marketplace whose scale and intensity was unprecedented in the New World. No enclave economy, Potosí: it drew commodities from Europe, Ecuador, Chile, and the ranches, workshops, and farms scattered widely across the vast mountainous interior of Peru and Bolivia. Together with Lima, Potosí was the growth pole that shaped the contours of Peruvian "economic space" and fueled an internal colonial market. At the famous marketplace of Potosí, the most prosaic goods (of both native and European origin) were transformed into commodities fetching fabulous prices.[1] All across the viceroyalty, European colonizers, mestizos, and enterprising Andeans engaged in petty commodity production to capitalize on the extraordinary commercial opportunities afforded by mining communities and colonial administrative centers.

But the scale of market operations at Potosí and the rapid commodification of indigenous staples should not obscure our vision of the enduring cultural patterns that shaped daily economic activities in the interior of Andean rural society in this heady age of mercantile capitalism. Even as Andean kingdoms and extended kin groups saw their world invaded and, to some degree, restructured by the imperatives and institutions of colonialism, native people sought strategies to preserve the most basic ideals that governed their social organization and gave meaning to their work and life. Andean ethnic groups sought self-sufficiency by holding onto and legitimating (in the new colonial context) land rights that gave them access to resources in diverse ecological niches, even as colonial policies tried to undermine their extensive "vertical control" over peripheral *mitmaq* colonies in distant lands and reduce them into tidy, contiguous *comunidades*.[2] Kinship and community continued to provide a language and ideology that bound most Andean people together in a web of mutual rights and responsibilities to the collective, even as the new tributary burdens strained the social fabric.

Within this cultural matrix, there was little fertile ground to cultivate economic self-interest and individual enterprise. And yet from the advent of silver mining and the organization of marketplaces, Andean people actively participated in commodity exchange. In the 1540s and 1550s, they cleared the thick undergrowth along the tropical eastern slopes of the Andes to plant coca for export to Potosí.[3] They prepared and carried by llama caravan vast quantities of *chuño* to market, served as muleteers and middlemen, and worked for wages in the mines. Andean society was never sealed off from the market. But as long as ethnic groups protected the bedrock of subsistence rights and preserved some degree of community solidarity and cohesion, they could partially shield themselves from trade cycles and exercise some control over the conditions under which they would engage in commercial transactions. Furthermore, the proceeds from commercial activities might be channeled into community resources to cover tribute, purchase land titles, or pay for colonial litigation to resolve a dispute between the community and outside claimants.[4]

At issue, then, is the extent to which Andean people could determine or affect the conditions and terms of their participation in the colonial marketplace. If they engaged in commercial transaction on relatively favorable terms, under their own aegis, and for their own ends, then market activity posed relatively little threat to the social reproduction of the Andean community. And their market activities would continue to be mediated by kinship or communal priorities. But here, of course, was the rub. For as long as indigenous market participation was primarily volitional and peasant labor bound up in subsistence economies, market forces in colonial Peru might be sharply curtailed or subject to the inner cultural dictates of Andean society (see Chapter 3 in this volume).

In the eighteenth century, before the introduction of Bourbon political reforms, the colonial state had lost much of its earlier capacity to set the parameters of extraeconomic force applied to the Andean population. The twin extractive institutions, tribute and mita, that Toledo had first applied on a viceregal scale had foundered and disintegrated by the early eighteenth century. Recurrent efforts to resurrect the mita on its original scale and extend tribute to the massive, uprooted population of Indian *forasteros* were to little effect.[5] The relatively weak presence of viceregal authority, especially in Alto Perú, and the long period of "salutary neglect" of colonial authorities at the regional and local level left wide open the scope and tactics by which political strongmen could force Andeans to comply with their (legal and illegal) demands. In other words, the mature colonial state (prior to the 1781 rebellions and the advent of Bourbon reorganization) had virtually abandoned its efforts to channel and contain the use of extraeconomic force toward high-level imperial ends.[6] Instead, the Crown opted for a rentier policy of selling *corregimientos* to ambitious colonialists who deployed political power to serve their own material interests. Buttressed by political tactics and royal consent (explicit and official after 1754), entrepreneurial behavior in the eighteenth century assumed dimensions capable of opening a vast, compulsory market among Andean peasant communities. As the terminal point of the mercantile exchange, the *corregidor* diffused the "marketplace" from the particular physical sites (in cities and towns, ports and mining camps, and at transit crossroads) to peasant villages throughout the rural hinterlands. The eighteenth-century marketplace traveled, unbidden, to the Indian community.

Apart from this "artificial market," there operated a more "spontaneous" product market in the cities and towns where prices fluctuated seasonally and cyclically, largely in response to harvest conditions and the supply of food crops and livestock (and a few manufactured goods, such as crude textiles). Like other preindustrial markets, a host of social, political, and meteorological conditions determined the volume and market value of commodities that oscillated from year to year.[7] Especially in the colonial context, where political authorities might preempt, undermine, or thwart Indian market participation, extraeconomic factors played an important role in local price-making.

Yet, on a more macro level, it is possible to trace the cyclical and seasonal patterns of agricultural and livestock prices of commodities sold at Potosí over the course of the eighteenth century. Enrique Tandeter and Nathan Wachtel have reconstructed price series of a number of staple commodities marketed at Potosí between 1719–1720 and the turn of the nineteenth century.[8] Through their price data, they have identified a series of subsistence crises that followed two or three years of drought. The years 1723, 1734, 1741, 1755, 1783–1784, and 1805 loom as moments of acute food shortage and peak agricultural prices. Apart from the cyclical crises of subsistence that plagued all preindustrial economies, the authors have traced two secular swings in the serial price data for the eighteenth century. As Peru and Alto Perú emerged from the nadir of indigenous population decline (around 1719–1720), agricultural production and prices began to rise slowly, except for those moments of violent fluctuation due to successive harvest failure. A turning point was reached, however, sometime in the late 1750s. By then, apparently, agricultural production was beginning to outpace population recovery, and prices stagnated or declined.

The conjuncture of intensifying political pressures in this period (as the Crown sanctioned or ignored abusive economic behavior on the part of the corregidores) and the secular decline or stagnation of prices of most agricultural goods on Alto Perú probably undermined the bargaining position of many Andean people who engaged in commercial transactions in the marketplace. The political "squeeze," together with the general deterioration in terms of trade for small-scale agricultural traders, narrowed the "small spaces" for commercial gain, vis-à-vis market transactions, for many Andean peasants. How particular *ayllus* or Andean communities responded to these political and economic conditions varied, of course. In the later eighteenth century, some ayllus thrived from their trade in wheat, coca, cloth, and pack animals. But those communities that did not exercise control over highly marketable commodities had few ways to offset the growing and increasingly arbitrary pressures of colonial authorities.

In many ways, the town of San Augustín de Tapacarí was a microcosm of the complex and ambiguous nature of the colonial market. It was the site of interregional commerce in grains, especially wheat and maize, thanks to its location alongside a riverbed which served (during the eight-month dry season) as a catchment area and major transit route between the altiplano and the central valleys of Cochabamba. San Augustín was also a local administrative center, the site of colonial authority in the largest Indian district in the province of Cochabamba: the pueblo real de Tapacarí. The town was the locus of two colonial, commercial circuits and modali-ties of exchange: one ostensibly mediated by prices on the "open" market but where monopolistic middlemen manipulated the cyclical oscillation of cereal prices; the other more openly coercive, with terms, volume, and forms of exchange commandeered by the local political elite, including Tapacarí's native authorities. Let us turn first to explore the social character and rhythms of the grain trade in this Indian community.

As mentioned, Tapacarí's importance as a grain market derived, in good measure, from its geographic location and topography. Traditionally, the Tapacarí River carved one of the only transit routes through the sierra to Paria and other sites along the western altiplano. Well before the European invasion, the Tapacarí river valley served as a vital link in the Inca road sys-tem that traversed the cordillera in the passage from the western altiplano down into the rich agricultural valleys of Cochabamba. Under Huayna Cápac, these eastern valleys became a crucial area of colonization, agricul-ture, and military fortification, and the Paria-Tapacarí-Cochabamba road became a major transit route for soldiers, colonists, state administrators, and agricultural produce under the Incas.[9]

Under Spanish rule, the Tapacarí valley and highlands (and the parallel river valley route through the town of Arque) continued to serve as a stra-tegic interecological zone and transit route between the western altiplano and the eastern valleys. Throughout the colonial period, commercial cereal agriculture on Cochabamba's haciendas was cut off from direct access to the major, north–south trade routes along the altiplano and the mining town markets of Potosí, Oruro, and Choquiabo (near La Paz). To export grains and other products to highland marketplaces, either producers or consumers themselves had to transport the commodities overland through the parallel river corridors of Tapacarí or Arque. In the eighteenth cen-tury, this long-distance, overland trade was considerable. One well-known contemporary source estimates the volume of cereal exports in 1788 to be some 200,000 *fanegas* of wheat and maize, alone.[10] More cereal moved out of the province in the form of wheat and maize flour. Other commodities, such as *tocuyo* (crude cotton cloth), were also exported in large quantities—at least toward the end of the century. The sheer magnitude of overland trade, and the fact that it followed one of two main intermontane trade corridors to the central altiplano, naturally gave Tapacarí a strategic advantage over many other valley towns in the Cochabamba province.

Tapacarí's location bestowed other advantages. At the confluence of three rivers that spilled out of the high sierras to the west, Tapacarí was rich in water power. Numerous mills flanking the riverbanks harnessed the water power to grind wheat and maize into flour (the latter especially important for the production of *chicha*). Aside from its marketplace, then, Tapacarí had a local industry that attracted buyers and sellers of grain. In addition, the town's attraction for large-scale grain dealers was that it lay out of the orbit of municipal price control. The Intendent Francisco Viedma, the same man who provided the global estimate of Cochabamba's "export trade" to other provinces, noted with some concern the impossibility of regulating grain prices in a "port town and a gateway to the western provinces."[11] Prices not only fluctuated more widely in the inland "port towns" of Tapacarí and Arque, but the market value of a fanega of grain was often 20 or 25 percent higher in those towns than in the market towns of the central valleys and heartland of Cochabamba.

The stated preference of grain dealers for *la saca,* as the inland export trade was called, reflected several social conditions of market exchange in Tapacarí. Clearly, from the perspective of the valley landlord, the terms of trade seemed to be better in the western river valley town than in the marketplaces of central valley towns where municipal price controls may have been more effective and where landlords faced competition from small-scale cereal producers who marketed surpluses during years of ordinary and abundant harvest. In contrast, the western market towns of Tapacarí and Arque were beyond the southwestern periphery of the valley region and out of the commercial orbit of most small-scale producers in the central valleys who could not supply their own pack animals or pay for freight costs. Second, the marketplace at Tapacarí specialized in long-distance trade. Grain sellers depended on highland merchants to purchase grain wholesale for cities and mining camps on the altiplano and on highland peasants to engage in retail transactions at the local marketplace. To be sure, Potosí no longer absorbed vast quantities of Cochabamba cereal, as part of a perennial pattern of trade that flourished in the late sixteenth century. In the eighteenth century, transregional trade and commercial profits in valley grain were subject to seasonal and cyclical fluctuation of harvest yields. Thus, Tapacarí's grain trade flourished in years of mediocre to poor harvest—when small-scale producers had little surplus to market and when dearth forced peasants into the marketplace to purchase subsistence crops and seed. Those years of high grain prices and scarcity of supply were moments when external traders, *hacendados* of the Cliza and Cochabamba valleys, and tithe speculators exercised virtually monopoly control over Tapacarí's local market and the carriage trade. Aside from a local group of creole and mestizo muleteers and millers and Tapacarí's small Indian elite, which engaged in trade and owned grain mills, the marketplace was in the hands of outsiders who used it as a conduit for cereal exports to the altiplano.[12]

During most years of mild to moderate harvest fluctuations, Tapacarí's grain market followed a seasonal rhythm. Even then, grain sellers depended on highland peasants to purchase and carry out a considerable share of the crop. During a 1799 royal inspection of grain mills in Tapacarí, a creole miller described the seasonal commerce with "puna Indians who journey down to Tapacarí to buy grain and grind it in our mills":

> The Indians who wander through this *quebrada* are from the Intendencies of La Paz and Puno. They purchase grain and grind some into flour during the first three months [after harvest, June, July, and August]. Most do not return for at least another year, and in the month of September and thereafter, few Indians bring their grain to our mills.[13]

Seasonal migration of highland peasants swelled the marketplace of Tapacarí and turned that town into the nexus of Andean, subsistence-oriented agriculture of the puna and Spanish cash-crop agriculture of the central valleys. The local marketplace articulated two ecological and cultural zones, modes of agricultural production, and ethnic and class groups. As in most such market situations, the hacendados and grain dealers who owned or controlled the scarcer or more necessary good (in this case, lower altitude crops that both complemented and served as subsistence insurance against frequent crop failure in the arid highlands) could outwait or outexchange the vulnerable highland people who, in most cases, lived at the margin of subsistence.

But what about years of abundant harvest when, presumably, peasants channeled a small portion of their harvested crop to the local market? Was it not in these years that local peasants, the Indians of rural Tapacarí, participated in the grain market to obtain cash to cover their tribute dues, *reparto* debts, and other monetary levies? Since such retail transactions went unrecorded, it is difficult to gauge the extent of peasant commerce after abundant harvests. But we suspect that the peasant retail trade at Tapacarí was relegated to the margins of the marketplace. Most ayllu Indians held little irrigated land and could not compete with the valley landlords in supplying a variety of high-quality maize. Second, as we shall see, many peasants were subject to multiple liens on their harvested crop that, in most cases, left little for market disposition even in good years. In addition to the usual colonial exactions on Indian households, the majority of Tapacarí's peasant population (classified on the tribute rolls as forasteros) was subject to the *veintena,* a twentieth of their wheat harvest allocated for the church.[14] This tax cut sharply into small surpluses of wheat, one of the principal crops cultivated in Tapacarí's highlands. Of course, the Indian community did export some wheat to the western highlands, but grain commerce seemed to be in the hands of Tapacarí's native elite.

Finally, there is the role of barter between peasant producers of complementary goods as an alternative exchange relation that functioned in years of normal or abundant harvest yields. The urban perspective from San Augustín de Tapacarí is one of a seasonal marketplace that flourished each year during the dry winter months when highland Indians descended to the town to purchase grain supplies. But we still know little about the magnitude or patterns of nonmonetary exchanges between Tapacarí peasants and puna Indians from Carangas, Sicacsica, and more distant places. Ritualized exchanges through kinship ties that bound clusters of valley peoples to their original highland ayllus or ethnic groups located across the provincial border are not yet visible in the Tapacarí case (as they are for some Indians in the nearby pueblo of Capinota).[15] But, as still happens today, highland Indians of Carangas and other parts of the central altiplano must have embarked on seasonal trading journeys to Tapacarí in order to exchange specialized products like salt, livestock, and other highland staples for maize. These itinerant trading patterns cushioned peasant households and estancias against subsistence scarcity, but they did not exercise a broader stabilizing effect on local prices of maize or wheat.[16] As we saw, cereal prices at Tapacarí's marketplace fluctuated widely from year to year and soared during subsistence crises that plagued Alto Perú every ten or twelve years during the eighteenth century. The existence of inter-ethnic barter networks among Andean inhabitants of different ecological tiers provided an apparently weak line of defense against dominant market forces, especially in times of acute subsistence need, when multitudes of highland peasants entered the product market as consumers.

A town noted for its interregional commerce, San Augustín de Tapa-carí was also the domain of ethnic authority, and we cannot appreciate the social character of mercantile transactions without embedding it in the broader context of shifting power relations inside village society. In 1788 the total population of the Indian district was 7,700 people, of whom about 6,849 were classified as "Indian and African slaves."[17] Over time, Tapacarí had shielded itself against the intrusion of creoles and mestizos, as almost 90 percent of its population was categorized in the colonial period as "Indian." Yet over the course of the colonial period, Tapacarí had seen the influx of Andean immigrants from other highland communities. The first systematic tribute count of *originarios* and forasteros, conducted in 1786, reveals the striking imbalance between the two groups. There were 150 adult, male originarios (who belonged to vestiges of the original ayllus and who identified themselves as members of the community with the atten-dant social obligations and rights, including land rights), as compared to the 1,315 adult, male forasteros (who inhabited communal lands, presum-ably through tenancy arrangements).[18] Apart from this internal division, Tapacarí's population was split between its traditional moieties, Anansaya and Urinsaya. At the subcommunity level, the moiety was the principal administrative unit, governed by a cacique and responsible for generat-ing its own tribute quota. Except for the town of San Augustín and its surroundings, the moieties were spatially segregated in distinct *anexos*.[19] For example, originarios and forasteros who belonged to Anasaya inhab-ited the hamlets and estancias of the anexos Tallija and Tirata, whereas the people of Urinsaya lived in Muclli and in the lower altitude hacienda zones of Ramadas and Calliri. Even where moieties intersected in the same anexos (Guaico, Chicmuri, Itapaya), estancias were separated by moiety. As in most bifurcated Andean communities, Anasaya was the superior half—with its larger number of tributaries (1,079 in 1786 compared to 692) and its concentration of people in the hinterlands of the river valley.[20] But the town of San Augustín marked the administrative convergence of the moieties: where Tapacarí's native hierarchy that ruled over the moieties, and through strategic alliances with colonial authorities, mediated most exchange between the satellite peasant villages (called interchangeably "anexos" and "ayllus") and the larger political economy.

In the 1740s and 1750s, two cacique families sat at the apex of Tapacarí's native hierarchy. The Liro de Córdova lineage ruled Anasaya for most of the century. Urinsaya's cacique was Pedro Condori, an Indian appointed as *gobernador* by the corregidor of Cochabamba.[21] As customary, they were responsible for overseeing the distribution of community lands, as well as the collection of tribute and the veintena. They also dispatched *mitayos* to Potosí and rounded up laborers for the local Augustine monastery and priests in the village. The caciques worked through a network of *hilacatas* and *cobradores* that imposed the levies on peasant households scattered widely across the broken landscape to the west and southwest of the *quebrada* and enforced the movement of goods and labor from the peripheral estancias to the vicinity of San Augustín.

Around mid-century, the caciques were mandated to forcefully distribute commodities among the estancia Indians. Tapacarí Indians were forced to accept a share of the repartos that the corregidor of Cochabamba was permitted to distribute in the province. As the largest Indian village, it was a target of the provincial repartimiento in such commodities as mules, local *bayeta* (flannel) cloth, Ecuadorian cloth, iron plow shares, coca, and imported clothing.[22] Both Liro de Córdova and Condori participated in the repartimiento de mercancías, either independently or as middlemen. Litigation from that period provides abundant testimony by Tapacarí peasants against the abuse of political office and the use of force in opening a "compulsory market" in the interior of village society.[23] Both Liro de Córdova and Condori (and a host of other authorities both inside and outside the pueblo real) were accused of abusive treatment of estancia peasants and other inhabitants of the pueblo real. Grievances cut across the ethnic and political boundaries of moiety and the fiscal and social categories of originario and forastero. The juridical protest did not simply reflect traditional rivalry between moieties or between caciques, one appointed and one hereditary. The trial records, specifically the testimony of the rival caciques, suggest that the economic and political behavior of the ethnic lords was perceived as a threat to the ideals of self-sufficiency, kinship, and community. Long before the outbreak of the 1781 rebellions, Tapacarí was racked by divisive forces that contributed to a climate of political and moral crisis.

It might be argued that the market initiatives of Tapacarí's caciques, including their participation in the forced distribution of goods, did not necessarily pose a serious threat to the collective interests of the moiety or community. That Liro de Córdova commercialized some of the grain harvested from community lands and then invested some of the profits in haciendas, livestock, and urban real estate in Quillacollo and other locations outside the village domain might be considered a privilege derived from his interstitial status as cacique of Anansaya. And Tapacarí peasants might even dismiss infrequent transgressions of community norms, as caciques (pressed into serving the interests of colonial authorities) forced peasants to accept repartos. After all, it was expected that caciques engage in commercial activities and expedite the collection of tributes (including debts from the repartimiento). At issue, therefore, were the underlying values and interests that motivated the economic and political behavior of Liro de Córdova and Condori and the longer-term consequences of their behavior. In the 1740s and 1750s, popular perception seemed to stigmatize one or both of the Andean chiefs as men motivated by economic self-interest and political ambition at the expense of communal well-being. The moral and institutional safeguards against the aggrandizement of Andean individuals or families who sought material wealth had broken down somewhere along the way. In the process, the caciques had jeopardized their social standing, assets, and claims in the community.

The central issue that emerged in the testimony, accusations, and counteraccusations against one or both of the cacique families was communal landholding. Each cacique accused his rival of appropriating communal or "reserve" land for his own use and personal gain. The appointed cacique, Pedro Condori, and later his son, Blas, testified before the *audiencia* of La Plata that Tapacarí was rich in cultivable lands where wheat, quinoa, *oca*, potatoes, *maz blanco*, and *morocho* flourished under good growing conditions. And yet, he stated, the moieties were always in arrears in meeting their tribute obligations. The problem rested, he noted, with the vastly unequal distribution of lands and the privatization of reserve land by the Liro de Córdova family. To press his case, Condori presented an inventory of the "excessive amount" of land in Liro de Córdova's possession. His list included whole estancias, *chacras*, and haciendas within the domain of the Indian community.[24] Further, he accused Liro of transgressing communal norms by parceling out communal lands to his loyal followers, all "newly arrived forasteros . . . because they are his partisans and part of his faction." Not surprisingly, Liro de Córdova launched counterattacks on the Condoris, enumerating the "great number of chacras" held by the Urinsaya cacique who "neither pays tax nor covers the expenses of the community."[25]

How to assess this testimony? Was the mutual accusation of private appropriation of communal land simply a trumped up charge in the heat of political rivalry? These charges cannot be so easily dismissed. Other evidence corroborates the testimony about cacique usurpation of communal resources. Peasant witnesses during the same trials offered testimony about the private estates of one or another of the caciques and obligatory agricultural labor on their private lands carved out within the community.[26] A 1781 inventory of Liro de Córdova's wealth also confirms the earlier testimony about the family's extensive holdings in the community—holdings that were managed, ironically, by a creole overseer.[27] Finally and paradoxically, the caciques themselves admitted at points during the endless testimony that they did indeed hold reserve lands in Tapacarí. While they rationalized their "right" to control agricultural production and distribution of crops on certain reserve lands, they nonetheless conceded that they held (and, in some cases, bequeathed) parcels of cultivable land throughout rural Tapacarí.[28]

To what extent did they still honor the accepted code of generosity, redistributing the fruits of their (de facto) private lands to members of the community or channeling surpluses to cover communal debts to the corregidor, state, or church? The answer to that question, of course, depends on the perspective of the interlocutor. The caciques assured the magistrates of Chuquisaca that they carried out their social commitments to the community, while each cacique accused his adversary of failing to do so. But again, the perception of many Tapacarí peasants who testified diverged sharply from the caciques' platitudes about their own gestures of generosity to the community. Indian witnesses complained of having to cover the large deficits they incurred when, as cobradores, they were assigned to collect semi-annual tribute dues; of having to pay tribute even in their widowhood; of facing arbitrary taxes and the impossible burden of repartos.[29] And the *subdelegado* of Tapacarí, during his two-month tour of the pueblo real in 1785, found vast inequity in the distribution of community lands to originario kin members of the village. Viedma's famous 1788 report presented his findings and deplored the situation where many originarios did not have access to sufficient lands or subsistence guarantees, while "caciques and *principales*" controlled "50, 60, or more fanegadas" of land.[30] Five years later, Viedma would oversee the redistribution of lands in Tapacarí in an effort to equalize landholding patterns and reclassify some forasteros as landholding originarios.[31]

Over the longer term, the participation of Tapacarí's native elite in the colonial market had destructive consequences for traditional social relations in the heart of village society. Mercantile colonial forces penetrated to the very core of village life, corroding the bedrock of subsistence guarantees for members of the extended kin group, destroying the content (if not the form) of reciprocal relations between the cacique and the moiety, and weakening the cultural cohesion of the community as a whole. Acute social tensions accompanied the development of class relationships within rural society, as traditional rivalries were increasingly subsumed in deeper social divisions defined by differential access to private property, wealth, and patronage. Of course, class relationships were still crystallizing, and peasants used "juridical warfare" and other means to censure the moral transgressions of their ethnic authorities. Further, Tapacarí's caciques did not yet monopolize control over all communal resources, and most peasants were not directly subordinate to an ethnic overlord for their own means of subsistence. Class tensions were still submerged in paternalist relations. In order to blunt the raw edge of class relations, ensure the supply of local laborers on their private properties, and conform to colonial standards of legitimate cacique behavior, the caciques subscribed publicly and selectively to Andean norms of reciprocity, gift giving, and feasting (much as their creole hacendado counterparts did on valley estates outside the pueblo real).[32] To be sure, neither wage incentive nor compulsion alone was a sufficient device to recruit or hold laborers. But such documentary evidence of cacique behavior—particularly the self-representation of cacique generosity in court testimony—should not conceal from the historian's view the possibility that Andean lords used the theater of symbolic reciprocity to advance their private economic interests in an internally divided and factious Andean community. Cacique engagement in western-style modes of commodity investment on the interregional grain market was embedded in colonial-Andean forms of paternal exploitation that under-girded a predatory, extractive economy internal to the Indian community. That these ethnic lords manipulated paternal ideology in pursuit of personal gain certainly did not seem to deceive most peasants subject to their demands! While the ideals of kinship and community still governed quotidian agrarian relations among peasant households in the hinterlands of San Augustín de Tapacarí, they barely masked the coercive nature of exchange between Andean lord and peasant. Pressures of forced commercialization turned many commoners against their own caciques in a series of litigious and discursive conflicts that festered in the decades preceding the great pan-Andean rebellion of 1781.

The conflictual power relations in this village were not uncommon in the eighteenth century, as the historical literature has amply documented. But it would be erroneous to imply that the social consequences of Andean intervention in the colonial market was the gradual "cultural contamination" of traditional norms of reciprocity and community. As many of the contributions in this volume show, Andean ayllus and communities assimilated many elements of commercial capitalism into their preexisting social organizations—sometimes with considerable success. That is, many communities were able to harness commercial activity to their own corporate village projects: to consolidate distant lands and diversify their resource base; to rebuild communal stocks of wealth; to finance the ritual and ceremonial life of the community; or to wage a battle in the colonial courts over disputed Indian lands or jurisdiction. Documentation for the early colonial era is replete with examples of Andeans engaging in mercantile practices for social purposes very much at odds with accumulative values. The same is true for the late colonial period. But by then, two centuries of colonialism had left their mark on the rural Andean landscape—eroding, fragmenting, and differentiating Andean communities—leaving many of them with depleted resources and diminished capacity to respond creatively and selectively to mercantile forces. Furthermore, the social character of commercial exchange in the mid-eighteenth century (as compared to the earlier period) became more violent, arbitrary, and rooted in coercive institutions. The margins narrowed for Andeans (both lord and peasant) struggling to negotiate the terms of exchange within the domain of the colonial market. For a variety of reasons, some Andean communities continued to thrive in the mid-eighteenth century, sustaining self-sufficiency while strategically engaging the colonial market and bureaucracy. But those villages that could not effectively censure the coercive practices of ethnic authorities suffered political strife throughout much of this period. Tapacarí, then, was no anomaly in the middle decades of the eighteenth century.

Yet the incursion of colonial market forces and their destructive impact on traditional social relationships in the southern Andes was neither historically inexorable nor progressive. Under different historical circumstances—for example, with the relaxation of extractive pressures in the postcolonial period—the participation of Andean peasants in market transactions might serve to strengthen communal institutions and enhance group self-sufficiency. Market transactions might be subordinated to cultural practices of reciprocity and labor sharing that governed and constrained peasant interactions with outside merchants and labor contractors. We now turn to consider the social significance of local rural markets in present-day Tapacarí.

Reinventing the Marketplace in Twentieth-Century Tapacarí

The contemporary scene of a backwater town, sealed off from the hustle and bustle of Cochabamba's central valleys, has its origins in the political and economic changes that San Augustín experienced around the turn of the twentieth century. The advent of liberalism in the late nineteenth century unshielded Tapacarí, and all corporate Indian communities in Bolivia, and exposed communal lands to outside investors anxious to accumulate property. Tapacarí lost its juridical status as pueblo real and official state sanction of corporate landholding. Thus while the Liro de Córdovas and the Condoris (who continued to dominate the *cacicazgo* after independence) lost state sanction of their status and function as ruling lineages of the former pueblo real, they could deploy the land reforms of the late nineteenth century to expand and legitimate (in Western terms) their private holdings in Tapacarí.

But while the loss of de jure status of communal holdings was a blow to many Andean communities,[33] it was not an unmitigated disaster for Tapacarí peasants in the outlying hamlets and estancias of the district. It spelled the partial dismantling of the political apparatus that had intervened in all facets of peasants' life and work—at least during the heyday of colonialism. No longer could an ethnic elite, based in San Augustín, mandate and enforce labor prestations or the extraction of surplus crops to the state or members of the political hierarchy. The nineteenth-century liberal reforms decentralized regional power and shifted the locus of indigenous authority to Tapacarí's anexos and other hamlets (or comunidades, as they are called today). Muclli, Tallija, Japo, Chaupichalla, Yrutambo, and other rural sites became focal points of communal groups where authority was vested in a local religious and political hierarchy that rotated among comunidad members.[34] Today, the majority of these comunidades are composed of Aymara-speaking peoples who inhabit estancias in the western highlands of Tapacarí. At the local level, traditional principles of reciprocity and redistribution govern patterns of production and exchange in a landscape that affords some degree of verticality and complementary crop production and pastoralism.

The persistence of Andean life ways in the western highlands of Tapacarí bespeaks the uneven effects of successive liberal reforms in the late nineteenth and twentieth centuries. While nineteenth century reforms effectively leveled the indigenous political hierarchy by removing the hereditary caciques, they did not usher in "the age of the latifundium" in Tapacarí. The expansion of private landholding was gradual and mostly confined to the river valley itself.[35] Investors coveted the irrigated lowlands in easy access to the main transit route along the river, and haciendas advanced slowly from Itapaya upland toward the town of San Augustín. The town itself increasingly became the residence of local landowners, merchants, and shopkeepers. Following the agrarian reform of 1953, many of these estates were broken up and the lands parceled out among former *colonos*. But other haciendas remained intact or were reassembled by influential members of the MNR, commercial dealers, and truckers—all of whom constituted a new economic and political elite in the region.

Yet the changing political complexion of San Augustín and the river valley did not encompass the outlying comunidades in the western highlands. By the middle decades of this century, Tapacarí had lost all the earlier advantages of its location and topography that once made it a major commercial thoroughfare and grain marketplace. The arrival of the railroad in 1917 linking Cochabamba to the altiplano provinces and the construction of an all-weather road that traversed the western highlands of Tapacarí diverted most long-distance traffic and trade from the river valley. The old *camino real* was left to decay, and the river was now seen as an obstacle to overland travel rather than as a natural corridor into the western highlands. Several major floods have contributed to the economic isolation and atrophy of San Augustín in recent times. Against this grim backdrop, the focus of economic vitality has shifted from urban center to the rural "periphery": that is, to the southwestern and western highland communities of Tapacarí. The highland peasants have created alternative retail markets responsive to their own economic needs and cultural norms.[36]

Over the past thirty years, Tapacarí peasants have intervened in the market and gradually established a network of subsistence marketplaces, where peasants exercise a considerable degree of control over the terms of exchange and conduct their trading relations in the lingua franca of Quechua (map 4). These ferias have designated market days, coordinated to facilitate the circulation of commodities, buyers, and sellers throughout the region. Some ferias (Japo, Soraje, and Leque) are located in remote niches of the *serranía*, not easily accessible to "outsiders" except by mule or foot. In these marketplaces, barter predominates among traders who exchange the staples of the *canasta familiar*: chuño, potatoes, grains, *huiñapu*, small livestock, wool, textiles, and some folk arts and crafts. Other ferias (Ramada, la Cumbre de Challa, and Pongo) are larger and more accessible to outside traders. They attract some itinerant traders (*ranqueros*) from distant valley towns, such as San Augustín and Quillacollo, and a few wholesale merchants and truckers (*rescatistas*) from the cities of Cochabamba and Oruro.[37] These marketplaces offer a wider variety of commodities, including some "luxury" foodcrops and processed goods (onions, chili peppers, tomatoes, bread, sugar, noodles, and wheat flour), as well as small, manufactured items (tools, candles, matches, aspirin, shampoo, elastic bands, safety pins, and the highly coveted jars of menthol cream). Barter predominates among the highland traders who regularly frequent these ferias, but they simultaneously engage in some monetary transactions with the ranqueros and rescatistas who import luxury and manufactured goods from distant towns and cities.

The ferias are differentiated by a limited degree of specialization. The Ramada feria, for example, is located in the Tapacarí river valley (at an altitude of about 2,900 meters), where ex-colonos and small landowners have begun to shift from maize agriculture to truck farming. Ramada specializes in vegetables and other valley crops and is much more linked to the urban markets of Quillacollo and Cochabamba than to the highland ferias. At the other end of the ecological spectrum, located at an altitude above 4,000 meters, the new feria of la Cumbre de Challa specializes in highland provisions, especially potato and wheat seed. The remote, "inland" feria of Japo, on the other hand, is known for its ceramics.

More important than the variety and range of these markets is the internal organization that peasants have imposed on the forms and terms of exchange. In stark contrast to the big grain market that operated during the eighteenth century at San Augustín, these small peasant retail markets are not dominated by monopolistic hacendados or political overlords. Peasants themselves participate in the markets as both small-scale sellers and buyers of subsistence goods, and even where they engage in monetary transactions with itinerant traders, they have imposed the ethical "rules of the game" within which trade and negotiation take place. At base, the socially defined purpose of trade is the circulation of subsistence goods and the maintenance of the basic social referents of "equitable exchange." In their trading interactions with the itinerant *vallunos* (traders of the valley), the highland peoples of Tapacarí have experienced a long-term decline in the mercantile value of their staple products, as have most highland peasants throughout Bolivia. They have found themselves increasingly marginalized as suppliers of urban markets over the past century. But the local cultural norms of exchange in these ferias provide a small measure of defense against the secular decline of agricultural prices. The feria provides an informal political and moral forum for peasant participants to monitor, discipline, and sometimes censor the economic behavior and practices of itinerant traders. The ranqueros and rescatistas are permitted to conduct their transactions under the vigilence of peasant traders, who outnumber them and engage primarily in horizontal exchanges among themselves. While economic transactions between highland peasants and urban traders are skewed against the peasant producer, the normative order of the highland feria imposes sharp symbolic limits on coerced commerce and oligopsonic privilege. The stereotypic mestizo middleman has no place in this peasant marketplace (see Chapter 12, the conclusion to this volume).

As in many other peasant markets, barter serves as one safeguard against the unleashing of commercial competition in the marketplace.[38] Barter relations ideally bind peasant producers through ongoing interchanges of equivalent values (determined by traditional Andean bulk measurements, rather than by weight). Under ideal conditions, it serves to equalize exchange relations, buffering each trading partner from price fluctuations in the larger market, while marginalizing the role of commercial intermediaries. Of course, in practice, barter takes many forms and may not always represent the exchange of equivalent values. But in general, peasant participants in these ferias have established an etiquette of fair exchange that defines and limits the scope and terms of trade and reduces the vulnerability of peasant households to price fluctuations.

Furthermore, these ferias serve other purposes that interlace the rural estancias and comunidades. They are nodal points of communication, where gossip and news interconnect the communities. They are places where villagers can encounter marriage partners. And, at various times in the agricultural and ritual calendar, the ferias become week-long religious fiestas, where the *hilacatas* and other village authorities converge to participate in intercommunal rituals of *tinqu,* watch their young men compete in soccer matches, and conduct business among themselves. In these special moments of the year, the ferias become a synthesis of quotidien exchanges among peasant communities, reinforcing their mutual dependencies and rivalries that continually redefine local ethnic identities, alliances, and power relations. These moments affirm the feria as the economic and cultural domain of highland peasant traders, consumers, and revelers.

The effort to institutionalize and enforce the morality of exchange is evident in the way peasants have distributed physical space to traders at la Cumbre de Challa, one of the most important highland ferias which was recently relocated. In 1982, highland peasants—who once traded at Challa, a high mountain pass where the old Inca road passed en route to the altiplano—initiated action to relocate the feria at la Cumbre de Challa after the new, paved road opened there (see map 4). But while they seized the opportunity to break their isolation and open trade to the "outside world," these people were unwilling to surrender collective control over the cultural norms of their subsistence retail market. When peasants met to organize the new market, they insisted on imposing strict rules governing local commodity exchange. In guild-like fashion, they agreed to allocate designated places around the market square to known and trusted traders who had an enduring clientele from surrounding peasant communities. The organizers of the new market carefully measured out lots of equal size and assigned them to certain individual traders who "belonged" to the former feria at Challa, as well as to representatives of the estancias and communities of western Tapacarí, whose kin members had traded regularly at the old feria of Challa. The distribution of physical space, which legitimated a trader's regular participation in the marketplace, was governed by noneconomic criteria. Market space was not put up for rent; it was bestowed as a right to certain, familiar traders who conformed to the noncompetitive norms governing exchange and who represented one of the comunidades that participated in the circulation and exchange of agricultural products. In this way, peasants tried to establish a delicate balance among legitimate traders and preempt outside individuals or families from monopolizing market stalls or cornering the market in certain staples.

The cultural logic of the marketplace is also encoded in the staging and choreography of trading interactions over the course of a day. At the feria of la Cumbre de Challa, peasant women of the surrounding highland communities dominate the interior space of the marketplace. They arrive early in the day, carve out their customary niches in the trading space alloted to their community, cover their produce with their dark-colored *aguayos*, and await the gradual arrival of other traders. Most intercommunity exchanges are conducted by peasant women, who spend long days waiting, watching, conversing, and quietly haggling over the balance and importance of the interchange. As the itinerant traders arrive at the feria, the peasant women will wait for the propitious moment to approach their customary *ranquera* to initiate the long, intricate process of negotiation over the relative value of the exchange. To the outsider's eye, their market etiquette is extremely subtle, almost invisible. Aymara- and Quechua-speaking women conduct their negotiations primarily in Quechua through patterned exchanges of whispers, silences, and gestures meant to coax, pressure, or appease their trading partners. The itinerant male peddlars stand in vivid contrast to the market women. Greatly outnumbered by the market women selling all manner of foodcrops and products, the men are purveyors of luxury, manufactured goods who stand "offstage"—at the margins of the feria's interior "feminine space" of quiet, intense negotiation over the staples of life. The most conspicuous male trader is the *ranquero*, the dazzling ambulatory peddlar who shouts out the exotic wares he has to offer. Draped with long, colorful strings of batteries, hair clips, ribbons, mirrors, combs, and shampoo packets, luminous and brilliant in the morning mountain light, the occasional ranquero is the agile harlequin of the marketplace, a magician of modernity. As the flashy "city slicker," whose wares are meant to tempt and delight, he is the perennial outsider whose mercantile behavior violates the norms of serious barter and trade among the women. Cast in the role of harlequin, his outlandish behavior poses little threat to the norms and practices of fair exchange among the women traders. This engendering of mercantile norms thus creates an interior social and ethnic space within which peasant women struggle to protect themselves from extortionist practices.

We are still a long way from understanding the complex and subtle "feedback" effects of the rural markets on social relationships within and between highland rural communities. In what ways has the creation of a subsistence marketing pattern in Tapacarí reinforced or altered reciprocal labor relations among kin members in a given community? To what extent has participation in these subsistence markets led to differentiation among the communities, with some gaining more advantages than others? These questions await further analysis. As we suggested earlier, the circulation of people, goods, and information through the ferias of highland Tapacarí probably has thickened the web of reciprocities and mutual aid among the participating peasant communities. Certainly, the rise of the ferias has not eroded nonmarket forms of circulation. Seasonal exchanges of labor and goods continue to be practiced widely among peasant households belonging to the same or different villages. And itinerant traders from the altiplano also extend the ecological reach of Tapacarí highland and valley communities through their seasonal exchange of specialized products. Still today, traders from the arid plains of Carangas follow llama caravans down through the cordillera into the western highlands of Tapacarí during June, July, and early August, bearing salt in exchange for maize, chili peppers, and other low-altitude crops as they ripen for harvest.

And yet while Tapacarí peasants who participate in the ferias have gained relative autonomy over market conditions, they are not entirely insulated from changes in the national economy. Peasants often must obtain cash to purchase basic processed and manufactured goods in the *ferias mercantiles* of Quillacollo and Cochabamba. Traditionally, highland *tapacareños* have had considerable success in marketing certain strains of potato and grain seed, as well as animal manure in the central valleys of Cochabamba. Valley farmers value these agricultural inputs because they are untainted by chemical fertilizers (unlike the seeds and crops grown in parts of the central valleys). The *chicheras* of Quillacollo also covet the fermented grain (*hui-ñapu*) of *yanahuma*—a sweet, dark wheat seed that is especially favored in the chicherías of Quillacollo (and distinctive from the famous maize chicha of Punata and other towns of the Cliza valley).

Yet however marketable these products, there are social risks involved in such transactions on the "open market" of the Cochabamba valleys. Rigid and unfavorable terms of trade undermine the bargaining position of small-scale sellers from the highlands. Furthermore, with the frequency of drought and poor harvest, many peasant families must sell most of their potato seed, cutting into their subsistence stock and diminishing their capacity to barter with other rural producers. Under these conditions, Tapacarí households are forced to seek temporary, seasonal, or daily wage work outside their rural world. During the 1970s, many Tapacarí peasants migrated seasonally to work in the nearby Kami mines, although the economic recession of the 1980s diminished opportunity for temporary, unskilled workers at Kami. Today, some Tapacarí peasants find casual day labor in the Cochabamba valleys: quarrying lime, making adobe bricks, and as porters hauling sacks of flour and vegetables between trucks, shops, and stalls in the weekly urban markets of Cochabamba and Quillacollo. To the east of Cochabamba, the tropical coca fields and cocaine factories of the Chapare beckon the cash-poor peasant.

Peasant intervention in the contemporary market, then, has set in motion two contradictory tendencies. One tendency derives from the initiatives of Tapacarí peasants to create their own, internal marketing network that draws communities and households together and partially shields them from monopolistic practices and unfavorable terms of trade. Peasants have harnessed commodity exchange to traditional, nonmarket strategies of subsistence and exchange that help peasant households spread risk and extend their reach beyond the narrow limits of their own productive resources. But such hybrid strategies cannot insulate peasant households from the larger commercial forces that draw on the casual labor of peasants subject to corrosive ecological and population pressures. Periodically, subsistence need drives peasants into the wider market economy, where they are subject to impersonal, price-making mechanisms, reduced to common day labor, and stigmatized by valley people as *laris*, or rustic mountain folk.[39] Yet, it is not clear that commercial penetration will undermine peas-

ant control over their retail subsistence markets, forcing more Tapacarí
people to migrate for long stretches of time to tropical coca fields where
wage work is sometimes available, or to enter the bloated informal sector
of Bolivian cities. During the years not plagued by drought, most Tapacarí peasants still maintain an oscillating and precarious balance between
subsistence agriculture and commodity exchange, engaging in commercial
transactions outside the region on a very selective basis. Few people leave
the orbit of their villages, lands, and ferias for periods longer than two
weeks at a time. Subsistence requirements continue to serve as the moti-
vating drive behind peasant participation in the distant, mercantile ferias;
Tapacarí peasants carry their huiñapu and seed bags to Quillacollo and
Cochabamba infrequently—usually when their acute consumptive needs
require it.

For the moment, then, these contradictory market forces do not appear to threaten the social webs of exchange among the peasants of western Tapacarí. However, the plight of the rural and urban poor continues
to worsen under Bolivia's recent neoliberal state policies. The current
national economic crisis has evaporated wage work opportunities in Kami
and in the major tin mines. Small-scale agricultural producers and wage
workers across Bolivia have suffered a deterioration in living standards and
have increasingly resorted to the spreading "hustle economy" of smuggling, cocaine processing, and informal urban marketing.[40] The degree to
which Tapacarí peasants can continue to narrow the margins of unequal
exchange among participants in the rural ferias and contain potentially
divisive class forces within the regional marketing system may serve as an
everyday strategy of defense against Bolivia's deepening economic crisis in
the face of the state's commitment to neoliberalism.

Notes

This chapter is the result of ongoing conversations over several years, encouraged
by Jorge Dandler and Jorge Balán, who first urged the authors to develop this
comparison. Their work on Tapacarí appears elsewhere in more elaborated form.
See Brooke Larson, *Colonialism and Agrarian Transformation in Bolivia: Cochabamba, 1550–1900* (Princeton, 1988), ch. 4, and Rosario León, *Nido de Hombres*

(Cochabamba, forthcoming). All translations from the original Spanish sources in this chapter are by the authors. All abbreviations for the archival material cited here are listed on the first page of the bibliography.

1. Carlos Sempat Assadourian, *El sistema de la economía colonial: Mercado interno, regiones y espacio económico* (Lima, 1982), esp. chs. 1, 3, 4, 6; Assadourian, "La producción de la mercancía dinero en la formación del mercado interno colonial: El caso del espacio peruano, siglo XVI," in Enrique Florescano, ed., *Ensayos sobre el desarrollo económico de México y América Latina, 1500–1975* (Mexico City, 1979), 223–292; Gwendoline B. Cobb, "Supply and Transportation for the Potosí Mines, 1545–1640," *Hispanic American Historical Review* 29:5 (1949): 25–45; and Luís Miguel Glave, "Trajines: Un capítulo en la formación del mercado interno colonial," *Revista Andina* 1.1 (1983): 9–67.

2. On the concept of "vertical control" of multiple ecological tiers through kinship and political networks and dispersed settlement patterns, see John V. Murra, "El 'control vertical' de un máximo de pisos ecológicos en las economías de las sociedades andinas," in Murra, *Formaciones económicas y políticas del mundo andino* (Lima, 1975), 59–116. See also Chapters 2 and 4 in this volume.

3. See the 1557 report of *encomienda* labor deployed for commercial coca production for export to Potosí: "Visita a Pocona, 1557," *Historia y Cultura* (Lima) 4 (1970): 269–308.

4. On Aymara lords' engagement in lucrative commerce, the proceeds of which were channeled toward communal ends, see John V. Murra, "Aymara Lords and Their European Agents at Potosí," *Nova Americana* (Turin) 1 (1978): 231–244; Silvia Rivera Cusicanqui, "El mallku y la sociedad colonial en el siglo XVII: El caso de Jesús de Machaca," *Avances* (La Paz) 1 (1978): 7–27; and Roberto Choque, "Pedro Chipana: Cacique comerciante de Calamarca," *Avances* 1 (1978): 28–32.

5. Forasteros were officially liable for tribute payments, beginning in 1734. But tax collection remained irregular and inefficient in Alto Perú until after the Indian rebellions, in the late 1780s. On tribute and Indian labor, see Nícolas Sánchez Albornoz, *Indios y tributos en el Alto Perú* (Lima, 1978). See also Larson, *Colonialism and Agrarian Transformation in Bolivia*, ch. 3.

6. Of course, the Bourbon state sanctioned and regulated the *repartimiento de mercancías* in order to curb excesses and also to tax the value of repartimientos. But it was quickly recognized that royal regulation was to little effect. Viceroy Manuel de Amat (1761–1776) openly admitted the futility of royal regulation and conceded the fact that the official tariffs served royal, not Indian, interests. Manuel de Amat y Juniente, *Memorial de gobierno*, ed. V. Rodríguez Casado and F. Pérez Embid (Seville, 1947), 189.

7. See Enrique Florescano, *Precios de maíz y crisis agrícolas en México, 1708–1810*

(Mexico City, 1969); also, Lyman J. Johnson and Enrique Tandeter, eds., *Essays on the Price History of Eighteenth-Century Latin America* (Albuquerque, 1990).

8. Enrique Tandeter and Nathan Wachtel, *Precios y producción agraria: Potosí y Charcas en el siglo XVIII* (Buenos Aires, 1983). This article was published in English in Johnson and Tandeter, *Essays on the Price History of Eighteenth-Century Latin America*, 201–276. However, all citations here are to the original Spanish version.

9. Nathan Wachtel, "Los mitimas del valle de Cochabamba: La política de colonización de Wayna Capac," *Historia Boliviana* (Cochabamba) 1.1 (1981): 21–57; reprinted in English in George A. Collier, Renato I. Rosaldo, and John D. Wirth, eds., *The Inca and Aztec States, 1400–1800* (New York, 1982), 199–235. See also John Hyslop, *The Inca Road System* (New York, 1984), ch. 9.
In pre-Hispanic times, Tapacarí was part of the cultural zone of the Aymara-speaking Charcas, who were subdivided into at least four kingdoms (the Soras, Quillacas, Carangas, and Uros). Of those groups, the Soras predominated in the Tapacarí highlands and river valleys. Their reach extended into the Cochabamba valleys, although there is some uncertainty as to whether the Soras expanded into Cochabamba before or during Inca rule, as a result of Cuzco's colonization policies. In any event, the Soras continued to be the predominant ethnic group in the Tapacarí region before and after the Spanish Conquest. See Mercedes del Río, "Simbolismo y poder en Tapacarí," *Revista Andina* 8.1 (1990): 77–106.

10. Francisco de Viedma, *Descripción geográfica y estadística de la Provincia de Santa Cruz* [1788] (Cochabamba, 1969), 137.

11. Francisco de Viedma to Consulado, Buenos Aires, Archivo General de la Nación [hereafter AGN], IX, Intendencia, Leg. 5, 8, 4, September 1, 1787. Viedma was actually describing Arque, Tapacarí's "sister inland port." Tapacarí's grain markets had similar characteristics. Viedma's reports on seasonal and cyclical price movements and harvest conditions are analyzed in more detail in Larson, *Colonialism and Agrarian Transformation in Bolivia*, ch. 6.

12. Viedma to Consulado, AGN, IX, Intendencia, Leg. 5, 8, 3, January 3, 1787; IX, Tribunales, 37, 3, 2, Leg. 124, Exp. 18 and 27 (1798); Viedma, *Descripción geográfica*, 63.

13. Real visita a las molinas de grano, 1799. Archivo Histórico Municipal de Cochabamba [hereafter AHMC], Leg. 1213.

14. Regulations governing church taxes on Indians: Archivo Nacional de Bolivia [hereafter ANB], Exp. no. 192 (1772), and no. 41 (1775); AHMC, Leg. 1181 (1776–1778).

15. Sánchez Albornoz notes that a 1785 *padrón* mentions one link between Tapa-

carí people and the Indians of Poopó, in the province of Paria. Sánchez Albornoz, *Indios y tributos en el Alto Perú,* 160.

16. Tandeter and Wachtel argue that the prevalence of barter of certain indigenous crops (chuño and quinoa) had a stabilizing influence on the fluctuation of prices of those crops in the eighteenth century. *Precios y producción agraria,* 59.

17. Viedma, *Descripción geográfica,* 63–64. For an extended discussion of village society in Tapacarí and other pueblos reales of Cochabamba, see Larson, *Colonialism and Agrarian Transformation in Bolivia,* ch. 4.

18. AGN, XIII, Padrones, 18, 2, 1, Leg. 46; 18, 2, 2, Leg. 47; and 18, 2, 3, Leg. 48.

19. Anexos were composed of several estancias, and were spatial and perhaps kinship units. In certain documents, "anexo" is interchanged with the word "ayllu," which suggests that the Spanish adapted native units of kinship to organize the spatial distribution and administration of Indians in the large Indian district. However, estancias were the microunits of residence, work, and tax collection. It is difficult to determine the extent to which ayllu organization continued to function in the different anexos, especially since forasteros made up the overwhelming majority of tributaries.

20. Sánchez Albornoz, *Indios y tributos en el Alto Perú,* 147.

21. Pedro Condori was appointed cacique gobernador by the corregidor, Bartólome Fiorilo Pérez, and was challenged by Juan Guillermo Liro de Córdova. A partial transcript of the trial is found in the ANB, Exp. no. 46 (1753), *Juicio en grado de apelación sobre los capítulos que se lee a don Juan Guillermo Liro de Córdova, por el indio Blas Condori, sobre las tierras en el pueblo de Tapacarí* (136ff). Another record of the trial, including testimony against the corregidor, is in the Archivo General de las Indias [hereafter AGI], Seville, Charcas, Leg. 367 (1746), *Testimonio de Liro de Córdova contra Pedro Condori.*

22. AGN, XIII, Padrones, 18, 1, 5, Leg. 45.

23. ANB, Exp. no. 139, *Testimonio del teniente de Ayopaya contra el Corregidor de Cochabamba* (1773); AGI, Charcas, Leg. 367 (1746), ff. 197–220 and passim.

24. ANB, Exp. no. 46 (1753), ff. 4–6.

25. Ibid., f. 35.

26. AGI, Charcas, Leg. 367 (1746), ff. 217v.–219; ANB, Exp. no. 46 (1753), ff. 22–23 and passim.

27. ANB, Exp. no. 84 (1782), *Cuaderno de cuentas dadas . . . de las cosechas de las sementeras de los caciques de Tapacarí.*

28. ANB, Exp. no. 46 (1753), ff. 4–6.

29. AGI, Charcas, Leg. 367 (1746), ff. 64v–66v, 73, 219.

30. Viedma, *Descripción geográfica*, 64.

31. AGN, XIII, Padrones, 18, 2, 1, Leg. 47; 18, 2, 2, Leg. 47; and 18, 2, 5, Leg. 150; Sánchez Albornoz, *Indios y tributos en el Alto Perú*, 180–185.

32. ABN, Exp. no. 46 (1753), f. 48v.

33. See, for example, Tristan Platt's discussion of the "first agrarian reform" of the late nineteenth century and its impact on the ayllus of Chayanta: *Estado boliviano y ayllu andino: Tierra y tributo en el norte de Potosí* (Lima, 1982).

34. Ethnographic observations were recorded by León, during several periods of fieldwork in rural Tapacarí, carried out between 1978 and 1983.

35. ANB, Ministerio de Hacienda, Leg. 3 (1870). *Cuadro demonstrativo de las tierras sobrantes . . . de Tarata y Cochabamba, 1866–69*; Federico Blanco, *Diccionario geográfico de la República de Bolivia* (La Paz, 1901), 2:128.

36. The following discussion is based on León's field notes on Tapacarí's ferias, particularly the feria of la Cumbre de Challa. Our analysis of the social significance of these marketplaces draws on some of the literature on peasant marketing systems in other contexts. See especially, Karl Polanyi, *The Great Transformation: The Political and Economic Origins of Our Time* (Boston, [1944] 1957), chs. 4–5; Sidney Mintz, "Internal Market Systems as Mechanisms of Social Articulation," in Vernon F. Ray, ed., *Proceedings of the 1959 Annual Spring Meeting of the American Ethnological Society* (Madison, 1959), 20–30; Carol A. Smith, "How Marketing Systems Affect Economic Opportunity in Agrarian Societies," in Rhoda Halperin and James Dow, eds., *Peasant Livelihood* (New York, 1977), 117–146; Barbara Bradby, "Resistance to Capitalism in the Peruvian Andes," in David Lehmann, ed., *Ecology and Exchange in the Andes* (Cambridge, 1982), 97–122; and Antoinette Fioravanti-Moliniè, "Multi-leveled Andean Society and Market Exchange: The Case of Yucay (Peru)," in Lehmann, *Ecology and Exchange*, 211–230.

37. In popular usage, "ranquero" refers to an itinerant peddlar, most often a woman (*ranquera*), who purchases wholesale allotments of goods, a small portion of which she transports and sells retail in the peasant marketplaces of the western highlands (*las ferias de arriba*). Popular stereotypes of the ranquera who frequents the ferias of Tapacarí construct images of a *chola* trader, who engages in a variety of livelihood activities, including small-scale agriculture, chicha-making, and itinerant trade. She is one who maintains ongoing, personalized relations with her highland trading clients of the ferias. For a somewhat different characterization of the ranquera in the Tiraque area on the eastern edges of the Cliza basin, see María L. Lagos, *Autonomy and Power: The Dynamics of Class and Culture in Rural Bolivia* (Philadelphia, 1994), 103, 112. The more common term, rescatista or *rescatiri*, indicates a wholesale dealer, often a muleteer or trucker, who sells mainly manufactured products.

38. For theoretical discussion, see Polanyi, *Great Transformation*, 56–62, and Bradby, "Resistance to Capitalism." For a pointed summary of different approaches to the issue of barter and cash sale, as well as a fascinating case study, see Benjamin S. Orlove, "Barter and Cash Sale on Lake Titicaca: A Test of Competing Approaches," *Current Anthropology* 27.2 (1986): 85–106.

39. In Inca and early colonial times, the Aymara word *lari lari* identified the highland inhabitants of western Tapacarí, who trapped vicuña for their fine-quality wool. Under the Incas, the Soras of the valley of Sipesipe wove the vicuña wool into fine *cumbi* cloth for export to their imperial overlords. (See Mercedes del Río, "Simbolismo y poder en Tapacarí," p. 101.) Today, *lari* is used by Spanish and Quechua-speaking people of the valleys to stigmatize an Aymara-speaking person of highland Tapacarí, Arque, or Ayopaya; *lari* signifies a "poor, ignorant Indian."

40. Further, the ayllus of highland Tapacarí have confronted the onslaught of nongovernmental organizations (NGOs) since the mid-1980s. These organizations, along with leftist political parties, have become important political actors in many regions of Bolivia, engineering microdevelopment projects and clientelistic forms of organization in the interior of ayllu society. The local impact of these new forms of political intervention, attendant upon the reestablishment of democratic government committed to economic liberalization in Bolivia since the early 1980s, merits more critical social analysis. But see Silvia Rivera Cusicanqui, "Liberal Democracy and Ayllu Democracy in Bolivia: The Case of Northern Potosí," *Journal of Development Studies* 26.4 (1990): 97–121, and Filemón Escobar, "El neoliberalismo apunta de muerte a las culturas originarias," *Autodeterminación* (La Paz) 9 (1991): 43–50.

IV

Negotiating the Meanings of Market

Exchange: Community and Hierarchy

in Three Andean Contexts

9

Ethnic Calendars and Market Interventions among

the *Ayllus* of Lipes during the Nineteenth Century

TRISTAN PLATT

> If the Indian did not have to pay tribute and tithes, if he were not obliged to pay for feast days and to pay a duty to the parish on the occasions of birth, death, and marriage, and if he had not created for himself the need to get drunk at all these religious festivals . . . then he would certainly work a lot less than he does today . . . , because the Indian has no concept of accumulation, no idea of wealth. He works only because force and custom have imposed these needs upon him.—Pedro Vargas, Potosí, 1864

> The native of Lipes is a person worthy of our admiration. . . . He pays his tribute punctually; he is the support of the mine owner; his time is perfectly allocated; and in the family no one is exempt from a share in the work.—Demetrio Calvimonte, Sucre, 1884

Writing in the middle of the last century, Pedro Vargas, a mine owner in Republican Potosí, paints a liberal picture of the tribute-paying Bolivian Indian as an irrational being on account of his stubborn "resistance to the market."[1] In some studies devoted to present-day Andean societies, the idea of indigenous "resistance" to the market is still present: it was encouraged when it became clear how limited the development of marketplaces in pre-Hispanic altiplano societies had been, with their tendency to favor redistributive methods for ensuring the circulation of goods and services between different ecological and social milieux. The existence today of nonmercantile systems of "vertical distribution" is therefore interpreted as evidence of the "survival" of a preexisting "ideal of self-sufficiency" in the face of gradual mercantile erosion.[2] Elsewhere, while restoring its historical dimensions to the role of the Indian population in the Potosí mining market during the colonial period, Carlos Sempat Assadourian also postulates a process of "subordination" of Andean social organization to the "power of the commodity."[3]

Both accounts privilege the notion of *violence* as the driving force behind Indian market participation. This is understandable, given the importance of fiscal and religious pressures on the domestic and collective economy of Andean ethnic groups. In certain circumstances, protests by Indians facing the problem of finding money for tribute do suggest a situation of "forced commercialization,"[4] in which peasant products must often be sold at "very low prices."[5] Nevertheless, other studies have shown how the commercial success of some *mallku* (Aymara lords) could guarantee the survival of their ethnic groups in the face of fiscal pressures.[6] The preference shown by certain ethnic groups for the commutation of labor (*mit'a*) to money through successful intervention in the Potosí market[7] also confirms that market participation was sometimes considered a positive option in a context where money had penetrated and unified many "spheres of exchange"[8] which, before the European invasion, had been kept separate. From this point of view, protests against "forced commercialization" may often reflect either a specific conjuncture of commercial crisis or a negotiating tactic on the part of the indigenous population, rather than any formal incompatibility between distinct forms of economic reasoning.

If we accept that intervention in the market could represent an *Indian strategy* rather than simply a colonial imposition, how did Andean ethnic groups manage to establish a balance between their own systems of production, nonmonetary exchange, and commercial transactions? What level of monetarization was desirable for their social reproduction in any specific conjuncture? What factors might combine to modify the relationship between the different kinds of exchange? One hypothesis proposes a direct link at the end of the eighteenth century between production, prices, and the volume of goods designed for barter.[9] Here, extremely high or low prices produce the same result: whether because of the high price of consumer goods in the market or because of a lack of sufficient revenue to make the customary purchases, saleable commodities are diverted toward nonmonetary exchange between direct producers, apart from those whose sale is forced by fiscal pressures. In both cases, contrary to the hypothesis of pure "violence," peasant behavior is thought to be based rather on economic calculation and a "rational" sensitivity on the part of the mass of Indian tributaries to annual fluctuations in prices. In this sense, then, these authors seem to imply that the increase of nonmonetary exchange, resulting from the reduced demand for costly consumer goods and/or the "forced commercialization" of cheap Indian products, operates as a kind of price regulator that pulls prices back toward the mean.

One problem[10] with this elegant hypothesis lies in its apparent incompatibility with an aspect of nonmonetary exchange brought out by ethnographic studies.[11] The exchange relationship cannot be broken off and then resumed at any given moment; it represents a long-term security for the two parties involved, in the face of fluctuations in their respective conditions of production, which requires both elasticity in the terms of exchange from one year to the next and the forging of a durable sociocultural link. Where does this leave us, then? Can we combine certain elements from each hypothesis without resorting to either extreme: the violence of resistance and subordination on the one hand, and pure commercial reason on the other?

The apparent contradiction can be attributed, to some extent, to a perspective developed *from* the market. Here I shall adopt the opposite approach, on the basis of ethnographic research in Andean peasant communities.[12] A case study will allow us to situate the commercial activities of tributary Indians within the wider context of their reproductive strategies, which follow the seasonal rhythms of an annual calendar marked by Catholic religious feasts. This calendar includes the collective organization and distribution of certain productive resources, the local movement of goods and services, and the development of important interregional circuits of monetary and nonmonetary exchange. Thus, the desire for coin will appear, in the first instance, as *one* specific use of *mensual time*, which must be coordinated with the rhythm of the productive process, the six-monthly payment of tribute, and periodical cues for increased expenditure (especially during religious feasts). In this way, we can understand how an interest in profit maximization can be uppermost at certain times of the year, while at other times it may occupy a lower position in the Indian scale of priorities: various "economic" rationalities may be adopted in turn by the same subject to fit in with his calendar of activities.

The choice of a case study from the nineteenth century has obvious disadvantages over a contemporary ethnographic example: documentary information is necessarily less complete than fieldwork for an understanding of local strategies. It will allow us, however, to demonstrate the possibility, given adequate documentary resources, of interpreting ethnic economic behavior during the early Republican period, for which very few case studies exist. Questions raised will suggest avenues for similar studies in the colonial period, as well as transforming the perspective from which we can view later twentieth-century developments. A long-durational approach will also show how these local cultures and economies changed in relation to transformations in the national and international context, shedding new light on the Bolivian rural experience of liberal economic policies.[13] The effort to establish the "lower limit" of monetarization required by tributary obligations ("forced commercialization") provides a methodologically necessary point of departure for determining the circumstances in which higher levels of domestic monetarization could also be achieved by certain social groups.

The study is drawn from the experience of sixteen *ayllus*, or ethnic groups, spread over the three cantons of the Potosí province of Lipes (Table 9.1). This province lies in the far southwest of Bolivia, and its vast spaces, swept by wind and biting cold,[14] offer the full range of high Andean natural resources. Here people hunt for rhea, vizcacha, vicuña, and chinchilla; flamingo eggs are gathered on the shores of the lagoons; cacti are cut for roofing and house doors;[15] and *llullucha* (freshwater laverbread or kelp[16]) and salt are used as items of exchange with people living on the eastern slopes of the cordillera. Farming is both pastoral, involving the raising of vast herds of camelids and other animals, and agrarian, with a land-extensive agricultural system based on long cycles of rotation appropriate to these high altitudes (nearly 4,000 meters above sea level). Mineral resources are equally abundant,[17] although in the nineteenth century the province remained on the fringe of the great silver boom that took place in other provinces of Potosí between 1870 and 1900.[18]

Archival evidence enables us to observe how the impact of liberal policies in the second half of the nineteenth century marginalized many ayllus that, at the beginning of the Republic, had enjoyed greater commercial opportunities. This is important in order to rebut the common Whig assumption that Indian approaches to the market only began to intensify

Table 9.1. Distribution of the Tributary Population of Lipes (1841–1877)
According to *Ayllu* and Canton

Canton and Ayllu	1841	1846	1854	1862	1867	1871	1877
San Cristóbal							
Cañiza	208	230	266	251	273	283	336
Colcha	104	118	137	150	157	165	175
San Pedro de Quemes	16	23	24	24	22	24	34
Santiago	46	57	59	67	71	82	87
San Juan	43	47	39	48	55	57	60
San Agustín	55	55	65	73	79	85	92
Subtotal	472	530	590	613	657	696	784
Llica and Tagua							
Aillo Grande	76	74	74	81	95	103	104
Caguana	71	66	76	82	90	90	91
Guanaque	28	27	37	38	39	41	47
Hornillos	68	79	93	100	108	116	147
Tagua (Aransaya y Maransaya)	98	111	133	154	184	206	239
Subtotal	341	357	413	455	516	556	628
San Pablo							
Pololos	143	148	145	140	140	153	155
Santa Isabel	82	78	77	70	78	75	91
San Antonio de Lipes	25	34	32	32	35	34	37
San Antonio de Esmoruco	64	67	75	63	69	70	66
Lagunillas	54	55	48	38	38	41	44
Subtotal	368	382	377	343	360	373	393
Total	1,181	1,269	1,380	1,411	1,533	1,625	1,805

Source: ANB Revistas Nos 228a, 228b, 229a, 230, 231a, 233, 234. *Estados Generales de la Provincia.*

during recent decades of "development" in a unidirectional advance toward "progress." Only in 1872 was the smuggling of silver bullion abroad legalized, thus reducing the number of marks coined in the mint at Potosí and initiating the transnationalization of mining capital and the partial conversion of the mining camps into economic enclaves connected directly to the ports of exportation. Money was exported abroad as bullion, leaving the rural areas destitute. The scarcity of money was exacerbated by the payment of dividends to shareholders living overseas;[19] above all, mining fever after the Pacific War (1879–1883) unleashed a wave of speculation during which foreign goods were imported that could only be paid for by exporting yet more silver currency.[20] Further aggravated by the arrival of the railway from Antofagasta to Uyuni (1889) and Oruro (1892), these factors produced a monetary crisis that threatened to eliminate the petty transactions of many Lipes tributaries.

The rise in the importance of nonmonetary exchange at the end of the century was due not so much to the calculations that the ayllus made in the face of annual price fluctuations (as suggested by Tandeter and Wachtel), but rather to a profound change in the nature and orientation of urban and mining demand. At the beginning of the twentieth century, many tributaries in fact found themselves more "marginalized" in relation to the market than at the beginning of the Republic, and prices were in no way "regulated" as a result. Paradoxically, this was due to the economic success of that very liberalism which, in the middle of the nineteenth century, had denounced their attitudes as "premercantile" and irrational.

Ethnic Calendars in the Province of Lipes

During the early decades of the Republic (declared in 1825), the Bolivian "Tributary State" was sustained, though on a reduced scale, by the economic system established during the colonial period. Silver production in Potosí continued to supply the raw material for the state monetary industry. Refined metal was transported by pack animal from many local refineries to Potosí, where it would be bought at fixed prices by the Banco Nacional de Rescates. Once the silver had been purified to a common standard, the Bank re-sold it to the National Mint to be turned into coin. Mining inputs (with the exception of mercury and iron, imported from Spain), including the laborers and their means of subsistence, were provided by the various provincial economies, within the framework of a regional division of labor. We shall attempt to identify the role played by the ayllus of Lipes within the mercantile area articulated by Potosí coin.

On the other hand, the ecosystem of the Lipes altiplano is character-

Table 9.2. Animal Distribution in Lipes, 1843

Animal	San Cristóbal	San Pablo	Llica and Tagua	Total
Llamas	17,201	12,810	4,000	34,011
Sheep	5,389	7,381	2,346	15,116
Mules	244	6	10	260
Donkeys	2,030	585	358	2,973
Horses	30	1	0	31
Cows	109	14	9	132
Goats	526	1,225	0	1,751

Source: ANB MH T 94, No 35. *Rasón estadística formada en San Cristóbal, Capital de la Provincia de Lipes en 8 de Diciembre de 1843.*

ized, to an extreme degree, by the climatic instability that compels some high-Andean societies to complement their local resources with sources of subsistence in the area.[21] Privileged access to pack animals, and to a range of products foreign to the valleys and lowlands, has favored an ancient model of seasonal migrations, directed toward the exchange of products between the two ecological zones.[22] Although during the nineteenth century Lipes pastoralists kept up these vertical relations with both sides of the cordillera, they had no *direct* access to valley lands. The rich resources of the high Andes favored a modification of practices that were common further north: instead of the bizonal or "vertical" production, typical of the province of Chayanta for example,[23] ecological complementarity in Lipes was based on an intensification of long-distance exchange relations.[24]

The increasing aridity to the south of the province[25] is reflected in the differences between the agricultural and stock-rearing resources of each of the three cantons (Tables 9.2, 9.3, and 9.4; see Map 5). In the north, agricultural production in Llica and Tagua is characterized by a strong preponderance of nonirrigated land (with the exception of the ayllu of Caguana); animal resources too are limited, though still important as a source of manure and transport. In the south, San Pablo is barely able to produce a tiny amount of fodder for its donkeys and is devoted almost entirely to raising pastoral animals for transport and for wool—mainly llamas and sheep. In the center, San Cristóbal combines both kinds of production, including a large number of mules, cows, and horses, thanks

Table 9.3. Seed Sown (Production in Quintales) in Lipes, 1843

Canton	Quinoa	Potatoes	Barley
Llica and Tagua	3,425	400	140
San Cristóbal	350	200	220
San Pablo	—	—	60

Source: See Table 2.

to a substantial yearly crop of barley on well-irrigated land: only the ayllu of Cañiza shares San Pablo's lack of cultivated land.

The paths traced by the *llameros* across the breadth of the cordillera must be seen as related not only to human subsistence, but also to the reproduction of their herds. In contrast to the damper pastures of southern Peru,[26] those of the altiplano of Lipes suffer regularly from droughts that precede the first rains of December.[27] Here, the descent of the herds from the beginning of April, when the dry season begins, must also be considered as a way of incorporating into the herding cycle the pastures of Chichas and Tarija in the eastern valleys and the oases of Atacama and Tarapacá in the desert region of the Pacific.

Upon the seasonal rhythm of the climate is superimposed the six-monthly pressure of the fiscal calendar: the gathering of tribute makes for two other fixed dates in the overall provincial calendar. Although the two ceremonies were named after the solstice festivals—St. John's Day and Christmas—the precise dates for payment varied in each province according to the demands of each ethnic calendar.[28] In 1835, the governor of Lipes referred to "the long-established custom whereby these [Indian] collectors deliver in February the tribute due at Christmas, and at the end of August that due on St. John's Day."[29] Every six months, tributaries had to make a payment of 3 pesos 4 reales to their collectors. We must therefore ask how this tributary coin came to be acquired in the months preceding the dates when it was to be paid, then look for factors that may have permitted higher levels of monetary income to be reached under certain circumstances.

Table 9.5, which shows the declared occupations of 181 tributaries in 1867, gives us the first hint of the Indians' trading activities. The differences already mentioned between the economic resources of each canton

Table 9.4. Distribution of Lands and Tributaries in Lipes, 1856

| Canton and Ayllu | Tributaries with Land | | Cultivated Land | |
	"Eligible"	"Underage"	Nonirrigated	Irrigated
Llica and Tagua				
Aillo Grande	74	25	479	0
Caguana	76	17	190	93
Hormillos	93	20	298	1
Guanaque	37	10	115	6
Tagua	133	32	847	10
San Cristóbal				
Cañiza	266	64	0	0
Colcha	137	39	290	23
San Pedro de Quemes	24	6	0	27
Santiago	59	23	16	62
San Juan	39	14	15	8
San Agustín	65	27	8	28
San Pablo				
Pololos	145	37	0	0
Santa Isabel	77	15	0	0
San Antonio de Lipes	32	20	0	0
San Antonio de Esmoruco	75	8	5	5
Lagunillas	48	7	0	0
Total	1,380	364	2,238	266

Source: AHP PD 830, No 19. *Cuadro que precenta el Gobernador de la Provincia de Lipez, por orden de SSY el Prefecto del Departamento.* Juan Bta Aramayo, San Cristóbal, Junio 26 de 1856.

are clear. Farming is clearly predominant in Llica and Tagua; nevertheless, we shall see how some tributaries depended more on their pack animals, which were driven to the Pacific oases after the harvest.[30]

In San Pablo, 25 percent appear to be male weavers (*tejedores*), a figure which is clearly related to the importance of sheep-farming in the canton (Table 9.2),[31] although most of the inhabitants of San Pablo fall within the category of drovers (*arrieros*). Multiple activities can be observed as well in San Cristóbal, where salt traders (*salineros*) used their own herds

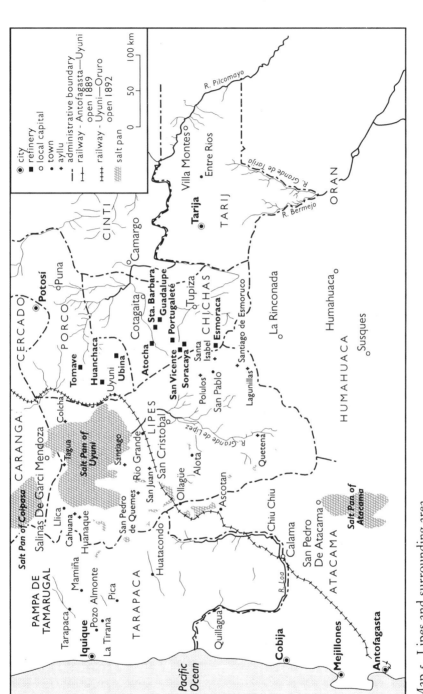

Map 5. Lipes and surrounding area.

Table 9.5. Declared Occupation of the Tributaries of Lipes, 1867

Occupation	San Cristóbal		Llica and Tagua		San Pablo		Total	
	No.	%	No.	%	No.	%	No.	%
Drovers	27	26	0	0	42	75	69	39
Farmers	4	4	21	91	0	0	25	14
Salt traders	68	67	0	0	0	0	68	37
Miners	2	2	0	0	0	0	2	1
Weavers	0	0	0	0	14	25	14	8
Others	1	1	2	9	0	0	3	1
Total	102	56	23	13	56	31	181	100

Source: ANB Revistas 231a. *Documentos pertenecientes a la revista de la Provincia de Lipes practicada por el Apoderado Fiscal Antolin Murillo en el pasado año de 1867* . . . The sample consists of Indian witnesses to Certificates of Absence, who had to declare their occupations.

to transport salt to the silver refineries and to consumers in the eastern valleys.[32] But here the distinction between salt traders and drovers marks an important contrast among the inhabitants (as we shall see); and the smaller number of farmers (*agricultores*) can be explained, in relation to the information given in Table 9.4, in terms of the predominance of barley production among the drovers who needed fodder for their donkeys and mules (Tables 9.2 and 9.3).[33] We shall now examine the precise situation within each canton in greater detail.

Llica and Tagua: Speculation and Security

This canton, with its essentially Indian population,[34] is situated on the edge of the great salt pan of Uyuni. The road to the Pacific coast crosses its territory, linking the neighboring ayllus of Salinas de Garci Mendoza (Department of Oruro) with the "Province of Tarapacá and the important towns of Pica and the rest . . . and to their sea-ports of Iquique and Pisagua."[35] Looking down toward the nitrate fields of Peru and the oases of the coastal desert, Llica and Tagua present us with a paradox: on the one hand, abundant sources of wealth—flourishing potato and quinoa production (Table 9.3) and a high level of trade—and, on the other, great instability due to the uncertainties of the climate that regularly encourages both seasonal and definitive emigration.

In 1860 we find evidence from Tagua of the productive capacities and volume of trade handled by sixty-four tributaries, who had been allotted "innumerable little plots of land" during the government of Belzú (1848–1855). According to Carlos Enrique Quiróz, the land inspector:

> [their allotments were] in excess of 100 *cordeladas* for each tribute-payer, and of such fertile land that even 20 *cordeladas* are still excessive, because in Chayanta one or two *cordeladas* are shared out and from this they pay their tribute, rents, tithes, first-fruits and a thousand other tasks and labors, and these people pay no more than their 7 pesos a year, harvesting 600 loads of potatoes, and from one to two hundred loads of quinoa, both the most exquisite products in the Republic, which they then sell in the nitrate-works at Pica at 5 or 6 or sometimes even 12 pesos the load.[36]

The suggestive comparison with the more northerly province of Chayanta confirms the need for long-term cycles of crop rotation and land-extensive agriculture in the arid plateau of northern Lipes: significantly, this "marginal" land was capable of sustaining a flourishing trade with the towns of the nitrate desert.

Journeys down to the desert were concentrated in August, when farming jobs were finished. As the provincial subprefect tells us at the end of July 1895, "this is the time of year in the Canton of Llica and the Vice-Canton of Tagua when all the Indians come together, but later on they set off."[37] They return for the big festival at Colcha in September. At this high point of the year, even the natives of Chichas and Tarapacá make their way up to the altiplano to exchange products from both sides of the cordillera.[38] In September, tributaries also had to find the 3 pesos and 4 reales that made up the St. John's Day tribute. In 1860 Quiroz suggests that the annual tribute (7 pesos) seldom represented more than two llama loads of four *arrobas* each (one arroba = twenty-five pounds). If we assume an average of six load-bearing llamas per tribute payer between 1841 and 1843,[39] they would still have enough loads left to exchange in the oases, and also to sell in order to be able to make purchases locally or, on their return, at the fair in Colcha. In this way, farmers were able to remain on the altiplano during the growing months (December–May), and Christmas tribute payments in February were managed without another journey before the following August.

But the agricultural risks at these altitudes are great. As the representatives of the *ayllus* declared in 1866: "The harvest . . . depends on the year: if it is a rainy year, then we gather in some sort of harvest, but if it is not, and the frosts come, as is always happening, then the seed, the money invested, the labor all is lost."[40] Commenting on the critical situation of 1861–1862, which had forced some tributaries to emigrate, they explained:

Because of the frosts, and because they had nothing with which or from which to pay the unavoidable tribute, force and necessity drove them to give it up, and to give themselves up to looking for work in order to make a living, as do many Indians by working in the nitrate-works (*oficinas*) on the coast.[41]

For some, therefore, the return to the altiplano would be postponed for several years: their migration could become definitive.[42] In the case of Pedro and Eugenio Condori from San Pedro de Quemes (San Cristóbal), the Peruvian lieutenant governor of their new town of residence, Huatacondo, sent a letter to the Bolivian governor of Lipes in 1867, requesting that their names be struck off the cantonal register of tributaries (*padrón*), so as to save the collectors the trouble of traveling all the way to the coast to collect tribute from the absentees.[43]

The places of residence of those who left the province "for good" in 1867 are indicated in Table 9.6. As we would expect, migrants from Llica and Tagua are to be found in the nitrate fields of Tarapacá; those from San Pablo, on the other hand, are to be found on the eastern slopes of the cordillera; and those from San Cristóbal have divided themselves between both sides of the cordillera. The data suggest prolonged stays in the same places that the inhabitants of each canton were already familiar with from their seasonal movements, but without ruling out the possibility of occasional return visits to their places of origin.[44]

Migrants would therefore have experience of seasonal work in Tarapacá before settling there for a longer stay. In July 1873, the corregidor of Llica noted that, "since we are situated near the coast, the tributaries always go to exchange their meager production, and to work in the nitrate-fields, and their bosses pay them for their labor with banknotes."[45] This suggests that the poorest farmers used a recurring strategy, which was also avail-

Table 9.6. Destination of Definitive Migrants from Lipes, 1867

Destinations	San Cristóbal		Llica		San Pablo		Total	
	No.	%	No.	%	No.	%	No.	%
Peru (Nitrate companies)	7	58	14	100	0	0	21	70
Mining centres (Chichas, Porco)	2	17	0	0	3	75	5	17
Tarija	2	17	0	0	0	0	2	7
Chiu-chiu (Atacama)	1	8	0	0	0	0	1	3
Oran (Argentina)	0	0	0	0	1	25	1	3
Total	12	40	14	47	4	13	30	100

Source: ANB Revisitas 231a (1867). *Documentos pertenecientes a la revisita de la Provincia de Lipes practicada por el Apoderado Fiscal Antolín Murillo en el pasado año de 1867. . . .* The sample consists of those migrants whose Certificates of Absence show the destination of their migration.

able as a contingency solution to those better off when hit by a bad year. Only the biggest producers (such as the sixty-four more fortunate ones in Tagua) would enjoy wider margins than the others, enabling them to take advantage of a general scarcity to the extent of asking for prices of up to 12 pesos a load in Tarapacá.

A final option was the transport of imported goods. In June 1854 we find one-third of tributaries already absent "down in the valleys, carrying goods from overseas to the consumers' marketplaces."[46] Some tributaries had their home base high up in the cordillera, above the upper limit of cultivable land (c. 4,200 meters above sea level), and they depended on being able to sell the labor of their pack animals if they were not to take wage labor in the nitrate fields. The rest of them supplemented their farm income with a certain amount of freight work, becoming part of the constant traffic that in the dry season plied up and down between the coast and the consumer towns on the altiplano.[47] In 1881, for example, we find a consignment of flour, Peruvian olive oil, tea, sardines, canned food, kerosene, cigarette paper, and writing paper ordered from Salinas de Garci Mendoza for consumption by this town.[48] And in 1890 the Indians of Llica consulted the prefect of Potosí concerning the dues they should pay "on rice, flour, sugar, medicines, and goods,"[49] all of which were brought from the coast under Chilean occupation since the Pacific War.

The importance of pack animals suggests the following interpretation of the available evidence concerning the economy of this canton. Although the highest monetary incomes (far exceeding the tribute) might come from agricultural specialization, the climatic uncertainties of the high Andes made farming alone a dangerously speculative occupation for most Indians. These domestic units found themselves caught between two extremes: on the one hand, a high degree of agricultural prosperity, which might nevertheless collapse into definitive emigration; on the other, a more secure base in the pack-animal business with the additional option of seasonal wage-labor. Out of the hazardous interplay between these two strategies came the opportunity for some to maximize advantages in such a way that a bad year would not bring them to the edge of ruin.

To sum up, then, the majority of tributaries from Llica and Tagua stayed on the altiplano during the months most favorable to farming (December–May), paying their Christmas tribute in February with whatever money they had accumulated during the previous year. A handful of drovers would perhaps take the long road to the coast before the first seasonal journeys of June and July. But as soon as August came, there would be a whole month of continuous journeys that would end in September with everyone returning to the altiplano for the festival of Colcha and the payment of the St. John's Day tribute.

San Cristóbal: Between Salt and Freight

San Cristóbal was the provincial capital throughout the nineteenth century. When Lipes was divided into two provinces in 1885, and what was left of the former province of Atacama (now mostly occupied by Chile and Argentina) was added to it, San Pablo rose in importance to become the capital of a new province—South Lipes; but San Cristóbal remained as the capital of the province of North Lipes. Situated in the middle, between Llica and San Pablo, and halfway between Potosí and Cobija, San Cristóbal gazes in both directions: toward the valleys and passes of the eastern slopes, and toward the western desert of Atacama. Each side of the cordillera is associated with a different commercial activity, and the tributaries of San Cristóbal had to adjust their relationship with each, according to changes in demand.

Table 9.7. Sales of Salt Made by the Salt Traders of San Cristóbal, 1842

Province	Refinery	Owner	Annual Con-sump-tion (qq)	Distance (leagues)	Price (reales)	Value (pesos)
Chichas	San Joaquín (Oploca)	José Calisto Yáñez	2,000	48	ND[4r]	1,000
	Guadalupe	José Sánchez de Resa	2,000	30	3r	750
	Soracaya	Diego Felipe de Obando	2,000	30	3r	750
	Concepción	Gregorio Ramírez	2,000	50	4r	1,000
	Atocha	Apolinar García	660	ND	3r	247.5
	San Ignacio	Manuel Antonio Yáñez	750	52	4r	375
	Carmen (Esmoraca)	Julian Mendivil	1,000	40	[4r]	500
Porco	Huanchaca	Mariano Ramírez	5,148 [2,574]	ND	2r	1,287 [643.5]
	Total		15,558 [12,984]			5,909.5 [5,266]

Source: ANB MH T.94, no 35 (1842). *Estado de la industria mineralógica.*
Note: Numbers in brackets indicate inferred or probable price.

Let us examine first the importance of salt, the collection and distribution of which had traditionally rested in the hands of the tributaries of those *ayllus* living on the edge of the great salt pan of Uyuni. Since the first decades of the Republic, the salt traders of San Cristóbal had kept their monopoly on the supply of salt to most of the silver refineries between Huanchaca and the Argentine frontier (see Map 5). Table 9.7 shows the amount of salt sold by the llama herders to the administrators of the refineries in 1842. Note that the price per quintal (100 pounds, or four arrobas) varied according to the distance between the salt pan and the point of sale: it was calculated according to the *animal labor time* spent on each journey. With the exception of Huanchaca, payment was entirely in hard cash; in Huanchaca, half the payment was in money, and the other half in kind—in other words, some 2,574 quintales had to be exchanged for money.[50] The total amount exchanged for money would then be almost 13,000 quintales, equivalent to the same number of llama loads of four arrobas each.

In general terms, it appears that the level of monetarization enjoyed by the salt traders during this period easily exceeded the "lower limit" represented by the tribute burden: in 1841, tribute paid by the entire canton amounted to $3,304,[51] and the monetary returns proceeding exclusively from salt came to $5,266 in 1842 (Table 9.7). But what proportion of the canton's population were salt traders? Table 9.5 suggests a figure of 67 percent in 1867. Given that the population of the canton was 657 tributaries in that year,[52] there may have been about 440 salt traders and 217 others, drovers who hired out their pack animals for freight. In 1841 the proportion of drovers was probably higher, for reasons to be discussed later. If, therefore, we reduce the proportion to 60 percent over a tribute-paying population of 472,[53] we get 283 salt traders and 189 pack animal owners. According to this hypothesis, each salt worker should receive about 18 pesos per annum, to give a total of $5,266.

A different calculation suggests that the llamas were mainly in the hands of the salt traders, with a corresponding concentration of donkeys and mules in the coastal transport trade. The advantage of llamas is that they find their own forage while traveling, but their labor is subject to seasonal limitations. In 1842 the director of the salt refinery at Guadalupe bought about 2,000 quintales of salt, "and there were employed in this exercise about 100 salt traders, who had charge of nearly 3,000 llamas,"[54] that is, roughly thirty llamas per salt worker. If we project this proportion onto the entire population of salt traders, we find that the 283 salt traders of the canton would own between them 8,490 pack animals. Data from San Pablo indicates that the herds were made up of more or less equal numbers of male and female animals,[55] and the figure of 8,490 in fact comes close to being half the 17,201 llamas registered in the canton in 1843 (Table 9.2). From this we may infer that each salt worker had to make some 1.8 journeys each year from Uyuni, to supply the total of 15,558 loads of salt consumed by the refineries in 1842 (Table 9.7), and earn an amount far greater than the 7 pesos a year required by the tribute collectors.[56]

We should not insist too much on the exactness of the figures: their purpose is simply to establish orders of activity and approximate levels of monetary income to see how they relate to the calendar and to the fixed amount of tribute. Moreover, it is clear that the administrators of the salt refineries could not count on getting a regular supply of salt all year round: in November 1842 and August 1856, they complained of irregularities in the supply, probably due to the fact that llama transport was seasonal.[57] Although we lack the sort of information that will allow us to analyze the San Pablo calendar in greater detail, a comment by the subprefect of North Lipes in July 1895 suggests that the salt traders of San Cristóbal were able to satisfy the demand only between January and June: "Concerning the Indians of this capital, Colcha and other places . . . the fact is . . . that in September they are all gathered together and at present all are off to the valleys in order to stock up with grains, flour, etc."[58] In other words, the visits to the refineries in fact represented only the first leg of a longer journey that took the salt traders and their llamas as far as "the valleys of Tarija, to find provisions in exchange for the salt they carry."[59] On this last stage, transactions were mainly carried out through exchange in kind, without using the medium of money. When September came, the salt traders would return to the altiplano to pay the St. John's Day tribute and to take part in the festival at Colcha, using the money saved mainly during the first half of the year. The Christmas tribute, on the other hand, would probably be paid in February with revenues from the first sales made in January to the nearest refineries (e.g., Huanchaca).

The expansion of the mining market in the second half of the century[60] also saw a great rise in the demand for salt: in 1894, for example, the refinery at Guadalupe enjoyed an annual consumption of 20,000 quintales of salt[61] as against a mere 2,000 quintales in 1842. How was this increase in demand satisfied? Moreover, the increase was temporary insofar as, during the decade of the 1890s, businesses began to take advantage of lower transport costs due to the construction of the Antofagasta railway, exporting crude ore to be refined outside the country. What impact did the disappearance of the industrial market in salt have on the ayllus of San Cristóbal? Before we answer these questions, let us look at the development of the transport business (*arriería*) that ran between Potosí and the Pacific.

New opportunities for Indian drovers had grown since 1829 when the small bay of Cobija was developed as a national port by the government of Andrés Santa Cruz (1829–1839).[62] Innumerable *pearas* (one peara = ten animals) began to take the desert trails, converging from Lake Titicaca (Huancané), Oruro (Challapata), Chichas, and northern Argentina.[63] The province of Atacama experienced a corresponding increase in its numbers of pack animals between 1832 and 1846. The participation of San Cristóbal drovers in the transport of goods between Calama and Potosí[64] was small in relation to the total volume, but the impact on the local Indian economy was immediate. Hence we find that in 1843 94 percent of mules and 74 percent of all the donkeys in the province of Lipes are concentrated in San Cristóbal (Table 9.2). To feed these animals and the rest of the mule caravans traveling between the trading posts and inns that had sprung up along the route,[65] barley production was increased from 50 quintales of seed in 1832 to 300 quintales in 1838.[66]

The level of monetarization among the families involved in the transport trade may be inferred, in general terms, from comments made by the governor of the province during the Spanish blockade of 1866–1867:[67]

> Payment of Tribute: although this province was once truly the most punctual in its payments, today this is no longer the case. Essentially dependent on animal transport, it lacks today this business from Cobija, as is well known, because overseas goods are no longer being brought into the country, so that the collection of tribute has posed severe problems.[68]

It may be this conjuncture that lies behind an exaggeration of the number of salt traders in Table 9.5, when many drovers would have been diverted into the salt-trading business: in this way, the transport of salt may have functioned as a security against the fluctuations in demand from overseas trade, just as the transport business did in Llica against the risks of high Andean farming.

But in Cobija's first years, the profits offered by the transport business seemed inexhaustible. The demand for transport was such that the state was forced to compete with private commercial houses in order to guarantee the importation of mercury, weapons, or other items needed by the army.[69] When goods arrived in port, the governor of Lipes was informed, and he would then try to gather together enough mule owners and llameros through the cantonal corregidor and the Indian authorities.[70] Half the carriage costs were paid in advance, and the other half were paid on delivery. Here are a few specific contracts: in September 1832 a mule owner transported seventy-four flasks (*frascos*) of mercury, using twenty-five mules, from Canchas Blancas (in the cordillera, between Lipes and Atacama) to Potosí and received a fee corresponding to seventy-five flasks "since he had undertaken this consignment on behalf of the state, in preference to private trade which would have brought him greater remuneration."[71] In February 1833, another mule owner transported 132 flasks of mercury using forty-four mules from Calama to Potosí, at the rate of 30 pesos the load, receiving a total of $1,320.[72] In 1838, one mule load of three flasks of mercury was carried from Calama to Potosí for 15 pesos; in 1841 the rate stood at 18 pesos.[73] In May 1835, "a cacique Cayetano" from the *ayllu* of Santiago, together with his uncle, Bernardo Siquile, carried a load of eighty bales of rifles and carbines, destined for the army, from Canchas Blancas to Potosí, at 11 pesos the load: these bales were part of a larger consignment, whose transport costs from Calama were reckoned at $4,500 at 20 pesos the load.[74]

These drovers enjoyed a level of monetarization higher even than that of the "rich" farmers of Tagua. The concentration of mules in the hands of the freight carriers, and the use of a team of ten mules as an accounting unit, suggest a privileged group of Indians whose caravans of mules were fed on an increasingly large barley crop grown on their irrigated land. In this way they could go on offering transport services even during the second half of the year, and the amount of financial revenue earned allowed them to spend more in the marketplace on provisions. Next to them we find a group of tributaries with diverse occupations, who, owning some donkeys and/or llamas, could take advantage of the occasional demand for transport, but could always revert to trading in salt if any crisis affected the import market (as in 1867). For these people, a double journey to Canchas Blancas would earn them enough to pay their annual tribute and leave a wide enough margin for local expenses (the festival at Colcha, for example) after a further journey to the valleys of Tarija in July or August.

We can now suggest a reconstruction of the long-term tendencies among the tributaries of San Cristóbal. The trade route between Cobija and Potosí became busier in the 1830s[75] when the proportion of Indians offering transport for hire was much greater than in 1867. The hire of animal transport continued to decline right up to the time of the Pacific War: with the Chilean occupation, and especially after the building of the railway in 1889–1892, the majority of drovers was forced to move into the growing salt market among the silver refiners on the eastern slopes of the cordillera. But at the end of the century, the contraction of the transport business coincided with the crisis in the refining industry, thereby hastening a process of gradual *demonetarization*. Nonmonetary exchange with the inhabitants of the Tarija valleys would grow correspondingly during the second half of the year, in order to compensate for reduced opportunities in the collapsing internal market. If the payment of tribute had been a minor nuisance in the domestic budget at the beginning of the Republic, by the end of the century it became a heavy burden, due to the impact of liberal policies on the twin bases of the canton's economy.

For the farmers of Llica and Tagua, the transport of overseas commodities was above all a security against the hazards of the climate; in San Cristóbal, by contrast, transport in the early days was even more important than the commercialization of such a valuable resource as salt. In San Pablo, this kind of transport business was indispensable for only two months of the year. More dependent than others on their pack animals, the llama owners of San Pablo could not avail themselves of international trade, nor did they possess their own salt deposits. Farming was of marginal importance; the former colonial mines at San Antonio de Lipes were now in ruins.[76] How did the southern *ayllus* manage to subsist and continue paying their tribute?

San Pablo: A Perfect Allocation of Time

Here improvization was impossible due to the intricate complexities of the calendar and the need to keep in delicate balance the relationships between its various components. Each activity was essential to the proper functioning of the whole; none could be marginalized (at least in the nineteenth century) in order to allow trading activity to expand unchecked. Consequently, the conjunctural subordination of the market to the ensemble of reproductive strategies is not something to be inferred from gaps in the documentary evidence; it can be found clearly expressed in the contemporary records.

A report written in February 1895 by the subprefect of South Lipes explains the difficulties of enforcing the communal work obligations on road maintenance (*prestación vial*) that had been made compulsory in 1891:

> The tributary Indians of this province live in their hamlets, looking after their llamas and cut off from one another by tremendous distances; at certain times of the year, when their llamas are in no condition to carry heavy loads, they make their living from hunting vicuña, rhea, and vizcacha. . . . As soon as the first rains of December allow sufficient grazing for their herds, they leave the neighboring provinces and are busy transporting metallic ores, thus enabling them to earn a modest income with which to buy foodstuffs and other things necessary for their subsistence. When carnival is over, they devote themselves to looking for salt and llullucha [laverbread] to take to Tarija to exchange for cereals. Then comes Easter, the only feast they keep, albeit only a third of them; once the religious festivals are over, all go down into the valleys to help with the maize harvest, in order to earn something in exchange for their services. . . . It is not until October of every year that each one is ready to take his turn with the communal repair work on the roads.[77]

According to the subprefect, then, the Lipes year began in December with the arrival of the rains and the greening of the pastures. Once the llamas had been watered[78] and recovered their strength, they and their owners left for the mining centers on the eastern slopes, to "bring down" (*bajar*) to the refineries the minerals stocked in the yard at the mine head (*cancha mina*).[79] In order not to arrive with empty sacks (*costales*), some carried fuel to sell—an abundant resource in the canton.[80] Part of their earnings would go at once on "food and upkeep" for the months to come.[81] This trading activity also provided the necessary money for the Christmas tribute in February.[82] The movable feast of carnival, which also stimulates festive spending by the participants, can be seen as the climax to this first tributary cycle.

We have no data that would enable us to estimate the level of income brought in by the transport of minerals (the *bajas*) toward the end of the century. But in 1842 we find an indication relating to the refinery of Guadalupe (Chichas), where they paid 10 pesos for every 5,000-pound *cajón* of ore over a distance of eight leagues between mine and refinery.[83] Information already presented might suggest, then, an average of thirty-five llamas for each tribute payer,[84] with approximately eighteen males in each herd.[85] However, the administrator of the Guadalupe refinery declared that "to bring down these minerals they used at least 100 men and between three and four thousand llamas" in an annual production estimated at 250–300 *cajones*.[86] It seems, then, that around four journeys were made by 3,500 llamas (split into about 100 caravans of thirty-five animals each) in order to shift 300 boxes and earn 30 pesos for their owners. Out of this, only 3 pesos 4 reales were needed to pay the Christmas tribute. In fact, by the end of the century, reference is made to great differences in the size of these animal caravans,[87] which points to an internal stratification among tributaries. Those who did not devote themselves to the *bajas* may have depended more on the sale of skins and furs.[88]

The second tributary cycle was shaped by two journeys with different aims: in the first, items of exchange were acquired; in the second, they were exchanged for food with only a minimum intervention of money. A more recent testimony sums up the cycle thus:

> The herds are gathered in winter and travel unloaded as far as the salt pan at Uyuni, where salt is acquired and transported to Tarija, Entre Ríos, and even Villamontes: they exchange it for cereals and then return to their hamlets. This journey lasts nearly three months; once the provisions have been brought back, they store them, working out how much they need to feed their families for the rest of the year, during which time the llamas stay grazing in their pastures.[89]

Nineteenth-century witnesses complete this summary. At the beginning of the new cycle, tributaries had to stock up with laverbread and salt. The gathering of *llullucha* took place in the little lakes of South Lipes; but, according to the subprefect, local deposits of salt yielded barely 100 *quintales* each year: "The peasants from communities in this province who transport large quantities of salt in blocks as far as Tarija, to exchange for cereals and flour, bring it from the neighboring province of North Lipes."[90] So a journey had first to be made to the salt pan at Uyuni, to collect salt with the permission of the tributaries of San Cristóbal.[91] This stage, which began with the end of carnival, ended with a return to the town of San Pablo to celebrate Holy Week—the only gathering of the year, and a moment of solidarity before the imminent diaspora, although not everyone waited to celebrate Easter before setting off on their journey.

The winter migration was longer than in the other cantons, where it took place between April to July;[92] here it took from May to August—and some did not return until September.[93] It involved an absence of between three and four months: the *llameros* of San Pablo traveled almost to the borders of the Chaco (see Map 5). But the food they acquired during this period had to last them until the beginning of the following year, when they were again able to acquire goods in the mining centers. These multiple transactions with a far-off network of clients constitute that spider's web of "minute flows" of salt which Carlos Sempat Assadourian contrasts with the "large commercial flows" carried to the silver refineries by the salt traders of San Cristóbal.[94]

But somehow the money needed for tribute had to be earned before the return to the altiplano, as the subprefect noted in May 1876: "the majority of Indians have left the province with the excuse that they need to find the wherewithal to pay the St. John's Day tribute."[95] In 1894 the price of a *quintal* of salt in North Chichas was 2 Bs., the equivalent of 2 pesos 4 reales in the old currency.[96] This represents an enormous rise over the price of 3–4 reales paid in the refineries of Chichas in 1842 (Table 9.7), due no doubt to the increase in mining demand toward the end of the century. In 1842, the 3 pesos 4 reales tribute could be earned with seven llama loads, whereas in 1894—assuming, say, 1 peso a load—only three and a half loads were needed, with a consequent increase in the volume available for nonmonetary exchange. In both cases, tribute money would be acquired on the margins of this direct exchange of most of the salt and *llullucha* for maize. Another way of obtaining it would be a little waged work: some *llameros* helped harvest and dehusk the maize "to earn something in return for their own labour,"[97] and part of their payment may have been the amount needed to cover the tribute.

In northern Lipes, the return to the altiplano coincided with the festival at Colcha. In the south, the return signals the moment for celebrating the

> enflowering [*enfloramiento*] of the llamas, . . . a festival in which woolen threads are pulled through the animal's ears, and little knots of the same colored threads are tied like flowerets over its coat. During this festival, they fortify the llamas by making them drink a concoction of *yareta*

[*Azorella*, a high Andean "cushion-plant" used as fuel], boiled in alcohol, after which the animals sleep in a drunken stupor and rest for several days; I had the opportunity of asking what the purpose of this drink was, and was told that it constituted a tonic, to restore the strength lost in traveling.[98]

Between September and the first rains of December, while the llamas rested, their owners devoted themselves to hunting vicuña and vizcacha, chinchilla and rhea.

The calendar of San Pablo supports the observations of Demetrio Calvimonte, who in 1883 confessed himself astonished at the "perfect allocation of time" shown by the Indians of South Lipes.[99] During the first cycle, the collection and sale of fuel and animal labor (the *bajas*) predominated. Income was used to buy food, as well as for paying the Christmas tribute in February. In the second cycle, salt and *llullucha* were collected for exchange against flour and maize down in the valleys, apart from a small amount of salt or labor sold to earn the St. John's Day tribute.

But these cycles also correspond to two different forms of economic reasoning. This can be illustrated with an example. Between 1885 and 1887, the Esmoraca Company, which worked the little mine at Buenavista, a few kilometers from San Pablo, found itself without a sufficient supply of *bajadores*. During the whole of 1885 and the first two months of 1886, 218 *cajones* of raw minerals had been extracted (one cajón = 5,000 pounds); but up until November 1886, only seventy-eight cajones had been taken to the refinery at Candelaria to be processed, and the rest remained stacked at the minehead at Buena Vista. This was partly due to the fact that the refinery is equipped to refine one *cajón* per day during those months of the year when water is in plentiful supply, decreasing gradually to half a *cajón* per day during the dry months.[100] Note here the irregularity in the supply of a key input—water—which influences the form of the miners' calendar as well as that of the peasants. But if we suppose that the first five months of the year were rainy and the following seven months dry, they would have refined 151 *cajones* during the first period and 107 during the second, which would have exceeded the amount of raw materials available. The problem stemmed not from the lack of hydraulic power, but from the scarcity of bajadores.

The first solution that the company came up with was to try to tempt the llameros away from their journeys to Tarija between May and August, by "offering them the same amount of provisions that they would have acquired from the proceeds of the journey, together with a wage four times greater than the amount they would have earned, and with less work though in the same amount of time."[101] The offer fell on deaf ears: for up to two whole months after their return, while their llamas are resting, this means of transport is unavailable.

Missing from the company's equation was, of course, the social relationship built up over the years between the llameros and the maize producers. The scarcity of grazing land on the altiplano made the journey down to the valleys a necessary one within the cycle of pastoral rotation; moreover, to fail to honor this relationship would have meant depriving their clients of salt and giving up their own sources of maize to the benefit of other llameros (from San Cristóbal, for example). They appear to have been unwilling to put in jeopardy a long-lasting relationship, in exchange for unlooked-for monetary gain, which was even unnecessary in the context of their calendar as a whole. Nor would the weakness of their animals allow them to work during the two months when pasture was most scarce.

But the refinery also had trouble with the llameros between December and February, when they were actively engaged in "bringing down" minerals. Here, however, a mechanism of supply and demand was in play: the close proximity of other refineries where the llama owners found it easier to earn a wage was another inconvenience that the administration had to struggle with.[102] During these months of the year, the mining centers were competing for access to a transport system operating between mine and refinery, whose costs of reproduction were mainly borne by the herding ayllus of the Lipes altiplano. For the Esmoraca Company, the only solution was to increase the rate of payments and "at the end of February of last year [1886], the refining process started up again at Candlemas with a supply of thirty-nine cajones of raw minerals, there being still 105 left at Buenavista."[103]

In this way, money can be seen as *one* medium of exchange, indispensable for some transactions during the first months of the year, but replaced by other means for acquiring cereals during the winter months. Reactions to the market were therefore different in each tributary cycle. The mining centers were obliged to compete for an elusive service, which would allow them to save on costs, but whose rhythm of supply remained unaffected during certain months of the year by a "tactical" rise in the price offered by the mining companies.

Conclusion

These characteristics, so salient in the case of San Pablo, can be recognized *mutatis mutandis* among most of the tributaries of Lipes. In general, the flow of money into the domestic economies corresponded to specific periods within each calendar. Farmers in Llica and Tagua looked for the greater part of their cash needs in July and August; the salt traders and freight transporters of San Cristóbal, between January and June; the bajadores of San Pablo, between December and February. These periods did not always correspond to the moments of greatest urban and mining demand, and a seasonal dislocation might easily be interpreted by the mining authorities as resistance to the market itself. But if it is incorrect to talk of the "subordination" of these peasant economies to the overwhelming forces of the market, neither does it make sense to talk about "Indian resistance" to market participation, so long as this participation did not unbalance the ensemble of ayllu reproductive strategies.

We can now understand the apparently contradictory reactions on the part of some ayllus to price fluctuations. No price series exist as yet for the Bolivian internal market during the nineteenth century, far less any series for those prices actually paid to different ethnic groups for their respective products. But it is clear that the market interventions of each group must be understood in relation to each tributary cycle. When circumstances produced low prices, for example, the "forced commercialization" of tributary surpluses could lead to the sale of a greater quantity of goods, given that the aim was to acquire a fixed sum of money. The same thing occurred in any situation where calculations were based on a fixed sum whose payment could not be postponed—buying food when the maize sacks were almost empty, perhaps, or covering the expenses of the next festival or tribute-paying ceremony. The requirement that money be paid out immediately here becomes a decisive factor,[104] although this does not mean that the ability was therefore absent to compare prices and calculate profits within the period set aside for market intervention.

In the case of the big freight transporters of San Cristóbal, we have suggested that their economy was more geared toward trade, perhaps because of the capacity they already possessed for responding to the new demand for animal transport throughout the year by increasing their production of animal fodder and the size of their mule caravans. Here the discrepancy in levels of trade suggests a preexisting inequality in the distribution of resources, whose roots should be sought in the colonial period or before.

It would be wrong, therefore, to assign to prices a metrological function sufficient by itself to orient the calculation by peasants of the comparative advantages of nonmonetary exchange and sale. In the first place, although our data do not allow us to reconstruct precisely the structure of domestic consumption (the implicit axis of Tandeter and Wachtel's hypothesis), it is clear that the consumer goods obtained by exchange or purchase do not always belong to the same spheres of exchange and are not, for that very reason, directly commensurable.[105] Moreover, the social relationships on which nonmonetary exchange is founded do not allow for an elasticity of response in the face of price opportunities to the extent proposed by Tandeter and Wachtel. In the ethnographic literature, such elasticity has been noted among certain specific groups of mestizo intermediaries—rescatadores, or peddlers—who may seek profit when they acquire by exchange goods whose commercial value has risen disproportionately in comparison with that of the objects given.[106] Such behavior describes a different type of economic actor, who is only rarely to be found on any scale in Lipes during the nineteenth century.

This is not to say that the exchange relationship remained fixed throughout the nineteenth century: calendars can be reorganized to fit in with changes in the sources of monetary supply. Once again the clearest example is to be found among the big transporters of San Cristóbal: when the arrival of the railway deprived them of their trade with the Pacific coast, they were able, first, to take advantage of the increasing demand for salt by the refineries between January and July. It may be at this time that the tribute-paying date was brought forward from September to Corpus Christi (May–June);[107] later, as demand waned and disappeared, they would become assimilated to the network of nonmonetary exchange with Tarija and share in the crisis of monetary scarcity at the end of the century.

We see here not simply a "rational" response to a conjunctural drop in prices, but a structural transformation in the nature of the demand, due to the construction of the railway and the opening of the Bolivian mines to the North Atlantic economy. It was precisely this global transformation that led to the "marginalization from the market" of the greater part of the south Andean peasantry and to a reduction of their monetary thresholds to a level much closer to the "lower limit" laid down by the forced commercialization of tribute-oriented production. As this limit was approached and even crossed, the idea of violence came into play again, but now as the direct result of a process of liberal rationalization, which had led to the exclusion of tributaries from their former markets.

The different ethnic calendars, elaborated and annually recreated according to each ethnic economy, explain the generally seasonal quality of their links with the urban and mining markets, during a period that witnessed the liberal assault on the old internal market of the Bolivian tributary state. This variety should be emphasized as a precondition for the elaboration of more detailed studies in the future. But these transformations of the calendar in time and space may also serve as a point of departure for a deeper analysis of Andean economic thought. What stands out here is the importance of fiscal ceremonies and religious feasts as cues for regular explosions of monetary expenditure, which express socioreligious thresholds and points of transition within each ethnic calendar.[108]

The analysis of different tributary calendars is essential, too, for understanding the growth of the mining export economy in Bolivia at the end of the nineteenth century. The seasonal nature of the Indian contribution acted as a brake on the accelerated growth in mining production that was required by mining capital from 1870 onward to counteract the drop in the world price of silver.[109] In the long debate between two polarized "national projects," represented by protectionism and Eurocentric laissez-faire, it is hardly surprising that the majority of tributaries in Potosí should have espoused the former: the violence that we find in the nineteenth century ends up opposing liberal reforms to the tributary state during the Civil War of 1899.[110] A study of southern Andean economic thought (indispensable if the changing role of Indian tributaries vis-à-vis the market is to be understood) must inquire after their capacity to articulate these new ideological elements within a symbolic language of their own. The persistence of an "Andean-protectionist" discourse well into the twentieth century, amid the debris of the old internal market, offers a point of departure for understanding the new political ideas that accompanied the Andean experience of Bolivian liberalism.

Let us end with an indication of Indian readiness to modernize where opportunities are available:

> The Indian of Lipes also aspires nobly to enlightenment, and though we do not provide him with the means, he finds them out and it is not uncommon to find a llamero who carries a map on his saddle. Their journeys to the Peruvian coast, to Potosí and other towns have made them familiar with some of our customs, lending them a certain varnish of culture; even in their houses, those modest dwellings lost in the pampa or hidden in some fold of the cordillera, one notes more comfort and cleanliness than in the huts of other Bolivian tribes. To recognize the good qualities of the *lipeño*, you must inspire him with confidence; then he is communicative, open and good-humored; he talks of his business deals, tells of his journeys, presents reports, offers his services, and becomes as appealing as before he was unknown. In sum, the Lipes Indian is an element of order and prosperity in Bolivia.[111]

This text shows the other face of Pedro Vargas's liberalism, though the frank paternalism characteristic of classic creole culture remains. Through this ideological filter appears a "modern" llamero, as might be expected on the route to the Pacific. Future studies must examine the terms of the debate opening between the protectionist majority, increasingly impoverished, and those who could exploit new opportunities as a result of the consolidation of the liberal project.

Notes

The materials used in this work were gathered as part of the Proyecto Comparativo del Area Andina, under the sponsorship of the Instituto de Estudios Peruanos (Lima), with funding from the Inter-American Foundation. I wish to thank Gunnar Mendoza, the late director of the Archivo Nacional de Bolivia (Sucre), and Mario Chacón, the late director of the Archivo Histórico de Potosí, for their kind cooperation; likewise, the postgraduate students of the M.A. program in Andean history, mounted by FLACSO-Quito in 1984, for their stimulating comments on an earlier version presented to the Congress of Americanists (Manchester, 1982), which was finalized as the article published in Harris, Larson, and Tandeter, eds., *La participación indígena en los mercados surandinos* (La Paz, 1987). This shorter version was prepared as part of the ESRC-CNRS Franco-British Project on "State Control and Social Response in the Andes" (1985–1987) for publication in *Annales ESC* (1987). It has been translated by Anna Crowe. All translations from the original Spanish sources in this chapter are by Anna Crowe. All abbreviations for the archival material cited here are listed on the first page of the bibliography.

1. The concept of the "market" is freshly problematized in Roy Dilley, ed., *Contesting Markets* (Edinburgh, 1992). For the clash of different moral and economic concepts in nineteenth-century Potosí, see my contribution, Platt, "Divine Protection and Liberal Damnation: Exchanging Metaphors in Nineteenth-century Potosí," 131–158.

2. See John V. Murra, *The Economic Organization of the Inca State* (Greenwich, Conn., [1955] 1979); Murra, *Formaciones económicas y políticas del mundo andino* (Lima, 1975). Also Shozo Masuda, Izumi Shimada, and Craig Morris, eds., *Andean Ecology and Civilization: An Interdisciplinary Perspective on Andean Ecological Complementarity* (Tokyo, 1985).

3. Carlos Sempat Assadourian, *El sistema de la economía colonial: Mercado interno, regiones y espacio económico* (Lima, 1982).

4. Witold Kula, *Théorie économique du système féodal* (Paris, 1974).

5. Archivo Nacional de Bolivia [hereafter ANB], Ministerio de Hacienda [MH] vol. 51 (1835); cf. Archivo Histórico de Potosí [AHP], Prefectura Departamental-Expedientes [PDE] 837a (1835), *Oficio contra el gobernador de la Provincia de Chayanta por pesos que adeuda por restos de los tercios de Navidad de 1833 y de San Juan de 1834.*

6. E.g., Silvia Rivera Cusicanqui, "El mallku y la sociedad colonial en el siglo XVII: El caso de Jesús de Machaca," *Avances* (La Paz) 1 (1978): 7–27; John V. Murra, "Aymara Lords and Their European Agents at Potosí," *Nova Americana* (Turin) 1 (1978): 231–244.

7. Thierry Saignes, "Notes on the Regional Contribution to the *mit'a* in Potosí in the Early Seventeenth Century," *Bulletin of Latin American Research* 4.1 (1985): 65–76. Cf. Assadourian, *Sistema de la economía colonial*; Peter J. Bakewell, *Miners of the Red Mountain: Indian Labor in Potosí, 1545–1650* (Albuquerque, 1984).

8. Fredrik Barth, "Economic Spheres in Dafur," in Raymond Firth, ed., *Themes in Economic Anthropology* (London, 1967).

9. See Enrique Tandeter and Nathan Wachtel, "Conjonctures inverses: Le mouvement des prix a Potosí pendant le XVIIIe siècle," *Annales ESC* 3 (1983): 53–59.

10. There are others, in particular the precise nature of the commercial dealings of the monastery of Potosí, whose account books provide the basis for this price study.

11. E.g., César Fonseca, *Sistemas económicos andinos* (Lima, 1973); Olivia Harris, "Labour and Produce in an Ethnic Economy, Northern Potosí, Bolivia," in David Lehmann, ed., *Ecology and Exchange in the Andes* (Cambridge, 1982), 70–96.

12. E.g., A. Camino, J. Recharte, and P. Bidegaray, "Flexibilidad calendárica en la agricultura tradicional de los vertientes orientales de los Andes," in Heather Lechtman and Ana María Soldi, eds., *Runakunap Kawsayninkupaq Rurasqankunaqa* (Mexico, 1981); Lehmann, *Ecology and Exchange in the Andes;* CAAP, *Estrategias de supervivencia en la comunidad andina* (Quito, 1984); Masuda et al., *Andean Ecology and Civilization.*

13. Cf. Tristan Platt, *Estado tributario y librecambio en Potosí durante el siglo XIX* (La Paz, 1986); also Platt, "The Andean Experience of Bolivian Liberalism, 1825–1900: Roots of Rebellion in 19th-Century Chayanta (Potosí)," in Steve Stern, ed., *Resistance, Rebellion, and Consciousness in the Andean Peasant World, 18th to 20th Centuries* (Madison, 1987), 280–323.

14. Bernabé Cobo, *Historia del nuevo mundo* [1653] (Madrid, 1964); S. Hurlbert and C. Chang, "Ancient Ice Islands in Salt Lakes of the Central Andes," *Science* 224 (1984): 299–302.

15. AHP, Prefectura Departamental-Correspondencia [hereafter PDC] 1801 no. 37 (1881). Bowman mentions a significant trade in cacti in the Puna de Atacama, which I have been unable to locate in the sources consulted for Lipes. See Isaiah Bowman, *Desert Trails of Atacama*, (New York, 1924).

16. Cf. Shozo Masuda, *Estudios etnográficos del Perú meridional* (Tokyo, 1981).

17. At the end of the sixteenth century, Lozano Machuca wrote that "throughout the district of Lipes, and in the houses and farms of the Indians, there are small furnaces for the smelting and refining of silver, as well as a great many *guairas* [portable wind-furnaces] in the hills, and all the people are engaged in exploiting and extracting silver." See "Carta [1581] . . . al Virrey del Perú en donde se describe la Provincia de los Lipes," in M. Jimenez de la Espada, *Relaciones geográficas de indias* (Madrid, 1965), 61. Cf. Alonso Barba, *Arte de los metales* [1640] (Potosí, 1967), passim; Cobo, *Historia del nuevo mundo,* 1:126–127; 2:166; Juan Pino Manrique, *Descripción de la villa de Potosí y de los partidos sujetos a su intendencia* [1787] (Buenos Aires, 1836); Demetrio Calvimonte, "Relación," in *Compañia Lipez: Datos sobre su importancia* (Sucre, 1885); Carlos Abecía, "La Provincia 'Sur Lipez,'" *Boletín de la Sociedad Geográfica y de Historia de Potosí* 40.12 (1953): 97–123. Minerals for medicine, mineral solvents to be used in smelting, turquoises, amethysts, salt pans and rock salt, alum, saltpeter, sulfur, borax, and metallic ores are found in abundance in the pampas and cordilleras.

18. See Antonio Mitre, *Los patriarcas de la plata: Estructura socioeconómica de*

la minería boliviana en el siglo XIX (Lima, 1981). San Cristóbal had seven Indian miners in 1829, and San Pablo twenty-three; AHP PDC 62 no. 24 (1829). The number of miners in San Pablo rose to 151 in 1887 (Compañía Lipes, *Tercera Memoria* [1887], 17), but it fell again to thirty in 1895; AHP PDC 2604 no. 22 (1985). Those from San Cristóbal rose to 283 in 1900, although the majority were Chileans or from other provinces; AHP PDC 2842, s/n (1899 [1900]).

19. Mitre, *Patriarcas de la plata*, 73–74.

20. Platt, *Estado tributario y librecambio en Potosí;* Antonio Mitre, *El monedero de los Andes* (La Paz, 1986).

21. Cf. Brook Thomas, "Energy Flow at High Altitude," in P. Baker and M. Little, eds., *Man in the Andes* (Philadelphia, 1976).

22. Cf. Lautaro Nuñez and Tom Dillehay, *Movilidad giratoria, armonía social y desarrollo en los Andes meridionales: Patrones de tráfico e interacción económica* (Antofagasta, 1979).

23. See John V. Murra, "El 'control vertical' de un máximo de pisos ecológicos en la economía de las sociedades andinas," in Murra, *Formaciones económicas y políticas del mundo andino;* Tristan Platt, *Estado boliviano y ayllu andino: Tierra y tributo en el norte de Potosí* (Lima, 1982); Platt, "Liberalism and Ethnocide in the Southern Andes," *History Workshop Journal* (London) 17 (1984): 3–18; Harris, "Labour and Produce in an Ethnic Economy."

24. Frank Salomon, in his typology of Andean institutions of ecological complementarity, refers to this system as "household expeditionary trading," although it should be remembered that the activity of all households is coordinated to the extent that the traders share collective calendars. See "The Dynamic Potential of the Complementarity Concept," in Masuda et al., *Andean Ecology and Civilization,* 511–531.

25. Carl Troll, *Geo-ecology of the Mountainous Regions of the Tropical Americas* (Bonn, 1968); Martin Cárdenas, *Disertaciones botánicas y amenidades biológicas* (Cochabamba, 1969).

26. See Felix Palacios, "Tecnología del Pastoreo," in Lechtman and Soldi, *Runakunap,* 217–232.

27. AHP PDC 2604 no. 16 (1895).

28. Harris, "Labour and Produce in an Ethnic Economy"; Platt, "Liberalism and Ethnocide."

29. AHP PDC 200 no. 9 (1835).

30. AHP PDC 772 no. 7 (1854); AHP PDC 1635 no. 20 (1877).

31. Textile production here includes the woven bags (*costales*) that the llamas were loaded with, and which appear in one source as articles of exchange in the valleys. AHP PDC 136 no. 8 (1832).

32. AHP PDC 829 no. 19 (1856), and table 7.

33. AHP PDC 288 no. 72 (1838).

34. AHP PDC 383 no. 60 (1841); AHP PDC 575 no. 6 (1847).

35. AHP PDE 915 (1836), *Expediente de indios de Salinas de Garci Mendoza, averiguando de 4 mulas perdidas en el Cerro Tunupa*, f. 16r.

36. AHP PDE 4642 (1860), *Obrados referentes a la deuda de 7000$ de los indígenas de Tahua a favor del fisco.*

37. AHP PDC 2594 no. 44 (1895).

38. AHP PDC 772 no. 20 (1854); AHP PDC 808 no. 17 (1855); AHP PDC 2637 no. 27 (1896); AHP PDC 2842 s/n (1900). One reference indicates a trade in coca with Tarapacá: "One Andrés . . . had introduced two loads of coca going in the direction of Pica." AHP PDE 915 (1836), *Expediente de indios de Salinas de Garci Mendoza . . . .*

39. On a hypothetical level, we can extrapolate from data provided by Abecía, who alleges that "how rich an Indian is can be worked out by counting the pieces of bone the llama owner wears around his neck, threaded like a necklace; each bone stands for a male animal, so that, in order to find out how many animals the Indian owns, one must double the number of bones in the necklace" ("La Provincia 'Sur Lipez,'" 118). The provisional figure of six pack-llamas is arrived at by dividing the number of llamas in the canton in 1843 (Table 9.2) by the population figure given for the canton in 1841 (Table 9.1), and then subtracting the half that stands for the number of females.

40. AHP PDE 5100 (1856), *Tasación de los terrenos del Cantón de Llica i Tagua en la Provincia de Lipes*, ff. 17r–18r.

41. Ibid.

42. Three tribute payers from the ayllu of Caguana, for example, "have been absent, they and their entire families, for the space of five or six years, and that year there was no harvest at all, since everything was killed by frost, and this is why they moved away, looking for their daily bread: their whereabouts is known to this [witness] to be Tarapacá in the Republic of Peru." ANB Revistas 231a (1867) VIII 2, *Documentos pertenencientes al Canton de Llica y Tagua.*

43. ANB Revistas 231a (1867) VII 58, *Documentos pertenecientes al Canton de San Cristóbal.* The need to pursue absent tribute payers in order to recover their six-monthly quota is the burden of complaints from the Indian authorities, both in the nineteenth and earlier centuries (cf. Saignes, "Notes on the Regional Contribution").

44. Ibid. As the Peruvian lieutenant governor said, referring to the two Condoris, "They have settled, together with their families, without any hope of re-

turning to their Republic, of returning to live there, *except for their private affairs, when they go and come back again*" (my italics).

45. AHP PDC 1449 no. 21 (1873).

46. AHP PDC 772 no. 7 (1854).

47. See Bowman, *Desert Trails of Atacama*, 24.

48. AHP PDE 6501 (1881), *Se pide paso libre para víveres que internan por la frontera peruana*. Cf. AHP PDE 6440 (1881), *Pide se le permite la importación de mercaderías por Tarapacá.*

49. AHP PDC 2299 no. 8 (1890).

50. ANB MH vol. 94 no. 35 (1842), *Estado de la industria mineralójica ff. 30r–v.*

51. Calculated on the basis of Table 9.1, at 7 pesos per taxpayer.

52. See Table 9.1.

53. Ibid.

54. ANB MH vol. 94 no. 35 (1842), *Estado de la industria mineralójica*, f. 17v.

55. Cf. note 39.

56. In 1.8 journeys each troop of thirty llamas would carry forty-eight quintales of salt, equivalent to 18 pesos at 3 reales per quintal. Deducting the 16.5 percent paid by the Huanchaca Company in kind, we are left with something over 15 pesos earned by each salt trader.

57. ANB MH vol. 94 no. 35 (1842), *Estado de la industria mineralójica*; AHP PDC 829 no. 19 (1856); cf. AHP PDC 898 no. 7 (1858).

58. AHP PDC 2594 no. 44 (1895).

59. AHP PDC 2480 no. 47 (1893); cf. AHP PDC 1480 no. 46 (1893).

60. See Mitre, *Patriarcas de la plata.*

61. AHP PDC 2555 no. 88 (1894).

62. Valerie Fifer, *Bolivia: Land, Location and Politics since 1825* (Cambridge, 1972); Fernando Cajías, *La provincia de Atacama (1825–1842)* (La Paz, 1975); Roberto Querejazu, *Guano, salitre y sangre* (Cochabamba, 1979).

63. AHP PDC 288 no. 39 (1838); cf. M. Leon Favre, French Consul and Chargé d'Affaires, "Apuntes sobre la navegación de los ríos de Bolivia," *El Orden y Progreso* (Biblioteca Nacional de Bolivia [BNB] PB Potosí 7) vol. 1 no. 54, 1/5 1854.

64. The Lipes drovers refused to travel as far as the port itself: "There is not one muleteer who wants to go there, and even the governor himself cannot compel them to do so." AHP PDC 200 no. 12 (1835). The reason was probably the dearth of water, forage, and food in the desert beyond Calama.

65. AHP PDC 62 no. 35 (1829); AHP PDE 234 (1830), *Solicitud de trabajar 5 postas en la Provincia de Lipes para la Carrera de Puerto Lamar;* AHP PDE 549

(1833), *Propuesta de Bartolomé Navarrete para el establecimiento de cinco postas principales del camino del puerto a Potosí y Oruro en los puntos de Cobija, Calama, Canchas Blancas, Agua de Castilla y Popó.*

66. AHP PDC 288 no. 72 (1838).

67. Querejazu, *Guano, salitre y sangre.*

68. AHP PDC 1215 no. 26 (1867).

69. AHP PDC 200 no. 12 (1835).

70. AHP PDC 200 no. 22 (1835); AHP PDC 200 no. 45 (1835).

71. AHP PDC 136 no. 33 (1832).

72. AHP PDC 159 no. 2 (1833).

73. ANB MH vol. 69 no. 17 (1838), *Banco Nacional de Rescates* at Potosí; ANB MH vol. 85 no. 20 (1841), *Banco Nacional de Rescates* (one *frasco* = seventy-five pounds = 0.75 quintales).

74. AHP PDC 200 no. 36 (1835); AHP PDC 200 no. 45 (1835).

75. See Cajías, *Provincia de Atacama.* In 1835 a customs union was formed between south Peru and Bolivia in the port of Arica, whose development diverted some imports toward the drovers of Tarapacá and Pacajes. A short time later, Cobija ceased to be a free port.

76. AHP PDC 136 no. 8 (1832).

77. AHP PDC 2604 no. 16 (1895).

78. Cf. the symbolic association between llamas and pools of water analyzed by Gabriel Martínez, "El sistema de los Uywiris en Isluga," in *Homenaje al Dr Gustavo le Paige S. J.* (Santiago, 1976); Martínez, "Los dioses de los cerros en los Andes," *Journal de la Société des Américanistes* (Paris) 69 (1983): 85–115.

79. See also AHP PDC 2604 no. 16 (1895).

80. Ibid.: "Having to look for the means of existence by carrying metal ores and introducing fuel to the refineries and mines in exploitation."

81. After 1889, an alternative at this time of year became the transport of goods to the railway at Uyuni. AHP PDC 2471 no. 11 (1893).

82. In San Pablo this date remained unaltered throughout the century: AHP PDC 200 no. 9 (1835); AHP PDC 1030 no. 30 (1862); AHP PDC 2668 s/n (1896 [1894]). Only in San Cristóbal are there any indications that payment of the St. John's Day tribute could be brought forward from September to Corpus Christi. This is probably due to the concentration of the trading activities of most people in San Cristóbal in the period between January and June. AHP PDC 2480 no. 12 (1893).

83. ANB MH vol. 94 no. 35 (1842), *Estado de la industria mineralójica,* f. 17v. The *buitrón* was the receptacle in the patio of the refinery in which ore and mer-

cury were amalgamated (traditionally by Indian feet) and fired. It was divided into six cajones of fifty quintales.

84. See Tables 9.1 and 9.2.

85. Cf. note 19.

86. ANB MH vol. 94 no. 35 (1842), *Estado de la industria mineralójica*, f. 17v.

87. AHP PDC 2490 no. 91 (1893).

88. The most valuable skins were those of vicuña and chinchilla. In spite of the ban on chinchilla hunting brought in by the government of Belzú in 1855 (AHP PDC 808 no. 15), by the end of the century the animal's extinction was considered imminent due to excessive hunting "throughout that year, even down to the killing of the young": AHP PDC 2910 s/n (1900). Skins were sold on the coast and at the yearly festival at Huari (May): AHP PDC 808 no. 15 (1855); AHP PDC 1250 no. 5 (1868).

89. Abecía, "Provincia 'Sur Lipez,'" 118.

90. AHP PDC 2535 no. 10 (1894).

91. I have found no indication as to whether the llama owners of San Pablo would have to buy the salt from the ayllus that bordered the salt pan: if so, it would be necessary to assign more time to the bajas of the first tributary cycle. A comparable situation at the salt pan of Coipasa, further north, is described by Gilles Rivière, "Sabaya: Structures socio-économiques et représentations symboliques dans le Carangas, Bolivie," Ph.D. dissertation (Ecole de Hautes Etudes, 1982).

92. AHP PDC 2604 no. 15 (1895).

93. AHP PDC 2471 no. 11 (1893).

94. Assadourian, *Sistema de la economía colonial*, 224.

95. AHP PDC 2638 no. 33 (1896).

96. AHP PDC 2545 no. 53 (1894). Cf. Platt, *Estado tributario y librecambio en Potosí*.

97. AHP PDC 2604 no. 15 (1895).

98. Abecía, "Provincia 'Sur Lipez,'" 118.

99. Calvimonte, "Relación," 12.

100. Compañía Esmoraca, *Segunda Memoria* (Sucre, 1886), 10.

101. Ibid., 9.

102. Ibid.

103. Ibid. In June 1887, the president of the board of directors complained once again of the absence of the llameros, confirming that they were not prepared to bring metal ores down from the cordillera during those months set aside for their journeys to Tarija. Esmoraca Company, *Tercera Memoria* (Sucre, 1887), 10.

104. See Platt, *Estado tributario y librecambio en Potosí*.

105. Harris, "Labour and Produce in an Ethnic Economy." Hiroyasu Tomoeda, "The Llama Is My Chacra: Metaphor of Andean Pastoralists," in Masuda et al., *Andean Ecology and Civilization,* 277–300.

106. Fonseca, *Sistemas económicos andinos;* Jorge Flores Ochoa, "Interaction and Complementarity in Three Zones of Cusco," in Masuda et al., *Andean Ecology and Civilization,* 251–276.

107. AHP PDC 2480, no. 12 (1893). No indication has been found of a similar modification in the other cantons, probably because of differences in the dates assigned to the acquisition of tributary coin. Cf. note 58.

108. Future fieldwork will allow comparison between the changing economic constraints on the form of fiscal and religious calendars with the more stable perspectives opening up from astronomical calendrics. Cf. R. T. Zuidema, "The Inca Calendar," in Anthony Aveni, ed., *Native American Astronomy* (Austin, 1977), 219–259, and Gary Urton, *Crossroads of the Earth and the Sky* (Austin, 1981).

109. Cf. Mitre, *Patriarcas de la plata.*

110. Ramiro Condarco M., *Zárate, el temible Willka* (La Paz, 1965); Marie-Danièle Demelas, "Jacqueries indiennes, politique créole," *Caravelle* (Toulouse), 44 (1985); Platt, *Estado tributario y ayllu andino.*

111. Calvimonte, "Relación," 12.

The Sources and Meanings of Money: Beyond the

Market Paradigm in an *Ayllu* of Northern Potosí

OLIVIA HARRIS

Some years ago the semantic complexity of money was brought home to me during the festival of the Virgin of the Assumption (August 15), the patron saint of the tin-mining center of Llallagua. After two days watching the processions of dancers, I had met up with a group of Laymi men who were preparing to return home to their villages some eight hours' walk away.

It was eight o'clock in the morning and they were pouring libations in the spirit of the preceding festival, as well as to ask protection for the journey home. With my arrival, more cheap rum (*alcohol de caña*) was purchased and we began a new round of libations, starting in the proper way by drinking for god and his consort the moon, then for the mountains and for *pachamama,* the earth. Next, since it was her feast, we drank for the Virgin of the Assumption (*mamita asunta*) and the money that she brings to her worshipers. The morning wore on, the sun moved across the sky, we bought more rum and continued pouring libations, with greater and greater fervor, to all the divinities honored by the local Andean population but especially to money and the sources of money. My drinking companions told me that mamita asunta's "husband" was Saint Michael, and that he is the *segunda mayor* of the mine (the term is that used in northern Potosí for the highest-ranking indigenous authority). Saint Michael's is the other important feast day in the mining district, celebrated in a spirit of both rivalry and complementarity in the nearby town of Uncía.[1] He is also represented at the head of one of the dance troupes—the *diablada,* or devils' dance. We also poured libation after libation for the "devils," the

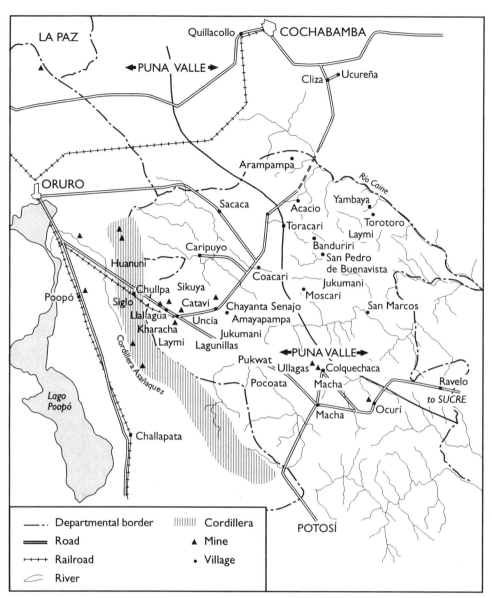

Map 6. Northern Potosí.

guardians and owners of the mine, frequently referred to in ritual language as *tío* and *tía* (*Sp.,* uncle and aunt). They live underground in the mines and also inhabit banks. They are distinguished from the Virgin and Saint Michael, according to one man, because "they do not have names."

Talking about money leads on to other, more secret aspects. They contrast today's money with that of ancient time (*layra timpu qullqi*); this is "Inca money" and has stamped on it the head of "Hernando" with long, loose hair (*ch'aska jirnantu p'iqimpi*). (Hernando is almost certainly the late eighteenth-century Spanish King Ferdinand VII, whose reign marked the end of effective Spanish hegemony over the Andean region.) Unlike present-day money, Inca money is very good. And there is yet a third, different sort of money, *chullpa qullqi,* which is buried underground.

The irony in this fervent pouring of libations became clear as the day wore on. My companions knew they should set off for home, and yet they stayed on, each of us in turn buying another round, in order to honor the local sources of money. The paradox was that in the name of ensuring continued access to money, and the overall reproduction of their society, they were drinking away cash which could, as I thought, be put to other uses.[2] Some Laymi would have agreed with me. One old man asked me a few days later if I knew where he could go to become a Protestant, since he had heard that they outlawed festive expenditure. He himself thoroughly disapproved of the waste of time, but more particularly of the squandering of money, in the long days devoted to pouring libations to honor all the sources and supports of life. Some women, too, are cynical about the drinking bouts carried on in the name of religious devotion, but while they may dislike the drunkenness, and the violence that often ensues, they direct their complaints more against the squandering of money, since worship of the mountains and earth requires the consumption of large amounts of liquor.

The incident conjures up the specter of the so-called irrationality of peasants. Why were these men not affected by the Protestant ethic? Why in a situation of scarcity were they spending their resources in such a nonutilitarian way? We can readily understand that they should pray to the contemporary sources of money, but talk of Inca coins and pre-Inca money is more mysterious.

Such questions are of course based on a naive European rationality. Those who study the workings of other economic systems would be unlikely to ask them in such a way, but the dilemma remains that while we know that people have different cultural canons of economic rationality, we assume that money itself can be subject to scientific scrutiny, and its behavior analyzed in terms of universal laws. The significance of money extends beyond the limits of any particular culture; it is an international language, which since the development of the modern world market has by definition transcended political boundaries. It is ambiguous, created by the state, and yet not fully controlled by the state. It is a human invention, but it evades our complete understanding.

Money in European Discourse

If the objective behavior of money eludes comprehension, its ambiguity is heightened by its symbolic multivocality. Probably the primary signifying function of money in Europe—at least since the early modern period— is to refer to the value of what is exchanged;[3] thence it comes to signify not only exchange value but exchange itself. The fact that economic textbooks constantly reiterate that money has other functions apart from that of the means of exchange only serves to reinforce this primary semantic identification.

The discursive functions of money are multiple, but two major currents can be identified, both of which have played an important role in how Andean history is represented. The first is romantic and nostalgic, treating money as the sign of alienation, of individualism, and the breakdown of social and communal values. The second is based on liberal philosophy and, by contrast, sees in money the advent of rational behavior and the sign of civilization, freeing human beings from the shackles of dependency.

Discourse of Nostalgia

The history of the Europeans' annexation of the region is hard to recount without invoking their lust for precious metals. Christopher Columbus had written eulogistically from Jamaica in 1503: "Gold is a wonderful thing! Its owner is master of all he desires. Gold can even enable souls to enter Paradise."[4] And Waman Puma's drawing of the first encounter between European and Inca makes the point with heavy irony: the "Spaniard" Candia (he was in fact Greek) is depicted kneeling before the Inca Wayna Qapaq, who offers him a dish filled with pieces of gold, asking him, *cay coritachu micunqui?* (It is this gold that you eat?); Candia replies, *este oro comemos* (We eat this gold).[5]

In Andean cultures, precious metals were closely linked to the holy, but for the Europeans the gold and silver objects were specie to be melted down and exported. "Peru" became in European tongues synonymous with fabulous wealth; to this image was added that of Potosí, the "rich mountain," whose veins of silver fulfilled their most extravagant hope of the fortunes to be made in the new colonies.

Such images have been used to powerful effect by generations of writers on Andean history; indeed, the inherent drama of this moment of European colonial expansion is not uncommonly enhanced by portraying the native Peruvians as morally superior to the Europeans. Bartolomé de Las Casas, the Dominican champion of the American peoples, set the tone in the 1550s:

> That which led the Spaniards to these unsanctified impieties was the desire of Gold, to make themselves suddenly rich, for the obtaining of dignities and honours which were in no way fit for them. . . . I am an eye-witness, and do affirm upon my knowledge that the inhabitants of Peru were a Nation very courteous, affable, and loving to the Spaniards.[6]

John Phillips, the English translator of Las Casas at the height of anti-Spanish feeling in the mid-seventeenth century writes of "these sad Relations of the devout CASAUS [Las Casas], by reason of the cruel Slaughters and Butcheries of the Jesuitical Spaniards, perpetrated upon so many Millions of poor innocent Heathens, who having only the light of Nature, not knowing their Saviour Jesus Christ, were sacrificed to the Politick Interest and Avarice of the wicked Spaniards."[7]

This tendency to idealize the pristine Andean world finds expression today in the view of Tawantinsuyu as a sacred, harmonious state in which exploitation was minimized through the reciprocal relationship uniting ruler and ruled, in contrast to the mercenary Europeans' desire for individual gain and their desecration and sacking of holy places. The contrast can be further emphasized in that the Inca economy was organized in such a way as to preclude the circulation of a generalized standard that we would recognize as money, and it lacked trade and markets. Since Murra analyzed these key features of the Inca economy, money and markets have been used by many as a key signifier of European domination, of the rupture with the Andean past.[8]

The contrast between nonmonetary and monetary economies is also built into the structure of anthropology as a discipline, whose theories are so often articulated around a play of oppositions. The appearance of Western money in an economy where circulation was previously organized on some other basis easily comes to imply a whole teleological sequence in which the values attached to collective interests and social ties are destroyed and replaced by accumulation for individual gain.

Such a contrast, particularly in the form of self-sufficiency versus exchange, has long historical antecedents in European thought. Aristotle in the *Politics* wrote of self-sufficiency as the perfect state: there was a "natural" (*oikonomike*) use of money which satisfied wants, but there was also an "unnatural" (*chrematistike*) use, in which obtaining wealth was an end in itself.[9] It was on the basis of Aristotle's formulation that Thomist law and the medieval church banned usury.

However, there is a common slippage in which money itself comes to be seen as evil or unnatural. For example, Mammon, meaning the devil of covetousness, is frequently used to mean simply money. Similarly, the original biblical statement that "the love of money is the root of all evil"[10] is usually cited as "money is the root of all evil." In these elisions, money is treated as identical with some of the more baneful consequences of its generalized use. Whether it be Christ throwing the moneylenders out of the Temple; or Luther fulminating against the sale of indulgences; or the poetry of those early romantic opponents of the industrial system, Blake and Shelley—the theme of money haunts the European imagination.

Since money frequently signifies the interest of individuals as opposed to that of the community, it is easy to see how it comes to be the antithesis of the holy. The religious community has itself often been defined in opposition to money.[11] Moreover, since it is a potent symbol of the evils of capitalism, its abolition has often been proposed by socialist or anarchist projects. The Owenites in the 1820s and 1830s, the rural anarchists of Catalunya and Andalusia in the 1930s, Pol Pot's regime in Cambodia in the 1970s—all aimed to abolish money.[12]

Discourse of Civilization

The discourse that attributes similar powers to money, but sees them as positive rather than as destructive, finds perhaps its fullest expression in nineteenth-century liberalism, which emphasizes the capacity of money to erode and destroy previous forms of social hierarchy. According to this view, it is "a radical leveller, it extinguishes all distinctions." [13] For liberal philosophy, the breaking down of any hierarchy that does not arise out of the "natural" mechanisms of free competition and market forces is progressive, and money is accordingly the signifier of progress.

In the Andean republics, liberal philosophies underlay repeated attempts to break up the *ayllus* (Indian communities), dissolve their communal lands, and replace them with individual private property. As Platt has shown, resistance by the Indians was seen as evidence of their irremediably savage state: according to the evocatively named "Law of Unchaining the Peasant Communities," enacted in 1874, individual titles were to be issued to create a market in land and thus draw the Indians into the sphere of its civilizing influence. A land inspector of the time commented that the need was "very applicable in the case of our Indians, since while they do not entirely avoid exchange, they practice it in such minute quantities that they perceive none of its beneficial effects." [14] But while the official liberal discourse castigated the ayllus for "refusing" to engage in commerce, other evidence suggests that local landowners and mestizo intermediaries were in practice actively preventing their access to markets. [15]

Money according to this view does not merely embody the beneficial effect of destroying unnatural constraints on its own operations, but represents rationality itself. In the language of development and underdevelopment, those who fail, or refuse, to participate fully in the market, or who use their profits for religious expenditure rather than accumulation and investment, are seen as irrational.

Andean Participation in Colonial Markets

Given the strength of both the liberal and romantic discourses, it comes as something of a surprise to discover that the early decades of European colonial rule witnessed the rapid, massive, and above all successful intervention of Andean peoples in the expanding market economy. Although money and markets were not developed in the Inca economy, it is mistaken to deduce, as many have done, that Indians of the early colonial period only engaged in commercial activity under pressure, or that they resisted money. A series of publications has provided conclusive evidence to the contrary,[16] and the evidence of sixteenth-century eyewitnesses is explicit. Cieza de León, for example, writes of the city of Potosí in the 1550s: "Business was on such a scale that between Indians alone, without the participation of the Christians, each day in times of prosperity in the mines twenty-five or thirty thousand gold pesos were sold, and sometimes more than forty thousand."[17]

Circulation in the Laymi Economy Today

Both the romantic and liberal currents can be found in contemporary writings on the Andes. Lest it be thought by implication that the Indians are immune to such attitudes, let me quote two opinions commonly voiced by peasants of my acquaintance, which illustrate the contradictory values attributed to money. I have heard it said that miners in the tin-mining towns are kinder and less abusive when they have little money (a "romantic" position that sees money and solidarity as antithetical and money itself as a corrupting influence). A contrasted opinion equates money with civilization: Indians often observe that those who live in the highlands (i.e., nearer the markets) are more civilized than valley dwellers since they understand better how to use money. By a similar logic, men in general are said to be more civilized than women since they have more experience in handling money (echoing liberal discourse).

However, these views by no means exhaust the signifying functions of money in Andean culture. In order to examine these, I shall first outline the ways in which money circulates in rural northern Potosí today.

For four centuries, tribute paid to the state in the form of money shaped the economic life of the ayllus. The Agrarian Reform Law of 1953 abolished the previous tributary system, but the fiscal obligations of the independent Indian communities remained ambiguous. With the inability of the state to institute a new system of rural taxation, the ayllus continued to pay the old tax voluntarily.

These days, the amounts are symbolic and are no longer a burden on household income. However, payment of the tribute retains its significance, both politically and symbolically, for the ayllus. They are proud of their regular delivery and see it as an essential means of regulating and reproducing their relationship with the state, and hence of maintaining the existing tenure system.[18] As we shall see, tribute payment and the mining economy have both structured the meaning of money in this region. Andean peasants produced the money in a literal sense for centuries and provided the fiscal basis for the state. While the money introduced by the Europeans was and is used for exchange, this does not exhaust, or even dominate, its meanings. The usurer and the miser, key figures in the European mythology of money, whose characteristics derive from its exchange function, seem strikingly absent in Andean folklore.

Moreover, the southern Andean economies have long been structured by a particular form of circulation that derives from the intense differentiation of the tropical mountain environment. Each unit had access to a wide range of ecozones whose different products circulated primarily within the group, transported by the producers or consumers themselves, and not by outsider intermediaries.[19] In recent decades, in spite of the pressure by the Bolivian state on collective control of ayllu land, a reduced version of this system has still operated in northern Potosí.[20]

The consequences of these forms of circulation is that there is little mystery for the consumers about where things come from or how they are produced. The typical indigenous traders of the central and southern Andes were and are not intermediaries; rather, they are people who traveled to obtain consumption goods from elsewhere for themselves and their kin. Bertonio, compiler of the first Aymara dictionary, is explicit: he contrasts "our sort of trader" with the "Indian style of trader," whom he describes as "he who travels to other areas to acquire food."[21] I suspect that this enduring economic system has profoundly affected the way money is represented, since its fetishistic quality derives in good measure from the way it appears to produce wealth—and thus the power to acquire everything—in and of itself.

Circulation in northern Potosí today is largely structured by ayllu membership. The central characteristic of what I have termed the "ethnic economy" is that the rates and forms of circulation, of both goods and labor, are different between ayllu members from what they are with members of other ayllus, or with townspeople.[22] The ethnic economy is thus not a "natural" or "use-value" economy, protected from the money form. Quite the reverse: many exchanges with outsiders cannot be realized through money, while transactions between ayllu members are often purchase and sale.

Cash enters the Laymi economy mainly through the sale of a species of potato (*papa imilla*) particularly favored by urban consumers. Laymi distinguish those potato fields that are planted "for food" (*maq'ataki*) from those that are planted "for money" (*qullqitaki*). However, the "cash crop" potato is also appreciated and consumed by Laymi households, so that when the harvest is poor it can be held back or withdrawn for domestic use. Money may circulate internally in the form of payments, debts, and small gifts between ayllu members, and above all for the highland potato producers to acquire maize and other temperate products from their kin living at lower altitudes. However, the two major uses of money these days are for external purchases—livestock and festive expenditure (coca leaf, cigarettes, rum), which is the single most important stimulus for entering into market relations. Compared with these expenses, purchases of food for household consumption or of clothing are small-scale.[23]

However, neither of these major forms of expenditure is a simple individual purchase. This is perhaps obvious in the case of festive expenses whose purpose is to acquire the necessary materials to communicate with the divine sources of power and so to reproduce the ayllu. Livestock purchases are at first sight more individually oriented, since animals are usually owned by individuals or by households, but in Laymi categories, livestock also symbolizes the wealth of the community and is harnessed to the reproduction of the ayllu as a whole.

In short, there are exchanges that involve money and exchanges that don't, but there is no systematic distinction between monetary transactions and barter. If townspeople visit the rural areas in search of potatoes and maize they must use barter; if ayllu members go to town, however, they prefer to sell for money. The logic is clear: when markets are far away, money is mainly avoided since there are few uses to which it can be put. The little cash that is needed in the remote valleys is accepted almost as a favor from close kin who find it more convenient than transporting loads of produce to exchange. There are no products that are exclusively exchanged for cash; conversely, everything that is obtained with cash may also be acquired without it. As we shall see, however, there are certain uses to which money or products cannot be put when they are acquired as gifts.

Money as such seems to have a largely neutral value; the flow of cash in the ayllu economy is limited for practical rather than for cultural or ideological reasons. In linguistic terms, there is no exclusive term for transactions involving money. The same root is used whether money is the medium of exchange or not: *alasiña*, or the Spanish-derived *kampiaña*. Moreover, the distinction between purchase and sale, derived from the monetary economy, is predictably slight in Aymara and is signaled merely by adding the suffix *-ja-*, which designates the separation of a part from the whole.[24]

A further example of the neutrality of money concerns the ceremonial gifts known as *arkhu*, made to cross-sex siblings when they sponsor a community feast. Arkhus usually take the form of cloth or clothing, but sometimes also money, which should be used to acquire livestock. Arkhu money is restricted in its use, not because money is profane in itself (it is after all offered as a ceremonial gift), but because it should only be used to acquire livestock, fundamental to the prosperity of the ayllu, and not for petty personal consumption. The worst thing one can do with it is to spend it on petty luxuries for personal consumption. Arkhu are reciprocal prestations, based on the principle of *ayni*, which reward those who take their turn to feast their neighbors and their divine guardians. Converting arkhu into livestock contributes to long-term recycling, whereas gratification through individual consumption is incompatible with this aim.[25]

Most men, however wealthy they are, work occasionally in the nearby mining centers for extra cash for personal or domestic consumption, usually as porters or building laborers, but remarkably few work in mining itself. Laymi who leave the ayllu for longer periods of wage labor used to go to Llica on the Chilean frontier, where in addition to earning some cash they are paid in livestock (llamas and donkeys) and *quinoa* (the protein-rich Andean cereal); today they go usually to the coca-producing Chapare region to the northeast where, in addition to money, they earn coca leaf and other tropical products. An important stimulus for such migration is either to acquire livestock or, more generally, to obtain produce and money for festive expenditure—that is, harnessed to the reproduction of collective prosperity.[26]

Circulation and Fertility

Money is therefore not seen per se as alien or threatening. Outside traders may be generous or they may be mean, but they are not as such seen as a burden on the ayllu economy. When Laymi complain that they are being "robbed" of their livelihood, they are not referring to prices and trading but to extraeconomic coercion. For example, sometimes in the mining centers they are intimidated into surrendering their potatoes at well below the going rate, or even for nothing, as happened in 1974, when the authorities in Uncía requisitioned peasant produce in order to cope with a severe shortage of food in town, and those who protested were put in jail.

I realize in retrospect that I had automatically assumed that the relationship between the Indian peasants and the mestizo traders was a hostile one and looked for evidence to support this view. I recall several conversations with Laymi householders in which I questioned their acceptance of what seemed to me to be exorbitant profits made at their expense by local traders. It transpired that they were fully aware of the inequality of particular transactions, but justified them by the convenience of the traders coming out to the countryside, thus saving them an arduous journey. One woman trader described as "bad" by most people did indeed wrest a living from the peasants by charging high prices or selling for credit to be repaid in kind at harvest time. However, it was not these activities that people were alluding to when they called her bad; rather, they meant that she was mean in not offering food and hospitality. Other traders who combined profit making with generosity were described as good (k'acha).

One of the constant complaints against me by Laymi friends was my refusal to enter into any kind of trading relationship with them. They would tell me I could finance my air trips to Bolivia by trading and complained because I did not bring with me for sale the special products of "Inkiltira," for example, local varieties of potato or clothing. Travel is always associated by them with the desire to acquire something not available locally. When someone goes off on a journey people ask: "What will you bring back?"

Indians consider that people who travel deserve to compensate their expenditure and effort by making a profit. Profit is explained as deriving from the costs of transport and travel, that is, the costs of circulation itself. In reality, profit is objectively visible only when a circuit of exchange begins and ends with the money form; money is unique in that it alone both initiates and completes a circuit of exchange. In principle it would be possible to calculate an increment in value even when exchanges are made by barter, by mentally converting what is exchanged to their monetary equivalents. Laymi do not make such calculation, but when they engage in petty trading, selling in the community what they have bought in bulk in town, they say that their money has "given birth" (*wawachi*). People who make money to give birth in this way are thought to perform a valuable social service. Money when it returns in the form of profit is fertile, not through the process of planting and maturation, but through exchange.[27]

The concept of debt also has close associations with fertility, not through the metaphor of giving birth but through that of manure. In the Aymara spoken by the ayllus of northern Potosí, the word for debt is the same as that for manure (*wanu*), whose Spanish rendering, guano, has become synonymous with the nitrate rich deposits of bird droppings along the Pacific coast. I do not think this association is a mere homonym, since a similar conclusion can be drawn from Bertonio's glosses for "debt" and "loan," both rendered in Aymara as *manu*. The Spanish *logro*, which can mean both profit and interest, is also translated by Bertonio as *manusitha*, with *mirani chasitha* as an alternative gloss. This second root, *mira*, means not only profit or interest but also increase (*multiplico*). *Mira marmi*, for example, means a fertile woman, and *miracatha* is translated as "the multiplication of money producing a profit." Furthermore, a synonym for *miracatha* is *hamacatha*, whose root, *hama*, means manure.[28]

Laymi believe that it is good to have both credit and debt relationships. In the metaphorical association of debt and credit with manure we can detect a vision of circulation itself—or rather delayed circulation—as a fertilizing force.

Seen from an economic perspective, money is of course not part of the subsistence base of the peasants of northern Potosí in the same way as the products of agriculture and herding, even though it may grow "like potatoes" in the entrails of the mines. However, the notion that profits "give birth" and that they arise from the time and effort expended in travel and transport suggests that for them circulation and production are part of a single process and that we should be wary of separating them. Of course, monetary transactions with outsiders to the ayllu inevitably mean that some wealth flows out—the "unequal exchange" postulate. This flow is I believe both recognized and tolerated by ayllu members. The ayllu is not a self-contained unit but is embedded in wider circuits of reproduction. Moreover the primary uses to which money is put—the purchase of ritual materials and the acquisition of livestock—counteract outward flow since they are productive and "reproductive." Ritual offerings harness the protection and fertilizing powers of the landscape. In Laymi thought, the metaphor used to represent libation, sacrifice, and other ritual offerings is not exchange: rather it is feeding. Humans must feed the sacred beings so that they will in turn provide food for human society.

It is not just because of its function in the reproductive process of the ayllu that money is associated with fertility and with the sacred beings who ensure fertility. In order to explore this connection further, let us return to the libations for the Virgin of the Assumption in the Llallagua festival and the link between money and religious worship.

The Sources of Wealth

In both Llallagua and Oruro (where the patron is the Virgin of the Mineshaft, celebrated during Carnival),[29] religious devotion is expressed particularly by dancing at the Virgin's feast for three successive years. To sponsor one of the dance troupes is a great financial outlay, and the sponsors walk at the head of the dancers bearing its banner and burning incense. In front of them come cars and trucks, decorated with silver objects and utensils. The dancers also make a major financial commitment since they must buy or hire their costume, and they rehearse with increasing intensity as the festival approaches. During the celebration they perform for hours on end, sometimes leaping and somersaulting through the streets under the midday sun, weighed down by elaborate costumes. The most renowned dance is the diablada. The performers wear full masks with long fangs and bulbous eyes, topped by four horns and lizards, and red satin cloaks decorated with snakes, except for the female devils (*china supay,* formerly acted by men in exaggerated and provocative female clothing, but nowadays by women). They are led by the figure of Saint Michael.

These devils who so proudly take over the streets are identified as *supay* or *tío,* the spirit owner of the mines. He gives mineral sometimes abundantly, sometimes sparingly, as well as on occasion killing those who work to extract the ore. Each mine or sector of the mine has its own image of the horned *tío,* phallus erect, mouth gaping, to which the miners make regular offerings. They chew coca leaf and offer cigarettes every day; once or twice a week they pour libations, and once or twice a year they make a sacrifice. The feast most explicitly dedicated to the devils of the mines is the beginning of August, known as the "month of the devils." At this time, the dead of winter, all the minerals buried underground rise to the surface, and hidden treasure is revealed. People say that to possess the treasure one must make a human sacrifice to the devils.

Devils are primarily masculine, and the guardian of the veins of ore is uninhibitedly so. However they also have female partners, who appear in a number of guises. In the diablada they are the china supay, as exaggeratedly sexual as is the tío himself. They are sometimes also known as *awicha,* in which form they intercede with the tío for the safety of the miners. In Laymi ritual libations they are usually referred to as the tía (aunt), an ambiguous figure sometimes identified with the devils, and sometimes with the Virgin of the Assumption. Tía, they say, is "like the moon" (*phaxsïma,* the common ritual term for money, silver like the moon). In the various identifications of the "aunt," then, there is an association between the devils who own the mineral, the metal that becomes money, and the Virgin who is the Christian patron of the mine.

The relationship between explicitly Christian figures (saints and advocations of the Virgin) and the devils is expressed in terms of contrasted spheres, which Laymi refer to as "God's part" (*tyusa parti*) and the "devils' part" (*saxra parti*). However, while these spheres are symbolically contrasted in many contexts, they sometimes merge. The feast of the Virgin of the Assumption in Llallagua is emphatically Christian, and I never heard it said that it was a feast of the devils, yet the Virgin is linked directly to the devil of the mine by being addressed as tía. It is hardly accidental, moreover, that the patron selected for the urban population of the mining area has her feast midway through the month of the devils.[30] The same duality is evident in Nash's description of the worship of the Virgin of the Mineshaft alongside the cult of the devils at carnival in the mining city of Oruro. In both fiestas, any potential ambiguity is neutralized by having the devil dancers remove their masks on the second day when the mass for the Virgin is celebrated.

In the Christian calendar, carnival heralds the beginning of Lent, but in this region it is known as the "feast of devils" and, at least in the country-side, is particularly a celebration of the fertility of flocks and fields.[31] The deity associated with the fertility of the crops is pachamama, identified both with the fields themselves and with the power that makes them fruit-ful, and often said to be the wife of the tío of the mines. In Laymi libations, tía usually refers to the pachamama, except during the feast of the Virgin of the Assumption.

Pachamama in Laymi religious classification belongs primarily to the domain of the devils (although there is ambiguity, as the association with the Virgin indicates). Today in northern Potosí and elsewhere in the Aymara world, the concept of devil (known variously as *yawlu, saxra, supay,* and *wak'a*) includes a whole spectrum of sacred beings: the moun-tains; the dead; powerful, untamed places such as gullies and waterfalls; and shrines where lightning has struck and killed an animal or human being; as well as the tío and the pachamama.[32] The defining character of these devils is not so much evil or malice as abundance, chaos, and hun-ger. Humans enter into and maintain a relationship with them by offering them food, whether a full sacrifice of blood (*wilani*) or merely coca leaf, cigarettes, and libations. In return, the devils may give unprecedented for-tune, or adequate prosperity, or they may "eat" their worshipers, making them ill or even die, if their own hunger—manifested by the ever-gaping mouth of the tío in the underground corridors of the mines—is not satis-fied. The devils are the source both of fertility and wealth and of sickness, misfortune, and death. They are unpredictable and very powerful.

Professional miners, including those with secondary education, talk of the need to make regular offerings to the devils. A local attorney who used to be a miner told me he had long ago realized that the tío was a mere super-stition; but almost in the same breath he related how his house used to be full to the rafters with food and stores and that after he stopped observ-ing the devil's cult, his luck had turned.[33] Among peasants similar stories are told. In the hamlet I know best there is one man who is strikingly well-off. The cynical observer might note that he farms large parcels of good land. His neighbors say that in addition to his good land, he has a special relationship with the pachamama whom he feeds liberally each year. The suggestions that such special relationships with the devils are a result of the distortion of the "natural economy" resulting from proletarianization therefore seems implausible.[34]

Devils are not associated exclusively with mining or with wage labor. On the contrary, Andean classification does not assign mining and agriculture to separate categories as the Western observer tends to do (the former belonging to the industrial, profit-oriented world, and the latter to the subsistence-oriented, traditional sphere), but links mining with agriculture and rearing livestock. The union between the primarily agricultural pachamama and the tío of the mines exemplifies this link. Moreover, there are striking similarities between the rituals performed for the fertility of the mines and those for the pachamama and other guardians of the fertility of fields and flocks, such as the mountains. It is widely thought that mineral grows in the mines like potatoes (a belief not unique to the Andes). Particularly striking lumps of ore are today called *llallawa*, the term also used to designate strangely shaped potatoes or double cobs of maize.[35] As Platt has described, there is an overall continuity of ritual practice between the huge state-owned mines and the rural cultivators, which is made evident in the rituals of small local mines, where peasants combine mining with agriculture.[36]

Laymi peasants today rarely work in the large mines and only work in smaller mining enterprises close to their own land and communities. Nonetheless, even those who have never worked as miners express a collective pride in the strength of "their" mines. Not only the small mines within their own territory, but also the huge tin mines around Llallagua continue to yield their mineral harvest, in part thanks to the efficacy of their own rituals. They compare Llallagua with the Potosí mine, which is now nearly exhausted. "Our mine is stronger," they say. "We have allowed it to rest and recuperate its fertility, and that is why it continues to produce. The Potosí mine was never allowed to lie fallow, and that is why the mineral no longer grows there."

This has always been an important mining region. One of the Incas' sources of gold lies on the edge of Laymi territory in Amayapampa, and there were also mines in operation in the local pre-Inca kingdoms.[37] The silver mine of Potosí lies not far to the south in the territory of the former Qaraqara kingdom. Throughout the period of Spanish colonial hegemony, Laymi tribute payers, together with other ethnic groups of the region, were a major source of mita labor for the Potosí mine.[38] The silver boom of the 1860s and 1870s brought new prosperity to the region. Of the major silver mines, Huanchaca lay to the south of Potosí, and nearby in Macha territory was the equally important Aullagas.[39] All these mines are remembered by Laymi today. And as the nineteenth century ended and silver demand declined, the mining economy was salvaged by the rising price of tin on the world metal markets. The mining operation around Llallagua constitutes one of the largest tin mines in the world, and it made its owner and entrepreneur Simón Patiño, who started life penniless and ill-educated, one of the richest men in the world.

When rural Laymi pour libations for the local mines, it is important that they are celebrating and entreating fertility not just for themselves, but for the whole universe of which they form part. The libations are for all the sources of wealth in whose circuits they are implicitly or explicitly involved, whether or not they personally have direct links with them. Prosperity, it seems, is not a competitive state, a "limited good," but is desired for everybody, hence the libations for the mines, where few if any of them work, and for the boom lowland city of Santa Cruz, as well as for more local sources of their subsistence. This I think is one of the reasons why there is little structured antagonism to traders from the towns or to the profits of the urban shopkeepers and chicha sellers. The generosity of the "devils" can benefit all.

However, it is not only mining that is associated with natural fertility, but also the money itself. Even in the mining centers the cult of the devils is not exclusive to miners. In Llallagua and Uncía the diablada is danced particularly by traders and shopkeepers; they say that this is because the miners cannot afford the financial outlay of the elaborate costume. All these towns owe their prosperity to the wealth produced in the mines, and the commercial sector—i.e., those who have profited most directly from that wealth—is also assiduous in its attentions to the devils.

In Laymi libations, the identification of money with fertility is explicit. Offerings to the most important deities are followed by libations for the three forms of abundance, addressed by their ritual names: *phaqhara*, llallawa, and phaxsïma. Phaqhara means literally "flower" and in ritual is used to refer to the increase of the flocks and to livestock in general. Lla-llawa, the name of strange-shaped tubers or maize cobs, stands for an abundant harvest, while phaxsïma ("like the moon") means money. The three concepts are so closely linked that libations are offered for "the three" (*kinsataki*). The same triad is repeated in a different form by pouring libations not only for money, livestock, and crops but also for their containers—the "strong and enduring corral" (*chukhi uyu*), the "strong and enduring storage bin" (*chukhi pirwa*), and the "strong and enduring purse" (*chukhi bolsa*).[40] Far from being treated as antithetical to the sources of fertility on which the economy is based (agriculture and livestock raising), money is closely identified with them. Placed in a wider setting, the ritual priority given to money and metals in the month of August forms part of a cycle in which all sources of well-being and increase are honored.

There is a close association between mining and money in this region, not surprisingly, since it was the silver of the Potosí mine that shifted the emphasis from gold to silver in the European monetary system.[41] The process of conversion of raw metal into money can have held little mystery in the Andes since the establishment of the mint beside the silver mountain in the early days of mining in Potosí.[42] Minting carried on in Potosí, with various interruptions, until the middle of this century. Today Laymi are still quite clear how money is made: "It is in the bank. The metal goes to the United States, and the money is made in a factory."

What then are Laymi addressing when they pour libations for phaxsïma? They aim to ensure the fertility of the mines, which not only produce money in the sense of minerals but are also the source of markets, of urban consumers cut off from the process of food production, and of monetary wealth. Also, the libations aim to ensure enough currency to buy the things they require, in particular to reproduce the wealth of the ayllu. But the meaning of phaxsïma is also more precise and more arcane than this.

The Raw and the Minted

Money comes from the same sources that ensure the potato and maize harvest, as well as reproduction of the flocks. By offering food, humans enter into communication with this source—the shadowy domain of the devils or saxra. But while money comes from the earth and the sphere of the saxra, it also paradoxically originates from the state, in that the state creates and guarantees its function as a means of circulation. The state apparatus and the authorities whose job it is to secure the functioning of social order belong not to the devils' sphere but to that of God. The devils' sphere is the source of abundance and of misfortune; above all, it is chaotic and unpredictable. God's sphere in contrast establishes and maintains order, morality, and "good government."

We have already noted that Judeo-Christian traditions are unusual in treating money as alien to, and potentially destructive of, the religious community. By contrast, the meaning given to money in Andean thought goes to the heart of religious understanding. Money is, of course, used by Indians for economic exchanges; it may also, as we have noted, in certain contexts be seen to threaten social bonds or as a symbol of civilization. But in Laymi concepts today, money relates primarily to the core values of prosperity and its reproduction on the one hand and the state on the other. Money is generated by natural fertility, in the same way as all aspects of wealth and abundance, but at the same time it is created by the state, as is evident from the very appearance of coins and bank notes. It derives, then, both from nature and from the law, and since these two sources are antithetical to each other, money itself has a dual, ambivalent character.[43]

This duality is evident in ritual practices, in the contrasted offerings made to the devils on the one hand and to God and the saints on the other. The devils are fed not with coins but with raw metal, for example, fragments of gold and silver leaf and sometimes other minerals too, or gold and silver paper, known by Laymi as "gold book" (*quri libru*) and tiny strips of multicoloured cellophane also called "gold" (*quri limphi*). In other areas, offerings include gold and silver leaf, or galena ore and iron pyrites representing gold and silver, or "crude" gold and silver scraped off larger lumps of metal.[44] Conversely, raw minerals are not offered to the saints, but worked metal sometimes is. For example, on patronal saints' days in the mining districts, silver plate is used to decorate the ceremonial arches and the motor vehicles that accompany the procession.

However, there are uses of money in rituals that do not at first sight fit this scheme of interpretation. For example, coins are part of the ritual gear of the Laymi shaman (the *wayuri*, known in other regions as *paqu* or *ch'amakani*). Not only does he keep a coin with his other instruments, but also those who employ his services to communicate with the devils have to given him a coin known as *silla*. It would be reasonable to assume that the silla is some sort of payment for services rendered. In a different context, gravediggers are also given silla coins, but this explanation cannot account for the coins kept by shamans in their bags of sacred instruments, nor does it throw any light on the name silla itself, seemingly of Spanish origin. A description by the Peruvian folklorist José Lira of a séance in southern Peru sheds light on the term. Before the shaman begins, he asks his client for a coin known as a *sellada*.[45] This Spanish word means "stamped, sealed, franked, or hallmarked" and is an obvious allusion to the way the coin is minted, with the symbols of the state stamped upon it. Why then do the shaman and the gravediggers have special need of minted coins to fulfill their functions? The beginnings of an answer can be made by piecing together fragmentary indications.

Tschopik, writing on the Titicaca region, offers one explanation. A typical séance round Chucuito started with the shaman telling all those present to place the coins on top of the stone *mesa* (table) to enable him "to see and think more clearly." These coins are called "eyes." Eyes, like coins, have multiple meanings in Andean cultures. In Laymi thought there is a close connection between eyes and mirror; mirrors are said to "have good eyes" (*sum layraniw*) or are actually called eyes. In addition, there are ways in which mirrors are directly associated with coins. The mirrors used by the Incas and their predecessors were usually small and round, made occasionally of silver and frequently of pyrite, which has a silver sheen;[46] today's Laymi believe that neither mirrors nor coins should be taken on fishing expeditions since they will cause the fish to disappear. As Platt has argued, mirrors in Andean culture represent duality, and duality as expressed in the Quechua concept of *yanantin* is the state of wholeness that typifies social order. This, it would seem, is why Macha say that mirrors are "the enemies of the soul of the dead" and are able to prevent a person from dying prematurely if they are posted at the entrance to the graveyard.[47]

This quality of mirrors that helps keep death at bay sheds light on yet another ritual use of coins. When Laymi prepare a mortuary bundle for a dead person to take on their long journey, they include not only food and personal effects but also a coin. However, the coin in this instance is not whole but deliberately broken or defaced. When I asked what these coins were for, people would tell me impatiently that they were for the dead to buy a house in the world they were going to. This seems unsatisfactory in that it fails to explain why the coin should be defaced. However, a comparison with the silla coins is illuminating. The name silla emphasizes the qualities that make the coin what it is: its "mintedness." By contrast, the coins given to the dead explicitly have their identity as coins defaced. Coins, as we have already noted, are able to "see" like mirrors, like eyes. They belong to ordered human society; stamped on them is the image of the state. The defacing of this image parallels the changed essence of the dead person. The living form part of ordered society, illuminated by the divine light of the sun; the dead, in contrast, form part of the shadowy world of the devils. A complete coin, like a complete mirror, would be antithetical to the condition of death.[48] Thus it seems that the need for coins by shamans and gravediggers is to protect and separate themselves from the dangerous powers of the devils and the dead. Silla coins in this interpretation have a comparable function to mirrors.

A further ritual use of coins by Laymi today reinforces their association with God's sphere, in contrast to the sphere of the devils. In 1973, several valley communities were racked by two disasters: the rains were two months late, and a virulent fever broke out, killing ten people in the course of only two weeks. As the crisis worsened, people began to agree that the individual misfortunes could no longer be interpreted singly, but were a punishment (*kastiku*) visited by God upon the whole community. To expel the destructive power, all households contributed to a collective rite known as the "money offering" (*qullqi arkhu*). This offering included various "cool" medicines: molle twigs, rice, coal, rosemary, and also silver coins. It was carried from house to house to expel the "heat," and the following day at dawn it was removed from the community and deposited far down the mountainside near the river where it would be out of harm's way. The offering was made to "ask pardon" from God, and, as on all the occasions when people ask pardon collectively from God, it was accompanied by a troupe of men playing bamboo pipes (*suqusu*) with two young girls (*mit'ani*) at their head waving white banners.

This troupe, known like the music they play as *wayli* (*Sp. baile*, dance), represents perhaps in its most concentrated form the communication of human beings with God; it is they who attend the feasts of saints celebrated in the different colonial parishes. The suqusu pipes should never be played during the rainy season for fear of offending the souls of the dead who are present in human society; this indicates that their sound is not a possible means of communicating with the sphere of devils, of which the dead form part. Given that the money-offering ritual is enacted by this troupe of suqusu players, who thereby implore God for pardon, we have here a further indication of the way that coins are associated not with the devil's sphere but with God, and are here used as a means of deflecting his righteous anger against his worshipers through the beseeching and granting of pardon. It should not be forgotten, moreover, that for nearly 400 years the relationship of the ayllus with the state was mediated by coins in the form of tribute, and the tribute payment was an important ceremony, maintained to this day by some ayllus of northern Potosí. In the Macha ceremony, the stone used to hold down the money (banknotes these days) is even known as an "inca."[49]

This apparent division between "raw" and "minted" does not exhaust the semantics of money in Laymi thought, however. Why does the ritual term phaxsïma, used above all in libations, refer in particular to old coins? Why is the "best money" that of the Inca, stamped with the image of the long-haired Ferdinand VII? And what is the other "money," said to be of the chullpa?

There was of course no money in the Inca economy; nonetheless, the profound significance of gold and silver (the "sweat of the sun and the tears of the moon") for the Inca cult, and indeed for all Andean civilizations, is well known. The Inca state controlled the production of metals that were paid as a form of tribute in kind by the mining nations. While in the Old World the important metallurgies established themselves in the domain of warfare, transportation, and agriculture, in New World societies metals served mainly symbolic functions, communicating power, status, and religious beliefs. As Lechtman has emphasized, "the most important property was color, and the two colors that were paramount in the New World metallurgical spectrum were silver and gold."[50]

Gold is still a significant attribute in ritual language. In Laymi libations the two words for gold (quri, chukhi) evoke strength and durability; on the other hand, the semantic identification of silver with money seems to outweigh all other associations for Laymi today, though they still emphasize color. The coins of the "Inca Fernando" are said to be the best because, among other reasons, they are "very white." But why the emphasis on old coins, and why are colonial coins said to be Inca money?

There still exist in this region many colonial coins from the reign of Ferdinand VII, much sought after by metal dealers. But Laymi treat their old coins with great respect and refuse to sell them even for good prices; people know which households own one, and they are extremely reluctant to show them to anyone, particularly to an outsider. This emphasis on secrecy surrounding the old coins leads us closer to a full understanding of their significance.

Some households own special amulets or stones that protect the herds and ensure their increase. Known as *illa*, these amulets are surrounded with secrecy and no one outside the social group—nor ideally anyone outside the immediate family—should see them. The mystery that surrounds old coins closely resembles this secrecy and suggests that they, too, are illa—not for the herds, but for money itself. The translations of illa in some Quechua dictionaries make this almost explicit. For González Holguin in the *Vocabulario* of 1608, illa is "whatever is very old and hidden away" (*todo lo que es antiguo de muchos años y guardado*). Lira's dictionary of 1973 defines illa as "brightness, transparency . . . Stone on which the lightning has struck, which is considered sacred . . . Precious coin."[51] The mystery and reverence surrounding the old coins surely derives from this source; those families that own them must treat them with great respect and make them offerings so that they fulfill their function of creating wealth and prosperity.

The statement that old coins are the "best money" can now be more readily understood: they are the best because as illa they are the powerful source of money. What then is their relationship to the devils, to the other source of money which we have already discussed? The beginnings of an answer can be traced by turning to the third form of money, that of the chullpa, distinguished by Laymi both from Inca money and from that of the present day.

The word chullpa in altiplano mythology refers to the monumental tombs that dominate the landscape in some areas, built for the rulers of the pre-Inca population itself, which is mythically associated with the moon. They shriveled up when the sun rose for the first time, heralding the new Inca age. The sun was for the Inca rulers their divine ancestor and was worshiped throughout the state. It was readily identified with the Christian God and is worshiped as God today. The chullpa, on the other hand, belongs to a shadowy world of half light associated with the dead and the devils.

There are many versions of what chullpa money is. Any interpretation is bound to be more schematic than is warranted by the medley of different and often vague beliefs held by people I have talked to, that accord well with the shadowy mythical status of the chullpa themselves. However for many people, chullpa money is not so much money, as what they call "treasure" (*tesoro, tapado*) and it is buried underground. (I have referred to it as money because in both the Andean and Spanish languages there is no lexical distinction between coins and the money-stuff—silver—from which they are ideally made). In the month of August, which it will be remembered is the devils' month, people say that this treasure comes to the surface and that those who are brave enough and who make a blood sacrifice—even a human sacrifice—will gain access to it.[52]

Chullpa "money," then, is also a primary source of money, but in this case it is not coins as currency that are emphasized, but rather the intrinsic value of the money stuff itself ("treasure"). Some beliefs surrounding chullpa money seem to link it directly with the veins of minerals hidden underground in the mines; in any event, the associations are close between the chullpa themselves and the sphere of the devils or saxra, between the "buried treasure" of the chullpa that comes to the surface in August and the buried riches of the mines, which humans may extract with the generous aid of the tío, whose special month is August. And blood sacrifices, it will be remembered, are made only to the devils, not to the holy beings of God's sphere. Like the wealth bestowed by the tío, chullpa money is conceived as an unpredictable source of riches.

The way that Laymi distinguish present-day money from ancient money, then, suggests not a historical comparison between the present and the past as a means of conceptualizing the ontological origins of money. As in so many aspects of Andean thought, the forces that engender money are located not in one past time but in two. The offerings of raw material belong to the saxra, while coins are in God's domain. In a parallel image, there are two sources of money: the most ancient, which lies underground, and a less ancient, which engenders the money of today. Both it seems are necessary to ensure the functioning of the economy.

Chullpa money, Inca money: the first is associated with the fertility of metal beneath the earth's surface, while the second, engraved with the "head of the prince" and the insignia of the state, constitutes the mysterious and sacred source of actual currency. Andean cultures harness the powers of the past in this way: remnants of bygone eras are put to work for the living and for the reproduction of the world.

Notes

The research in Bolivia—in the Laymi communities of Bustillos and Charcas provinces—was carried out at various times between 1972 and 1983. This is a revised version of Olivia Harris, "The Earth and the State: The Sources and Meanings of Money in Northern Potosí," in Jonathan Parry and Maurice Bloch, eds., *Money and the Morality of Exchange* (Cambridge, 1989), 232–268, and is published here with kind permission.

1. In 1986 as a result of monetarist policies and above all the 1985 tin crash on the London Metal Exchange, the mines of Siglo XX, Uncía, and Catavi were virtually closed down and the majority of the miners dismissed. See Latin America Bureau, *The Great Tin Crash: Bolivia and the World Market* (London, 1987).

2. The circumstances were even more poignant, in that the previous two harvests had been ruined by drought. If ever there was a moment for cutting back on festive expenditure, it was surely then.

3. Karl Polanyi, *The Livelihood of Man* (New York, 1977), ch. 9; Michel Foucault, *The Order of Things* (London, 1970), ch. 6.

4. Cited by Karl Marx, *Capital* [1887] (London, 1976), 1:229. In the words of Pierre Vilar: "It was gold which unleashed the conquest of America and ensured that it was carried out in a rushed, haphazard and dispersed manner." Vilar, *History of Gold and Money, 1450–1920* (London, 1976), 66.

5. Felipe Waman Puma de Ayala, *Nueva corónica y buen gobierno* [1615], ed. John V. Murra and Rodolfo Adorno (Mexico, 1980), 2:369.

6. Bartolomé de Las Casas, *Brevíssima relación de la destruyción de las indias* [1552], translated as *The Tears of the Indians* [1656], by John Phillips (New York, 1972), 4.

7. Ibid., 62. It should be noted that at the same time that Phillips was contributing to the Black Legend of Spain's imperial role, Cromwell was carrying out in Ireland similar policies to those of which the Spanish were accused in the Americas.

8. John V. Murra, "El 'control vertical' de un máximo de pisos ecológicos en la economía de las sociedades andinas," in Iñigo Ortíz de Zúñiga, 2 vols. *Visita a la Provincia de León de Huánuco* [1562] (Huánuco, 1972), 2:429–476; Murra, *The Economic Organization of the Inca State* (Greenwich, Conn., [1955] 1979). As Anthony Pagden notes, the great Spanish theologian, Vitoria, justified his argument that the Indians were men by reference to Aristotle's criterion of commerce, which he thought the Indians shared with Europeans. In contrast, the lack of iron, of writing, and of the arch were for Vitoria more serious problems, which required greater ingenuity to explain away. Pagden, *The Fall of Natural Man* (Cambridge, 1982).

9. Aristotle, *The Politics* (London, 1962), 59.

10. *The New Testament.* Tim. I:6:10.

11. As Thomas Crump notes, it is only the Judeo-Christian tradition among world religions that treats money as antithetical to the sacred. Crump, *The Phenomenon of Money* (London, 1981), 17, 285.

12. Pol Pot's imitators in Peru—Sendero Luminoso (Shining Path)—also tried to abolish exchange entirely in their early campaigns in the southern sierra. L. Taylor, "Maoism in the Andes: Sendero Luminoso and the Contemporary Guerrilla Movement in Peru," *Centre for Latin American Studies Working Paper* no. 2 (University of Liverpool, 1983), 29.

13. Marx, *Capital,* I:229.

14. Tristan Platt, *Estado boliviano y ayllu andino: Tierra y tributo en el norte de Potosí* (Lima, 1982), 98. See also Nicholás Sánchez Albornoz, *Indios y tributos en el Alto Perú* (Lima, 1978).

15. Silvia Rivera Cusicanqui, *Oprimidos pero no vencidos: Luchas del campesinado aymara y quechwa 1900–1980* (La Paz, 1984), ch. 2.

16. Assadourian detailed the Indian control of mining and marketing in the boom city of Potosí in the early *wayra* period of silver production; while Rivera, Choque, and Murra chronicled the substantial trading activities of different Andean lords and the wealth that they controlled, and Bakewell's work reaffirmed the significance of "free" Indian labor in early Potosí. See Carlos Sempat Assadourian, "La producción de la mercancía dinero en la formación del mercado interno colonial," in Enrique Florescano, ed., *Ensayos sobre el desarrollo económico de México y América Latina (1500–1975)* (Mexico City, 1979), 233–292; Silvia Rivera Cusicanqui, "El mallku en la sociedad colonial en el siglo XVII: El caso de Jesús de Machaca," *Avances* (La Paz) 1 (1978): 7–27; Roberto Choque, "Pedro Chipana: Cacique comerciante de Calamarca," *Avances* (La Paz) 1 (1978): 28–32; John V. Murra, "La correspondencia entre un 'Capitán de la Mita' y su apoderado

en Potosí," *Historia y Cultura* (La Paz) 3 (1978): 45–58; Peter J. Bakewell, *Miners of the Red Mountain: Indian Labor in Potosí, 1545–1650* (Albuquerque, 1984).

17. Cited in Assadourian, "Producción de la mercancía dinero."

18. Platt, *Estado boliviano y ayllu andino;* Ricardo Godoy, "The Fiscal Role of the Andean Ayllu," *Man* 21.4 (1986): 723–741. Because of the limited expansion of haciendas in the late nineteenth and early twentieth centuries, the Agrarian Reform Law of 1953 made relatively little impact in this region.

19. Murra, "'Control vertical' de un máximo de pisos ecológicos"; Jorge Flores, ed., *Actes du XLIIe Congrès International des Américanistes,* vol. 4 (Paris, 1978); Shozo Masuda, Izumi Shimada, and Craig Morris, eds., *Andean Ecology and Civilization: An Interdisciplinary Perspective on Andean Ecological Complementarity* (Tokyo, 1985).

20. Tristan Platt, "The Role of the Andean *Ayllu* in the Reproduction of the Petty Commodity Regime in North Potosí (Bolivia)," and Olivia Harris, "Labour and Produce in an Ethnic Economy, Northern Potosí, Bolivia," both in David Lehmann, ed., *Ecology and Exchange in the Andes* (Cambridge, 1982), 27–69 and 70–96.

21. Ludovico Bertonio, *Vocabulario de la lengua aymara* [1612] (La Paz, 1985), 1:314 "Mercader a nuestro modo: Mircatori, vel Tintani. Mercader a modo de indios. Haurucu, Alasiri"; 2:125 "Haurucu: El que va a rescatar comida a otros pueblos."

22. Harris, "Labour and Produce in an Ethnic Economy."

23. While this was the case until the mid-1980s, in recent years Laymi have largely abandoned their homespun clothes and now buy much of what they wear.

24. Bertonio states: "*Alatha,* to buy, and to sell, depending on the construction," *Vocabulario de la lengua aymara,* 2:9; N. Clearman England, "Verbal Derivational Suffixes," in M. Hardman, ed., *Outline of Aymara Phonological and Grammatical Structure* (Ann Arbor, 1974), 3:153.

25. It is not only money gifts whose use is restricted in this way. Gifts of cloth are also surrounded by the same taboos; they may be converted into money, but again only for the purpose of purchasing livestock.

26. This pattern contrasts sharply with that of the neighboring Jukumani ayllu where mining work is common. See Ricardo Godoy, *Mining and Agriculture in Highland Bolivia: Ecology, History, and Commerce among the Jukumanis* (Tucson, 1990). It seems that the Laymi steered clear of mining from the beginning of the tin boom. See Olivia Harris and Xavier Albó, *Monteras y guardatojos: Campesinos y mineros en el norte de Potosí* (La Paz, 1975). Today, however, the Chapare, one of the main cocaine-producing regions, acts as a magnet for migrant labor from

all over the country. In years of drought, earnings from the Chapare have staved off disaster for many households.

27. The metaphor of natural reproduction to signify monetary gain is of course not unique to the Andes. The Greek word *tokos* means both child and interest. Aristotle speaks of "currency born of currency" (*Politics*, 87), and Marx echoes the same idea. But their imagery refers to interest on loans and usury, whereas Laymi at the time of my original fieldwork apparently did not pay interest on monetary loans and used the imagery of money giving birth to denote profit from sale.

28. Bertonio, *Vocabulario de la lengua aymara:* 2:216 "manusitha: Tomar prestado algo"; 1:294 "logro: Manusitha. Mirani chasitha"; 2:222 "Mira: Multiplico, y también logro; Mira marmi: Mujer fecunda"; 2:51 "Collque miraatha: Grangear o tractar con la plata o dar a logro"; 2:115 "Hamacatha, miracatha: Multiplicarse así la plata dandola a logro." Francis Bacon in seventeenth-century England evokes the same image—"Money is like muck, not good unless it be spread"—in his *Essays* (London, 1625), no. 15, "Of Seditions and Troubles."

29. June Nash, *We Eat the Mines and the Mines Eat Us: Dependency and Exploitation in the Bolivian Tin Mines* (New York, 1979), 128–134.

30. Around La Paz, the month of August is ritually divided in two: the first half is particularly associated with the pachamama and the second (i.e., after the 15th) with the tío.

31. Olivia Harris, "The Dead and the Devils among the Bolivian Laymi," in Maurice Bloch and Jonathan Parry, eds., *Death and the Regeneration of Life* (Cambridge, 1982), 45–73.

32. Olivia Harris and Thérèse Bouysse-Cassagne, "Pacha: En torno al pensamiento aymara," in Thérèse Bouysse-Cassagne et al., *Tres reflexiones sobre el pensamiento queshwaymara* (La Paz, 1986), 11–59.

33. The attention of Simón Patiño to the cult of the tío is well known, even after he had consolidated ownership of the whole mine and become wealthy.

34. This is the core of Michael Taussig's argument in his book, *The Devil and Commodity Fetishism in South America* (Chapel Hill, N.C., 1980). The idea of contracts with the devil is mentioned by June Nash, and I have heard townspeople talk of it. On the surface, the stories told by Laymi seem to fit the same notion; however, their metaphor is that of feeding, which for Laymi is emphatically not exchange. Feeding is the proper behavior of human beings: you expect that other human beings will feed you; offering food is not an act of exchange. Humans must feed the devils to assuage their voracious hunger; but this does not guarantee these humans food or prosperity.

35. The same association was noted in the sixteenth century by the "extirpator

of idolatry," Cristóbal de Albornoz, with reference to the concept *mama* ("La instrucción para descubrir las guacas del Piru y sus camayos y haziendas [c. 1580]," *Journal de la Société des Américanistes* [Paris] 56.1 [1967]: 7–39). The name of the mining town itself—Llallagua—is obviously significant. Querejazu reports that the name was given because the shape of the mountain was like that of a llallawa potato: extraordinary and ritually important. Roberto Querejazu, *Llallagua: Historia de una montaña* (La Paz, 1978). I have been told that the name is in fact recent and was given to the burgeoning town because of the mineral llallawas found there. Whatever reason is historically correct, the connection between the fabled wealth of the tin mine and the ritual significance of unusual tubers is made explicitly by local inhabitants.

36. Tristan Platt, "Religión andina y conciencia proletaria: Qhuyaruna y ayllu en el norte de Potosí," *HISLA* (Lima) 2 (1983): 47–74.

37. Waldemar Espinoza Soriano, "El 'Memorial' de Charcas: 'Crónica' inédita de 1582," *Cantuta: Revista de la Universidad Nacional de Educación* (Chosica, Peru, 1969): 1–35; Espinoza, "El reino aymara de Quillaca-Asanaque, siglos XV y XVI," *Revista del Museo Nacional* (Lima) 45 (1981): 175–274.

38. Enrique Tandeter, "Forced and Free Labour in Late Colonial Potosí," *Past and Present* (London) 93 (1981): 98–136.

39. Antonio Mitre, *Los patriarcas de la plata: Estructura socioeconómica de la minería boliviana en el siglo XIX* (Lima, 1981).

40. Another symbolic reiteration of the same triad is found in the patron saints (*milagros*) of Muruq'umarka. During the patronal feast, there are five different celebrations; the first is for God (*suwirana*) and the last for the ancestors in the form of a skull (*t'ujlu*). The three intermediate days are devoted to Sts. Philip and James, the Virgin, and St. Michael, standing respectively for livestock, crops, and money.

41. Vilar, *History of Gold and Money*; M. McLeod, "The Atlantic Trade, 1492–1720," *Cambridge History of Latin America* (Cambridge, 1984), 1:34–88. In both French and Castilian to this day, the same term—*argent* and *plata*, respectively—denotes both the precious metal and money in general. The same is true for Aymara and Quechua *qullqi*.

42. This occurred in 1572 according to Pierre Vilar, while Benavides implies that it was established earlier (*Historia de la moneda en Bolivia* [La Paz, 1972], 11). With the replacement of silver by tin as the major source of mineral wealth, the direct connection between mining and money disappeared. However, in pouring libations, Laymi link the tin mines directly with money. Apart from the obvious fact that the tin mines are the source of monetary wealth for the whole region, raw metal can also form part of the miner's wage, either officially as in the colonial

corpa, or unofficially as in the "robbery" known as *kajcheo,* which supplemented low mining wages (Tandeter, "Forced and Free Labor," 134) or *jukeo* (Harris and Albó, *Monteras y guardatojos,* 17).

On the other hand, since 1869, when bank notes were introduced by President Melgarejo, silver has gradually ceased to be the base of the currency. Paper money has not replaced silver coinage in the symbolic discourse of money; however, it does have its own metaphorical attribution, known as "flowers."

43. In economic thought, there are two theories of the origin of money: the state theory, according to which money was created and guaranteed by a political system and functioned as a "token" or sign of the mutual obligations of the state and its citizens, and the commodity theory, which argues that the functions of money depend on its intrinsic value. See K. Hart "Heads or Tails? Two Sides of the Coin," *Man* (n.s.) 21.4 (1986): 637–656.

44. H. Tschopik, "The Aymara of Chucuito, Peru," *Papers of the American Museum of Natural History* 44.2 (New York, 1951): 137–308, p. 231; Billie Jean Isbell, *To Defend Ourselves: A View through the Andean Kaleidoscope* (Austin, 1978).

45. J. Lira, "El demonio en los Andes," *Tradición* (Cuzco) 1.1 (1950): 35–40.

46. J. Muelle, "Espejos precolombinos del Peru," *Revista del Museo Nacional* (Lima) 11.1 (1940): 5–12.

47. Tristan Platt, "Mirrors and Maize: The Concept of *yanantin* among the Macha of Bolivia," in John V. Murra, Nathan Wachtel, and Jacques Revel, eds., *Anthropological History of Andean Polities* (Cambridge, 1986), 247. Another link between mirrors and coins may be the imagery of lakes. Platt notes the symbolic connection between the lake and the mirror, and Tschopik relates that the Aymara of Chucuito used a silver coin to represent Lake Titicaca in certain rituals (ibid., 244).

48. An observation made by Pablo José de Arriaga in 1621 suggests an interesting parallel. Commenting on the use of silver coins in offerings to the *huaca* shrines, he writes:

They also offer silver in *reales* (coins); and in some places, for example in Libia Cancharco, fifteen *patacones* have been found with other small coins, while in the town of Recuay Doctor Ramirez found two hundred patacones in a huaca. *They usually beat them and dent them so that you can barely make out the royal coat of arms, and it appears that they are spattered with blood and with chicha, placed around the shrine.* In other circumstances the priests of the shrine keep this money and collect it for meeting the expenses of their feasts [my emphasis]. (Arriaga, *The Extirpation of Idolatry in Peru* [Lexington, 1968], 43)

One possible interpretation of such actions would be that the coins were offered to the gods whose cult at the beginning of the seventeenth century was already forbidden and operated in clandestinity; and that except for cases where they were used to cover ritual expenditure, the insignia of His Most Catholic Majesty were erased in order to make them acceptable as offerings to the indigenous deities.

49. Tristan Platt, *Estado tributario y librecambio en Potosí durante el siglo XIX* (La Paz, 1986).

50. H. Lechtman, "Pre-Columbian Surface Metallurgy," *Scientific American* 250.6 (1974): 56–63, p. 63. It should be noted that Europe had its own tradition of hermeneutic interpretation of precious metals—in the science of alchemy.

51. Quoted in J. Flores, "Enqa, enqaychu, illa y khuya rumi," in Jorge Flores Ochoa, ed., *Pastores de puna: Uywamichiq Punarunakuna* (Lima, 1977), 223.

52. In some areas, buried treasure is explicitly identified with the gold of the Inca which, it is said, went underground when he was garrotted by the Spanish and will only return to the surface when his decapitated head has grown a new body and the old order is renewed (e.g., the version of the myth recorded by J. Roel Pineda, "Version del mito de Inkarrí," in Juan Ossio, ed., *Ideología mesiánica del mundo andino* (Lima, 1973), 222–223.

11

"Women Are More Indian": Ethnicity and

Gender in a Community near Cuzco

MARISOL DE LA CADENA

This chapter explores the ways in which gender and ethnic relations have developed and intersected over time in Chitapampa, a peasant community in the district of Taray, which lies only half an hour by public transportation from the city of Cuzco. Chitapampa is a small community, which until the Agrarian Reform of 1969 had long struggled with a neighboring hacienda over their shared borders. Today the village is home to fewer than 100 *comunero*, or villager, families, who dedicate themselves to commercial and subsistence farming. They cultivate mostly maize and potatoes, although some families have cows and sheep. However, livestock is not a general or major source of income. Since agricultural lands are extensively subdivided and small, the sale of their produce does not cover their consumption needs. Consequently, Chitapampinos look for wage work in various places throughout the region of Cuzco. Although Chitapampa lies in close proximity to the city of Cuzco, and the peasants go there frequently, many Chitapampinos remain monolingual in Quechua and are illiterate. In this characteristic, Chitapampa resembles other rural communities in the region. What does distinguish Chitapampa from its neighbors is its recent history of land struggle and internal conflict.[1]

It was not this distinction, however, that made me challenge the received wisdom about Andean principles of complementarity and subordination as the basis of social organization. It was their conceptual inadequacy in describing and explaining the conflictive nature of gender relations and hierarchy in Chitapampa. According to many recent ethnological studies on the Andes, relations of complementarity between men and women have prevailed in traditional villages until gender equality was ruptured by "mercantile penetration" and women were assigned a peripheral place. More recently, the ethnohistorical work of Irene Silverblatt and ethnography of Florence Babb have explored the dynamics of gender hierarchy and market relations among Andean peoples in colonial and contemporary contexts.[2]

Certainly, the earlier emphasis on gender complementarity in rural Andean society is refuted by the evidence gathered from contemporary Chitapampa and neighboring communities. For while women actively participate in agricultural tasks, they are also verbally and physically abused by their own menfolk. Behind that behavior lie deep-seated assumptions about women's inferiority and infantility. Setting out to study gender complementarity, then, I discovered a radically different reality. Although the principle of complementarity governs the sexual division of labor, women occupy an inferior position in this normative order.[3]

If the subordination of Chitapampino women did not surprise me very much, I had not foreseen the task of having to explain ethnic differences within this peasant community. I had assumed the terms *misti* and "Indian" (so in vogue in the 1960s to explain inequalities in some regions of the sierra) would not be analytically useful. Instead, economic, or class, differences between and within communities would account for relations of domination in the countryside, as well as for the dominance of urban over rural areas. I further assumed that the Agrarian Reform Law of 1969 and its populist rhetoric had eradicated ethnic inequality along with abolishing servile relations. I never imagined that, under specific circumstances, differences between peasants from the same community, and even between spouses, would be framed in ethnic terms.

But I found the contrary to be true: although economic stratification was important, ascriptive ethnic identities structured and legitimated social hierarchies within Chitapampa. To understand the complexity of gender and ethnic inequalities, then, I have situated my analysis in the complex dynamic between the mental and material reality through which the comuneros, men and women, organize and apprehend their daily life.[4] From this perspective, the cultural values and ideology surrounding social relations are as real as the power relations themselves. Furthermore, popular notions of ethnicity form part of the historical process of ethnic identity formation and change. This occurs on two analytical planes: both personal interactions, on which day-to-day and face-to-face interactions take place, and the broader regional and national field of force, in which dominant ideologies shape and legitimate power relations. At the intersection of these levels, individuals construct or contest their ascribed ethnicity within specific social contexts of power and domination based on class and gender inequalities. Thus, while the social indicators of ethnicity (the everyday masks of Indianness or non-Indianness) might change, the ideology of ethnic hierarchy may endure at the macro or micro level. In the region of Cuzco, for example, material appearance (the disappearance of Indian homespuns, the spread of Spanish and urban cultural forms to rural areas) might on the surface indicate that "Indians are disappearing"; however, the discursive practices of everyday life on the edges of Cuzco or in the countryside continue to differentiate Indians from mestizos and even to deepen the stigma of being Indian for some sectors.

According to the hegemonic regional ideology, "Indian" and "mestizo" are closed, bipolar constructions, standing in diametric opposition. From this perspective, individuals have an identity, according to a cluster of characteristics that mark their personage. Thus someone is either Indian (Quechua-speaking monolingual, illiterate, and peasant or livestock raiser) or mestizo (a migrant or urban resident, bilingual in Quechua and Spanish, and literate). Contradicting this regional ideology of fixed, bipolar ethnic categories is the fluid, protean, and contingent process by which people attach ethnic labels to themselves or others. Depending on the circumstances of daily life, a person has almost limitless possibilities to construct, and mix, Indian and/or mestizo identities.[5]

Furthermore, in material reality, the categories of Indian and mestizo are inherently relational. Ethnic identities are constructed through complex interactions in accordance with the attributes that are recognized and confirmed, often through conflict, in particular power relations.[6] It is not unusual, for example, for someone to be seen and see himself as Indian in one ongoing relationship, while he self-identifies as mestizo in another.[7] The Chitapampino merchant who prepares to leave his community in the morning for the city is considered mestizo in his village, as he gives orders in Quechua to the workers who stay behind tending his crops and chats in Spanish with the other passengers in the truck bound for Cuzco. Once he arrives in the city, however, the wholesaler looks at him as an Indian and treats him as such, giving him orders in Quechua while speaking to others in Spanish. A recurrent experience among the Chitapampinos, this example suggests that in everyday, material life, both identities—Indian and mestizo—are acquired and lost through dynamic, conflictive processes rooted in implicit and established hierarchies, and legitimated by regional cultural norms.

Both ideological and material aspects of ethnic identity and hierarchy legitimate mestizos' subordination of Indians. However, the content of ethnic constructions is socially and historically contingent and can be shaped and wielded for different political ends—to oppress or empower; to legitimate or subvert authority. Historically, peasants and urban popular classes in the region of Cuzco have deployed ethnic labels and racialist discourses, often modifying the meanings or attributes of Indian and mestizo to suit their own purposes without necessarily undermining regional ethnic hierarchies. However, the Chitapampino case is interesting because the community has created its own ethnic hierarchy—superimposing mestizos over Indians. Thus where the dominant elites would see only Indians in Chitapampa, Chitapampinos themselves behold sharp ethnic inequality in the community.

The strategy used by the Chitapampinos to challenge the dominant view of peasants as a seamless category of Indians has been to identify mestizos in the peasant communities, in accordance with the level of contact that the comuneros have with urban sectors. This does not mean that the urbanization of rural people has not always existed, or that the difference between Indian and mestizo in the community is a new result of present-day migration. Nor does it mean that all migrants experience cultural *mestizaje*. But it is a truism in the local culture that an urbanized peasant becomes more mestizo in the eyes of his fellow comuneros. As we shall see, gender difference informs and reinforces ethnic identities in Chitapampa.

Ethnicity, Gender, and the Concept of Work

The peasants of Chitapampa, and probably those of other communities in the region as well, order their local worlds according to differences, in ways that incorporate and reinforce inequalities between men and women.[8] A mestizo woman, for example, can subordinate an Indian man but not a mestizo man; a mestizo man, on the other hand, enjoys superior status over all indigenous men and women and over mestizo women as well. Men can undergo cultural mestizaje whether or not they are married, while an indigenous woman who stays in the community will retain her Indian identity until the moment that she formalizes an engagement, at which point her ethnic mobility begins.[9] When Chitapampinos, both men and women, fold gender into ethnic categories, women lose ground. Indigenous women are the last link in the chain of social subordination: they are the least ethnically or socially mobile, and their Indian identity approaches closure.

Furthermore, the interweaving of ethnic and gender subordinations in Chitapampa reveals itself in patriarchal relations that begin in the nuclear family and hierarchically order relations within and between families, and within the community and between the community and outsiders.[10] Chitapampino patriarchs are heads of extended family groups, composed of two or more nuclear families. To be the head of one of these groups means to control the agricultural resources and properties of their children and, in some cases, grandchildren. They also exercise control over the labor of their descendants and monopolize decision-making about matrimony and transfers of property.[11] The Chitapampino patriarchs decide when and with whom their children marry, and which children should work with their parents if they hope to inherit family lands.[12]

The patriarch's power to mobilize labor and organize productive work derives from two factors: possession of land and capacity to work. The second factor legitimates the first. A patriarch who cannot work, because of age or whatever other reason, often must concede his rights to the land to his successors. On the other hand, as long as he can direct and participate in production, he dominates decision-making about work on his lands. Even when he has conceded the use of some plots to those of his children who have their own families, he remains the owner of the properties. His status as property owner gives him sufficient authority to ensure that his children work for him, in their fields or in any other activity, whether productive or festive.

The evaluation of men's and women's relative capacities to work also provides a source of gender inequality. For the Chitapampinos, men's capacity to work is greater than that of women, primarily because men can plow and women are traditionally excluded from that task. Further, a man's capacity to work is evaluated according to the degree of control that he exercises over a work group, familial or not. This is not to say that women see themselves as useless, or that they do not contest these values. In fact, they occupy strategic sites in the cycle of family reproduction, such as controlling seeds during the harvests and the daily sale of goods in city markets. Yet neither of these tasks is considered to be "work." On the contrary, they are perceived as activities demanding no physical or mental exertion: "women sit down to do their selling," say the men; "even children can do it," is another frequent comment. One consequence is to deny women access to status and power in the community. Instead, their social position is acquired through their male partner.[13]

The Chitapampinos' notion and valorization of work have been transformed and spread into the urban sphere, incorporating regional changes into local definitions of ethnicity. As we shall see, the city has assumed increasing importance as a source of economic power and political prestige. Urban work is valued more highly than rural work. "Urbanized" work encompasses certain craft skills (shoemaking, carpentry, masonry, or baking), as well as the skill of negotiating (the Chitapampinos refer to it as *conversando*, conversing) with urban functionaries, mainly ministerial officials, professors, and representatives of nongovernmental organizations. Thus defined, urban work serves to distinguish mestizos from Indians: "Indians don't know how to work as well as mestizos do" is a widely accepted assertion among the Chitapampino comuneros.[14] In popular discourse, women have no proficient relations with the urban world, given their incapacity to work there, and thus are stigmatized as being "Indian" in the community's ethnic hierarchy.[15]

In short, shifting, value-laden definitions of work are central to Chitapampa's ideology of gender inequality. With the redefinition of the valorization of work, the new construction of ethnic differences also affects the base of the patriarchal structure of Chitapampa, which in the near future might see itself threatened by a new patriarchal system structured around young, landless, but successful urban migrants. Changes in the meaning and value of work have occurred, together with transformations in the structure of landholding, as we shall explore next.

"Women Are More Indian"

Patterns of Inheritance and Peasant Patriarchy

At the beginning of this century, property in land was an important element of social stratification among peasant families of the community. Peasant patriarchs concentrated their landholdings through marital alliances and inheritance practices, thus consolidating various facets of local power in the hands of family groups whose genealogies can be followed until today. Because of differences in property holdings, siblings of the same parents were separated into different spheres of economic power and authority. The owners of the largest properties (see Table 11.1), who were the patriarchs of that time, were not brothers, but relatives—brothers-in-law—who belonged to the family groups that then controlled power in Chitapampa. The leaders of these groups had been the principal heirs of landed property in their respective families. Their siblings and direct kin appear among the other, lesser proprietors. Alliances might bring together brothers-in-law and cause conflict among brothers themselves for land, owing to the particular inheritance system that privileged some children at the expense of others. In particular, it discriminated against women.

At the turn of the century, Chitapampa husbands were the principal owners of family lands, while wives possessed only small parcels of land. This pattern was the logical outcome of local inheritance norms governing the distribution of agricultural lands.[16] Among male and female siblings, there were three categories of heirs: the primary descendant, the secondary descendant, and "others." In most cases, the first two were male. The primary heir usually inherited about 80 percent of the family property, while the secondary heir would receive between 10 and 15 percent.[17] Remaining lands were divided among the others, whether they were male or female.

Intimately related to the patterns of inheritance was the system of matrimony, which forged symmetrical or asymmetrical alliances among leaders of family groups in the community and in the region. At the moment of matrimony the classification of siblings revealed its importance: male children were designated either as principal or secondary heirs in order to cement strategic marital relations. As marginal heirs, female children did not bestow wealth or prestige to their in-laws; women did serve as strategic resources in negotiating extended kinship alliances. In practice, families tried to offset the liabilities of female heirs by exchanging pairs of

Table 11.1. Landed Property in Chitapampa (1900–1920)

Size of Property (ha)	No. of Proprietors	Average Size (ha)
Less than 1	50	0.75
1 to under 2	7	1.00
2 to under 3	6	2.00
more than 3	3	6.00
Total	66	

Source: Map and census of Chitapampa done by Margarita Huayhua and Liliana Sánchez in August 1987.

brothers and sisters. While the two brides were subordinated to their respective husbands, the latter would bestow property and prestige to their new families. Having exchanged sons and lands of roughly equal proportions, the two families—united by marriage—would have reproduced their symmetrical relations.

Over the last fifty years the social basis of patriarchal relations has changed, along with the criteria that rank the heirs. Heirs are no longer classified solely according to the quantity of land that they are going to receive. Furthermore, access to land appears to be more equally distributed. But if we step back from the local canvas of land tenure, we can better appreciate how the insertion of Chitapampa into the modernizing regional economy of Cuzco has sharpened gender inequalities in the community.

Changes in peasant communities like Chitapampa are closely linked to larger social and ideological "processes of modernization" in Cuzco and its surroundings, which began to accelerate at the end of the 1940s.[18] While the urban infrastructure underwent modernization in the 1950s (with the transformation of means of communication and the construction of buildings, both inspired by the boom in tourism and urban businesses), by the 1960s pressure from peasant and urban popular sectors began to elicit radical changes in social relations and cultural values throughout the region. Regional transformations culminated with the official restructuring of the landholding system, decreed by the Agrarian Reform Law of 1968 and implemented in the early 1970s. Released from servile relations and drawn by wage work, peasants began to migrate more frequently, to Cuzco, the subtropical *ceja de selva,* and distant provinces to earn money over two or more seasons. Many migrants hoped to begin life anew in the city of Cuzco. Some achieved their goals; others did not. What is certain is that the city's influences—its institutions and norms—became a daily presence in the life of peasants throughout the entire region. These urban influences were magnified in communities like Chitapampa, which lay in close proximity to the departmental capital. The collapse of urban/rural boundaries could also be seen in the city: Cuzqueños could no longer ignore the permanent and swelling presence of "urbanized" peasants.

Processes of land fragmentation and scarcity inside peasant communities gave further impetus to migration. Captives in a shrinking rural world, peasants looked to the economic opportunities the city offered, and urban employment began to supplant land as a symbol of status and power inside the community. The cultural devaluation of land was a result not only of its fragmentation but also of the normative degradation of peasant lifeways that took place as access to cities became easier and less mediated by the patrons of the earlier period.[19]

As value of land lost its material and ideological value, inheritance customs changed. Chitapampa men no longer looked on land as a source of status and wealth, and women, who once had been excluded from direct possession of land, now found themselves inheriting small, scattered land parcels. Landholding statistics tell the story: as the average size of landed property declined by almost one-half over the course of this century, the percentage of female heirs has almost doubled (see Table 11.2). If previous inheritance customs excluded women from owning land, once the main source of local prestige and wealth, contemporary practices permit women to inherit land now that its cultural value had declined. These more "democratic" patterns of land distribution effectively free community men to pursue alternative sources of income in the city. Men can afford to do this only when there is an "alternative" heir who stays behind cultivating food and managing herds and lands. Women fulfill this role in the domestic (household) economy and so remain more deeply invested in the rural sphere. Such household strategies of survival thus confine women to the ideological sphere of rural Indianness.

If landholding is no longer the social basis of local patriarchy, then, access to urban institutions, patrons, and employment certainly is. Rural patriarchal relations reach deep into the urban sphere, privileging male migrants over women and even local peasant patriarchs. Now one observes a

Table 11.2. Inheritance and Gender in Chitapampa

	Men	Women	Total No. of Heirs	Average Property Size[a]
1900–20	53 (78%)	15 (22%)	68	1.14
1940–70	112 (69%)	49 (31%)	161	0.91
1970 . . .	141 (60%)	94 (40%)	235	0.68

Source: Local Census and Genealogies of Inheritance (1987)
[a]The local unit of measure is the *topo*, which equals approximately 0.3 hectares.

chain of power that links countryside to city, and which is often expressed in ethnic and gender idioms.[20] Mestizo male migrants are most strategically positioned to exploit their knowledge, experience, and contacts in the city, while peasant women remain behind in the village—the last link in the chain of power, and the most "Indian" of all.[21] Wedged in between and jockeying for better positions among themselves, are peasant men, as well as mestizo women who have returned to the community. Let us now turn to examine how Chitapampinos have engendered ethnic categories to order and make sense of their changing world.

City and Country, Mestizos and Indians, Men and Women

In the first decades of this century, the peasants who migrated to the city often lost their ties to the community and entered into various forms of servitude under *hacendados, compadres,* and other patrons who facilitated their life and livelihood in the city. Our oldest informants recount the time when women migrated to the city more frequently than did men. Without good inheritance prospects, only those women who married under favorable conditions could afford to stay in the community and enjoy a legitimate place within the extended family.[22] Unmarried women were not simply marginalized in the community, but they were cast aside by family members. At the mercy of relatives that might (or might not) offer them sustenance, many unmarried women contemplated their future as servants of mestizo families in neighboring villages or in the city.

Indian women were frequently sold or rented to mestizo godparents, as payment for past or future favors. Male children were also given to mestizos in exchange for favors; however, urban prospects for men were better. Although both began as servants, most men soon left the domestic sphere of their urban patriarch or matriarch. Some Indian men learned trades and eventually became master craftsmen in artisan guilds. Women had fewer economic options: some remained as domestic servants; others became street vendors or went to work in *chicherías*. But unless they were able to peddle goods in the streets of Cuzco, most women remained tied to their mistresses.

This urban scenario began to change in the early 1920s, although the pace of urban change quickened in the 1940s and 1950s. In those years, the landed oligarchy fell on hard times, as new sources of monied wealth sprang up in the city. Traditional hacendado-servant relations, which had long defined ethnic differences, disintegrated under the force of peasant movements in the 1960s and the 1968 agrarian reform. Under General Velasco, the official discourse banished the term "Indian" and replaced it with "peasant," signifying the transformation of rural labor relations under the new regime, as well as the government's adoption of a decolonized, popular rhetoric. Although effaced from official rhetoric, ethnic distinctions and hierarchies surfaced in everyday discursive practices. But they were also adjusted to fit changing social conditions. Whereas landowner-ship once defined "mestizos" and "whites" as such, now urban residence, employment, or lifestyle determined who was "non-Indian." The city of Cuzco, which had once beckoned and harbored Indians in the early part of the century, became the site and symbol of "de-Indianiziation."[23] Similarly, the material markers of Indianness (*chullos, ojotas,* and *bayetas*—the distinctive hats, sandals, and thick woolen cloth of the indigenous people) faded before new, more subtle signs of ethnic otherness. These markers allow mestizos to distinguish themselves from Indians, although they are virtually invisible to outsiders and even to the Cuzqueño elite. These new identity markers pervade and order ethnic relations, but also reveal more fluid and permeable ethnic boundaries. After all, they are no longer associated with a tangible possession, such as land.[24]

In Chitapampa today only a small minority is identified in absolute or fixed terms—either Indian or mestizo. When one asks a Chitapampino

Table 11.3. Ethnic Differentiation in Chitapampa

	Males	Females	% of Population
Indians	4 (26%)	11 (74%)	15 (15%)
"In Process"	20 (37%)	33 (63%)	53 (52%)
Mestizo	24 (70%)	10 (30%)	34 (33%)

Source: Census of Chitapampa, August 1987, and "Local Ethnic Classifications." (Includes only adult couples.)

about the ethnic status of one or another villager, a common response is "he is neither one nor the other; he is 'in process.'" This observation points to the open-ended and contingent nature of ascribed ethnic identity. For Chitapampinos, the cultural process of mestizaje consists not only of changing clothing, food, or language, but of acquiring local status and prestige by "learning to work" or by studying. Crossing ethnic boundaries in Chitapampa does not entail ridding oneself of some cultural elements in exchange for others, but rather acquiring the cultural resources associated with, and necessary to, urban pursuits. Yet people who emigrate are not the only ones capable of assuming mestizo identity. Urban cultural influences are channeled through official education, which at times translates into various levels of literacy, no more. There are other, more subtle sources of urban (mestizo) identity: the type of music one listens to, the preferred drink and food (and expertise in preparing them), hair styles, and the mastery one shows over urban slang—all are indicators of ethnic status among Chitapampinos.

The idea of being "in process" as a stage in ethnic identity, in spite of its nonfixity and dynamism, implicitly supposes an acceptance of ethnic and racial bipolarity. Table 11.3 is an attempt to establish the broad parameters of putative ethnic identities, according to the classification used by Chitapampinos themselves. Among other things, it suggests the dynamism of ethnic identities in Chitapampa.[25] In Chitapampa, and probably in other parts of the region, the fixing of ethnic attributes is intimately connected to the gender of the social actors. As the table shows, the "mestizo" population is overwhelmingly masculine, while most "Indians" are women. If ethnic subordination distinguishes superiors from inferiors, this distinction holds for gender inequality as well. As we have seen, the engendering of ethnic hierarchy has very much to do with how women have been "sentenced" to life and work, in effect freeing men to move into the more privileged economic and cultural spheres of the city.

Historically, cultural mestizaje has developed within the parameters of local patriarchal values, which traditionally have devalued women's work. Even as women have become heirs and caretakers of family plots in recent decades, local gender ideology has marginalized them as economic providers or workers. On the one hand, Chitapampinos define work in terms of those tasks (such as plow work) requiring brute force. On the other, "common sense" holds that if women attempt these tasks "they will take ill, and do it poorly," damaging their biological reproductive capacities. By definition, then, women cannot "work" without putting their essential functions at risk. Even when women are potential heirs, their "incapacity" to work diminishes their possibilities to acquire landholdings unless that activity is mediated by the presence of a "working" male.

Furthermore, the feminization of the rural community has its counterpart in the perception of the city as the male domain. Not only are mestizo men "more capable of working" in the city, but the city represents "sexual danger" for Indian women. Such norms serve to prescribe female chastity, as well as to discourage women from leaving the community and violating their prescribed gender roles.

This is not to suggest that women are unfamiliar with the city or with urban culture. Quite the contrary: in keeping with the sexual division of labor, Chitapampino women are in charge of selling the community's carrots, potatoes, and onions in Cuzco's markets. Every day, women load their *q'epis* with produce and leave the community at dawn to travel in pick-up trucks to the city. They set themselves up in one of the markets where their regular customers can find them and busy themselves with sales until late in the afternoon. When their sales are over, they purchase small quantities of soap, kerosene, candles, noodles, and sugar. Then they make their way back to the community. Men and children accompany them only in the harvest season, when more than one person is required to carry the sacks and sell the abundant amounts of produce. However, this "women's work" is not recognized or valued as such: prevailing male views hold that the sale of products is not work because it is done "sitting down." For them this labor is secondary and derivative—the fruit of masculine work. Purchasing products for household consumption is denigrated as "spending money" earned from masculine labor.

The only other urban outlet for peasant women is domestic service. In that fact alone, not much has changed since the early part of the century. Contemporary stereotypes of this work are that it mainly entails cooking—merely an extension of the domestic tasks that women do within the community. Ironically perhaps, this type of work is virtually the only avenue of female social mobility in the urban context. The domestic skills they acquire can serve to push them (in spite of their gender) into the ranks of urban mestizos. In contrast to Indian women "who only know how to boil potatoes and make *lahuas* [a peasant soup]," mestizo women are valued as "very good cooks," who can make "stews, rice, and cakes," for which skills they are highly appreciated in community fiestas.

Thus, just like the men, women can acquire the status of mestizo through acquiring urban skills. Note that in Table 9.3 the majority of the women appear in the category "in process." But unlike those of the men, the skills and employment that women acquire in the city are not considered to be "work." Thus even urban feminine activities bestow a limited power within their own homes and community.

Conclusion

The historical fabric of power in Chitapampa is interwoven with various threads, among which ethnicity, class, and gender are the most important. In the region, ethnic differences between whites, mestizos, and Indians sort out and justify power relations, which historically were constructed on the basis of land monopolization. In the middle of this century, those foundations were threatened and destroyed by an insurgent social movement, so that today differences between Indian and mestizo are represented by perceived differences between country and city. Where once ethnic differences coincided effectively with class conditions (Indians being equal to landless peasants, and mestizos to landholders), today—in both regional practices and ideology—rural people are distinguished from city-dwellers, even when neither one group nor the other is purely urban or rural. Through traditional marital alliances with mestizo hacendados early in the century, reinforced by political alliances with insurgent regional leaders in the 1960s and intensified by recent migratory flows between city and country, Chitapampinos have reconstrued power, authority, and prestige in relation to regional ethnic differentiation. In this journey they have gone from accepting the indigenous condition of cultural inferiority to rejecting that condition through their own struggle to de-Indianize, first individually and then collectively.

The comuneros of Chitapampa distinguish among themselves as Indians, mestizos, and those halfway between—so aptly labeled as "in process." Patriarchal relations have been reordered, as Chitapampinos appropriated the dominant regional discourse on inequality to interpret and legitimate shifting power relations within their own community. Thus Chitapampa comuneros have ideologically integrated themselves within the dominant discursive framework, according to which Indians are inferior to mestizos. The cultural cost of appropriating this racialist discourse has been to import its symbolic violence into the very heart of communal relations. But it has also produced its ideological counterpart: triggering the "process" of ethnic mobility. Many Chitapampinos have resisted racialist violence by moving to the margins of Indianness, even though being "in process" presupposes a position of inferiority to which they might always "return." If, on the one hand, the ambiguity of the regional framework allows for the "process" of leaving behind Indian status in everyday relations, the possibility of taking on that status anew, when confronted with someone "culturally superior," always exists. It is in the intimacy of everyday relations in the street, marketplace, and village that implicit decisions and identities are made about who is, and who is not, Indian. Because the definition of a person's capacity to work is central to ascribed ethnicities, gender intersects with status to structure and legitimate ethnic inequality within the community and even within households. Thus, within the regional and local confines of modern patriarchy, modernization has reinforced the Indianization of women, while opening the option of cultural mestizaje to most men.

Notes

A preliminary version of this article was published as " 'Las mujeres son más indias:' Etnicidad y género en una comunidad del Cusco," in *Revista Andina* 9.1 (1991): 7–29. Fieldwork was carried out in 1987 by the author and two collaborators, Margarita Huayhua and Liliana Sánchez. I thank the members of the Cedep Ayllu, and in particular Alex Chávez, for their contributions to this study. The translation was done by Julie Franks and Brooke Larson.

1. Investigators and activists who have worked in the area share this opinion with neighboring villagers. While no one knows why the Chitapampinos are so "conflictive," most believe it has to do with the village's proximity to the hacienda. This explanation is not very convincing, however, since the three other communities also share borders with the hacienda and provide labor for its owner. What is certain is that Chitapampinos led the struggle against the owner and took over the recovered lands, apparently without much resistance from the neighboring communities.

2. Among the earlier, pathbreaking studies on gender complementarity, see Tristan Platt, *Espejos y maíz: Temas de la estructura simbólica andina* (La Paz, 1975); Olivia Harris, "Complementarity and Conflict: An Andean View of Women and Men," in J. S. LaFontaine, ed., *Sex and Age as Principles of Social Differentiation* (New York, 1978), 21–40; Billie Jean Isbell, "La otra mitad esencial: Un estudio de complementaridad sexual en los Andes," *Revista Andina* 5 (1976): 37–56; and Isbell, *To Defend Ourselves: A View through the Andean Kaleidoscope* (Austin, 1978). Compare Irene Silverblatt, *Moon, Sun and Witches: Gender Ideologies and Class in Inca and Spanish Peru* (Princeton, 1987), and Florence Babb, *Between Field and Cooking Pot: The Political Economy of Marketwomen in Peru* (Austin, 1989).

3. The manner in which both terms have been used lends itself to confusion. Generally the concept of "complementarity" has been used to mean "equality." I am using "complementarity" to explain the material reality in which the sexual division of labor occurs: the work of women is as necessary and well-defined as is that of men. On the other hand, I use the term "subordination" to refer to the explanations that peasants themselves use to make sense of gender inequality.

4. In this, I have benefited from the suggestion of Maurice Godelier, *L'idéal et le matériel: Pensée, économies et sociétés* (Paris, 1984).

5. For example, one might speak "better" or "worse" Spanish, and clothing might combine elements of mestizo and Indian dress.

6. In Cuzco, when identities are confirmed in the material reality of interactions, ethnicity acquires "volatile" characteristics that operate in spite of—and together with—an ideology that speaks of the solidity of interethnic barriers. De-

pending on the context, the fluidity of the material reality and the rigidity of the ideological reality vary. The ways in which rigidity and "volatility" interact in particular interethnic relations depends on the concrete historical situation.

7. Examples of this phenomenon are found in Erwin Grieshaber, "The Changing Definition of an Indian: A Comparison of the Bolivian Censuses of 1900 and 1950" (unpublished manuscript, 1984); and Penelope Harvey, "Muted or Ignored: Gender, Ethnicity and Politics in the Southern Andes," paper presented at the 66th Congress of the Latin American Studies Association, New Orleans, La., 1988. See also the pioneering article by Enrique Mayer, "Mestizo e indio: El contexto social de las relaciones interétnicas," in Fernando Fuenzalida et al., eds., *El indio y el poder en el Perú rural* (Lima, 1970), 87–152.

8. Various studies look at gender relations in the region of Cuzco. See Sarah Radcliffe, "Migración campesina de comunidades campesinas," *Allpanchis* 25 (1985): 81–121; Harvey, "Muted or Ignored"; and Linda Seligmann, "To Be In Between: The Cholas as Market Women," *Comparative Studies of Society and History* 31.4 (1989): 694–721.

9. If she migrates successfully, a woman can be considered mestizo upon her reentry into the communal context.

10. Generally speaking, the patriarchy could be described as control over productive resources, labor force, and reproductive capacities, based on notions of superiority and inferiority legitimated by differences in gender and generation. Patriarchal domination orders not only gender, but men themselves as a group. For another example in the Andes, see Susan C. Bourque and Kay B. Warren, *Women of the Andes: Patriarchy and Social Change in Two Peruvian Towns* (Ann Arbor, 1981). In Latin America, the historical manifestations of patriarchal systems incorporate, among other local cultural traits, ethnic and economic differentiation. The subordinate indigenous people, sometimes feminized and sometimes not, appear in the patriarchal structure as "minors" and therefore are incapable of exercising direct control over their economic and biological reproductive potential. See Silverblatt, *Moon, Sun and Witches,* for the Andes and Florencia E. Mallon, "The Conflictual Construction of Community: Gender, Ethnicity and Hegemony" (Unpublished manuscript, 1990), for Mexico. In *The Symbolism of Subordination: Ethnicity in a Guatemalan Town* (Austin, 1978), Kay Warren illustrates the case of Guatemala.

11. The Chitapampinos also have herds, but the possession of livestock does not significantly contribute to the modes of economic stratification. The herds are small, and grazing areas in the community are limited.

12. Inter- and intragenerational conflicts mostly revolve around property inheritance. Blows between potential heirs and between them and landowners are

* commonplace and create enduring conflicts in the community. At issue in these conflicts are the legitimacies of the patriarch and his successor.

13. According to the criteria of patriarchal hierarchies, unmarried daughters occupy the lowest of all positions within the family, and their potential as a future wife is what gives them a place in the familial matrix.

14. This assertion contradicts another commonplace in other areas, according to which "mestizos don't know how to work." Elsewhere different meanings adhere to mestizo and work. The mestizo who "doesn't know how to work" is exclusively urban, and the work he doesn't know how to do is agricultural. The folk wisdom cited in the text is specifically that of Chitapampinos and cannot be generalized beyond the situation described.

15. This of course is an ideal representation. Obviously, there are widows and married women who direct the process of work within their family units, in the absence of their spouses. Generally these women are considered to be mestizo in Chitapampa.

16. The scarce literature on patterns of inheritance in the Andes assumes that in peasant communities inheritance is bilateral, with men and women inheriting roughly equal portions of land. See, for example, Bernd Lambert, "Bilaterality in the Andes," in Ralph Bolton and Enrique Mayer, eds., *Andean Kinship and Marriage* (Washington, D.C., 1977), 1–27; Juan Ossio, "La propiedad en las comunidades andinas," *Allpanchis* 22 (1983): 35–60; and Isbell, *To Defend Ourselves.* However, the information that we collected in the community reveals a pattern of family property and a system of inheritance very different from what is commonly acknowledged.

To obtain information about landed property, my co-investigator, Margarita Huayhua, made a map of the parcels of land in Chitapampa as they existed at the time of our fieldwork. With the map in hand, together with a census of all of Chitapampa's resident families that we had previously done, we questioned owners about the origins of their parcels. We asked if they had been purchased or inherited from their mother or father; in the case of inherited property, we asked if they knew how their parents had obtained the land. We ended up with two maps that traced two generations back from the present owners.

The process of compiling the maps allowed us to cross-check the accuracy of the comuneros' responses. After all, although the number of parcels had grown, and the extension of each one would now be less than it had been, the total extension of the community was about the same (with some exceptions well known to all comuneros). Therefore, the oral information had to coincide for the map to take shape, as if every bit of information was a piece of a jigsaw puzzle. With our puzzle complete and the entire extension of the community accounted for, we could then go back to our informants, young and old, and correct errors.

17. The comuneros did not explicitly mention these terms; neither did I ask what Quechua or Spanish terms might be used to express this classification. The adjectives "principal," "secondary," and "others" are terms that we came up with in the process of analyzing information on the distribution of land. Nevertheless, they proved useful in explaining the relations upon which patriarchal power in Chitapampa is based.

18. See José Tamayo Herrera, *Historia social del Cusco republicano,* 2nd ed. (Cuzco, 1981); and José Luis Renique, "Kausachun Qosqo: La lucha del Cusco por la descentralización y el desarrollo regional (1900–1930)," (unpublished manuscript, 1990).

19. In some cases the devaluation of land was purely ideological since in spite of fragmentation, the yields per hectare increased, thanks to changes in methods of cultivation.

20. The objective in exercising community power is twofold. Urban-dwelling Chitapampinos are interested in augmenting their incomes with agricultural claims, just as those who stay in the community want to cultivate relations that will facilitate future migrations or their daily contacts with urban merchants. Community politics are also characterized by this double objective that organizes interfamilial power alliances. The formation of ties through marital alliances between rural and urban Chitapampino families is very common.

21. This in no way is meant to suggest that the women conserve traditional aspects of the peasant culture, while the men become modernized. In the first place, the fact that women now inherit land does not mean that they have no contact with the city or with modern aspects of peasant culture. By the same token, greater urbanization among men does not mean that they abandon traditional cultural practices. In the second place, the traditional/modern dichotomy is not equivalent to rural/urban, nor is it considered within the Chitapampino definitions of Indian and mestizo.

22. Those who did not marry inside the community often married peasants from outside. Intercommunity marriages are still frequent in the microregion today.

23. The de-Indianizing capacity of the city has been a theme in the discourse of the *indigenista* intellectual elite of Cuzco since the 1920s. One of the tasks accomplished by the 1912 census of the then-Provincia del Cercado del Cuzco, done by the university, was to make invisible the indigenous presence in the center of the city. The census takers accomplished this by defining the Indians living in

the most central streets as servants of hacendados, and therefore only incidental and transitory city dwellers. When the hacendados disappeared under the 1970 agrarian reform, this artifice disappeared as well, but the rhetoric that it produced had already introduced the city to its de-Indianizing potential. Thus, peasants who migrated to the city and established themselves there could use the images in circulation since 1912, to de-Indianize themselves. On this, see Marisol de la Cadena, "Decencia e indigenismo: La ciudad del Cuzco y los caballeros de 1920," *Revista Andina* (1994): 79–122.

24. I do not mean to suggest by this that Indian and mestizo were not materially fluid categories before the agrarian reform, but rather that their earlier representations were much less protean than now. The sharp ethnic images of an earlier age are disappearing from official and public rhetoric in the Cuzco region.

25. We obtained the information used to construct the chart by asking a group of informants about the ethnic identity of each of the comuneros, men and women. Using the community register and the census of domestic units, we put together a group of men and women and met with them in two sessions as they identified their families and neighbors.

V

Conclusion

12

Ethnic Identity and Market Relations:

Indians and Mestizos in the Andes

OLIVIA HARRIS

This volume has focused on the varying forms in which the indigenous population has participated in markets since the earliest days of the European presence. What, then, are the forms and limits of mercantile activities at different historical periods for those who are classified as "Indians"?[1] In what ways do ethnic labels structure the parameters of participation in different markets? Further, do market relations play a part in defining ethnic identity?

In the late twentieth century local merchants and traders who derive the greater part of their income from commerce, even on a petty scale, are mestizos.[2] By contrast, the people most unambiguously classified as Indians in the high Andes are those whose economic reproduction does not depend decisively on markets. This being the case, the very definition of Indian identity today is a function of their limited market participation and is often associated with poverty and backwardness. The arguments and the empirical data of the preceding chapters help to outline the fluctuating process by which, first from the complex economy admired by the Spanish in the 1530s and then from a colonial society in which some Indians were wealthy by any standards, the category of Indian is today identified with subsistence-oriented communities and usually also with poverty. This development was far from linear. However, there is a beginning—the wealthy Inca economy about which a certain amount is now known—and an end point in the form of the present-day difficulties of Indian communities in many parts of the Andes. In the process, while certain indigenous institutions and organizational principles maintain continuities, they have also been refunctionalized by changing economic and political conditions.

It is clear from many of the contributions to this book that the commonplace idea that Andean peasants were and are resistant to participation in commercial circuits cannot be sustained. This does not of course mean that they were docile pawns in the economic projects of their rulers. Resistance there certainly was, and is—but not to markets as such. Rather, it has been to certain forms of coercion by which they have been forced to hand over their surplus, to offer their labor and produce at disadvantageous or unjust rates, or to sell or give up land vital for the reproduction of their agriculture. The strategy of colonial and republican administrations was by and large to impose ever tighter control over the terms of Indian participation in different markets. What many of the chapters hint at, and what needs further exploration, is the unequal terms on which indigenous Andean populations so often entered—and still do—into market relations with others and how closely this inequality is linked to ethnic differentiation.

In the introduction, Chapter 1 in this volume, Brooke Larson discusses critically the dualism implicit or explicit in so many accounts of Andean economies, which contrasts market with nonmarket economic activities as though they were two independent spheres.[3] Nonetheless, a number of historical realities have given particular strength to dualistic models of Andean economies, of which three are especially significant.

First, the model for the economy of Tawantinsuyu provided by John Murra goes far beyond the common negative labels used to characterize economies not incorporated into the world system. In particular, given the absence of money and markets in the core Inca system, it provides a stark contrast to the mercantile order introduced by the Spanish. Murra and those who have elaborated his model have provided a set of positive concepts with which to understand its high productivity, as well as the complex system of circulation and distribution across enormous distances.[4] The political and economic system imposed by the European colonizers was in an absolute sense profoundly destructive of the unique and efficient economic order that was operating at the time of the last Inca kings, as Murra has repeatedly argued.

Some enthusiasts have appropriated Murra's model as a transhistorical slogan for what makes Andean cultures ineradicably different and have as a result favored a dualist model based on contrast. However, most of those who have studied the operation of "verticality" in Andean economies since the sixteenth century have taken pains to locate it within a precise historical and economic context, and to show how nonmercantile forms of circulation—albeit on a reduced scale in comparison to Tawantinsuyu and the early colonial period—were complemented by market distribution.[5] As a result, what at the moment of conquest were two opposed and incompatible systems, over time produced different varieties of hybrid accommodation and integration.

A second historical reality that appears to endorse a dualist model of Andean economic structures can be found in the consistent attempts of colonial governments from the time of the Toledan reorganization to preserve Indian communities and their independent control over resources. Motivated by the need to guarantee Indians' ability to pay tribute and especially to perform *mita* labor, the policy was legally formalized as the two republics—that of the Indians and that of the Spanish. The image of two separate worlds was thus enshrined in colonial legislation, even though an observer as early as Polo de Ondegardo recognized that in practice the two republics were heavily interdependent (Thierry Saignes, Chapter 6 in this volume).

A third historical reality that reinforces dualistic classification is the way in which social classes and economic activities are identified with different ethnic labels grounded in racial classifications. It is this issue that I wish to explore in the following pages. All too often the nature of Indian identity in the twentieth century has been read back onto the historical past. Today's commonplace alignment of those with high levels of participation in markets, or involved in smallholder agriculture, to a mestizo identity is the result of a long drawn-out historical evolution which has been little studied. Before this process had fully developed, the colonial category of Indian embraced a far wider range of social classes and occupational groups than it does today.

Ethnic Categories and Colonial Markets

Indians as a Fiscal Category

The term Indian, used from Columbus on to refer to the native inhabitants of the Americas, became in the Andes fundamentally a fiscal category by which the obligations of the native population to the colonial state were defined. Its role was to provide labor and rent for both the Crown and the church, and for individual Spanish conquerors. It was of course also colored by the concerns over "purity" of blood and depth of commitment to Christianity, which the Spanish brought with them to America.

The Indians' obligations to the Spanish king were formally similar to the role of the *hatun runa* under Tawantinsuyu, but the main form in which they paid surplus to the Inca state was in human energy; to the Spanish *encomenderos* and state, however, payment was in produce and then money. Spanish exactions also promoted the homogenization of the native population. The ethnic policy of Tawantinsuyu emphasized difference (for example the clothing regulations), and while some labor obligations were standardized, particularly that of cultivating state lands, in others ethnic difference was articulated in specialist obligations. By contrast, in the Spanish system fiscal differences were only regional, connected to productive specializations such as wool or coca leaf.[6] The Toledan reforms— by commuting most tribute to money and by specifying Indians as mita laborers regardless of their particular skills—made one Indian tributary formally the equivalent of all others. Spanish mita service might be in mining, in cloth production, agriculture, *tambo* service, or transporting ice to Lima, but there does not seem to have been a recognition of, or use of, ethnic difference in assigning mita Indians to different work.[7] This process of homogenization was furthered by mass migration and urban experience, especially in the mines.

The obvious racial and cultural contrasts between Spanish and Indians, legally inscribed as the two republics, were grounded in an economic distinction. "Indians" were those who were liable to tribute and mita, whereas non-Indians were not.[8] The *alcabala* sales tax and tithe regulations further emphasized the radical difference between the two categories. In both cases they were paid primarily by non-Indians, and native American produce from Indian lands was exempt. Tithes were only paid by Indians on crops from land rented from the Spanish, or from bought land, and on European crops and livestock; alcabala was paid only when Indians bought from non-Indians in order to re-sell. Tandeter makes clear that the official justifications for this policy shifted over time. In the sixteenth century the Indians were exempted on the ground of their "rusticity." By the eighteenth century the rationale had shifted, and Indian exemption was instead justified by the need to promote commerce among them (Enrique Tandeter et al., Chapter 7 in this volume). However, the reality may have been in practice to inhibit Indian commerce.[9] A similar observation can be made with respect to the labor market insofar as Toledo envisaged that one of the forms in which Indian labor would be employed was as mita. In other words, while both tribute and mita were closely tied to the development of the internal market, the formal structuring of the colonial economy envisaged the Indians as participating in the developing markets on different terms from those of the non-Indians—as the source of revenue rather than as its beneficiaries.

Indian Wealth in a Mercantile Age

The Toledan settlement also attempted to homogenize the Indian population in class terms by substantially reducing the numbers of lords eligible for privileges and exemptions and by limiting the amount of Indian service available for those who were eligible.[10] In reality, there were many ways in which Indians could reproduce their wealth, or become more prosperous in the new economic conditions, with expanding urban markets, new trades to be learned, and the need for pack animals to transport goods from the point of production to that of the market and of consumption. For one, there was the possibility of buying and selling land as a collective, and increasingly as a private, resource.[11]

The great wealth of many lords is now well established. They could draw on the free labor of their subjects or hire them out to Spaniards as *marahaques*. This is matched by Matienzo's concern, voiced in the 1560s, that the riches of some *kurakas* in Potosí enabled them to behave "like Spaniards."[12] In spite of Toledo's restrictions on the lords' access to labor, and in spite of the repeated accusations of malpractice and abuse, many of them amassed great wealth: seventeenth-century caciques owned haciendas and rented out land to Spanish and forasteros (Saignes, Chapter 6 in this volume); the estates of the Liro de Cordovas of Tapacarí were administered by a creole (Brooke Larson and Rosario León, Chapter 8 in this volume). The wealth and social position of the kurakas also made itself felt in the urban world where they sometimes owned extensive properties.[13] Stern emphasizes the ambiguities of some of the deals made by kurakas and the problems in ascertaining how far their motives were for personal gain or for the protection of their subjects, and their responsibility for the tribute and mita of their people (Steve Stern, Chapter 3 in this volume). By the late eighteenth century, Europeans and criollos were wont to complain of the "unfair advantages" of wealthy Indians, since in addition to their fiscal exemptions they did not have to pay wages.[14]

The kurakas were key intermediaries between state and people—between market and peasants. However there was also internal stratification among tribute payers. We know that there had been significant differences of wealth among the Lupaqa pastoralists in late Tawantinsuyu. With increased internal migration in the early seventeenth century, access to land became a new basis for social differentiation among tribute payers. Those who had abundant land were able to buy exemption from the mita as "money people" or *qullqi jaqi/runa*,[15] to rent out their lands, and to hire the labor of other Indians.[16]

One field that deserves further research is that of consumption. Susan Ramírez details the European produce listed in the wills of lords in the early decades of colonial rule, while the wills of commoners contain less mention of exotic consumption goods (Chapter 5 in this volume). In the mid-eighteenth century Indian levels of consumption became a major issue. The *repartimiento de efectos* can be read as evidence of the earlier success of Indian groups in determining the level of purchases in the commodity markets, in that they were a forcible means of increasing that level to what, in the calculations of the large Lima merchants, would resolve the crisis in levels of Indian consumption (Stern, Chapter 3 in this volume). On the other hand, the massive Indian consumption of stimulants (especially coca, and also *chicha* and wine) had played a key role in the development of the internal market,[17] and Scarlett O'Phelan argues that levels of market participation were high in the eighteenth century, indeed that they were a major cause of the great insurrection of 1780, especially since most of the leaders of the rebellion were involved in trade and *arrieraje*.[18] While much research remains to be done, one can at least conclude that government concern over levels of Indian market participation at different periods should not be taken literally, but be seen as reflecting a profound crisis in the whole economy.

Migration and Changes in Fiscal Categories

Labor markets reveal similar ambiguities. There were early efforts to stimulate wage labor, but it was easier to get wage laborers through the command of the lords than through direct monetary incentives. The massive population movements registered in documents from the seventeenth century on, and the rapid expansion of the category of forasteros, is a many-faceted phenomenon which to some extent reflects a partial commoditization of labor. Ann Zulawski's discussion of how and why a full labor market did not develop in Oruro (in contrast, for example, to Mexican mines) is useful in this context, emphasizing the significance of agriculture and ore theft in addition to wages for reproducing the labor force, as well as the effect of the mita obligation itself and prolonged demographic decline.[19] Moreover, the sector of Oruro's and other towns' Indian populations that was fully separated from agriculture and really dependent on earning money was not a mining proletariat but comprised mainly craftspeople and travelers who brought supplies to the city.

There are suggestive indications on who these forasteros were who left their communities of origin. The research of both Saignes and Zulawski strengthens the revisionist reading which, rather than assuming that forasteros were fleeing the burdens of tribute and mita, emphasizes that some of them kept links with their families and *ayllus* of origin, paying tribute and sharing the responsibility for the mita even though in the early colonial period they were legally exempt. Many of them had limited access to resources in their ayllus—for example, if they were illegitimate children whose rights to land would have been circumscribed. Their status in the communities in which they settled was generally subordinate: many forasteros paid rent to *originarios* and did mita duty for them. Others supplemented their resources by trade.[20]

The increase in the numbers of *yanaconas* is particularly striking since they were often highly mobile and over the generations lost any reference to a rural place of origin.[21] Their tribute dues were based on their occupation, and it was not necessarily assumed that they had a land base. They were not eligible for mita service, and this exemption led to a massive registration of Indians as yanaconas of the king in the seventeenth century, abandoning their ethnic affiliation, changing to European dress, and learning a craft or becoming traders. Women might register their children as having an unknown father in order to gain exemption from the mita. Free wage laborers, for example in Potosí, were also classed as yanaconas, as were the permanent laborers on the haciendas which expanded in the eighteenth century in some areas, for example, in Cuzco and Cochabamba.[22] In short, they were not under the authority of a cacique; their fiscal status was different; in employment, income, and lifestyle, they might be closer to the Spanish than to rural peasants, and yet they were still classified fiscally and legally as Indians. They were a permanent and expanding group of "urban Indians"—that category which in more recent times has become so much a transitional and an oxymoronic concept.

Changed though they were, forasteros and yanaconas remained within the republic of Indians. Accompanying this transformation was the increase in the numbers of mestizos.[23] Mestizos, whose expansion as a category was not envisaged when the principles of the Leyes de Indias were encoded, were classified as belonging to the "republic of Spaniards," although they were barred from many positions in colonial society. Thus they too were not liable to pay tribute, still less to perform mita service, and were forbidden to live in Indian villages and towns, though as their numbers grew this rule was increasingly hard to sustain. Many retained ties to their home communities; some sought leadership positions,[24] but others were scarcely distinguishable from forasteros, renting land from originarios and engaging in trade and handicraft production.[25]

Among the strategies used to "pass" into the category of mestizo, obviously the most direct was miscegenation. However as Spalding notes, in the Lima region the easiest way to pass to mestizo status was by highly mobile occupations such as that of sailor or *arriero*,[26] in other words by diminishing the ties with one's kin group and lying about one's origins. This denial is made explicit in Bertonio's dictionary where the Aymara term *huayqui haque* is translated in Spanish as "mestizo, neither fully Spanish nor fully Indian" and its cognate *huayquicchaa* is glossed as "illegitimate or bastard, and also someone who belonging to one nation or people says he is of another, or someone who denies his parents."[27] Real or claimed illegitimacy was another strategy by which women gained mestizo status for their children.[28] In other words, the process of *mestizaje* often involved denial of one's past or at least separation from one's origins. It is impossible to tell what proportion of mestizos by the end of the eighteenth century were products of miscegenation, however remote, and what proportion had dissembled. Be that as it may, the transition from the category of Indian to that of mestizo entailed a more profound rupture than that of forastero and yanacona migrants. Even in cases of miscegenation, fiscal categories privileged one remote European ancestor over many Indian ones and so promoted a vision of absolute difference between mestizos and Indians, rather than recognizing the ambiguities of mixed parentage.[29]

How far this difference was articulated culturally and economically is not yet clear. By the late seventeenth century "Indian" culture was thoroughly "mestizo" in the sense that all aspects of it were profoundly affected by European imports and vice versa. It is not clear that the difference between Indians and mestizos was expressed systematically in cultural terms, although a precondition for "passing" to mestizo status was the adoption of the Spanish language and dress. But there were certainly many poor rural mestizos as well as prosperous ladino Indians in cities. Land was a fundamental source of wealth, so that Indians who still controlled good land at the end of the eighteenth century were wealthy.[30] Access to land brought access to labor. The possibility of maintaining large herds and the existence of a functioning mercantile system limited the degree to which the Spanish authorities could control the access to wealth by Indians, and they also drastically altered the hierarchies within the republic of Indians as some commoners acquired new riches and therefore higher status.

Repositioning Mestizos and Indians in the Republican Period
Consolidation of Ethnicity as an Economic Relation

Early republican legislation was inspired by the desire to shake off the past, to take advantage of the economic benefits of independence from Spain and its colonial monopolies, and to create citizens out of the Indians by abolishing the colonial legislation that defined the category of Indian itself—tribute, labor services, the protected status of Indian land. However, these ambitions were short-lived, foundering on an economic reality of stagnation and disruption from the prolonged war. In such circumstances, the new republics turned back to their only secure source of revenue—the Indian tributes, which they had abolished on doctrinaire liberal grounds, although the change of name to "indigenous contribution" was designed to disguise the continuity and make it seem more voluntary than the old colonial tribute.[31]

In a predominantly protectionist environment, in which local production was shielded from competition because of the high cost of transport, the Indians' mercantile interventions continued and were not merely restricted to obtaining money for the tribute. Indian economic activities in this period of relative stagnation have been extensively discussed by Tristan Platt, for example the Lipes ayllus with their vast llama herds and their role in transport.[32] In fiscal terms there is some evidence that the highlands were "re-Indianized" in the first half of the nineteenth century, for example in the overall stability of fiscal categories until the 1850s, and the reclassification of some mestizos as (Indian) tribute payers in order to guarantee their rights to land they had been squatting.[33] How far such "fiscal Indians" accepted their new identification in cultural and social terms doubtless differed according to circumstance, and in some areas there was soon a significant increase in registration as mestizos, for reasons of social rank as well as financial considerations.[34]

While the broad structure of rural society might remain relatively stable in the first half of the nineteenth century, the institution of republican government had decisive long-term consequences for the "republic of Indians." As Andres Guerrero has noted for Ecuador, the reinstitution of Indian tribute meant de facto the continuance of the colonial structure of tribute collectors and land rights, but at the same time republican local government led to the growth of an alternative authority system, which gradually superseded that of the *curagas* and fragmented many Indian groups through the operation of new administrative units such as *cantones* and *parroquias*.[35] In the late colonial period there had been important changes in the incumbents of rural office. Hereditary kurakas were replaced by mestizos who made the most of their positions as tribute collectors to appropriate ayllu lands and to enjoy the obligatory labor of the Indians. They might also monopolize trade in the Indian communities.[36] The rural priests, too, were able to exploit their position; in one case in Atunhuaylas (Peru) the priest simultaneously acted as tithe collector, general trader, landowner, and subcontractor of the confraternity herds.[37] The position of the hereditary noble Indian families became increasingly ambiguous. In many cases, they intermarried with the local mestizo elite and took on administrative posts in local government. Christine Hünefeldt discusses a landowner subprefect of Azangaro in the 1830s who came from a cacical family, and Carlos Mamani Condori quotes the example of a hereditary cacique who became corregidor in Taraqu (Pacajes) in the 1860s. It appears that in many cases they became absorbed into the category of mestizos.[38] The contrast between tribute-paying Indians and those who enjoyed access to their labor and resources as intermediaries of the state was thus increasingly inscribed as an ethnic difference.

The mid-century boom in the various Andean countries was confined to a few export crops and raw materials; however, it was enough for tribute to be abolished in Peru in 1854 and in Ecuador in 1857.[39] As a result, to be an "Indian," no longer a fiscal classification, became more like a class position. In Ecuador, the category of Indian that was abolished along with the tribute was de facto re-created by the introduction of "subsidiary work" to be organized by the ethnic authorities,[40] and a similar process occurred in Peru with the introduction of compulsory road-building labor, to which in theory all were to contribute the same amount but which was in practice relegated to the Indians.[41]

Growth of Mestizo Control over Indians and Their Resources

The marked population rise[42] and the growth of urban markets in the second half of the century expanded the labor market and commercial opportunities. Erick Langer's account on the barley boom in Tarabuco, though focusing on the early twentieth century, is illustrative of a process that went on *mutatis mutandis* in much of the Andean highlands. The mestizos in the pueblos took advantage of the commercial expansion, lending money, renting Indian land or appropriating it in less legal ways, and buying Indian produce in order to resell.[43] Another well-documented case study is that of wool, the one "export crop" produced directly by the highland Indian communities, whose commercialization dominated the southern highlands of Peru in the second half of the nineteenth century. Much of its production remained in the hands of "free" Indians (although livestock haciendas also expanded); however, its commercialization was increasingly monopolized by mestizo middlemen who sold it to the exporting houses in Arequipa. In Caylloma near Arequipa, *llameros* from the communities took the wool to Arequipa themselves until the railway was built, bringing in mestizo intermediaries.[44] Manuel Burga and Wilson Reátegui emphasize the importance of *compadrazgo* in oiling the commercial relationship between mestizo intermediaries and Indian wool producers of free communities; for example, one mestizo trader in Sicuani claimed to have 600 Indian compadres. But Indians kept careful watch on price fluctuations of wool, and the profits that mestizos made came more from *astucia* and false weighing scales than from price-fixing itself.[45]

This pattern was a general one as Indians lost income from droving and transporting, and also the prices they could obtain for their produce on the domestic market declined as a result of external competition. Old people in the mining region of northern Potosí remember how they used to be rich, eating plenty of food bought in company stores when they worked with their llamas transporting mineral from the nearby tin mines in Uncía/Siglo XX before the railway was built. In many areas with the expansion of the railways, not only transport but also trade passed into the hands of mestizos, although not without resistance on the part of the Indians.[46] In the highlands of southern Peru, mestizo *gamonales* took over the management of both the local state and the market, and to some degree also of the Indian labor force.[47] In other regions Indians were expressly prevented from marketing their own produce.[48] However, the same long-term processes that undermined Indian income from transport and commercialization did open up new possibilities in labor markets, particularly in mining and plantation agriculture. Henri Favre writes of the highland communities of Huancavelica flocking down to the coastal plantations of the Cañete in the 1880s in order to break their dependence on the mestizos of the valley pueblos.[49] In the mining sector, too—for example, in Cerro de Pasco in the central Peruvian highlands—the use of a system of debt bondage (*enganche*) seems to have operated effectively as a means of recruiting labor from the second half of the nineteenth century, given the existence of poor peasants eager to escape dependence on local pueblos or with not enough land for subsistence.[50]

A market in land had been envisaged in early republican legislation as a means of stimulating Indian entrepreneurs. Mid-century attempts to make land available for purchase proved paradoxically to be a further means of excluding Indians from participation in commercial activities, for a number of reasons. Those Indians who were incorporated into the expanding estates at the end of the nineteenth century were excluded from commercial activity without becoming a rural proletariat. Moreover, very little investment went into land so that agricultural techniques were correspondingly rarely affected.[51] Much of the land that passed out of Indian control was not bought legally but changed hands in more dubious and ambiguous ways, for example through debt, compadrazgo, intimidation, and tactical use of the law, as well as the squatting on "vacant lands" from an earlier period. In view of such tactics, Jacobsen has argued that one should probably speak of the myth of a land market at this time—that is, a means of justifying the dubious acquisitions of the expanding landowners—rather than an actual land market in which land changed hands through voluntary sale and purchase.[52] "Free" Indians despised those who were subject to the new haciendas,[53] and the mass appropriation of Indian lands was met by many forms of resistance varying from armed uprisings to legal battles.[54]

There is evidence of profound contradiction between the ambitions of state legislators and local realities of power. The former, inspired by liberal ideologies, at various moments sought to do away with the category of Indians by abolishing the bases of their collective identity, particularly through landholding. In addition to the assaults on collective land, even Indian religious festivals were suppressed in Ecuador.[55] But there were strong local vested interests for maintaining a distinctive category of Indians. For example, service obligations continued in force in rural areas, ignoring the fine sentiments of legislation which officially abolished them. In Peru such legislation was repeated again and again throughout the nineteenth and early twentieth centuries, worth little more than the paper it was written on.[56] Indians thus remained a source of free or cheap labor, no longer to their lords and as mita workers, but to local landowners, merchants, and representatives of the state. Mestizos made handsome profits from them in other ways, too—in the low or nominal "prices" they paid for Indian produce and livestock, or in the high charges they levied for milling Indian flour.

In many spheres, mestizo economic activities were of very dubious legality—for example, their acquisition of (Indian) land and their appropriation of Indian labor and produce. For all the changes since the colonial period, then, the status of mestizos remained highly ambivalent, recalling the ambiguity of their legal position in much of the colonial period[57] and the direct illegitimacy or falsification of their origins in many cases.

Bases of Mestizo Identity

While some Indians might live in urban space (often a colonial pueblo), they were primarily defined as living in rural communities, working land that remained de facto communal even if de jure such a status was denied. By contrast, mestizos were identified with the "civilization" of nucleated urban settlements and individual ownership. They might make their living through agriculture, but it was organized along different lines from the Indians' productive activities. Those regions of the Andes such as southern Ecuador (Loja), northern Peru, and the Cochabamba valley, which had predominantly individual smallholder agriculture, were correspondingly classified as mestizo rather than Indian. After the abolition of the fiscal distinction between the two categories, the process of ceasing to be an Indian and becoming a mestizo was no longer an affair of the state, but it remained very much the concern of the local powerbrokers, whose position relied on the existence of a subservient Indian labor force and a local monopoly on trade and price-setting mechanisms. In southern Peru until the 1860s one could still find cases of prestigious and affluent Indians treated as equals by local notables, but in subsequent decades such equality became rare, as hacendados, merchants, and officialdom associated "Indianness" with backward peasants or estate *colonos* and further polarized rural identities.[58]

The social and demographic forces that produced a rise in the numbers of mestizos have been little studied as yet. Transition to mestizo identity is certainly connected with increased participation in the markets, a shift away from subsistence production to forms of trade, employment of the labor of others, or waged employment, even if on a very modest scale. For example, Carlos Contreras's study of the early republican central sierra of Peru notes that "Indians (*indígenas*) who were inserted in the mercantile sphere as owners of an estate or enterprize oriented to commercialization" were registered as mestizos. Such evidence makes it clear just how closely ethnic categorization was linked to economic activity. Contreras also describes the delicate set of calculations for Indians in the Mantaro region in the 1840s as to whether they should reclassify as mestizos, thereby ending their liability to pay the contribution, but instead becoming liable to pay the alcabala sales tax.[59] In the cities, as available land for cultivation by the urban Indian population was swallowed up in new urbanization, they became mestizos.[60]

The shift from Indian to mestizo within an individual's lifetime would usually involve migration—a break with one's place of origin in order to work at the lowest level of unskilled labor in cities, mines, or plantations or as domestic servants. Full incorporation into the category of mestizos involved denial of one's identity, one's past, one's origins. This denial frequently involved—and still does—changing one's family name (for example, among Aymara speakers, from Mamani to Aguilar, from Kamaqi to Camacho, from Wilka to Villegas) and thereby distancing oneself from one's kinsfolk.[61] Changing one's clothing, one's diet, and one's language were crucial indicators, and remain so today. We can hypothesize that the coercive control over Indian populations wielded by mestizos was certainly facilitated by their radical denial of similarity, even when this was contradicted by the ambiguous realities of everyday life. Within the category of Indians there were of course endemic conflicts, both within communities and between different groups. And "mestizos" in some circumstances shared close interests with Indians—for example, in their claims on Indian land.[62]

The practices of everyday life also involved all the ambiguities of daily encounters and mutual dependency, of identification and recognition, as well as of exploitation and rejection. In the pueblos, the mestizos usually spoke the same language, visited the same healers when sick, and celebrated their religious worship in similar ways.[63] And yet their self-definition required the establishment and reiteration of difference between themselves and Indians. In northern Potosí today, mestizo traders when they go to acquire foodstuffs in the Indian communities stay with Indian compadres and accept food from them. But they always re-cook it, or do the cooking themselves and offer food to their hosts in order to maintain the distinction that full commensality would blur. Assertions of hierarchy and difference are also made by established mestizos in urban rituals and fiestas in order to distinguish themselves from new migrants from the countryside.[64]

Mestizo superiority depended on a number of factors, including cultural prejudice, coercive force, and the maintenance of oligopsonic privilege. Mestizos acted as agents for hacendados and as government intermediaries; above all, they controlled peasant access to commercialization and credit. I have also often witnessed mestizo traders in northern Potosí keeping a close eye on the activities and prices of their neighbors and competitors, and harassing those who deviate from the norm and give better prices to the Indians. There is abundant piecemeal evidence in studies of the late nineteenth and early twentieth centuries of ways in which mestizos crushed the attempts of Indians to acquire the fruits of "civilization" and end their subordinate status. It has been difficult, if not impossible, for Indians to obtain schooling.[65] Even wearing non-Indian clothes could be punished: for example, Indians who returned to Acora in 1910 from working in the Chilean copper mines wearing manufactured clothing were beaten up by local mestizos.[66] Moreover, the Indian/mestizo art that had flourished in the colonial period disappeared in the nineteenth century. When the church expanded again toward the end of the century, plastic arts and cultural life were modeled on Europe rather than on the artistic heritage of the colonial period.[67] The economic polarization of rural society was matched by a comparable ideological polarization expressed in "modern" racist ideologies. These played their part in the evolution of the idea of a generic, homogeneous Indian, which was expressed both in legislation and in cultural representation.[68] Until the effects of agrarian reform modified the position of the mestizos in rural pueblos, their control over Indian produce and labor remained tight. They considered that the Indians belonged to them. A typical pattern was for mestizos from time to time to help themselves to Indian livestock, offering no more than token "payment."[69]

Over the course of the nineteenth century the category of mestizo was reorganized and redefined. From having been first a racial and then a fiscal and administrative category, in the republican period it became more clearly an economic and political grouping. The relationship between Indians and mestizos became a quasi-class one: ownership of land was often not at the center of the relationship, but increasing mestizo control over local government, the judiciary, and markets enabled them to dispose of the labor and produce of even "free" Indian communities. In fact, it is plausible to argue that it was precisely because the relationship between mestizos and Indians was not securely a class one that ethnic difference became so important a means for mestizos to legitimate their domination over the Indians. This would help explain the paradoxical nature of mestizo "identity," which in some cases seems to reside in nothing more secure than *not being Indian.*

Indian Communities and Individuals in the Late Twentieth Century
Collective Institutions, Indian Identity

Contrary to the hopes and expectations of generations of liberal reformers since the founding of the republics, economic and social differentiation has not been secured within the Indian population. By eliminating the large landowners, the agrarian reform laws had a dramatic impact on rural life in Bolivia and Peru (though far less so in Ecuador). But domination by mestizos continues—in local government, in commerce, and since agrarian reform especially in rural education—although it is less violent and more accommodating than in the first half of the century.

Indian communities as they exist today are profoundly transformed from the ayllus that functioned under Inca rule. The very system of common field agriculture may well be an import from Europe.[70] By creating a whole new apparatus of local administration, republican legislation substantially furthered the process of ethnic fragmentation, and the progressive erosion of "vertical" organization has meant a serious reduction in resources available to peasant households, and hence in their ability to spread risks. Nonetheless, in highland Bolivia coordination of economic activities and long-term bonds can still today incorporate groups far larger than the local community, even though the authority of caciques over such groups has been increasingly restricted, and in most cases the common lands belonging to the group have also long since been individualized. In spite of the fact that larger groups and their resources have been fragmented, in spite of marked differences in wealth and status between community members, and for all the conflict both within and between groups, however, the language of community is pervasive. "We are all the same" is a common response.[71] This discursive assertion of equality is reinforced by institutions such as festive sponsorship or collective work, both of which presume a formal equivalence of all households even though in reality they are stratified.[72] Differentiation is more likely to be pronounced in mestizo populations.

Many of the preceding chapters have argued against dualistic interpretations of Andean economies in favor of an integrated approach. However, while the "Andean" is inextricably linked with the commercial, participation in markets on whatever scale tends to be the affair of individual households. It is this combination of collective and individual strategies, including mercantile and nonmercantile forms of circulation, as well as the systematic application of differential rates to those within and those outside the ethnic group, that I have elsewhere termed the "ethnic economy." Collective organization guarantees the reproduction of the conditions of production and is oriented usually to subsistence crops. It is not at all incompatible with individual and household strategies of market exchange and accumulation. There is little evidence in the Andes of the corporate management of accumulation and commercial investment that has worked so well for kin-groups in some other parts of the world. Today, in contrast to previous centuries when wealth lay in land and in flocks, and when in at least some cases caciques orchestrated a collective participation in the different markets, the collective is generally associated with the nonmarket sphere, and intervention in markets is an affair for individuals, much in the time-honored vision of liberal philosophy.[73]

There are many reasons for the continuity of Indian communal organization and institutions, particularly deriving from the nature of highland agriculture and reproduced through their religious worship, which is closely bound up with collective reliance on the land and its fertility. The typical resource base in highland communities is a mix of agriculture and livestock raising. Since nowhere in the high Andes has it been found profitable or feasible to enclose pasture land, community control is essential to manage pasture resources and prevent livestock from damaging the crops. In addition, high-altitude nonirrigated fields (known variously as *laymi, moya, turno, liwa, muyuy, aynuqa,* and *manta*) are usually subject to collective decisions concerning length of fallows and when to bring them under cultivation again, both in order to coordinate with livestock raising and to guard against erosion and degradation.[74] Again, some forms of productive investment in agriculture, notably irrigation systems and terracing, require collective management.

Mutual aid is also based on institutions perceived by community members to be of long-term benefit, reproducing ties of interdependence, and in many cases representing a cost-effective way of distributing labor to land. They are particularly connected with communal forms of agriculture, but are also a resource that can be drawn on more widely in other environments and in times of crisis. For example, mutual aid is often used by new migrants to Lima and elsewhere. However, it appears that the collective institutions of the rural community rarely endure in the urban environment. Once migrants are well established, they turn away from mutual aid to a more limited family network.[75] Collective institutions are fundamental in the definition of Indian identity today. The Aymara movement of recent decades has placed much emphasis on the ethical quality of Indian life, expressed in the strong emphasis on collective responsibility and obligations.[76] In all the debates on whether ethnic identity in the Andes is based primarily on cultural or on economic factors, the role of collective institutions has received little attention. Their importance in defining Indian life is, it seems to me, one of the main reasons why a change in economic circumstances, for example through migration or the decline of community institutions in favor of smallholder agriculture, is expressed as a rupture in ethnic identity.

Seen from outside, the persistence of Indian identity among peasants facilitates their exploitation by non-Indians. However, from their own perspective, there are other, far more positive, reasons for their continuing classification as Indians, which have to do with their relationship with the land. While non-Indians may despise peasant culture, Indian peasants in their turn despise outsiders, who "do not know how to work" and who live by begging from them—for this is often how they perceive the exactions of mestizos. They even feel sorry for these people who have little or no land, who are afraid of real work, and who depend on others to produce food for them.[77] Mestizos from this Indian perspective are individuals who have lost their identity.

Another reason for the comparative lack of differentiation within Indian communities today is that both increased wealth and increased poverty are usually translated into separation from the community, both physically through migration and ethnically through the transition to mestizo status. A noteworthy exception to this general pattern is Otavalo (Ecuador). Many Otavaleños have become prosperous entrepreneurs but have not abandoned their Indian identity, partly because in the second half of the twentieth century they have made it a source of income through the sale of weavings and handicrafts to tourists.[78] But few other Indian groups have been able to capture and control a market for their produce in this way.

In part this is due to the limited possibilities for investment in highland agriculture. The subsistence products of Indians are different from those of city dwellers, the difference in diet being yet another precipitate of ethnic polarization. As a consequence, the market for Indian agricultural products is not particularly expandable.[79] Furthermore, even where there is demand, urban pricing policies are designed not to stimulate Indian supply but to cheaply satisfy urban demand.[80] These economic conditions, together with the objective limitations on what crops can be grown at high altitudes, inhibit investment in agriculture itself, particularly since the specialized and unusual conditions of highland agriculture are not appropriate for many of the solutions proposed by economists for other environments.

In the past, the major form of investment was livestock; today, it is increasingly motorized transportation—in Gilles Rivière's memorable phrase there has been a shift "from llama to Volvo"[81]—related to different forms of commerce. Parents also invest in educating their children so they will be able to obtain skilled or professional employment. These tendencies are particularly clear at high altitudes. In the flat valley lands, where productivity is more easily raised, and investment a more attractive proposition, it is correspondingly more common for rural cultivators to be, or to become, mestizos. The Mantaro valley in central Peru is a particularly instructive example, since it has long been famous as a region where, in Arguedas's words, the Indian population was "motivated by the stimulus of commercial activity and the spirit of modernity."[82] For example, the community of Llocllapampa has retained collective control over significant productive resources such as a silica mine and mineral water springs.[83] But today even in the fertile Mantaro region, many peasants who are able to accumulate prefer to invest outside the rural area, for example in urban enterprises in Huancayo.[84]

Dependence on Markets and the Crisis of Indian Communities Today

In recent decades, there has been a marked overall increase in Indian participation in markets. Agrarian reform and the curtailment of local mestizo and landowner control stimulated them to sell more of their produce.[85] But paradoxically, in many areas of the highlands the viability of agricultural subsistence has been undermined to the point where participation in markets is defensive, a symptom of crisis rather than of economic strength. Population growth was already increasing, and agrarian reform provided further stimulus. In many areas subdivisions of community land have reached a level where peasants can no longer produce their subsistence needs, and the crisis in the availability of firewood has resulted in both ecological degradation and increased consumption of bought foods, which require less fuel for preparation, and hence has led to further dependence on the market.[86] The droughts that affected the Andean highlands throughout the 1980s had similar effects particularly through wage labor.[87] In agriculture itself, there is increasing reliance on chemical inputs, such as fertilizer and insecticide, both because of a marked increase in blights and disease and because of the impact of development agencies who preach the gospels of chemical fertilizers and increased yields and of greater commercialization of agricultural and livestock produce. These policies have often been advocated with little regard for either their ecological or economic consequences.[88] It is not entirely clear what their wider rationality might be.

In view of the limited possibilities for investing in rural enterprises, Indian communities export increasing numbers of their members as temporary or permanent migrants, especially to the cities and colonization zones in the tropical lowlands.[89] But in labor markets, ethnic segmentation repeats the familiar structure by which those classified as Indians are the most disadvantaged. Indians are at the bottom of the wage level because of ethnic prejudice. In the cities, they work as porters, domestic servants, and masons. In cocaine production, it is mainly Indians who stomp the coca leaf, up to their knees in gasoline. In the mines, they do the least skilled, and often most dangerous, work. Small wonder, then, that many Indians now lead a double life in order to lessen the racial discrimination they suffer when they leave their land base, that the drift to mestizo status is pronounced in some areas, and that the boundary between the two is becoming more ambiguous. This ambiguity is especially pronounced for men as migrant labor, education, and military service have redefined their identity. Indeed, it has been argued that increasingly it is women who are the bearers of Indian identity in areas of high migration, and also women—the distinctive *cholas* with their marketing and trading activities—who are the prototypical mestizos.[90] In other words, women's ethnic identity is more clear-cut because of their relatively stable relationships with consumer markets. Peasant men, on the other hand, typically enter and leave markets in a more fluid and mobile way and their ethnic identity is correspondingly less clear-cut.

Social Mobility and Ethnic Change

The category Indian is no longer a fiscal category, nor even a class category, to the degree that it was half a century ago. However, as in earlier historical periods, Indian identity in the second half of the twentieth century is closely related to the ways that their own economic base, and the wider society, permit them to participate in markets. The enduring strength of community organization sets limits to the full mercantilization of the rural economy; conversely, in the context of intense discrimination in the Andean countries today, Indians are disadvantaged in both labor and product markets by being Indians. In spite of the greater fluidity brought by mass education and migrant labor, identity is still conceived today in terms of a dichotomous contrast, the assumption of rupture, and a relationship of opposition between the categories of Indian and mestizo.[91]

As we have seen, this ethnic contrast was inscribed in colonial legislation and was redefined in the nineteenth century by the clear class and cultural opposition between Indians and mestizos. But the lived reality has of course always been far more complex. Moreover, each generation has produced a new wave of Indian aspirants to the condition of mestizos, who may be referred to today as *cholos, mozos, en proceso, sabios,* and doubtless many other local variants.[92] The demographic shifts of the last fifty years mean that for the first time, Indian peasants are no longer the clear majority of the population. Indians may be numerically increasing, but proportionally they are in decline. In Bolivia, these new generations of migrants to the city have found their own distinct political voice.[93] There is evidence that in Peru, too, they have found a distinctive, if very different voice, for it is among the new mestizos that Sendero Luminoso appears to have made many recruits,[94] capitalizing on the conflict between those whose recent forebears were Indians and the older, established mestizos who have been used to exerting control over "their" Indians. Those who make the ethnic shift to mestizaje today hope to raise their status and make a better life for their children, but racism and prejudice remain an enduring reality, and in Peru in particular the possibilities for employment for those who complete an education and become "civilized" are ever smaller, given the current economic crisis affecting the country.[95]

What I am describing is in many respects a familiar pattern of the erosion of functioning peasant life because of changes and growth in the world economy. Migrants the world over always look down on their country cousins, and patterns of kinship and group solidarity are drastically modified. But what we see in the Andes is more than this, because of the ethnic labels that are associated with the process of transition. As Doña Matilde Qulqi, an Aymara woman, laments: "Boys from my village have studied and become doctors, lawyers, teachers. Now they don't understand us any longer. It's as if they were calling us 'Indian, Indian.'"[96] The Andes is unusual in the degree to which this contrast between community and individualism—which recalls the classic sociological opposition between Gemeinschaft and Gesellschaft—is expressed in ethnic terms. But the ethnicity involved is a curious one, because one of the two "ethnic" categories is in a way antiethnic, defined in terms of what it is not, rather than being a bounded group with minority status.[97]

Conclusion

With the current triumph of neoliberal philosophy, in which the positive values of monetary wealth and freedom are closely identified with "the market" and with free trade, the issue of peasantries in many parts of the world takes on a new urgency. Those populations that are not fully integrated into the market system are held to be backward, if not downright deviant, and there is little concern for the historical processes that have marginalized them. This attitude is not new. A recurrent preoccupation by governments throughout the centuries in the Andes has been the supposedly low levels of market participation by the Indians, while at the same time other policies and sectional interests have sought to limit and exploit it.

Three broad categories of market are of relevance in tracing the economic history of those classified as Indians in the Andes: that of land, that of products and transport, and that of labor. In the case of the first, land has been sold by Indians—especially by kurakas in the colonial period— to outsiders since money was introduced into the Andes. However, governments at various critical moments claimed rights to the land so that where sales were made it was the state and not the Indian communities who benefited.[98] Moreover, from the mid-nineteenth century the ways in which land was alienated from Indian control could not in many instances be said to constitute a land market, even though this was the ideological justification used. Indians might sell land at times of low population density, but as population rose and pressure on the land increased, what had been lost could rarely be recovered. In most cases, it became separated from communal ownership, however this was defined at different historical periods, and became private property. Therefore, although Indians sold and bought land, this process could be, and generally is today, one that leads to their abandoning Indian identity. Smallholders, those who own their land individually, are identified as mestizos; Indians are those whose land is administered communally.

In the second case, the product markets, Indian agriculture, livestock raising, and droving activities as llameros and muleteers have in the past generated large surpluses, in spite of the erosion of the resource base and population decline. While much large-scale trading went into the hands of the Spanish from early in the colonial period, the ethnic opposition so familiar today seems not to have been clearly demarcated until the nineteenth century. Those with commercial interests increasingly defined themselves as non-Indian, and by the end of the century the transporting and marketing of produce passed significantly out of Indian hands. Substantial population rise was accompanied by increased pressure not only on their land but also on their labor, and while the tribute was abolished or diminished, other less direct forms of appropriation replaced them, not least the consistent downward pressure on prices for agricultural produce in the expanding urban markets.

In the third case, the labor market, the Andean countries have been and still today are characterized by low levels of proletarianization. Mining is the most striking case: it generated a waged labor force in the colonial period; however, such people did not live solely from their wages but supplemented them with independent extraction of ore and sometimes with agriculture. They were, and still are, complemented by a large temporary labor force that combines waged work with agriculture, or at least retains long-term rights to land. Moreover, in agriculture there has been very little proletarianization except on coastal plantations: in the typical hacienda enterprise even commercial agriculture and livestock raising were usually combined with subsistence agriculture. Since the early colonial period, permanent migration to cities has created a class of urban artisans, traders, and other workers, and this has always involved a shift of cultural identity. During the colonial period, the shift was often from Quechua- or Aymara-speaking peasant to Spanish-speaking yanacona, but during the nineteenth century it was increasingly to mestizo. Recent migrants in the segmented urban labor markets do the dirtiest, often the hardest, and always the worst paid jobs. Only insofar as they distance themselves from their Indian origins do they move upward in the employment ladder. With the abolition of tribute as a defining criterion of Indian identification, the fixity of the category was weakened, but was at the same time reinforced ideologically by the growth of scientific racism with its obsessively repeated message that Indians are inferior and are responsible for the poverty and backwardness of the Andean countries.

Indians are a class to whom accumulation of resources has been progressively denied. The history of Indian identity in the Andes is for most regions a history of wealth turned to poverty. But this poverty is not only the result of colonial and neocolonial extraction, of the erosion of their lands and of their institutions, of preventing their participation on equal terms in labor and commodity markets, but also because of the process by which those who did accumulate altered their status and "passed" to mestizos. Especially since the founding of the republics the result has been a simplification of the category "Indian" to its current identification with those who maintain subsistence agriculture and participate in community institutions. My concern in this chapter has been with the evolution of Indian and mestizo as historical constructs. I have necessarily taken a general view of these notoriously protean and contested terms, and I have not attempted to include an appreciation of the complexity of the self-attribution of identity by different historical actors. Until the recent development of Indianist movements, and still today in rural areas, Indians do not think of themselves primarily as "Indians" but use the term ironically with reference to how they are classified by outsiders. They express their identity more in affiliation to local or regional groups.[99]

The process of rupture, of amnesia, and of denial that separates Indians from their more successful and entrepreneurial kin has, since the Toledan settlement, been part of a process of the reordering of classes, differentially exploited, with different access to the sources of wealth. At the same time, many mestizos, both in the past and today, find themselves in a situation of multiple illegality.[100] However, I am not arguing that Indian identity is reducible to a class position, a view espoused by those who with naive voluntarism sought to abolish the "Indian problem" by changed nomenclature, from "indio" to "campesino."[101] In recent years there has been belated recognition of the more profound and enduring nature of ethnic discrimination and hierarchy. Indians have participated in markets since markets were introduced into the Andean economy, but usually they have been disadvantaged. The multifarious historical processes which have inscribed economic and class mobility in terms of an ethnic transformation only serve to underscore this fact.

Notes

I wish to thank Brooke Larson and Enrique Tandeter for their detailed and invaluable comments on earlier drafts of this chapter. An earlier version was presented to the Andean seminar at the University of Liverpool, and I am also greatly indebted to the lively responses of the participants. Thanks also to Fleur Rodgers for transforming the system of bibliographic references.

1. I have chosen to use the term "Indian" to refer to those populations who are the bearers of native American traditions for a number of reasons. First, because this is the term employed throughout the colonial period, on which a good part of my argument rests. Second, although terminology changed in the Republican period to the more "scientific" term, *indígena,* which is used today especially in Peru and Ecuador, I want to emphasize the element of arbitrariness involved in defining some people as "native" and others not. For this reason, I find the term Indian—itself the product of historical contingency—preferable to indígena with

its pretensions to scientific objectivity and its associations with more recent colonial and racist ideas. Moreover, in Bolivia where I have done research, Indian identity has in recent decades been reclaimed by the Aymara movement and given a positive connotation.

2. In selecting the term "mestizo," inevitably I am begging many questions, as the chapter will make clear. While there is a wealth of terminology, both historical and current, to refer to the population that is "in between" whites and Indians, mestizo is the one most generally employed, both in colonial legal thought and in sociological discourse today.

3. Karen Spalding makes a sustained critique of dualist ideas: see her "Exploitation as an Economic System: The State and the Extraction of Surplus in Colonial Peru," in George A. Collier, Renato I. Rosaldo, and John D. Wirth, eds., *The Inca and Aztec States, 1400–1800* (New York, 1982), 321–342; see also Jonathan Parry and Maurice Bloch, *Money and the Morality of Exchange* (Cambridge, 1989).

4. John V. Murra, *The Economic Organization of the Inca State* (Greenwich, Conn., [1955] 1979); Murra, "El 'control vertical' de un máximo de pisos ecológicos en la economía de las sociedades andinas," in Iñigo Ortíz de Zúñiga, *Visita a la Provincia de León de Huánuco* (Huánuco, 1972), 2:429–476; and Murra, Carlos Sempat Assadourian, and Susan E. Ramírez, Chapters 2, 4, and 5 in this volume.

5. Giorgio Alberti and Enrique Mayer, eds., *Reciprocidad e intercambio en los Andes* (Lima, 1974); Jorge Flores Ochoa, *La complementariedad ecológica en los Andes* (Paris, 1978); David Lehmann, ed., *Ecology and Exchange in the Andes* (Cambridge, 1982); Enrique Tandeter and Nathan Wachtel, "Conjontures inverses: Le mouvement des prix a Potosí pendant le XVIIIe siècle," *Annales ESC* 38.3 (1983): 549–613; Shozo Masuda, Izumi Shimada, and Craig Morris, eds., *Andean Ecology and Civilization: An Interdisciplinary Perspective on Andean Ecological Complementarity* (Tokyo, 1985).

6. An obvious exception was the ethnic category of *urus* who paid a lower rate of tribute. Thérèse Bouysse-Cassagne has argued that they were not so much a distinct ethnic group but the survivors of Inca expansion and exterminist policies toward the Qulla in particular. See her "Le Lac Titicaca: Histoire perdue d'une mer intérieure," *Bulletin de l'Institut Français des Etudes Andines* 21.1 (1992): 89–159. Their low status and poverty became closely linked to their nonintegration into the mercantile system. See Nathan Wachtel, *Le retour de ancêtres: Les indiens urus de Bolivie, XXe–XVIe siècles* (Paris, 1990), 499.

7. Thérèse Bouysse-Cassagne discusses ethnic specializations in peasant obligations to Tawantinsuyu, in *La identidad aymara: Aproximación histórica, siglos XV–XVI* (La Paz, 1987). Discussion of different forms of colonial mita can be

found in Peter J. Bakewell, on mining, *Miners of the Red Mountain: Indian Labor in Potosí, 1545–1650* (Albuquerque, 1984); Luís Miguel Glave, on tambos, in *Trajinantes: Caminos indígenas en la sociedad colonial, siglos XVI–XVII* (Lima, 1989); Karen Spalding, on the ice mita, in *Huarochirí: An Andean Society under Inca and Spanish Rule* (Stanford, 1984); and John L. Phelan, on cloth, in *The Kingdom of Quito in the Seventeenth Century* (Madison, 1967).

8. This clear contrast was confused by the growth of the *forastero* category who were not formally obliged to pay tribute until the eighteenth century. See Nicolás Sánchez-Albornóz, *Indios y tributo en el Alto Perú* (Lima, 1978), ch. 2 and pp. 108–110. However, as Saignes and Zulawski show, forasteros often did make contributions to the caciques. See Thierry Saignes, Chapter 6 in this volume; Ann Zulawski, "Forasteros y yanaconas: La mano de obra de un centro minero en el siglo XVII," in Olivia Harris, Brooke Larson, and Enrique Tandeter, eds., *La participación indígena en los mercados surandinos: Estrategias y reproducción social, siglos XVI–XX* (La Paz, 1987), 159–192.

9. O'Phelan, for example, suggests that the alcabala limited incentives for Indians to enter forms of commerce other than the small-scale exchange of their own produce. However, hacendados also used Indians to commercialize hacienda produce illegally in order to avoid paying the tax. See Scarlett O'Phelan, *Un siglo de rebeliones anticoloniales: Perú y Bolivia 1700–1783* (Cuzco, 1988), 220–221.

10. The caciques attempted to secure the positions of their disinherited kin, for example by assigning them as lay assistants to priests, posts which were exempt from mita and tribute. See Salvador Moreno Yañez, *Sublevaciones indígenas en la audencia de Quito* (Quito, 1985), 383–384.

11. Glave and Stern give examples of land sales. See Glave, *Trajinantes;* Steve J. Stern, *Peru's Indian Peoples and the Challenge of the Spanish Conquest: Huamanga to 1640* (Madison, 1982), 152; and Stern, "The Struggle for Solidarity: Class, Culture and Community in Highland Indian America," *Radical History Review* 27 (1983): 21–45. Moreno Yañez (*Sublevaciones indígenas,* 49) relates that the caciques and Indians of Riobamba sold communal lands in part in order to escape mita obligations.

12. Juan Matienzo, *Gobierno del Perú* (Lima, [1567] 1967); also Assadourian, Chapter 4 in this volume.

13. In La Paz kurakas owned large tambos (where agricultural produce was sold) not only in the Indian parishes but also in the Spanish center. See Rossana Barragán, *Espacio urbano y dinámica étnica: La Paz en el siglo XIX* (La Paz, 1990), 49–50; Christine Hünefeldt mentions that Peruvian caciques had to own not only a house in the local pueblo but also a place in Lima. See her *Lucha por la tierra*

y protesta indígena: Las comunidades indígenas del Perú entre colonia y república (Bonn, 1982), 29.

14. Hünefeldt, *Lucha por la tierra*, 164–167.

15. Thierry Saignes, "Notes on the Regional Contribution to the Mita in Potosí in the Early Seventeenth Century," *Bulletin of Latin American Research* 4.1 (1985): 65–76.

16. Larson and León, Chapter 8 in this volume; Zulawaski, "Forasteros y yanaconas."

17. Carlos Sempat Assadourian, *El sistema de la economía colonial: Mercado interno, regiones y espacio económico* (Lima, 1982); Roberto Choque Canqui, "Los caciques aymaras y el comercio en el Alto Perú," in Harris, et al., *Participación indígena*, 357–378; and Glave, *Trajinantes*.

18. O'Phelan, *Siglo de rebeliones anticoloniales*, 282.

19. Zulawski, "Forasteros y yanaconas"; the topic is also discussed in detail by Enrique Tandeter, "Forced and Free Labour in Late Colonial Potosí," *Past and Present* (London) 93 (1981): 98–136, and Tandeter, *Coercion and Market: Silver Mining in Colonial Potosí, 1692–1826* (Albuqerque, 1993), ch. 3.

20. Saignes, Chapter 6 in this volume; Zulawski, "Forasteros y yanaconas." Daniel J. Santamaría notes that most *piqueros* trading in coca at the end of the eighteenth century were forasteros. See his "La participación indígena en la producción y comercio de coca, Alto Perú 1780–1810," in Harris et al., *Participación indígena*, 425–444.

21. As John V. Murra has emphasized, this category of people, separated from their community of origin, was already expanding by late Tawantinsuyu, so that the colonial phenomenon was not unprecedented. See his *Economic Organization of the Inca State* (Greenwich, Conn., [1955] 1979), ch. 8. Spalding (*Huarochirí*, ch. 7) points out that many yanacona artisans and merchants in Lima came from the minor nobility and did keep links with their place of origin. Glave (*Trajinantes*, 337) notes that women were not eligible for tribute and were therefore more available to move to cities permanently, to work as domestic servants.

22. Tandeter, "Forced and Free Labour in Late Colonial Potosí"; Luís Miguel Glave and María Isabel Remy, *Estructura agraria y vida rural en una región andina: Ollantaytambo entre los siglos XVI y XIX* (Cuzco, 1983); Brooke Larson, *Colonialism and Agrarian Transformation in Bolivia: Cochabamba, 1550–1900* (Princeton, 1988). By 1734 the numbers of agricultural yanaconas was such that thereafter they were registered as a distinct category. See Sánchez Albornoz, *Indios y tributos en el Alto Perú*, 43n.

23. The rise in numbers of mestizos is discussed by Larson, *Colonialism and*

Agrarian Transformation in Bolivia, 111–115, and Martin Minchom, "The Making of a White Province: Demographic Movement and Ethnic Transformation in the South of the Audencia of Quito 1670–1830," *Bulletín de l'Institut Français des Etudes Andines* 12.3–4 (1983): 23–39. The 1795 census of Viceroy Gil for the audiencias of Lima and Cuzco indicates that 57 percent were Indians, 23 percent were mestizos, and 13 percent were Spanish. See John Fisher, *Government and Society in Colonial Peru: The Intendant System 1784–1814* (London, 1970), 6, 251–252. However, in other areas the proportions were very different; for example, in the audiencia of Quito, where only 6.7 percent of the population were mestizos in 1785. See Galo Ramón, "El Ecuador en el espacio andino: Idea, proceso y utopía," *Allpanchis* (Cuzco) 35–36 (1990): 548.

24. Hünefeldt, *Lucha por la tierra;* Roger Rasnake, *Domination and Cultural Resistance: Authority and Power among an Andean People* (Durham, 1988); Ann W. Wightman, *Indigenous Migration and Social Change: The Forasteros of Cuzco, 1570–1720* (Durham, 1990).

25. Larson, *Colonialism and Agrarian Transformation in Bolivia*, 111–115.

26. Spalding, *Huarochirí*, 184.

27. Cited in Rossana Barragán, "Aproximaciones al mundo 'chulu' y 'huayqui,'" *Estado y Sociedad* (La Paz) 8 (1991): 85, 87.

28. Saignes, Chapter 6 in this volume; Thérèse Bouysse-Cassagne, "Incertitudes identitaires métisses: L'eloge de la bâtardise," *Caravelle* (Toulouse) 62 (1994): 111–134. Nicolás Sánchez-Albornóz discusses the assumption, embodied in certain laws, that mestizaje involved illegitimacy. See his *The Population of Latin America: A History* (Berkeley, 1974), 133. Magnus Mörner discusses the *gracias a sacar* certificate that could be purchased to change one's caste status in *Race Mixture in the History of Latin America* (Boston, 1967).

29. Much research remains to be done on shifting patterns of alliance and disaggregation between Indians and mestizos. There are many suggestive indications in the literature on the Great Insurrection of 1780–1783. For example, O'Phelan (*Siglo de rebeliones anticoloniales*, 281) states that many mestizos participated in the insurrection because they saw their position threatened by the Bourbon reforms. Alberto Flores Galindo, on the other hand, indicates that in some instances in 1780 the rebels identified mestizos with the Spanish, as enemies to be killed on principle. See his *Buscando un Inca: Identidad y utopía en los Andes* (Havana, 1986), 125–126.

30. Hünefeldt (*Lucha por la tierra*, 16) argues that in the early nineteenth century, as non-Indians began to take more interest in land, Indians began to react more violently, and their defense of their lands became more directly identified in ethnic terms.

31. Carlos Contreras, "Estado republicano y tributo indígena en la sierra central en la post independencía," *Revista de Indias* 48.182–183 (1988): 517–550. The 1812 Constitution prefigured both the abolition of colonial obligations and the change of terminology. See Sánchez-Albornóz, *Indios y tributo en el Alto Peru*, 189, and Hünefeldt, *Lucha por la tierra*, 164, 171.

32. Tristan Platt, Chapter 9 in this volume, and Platt, "The Andean Experience of Bolivian Liberalism, 1825–1900: Roots of Rebellion in 19th Century Chayanta (Potosí)," in Steve J. Stern, ed., *Resistance, Rebellion, and Consciousness in the Andean Peasant World, 18th to 20th Centuries* (Madison, 1987), 280–323; Platt, *Estado boliviano y ayllu andino: Tierra y tributo en el norte de Potosí* (Lima, 1982); and Platt, *Estado tributario y librecambio en Potosí durante, el siglo XIX* (La Paz, 1986).

33. Paul Gootenberg discusses the stability of fiscal categories in "Population and Ethnicity in Early Republican Peru: Some Revisions," *Latin American Research Review* 26.3 (1991): 109–157. Contreras notes the advantages of registering as *contribuyentes* in early years of the Peruvian Republic in his "Estado republicano y tributo indígena," 547, and Jean Piel takes up George Kubler's (1952) idea of re-Indianization. See Piel, "Las articulaciones de la reserva andina al estado y al mercado desde 1820 hasta 1950," in Jean Paul Deler and Yves Saint-Geours, eds., *Estados y naciones en los Andes* (Lima, 1986), 1:323–336; George Kubler, *The Indian Caste of Peru 1795–1940* (Washington, D.C., 1952). See also Platt, "Andean Experience of Bolivian Liberalism."

34. See Contreras on the Mantaro region in "Estado republicano y tributo indígena"; Ramón gives comparable data for Ecuador in his "Ecuador en el espacio andino," 549. Ramón also indicates that the *alzamiento de los pueblos* of 1843 was partly caused by a proposed "contribution" for mestizos, which they considered would lower their status by treating them as Indians.

35. Andres Guerrero, "Curagas y tenientes políticos: La ley de la costumbre y la ley del estado (Otavalo 1830–1875)," *Revista Andina* 14 (1989): 321–366. Also Ramón, "Ecuador en el espacio andino."

36. René Arze quotes Cañete who in 1789 criticized the "dominio privado de los caciques." He also refers to requests by Indians to replace with Indians the non-Indian caciques who "tyrannize" them. See Arze, *Participación popular en la independencia de Bolivia* (La Paz, 1987), 82–85. This theme is also discussed by Hünefeldt, *Lucha por la tierra*, 23, 30–32; see also Platt, "Andean Experience of Bolivian Liberalism."

37. Hünefeldt, *Lucha por la tierra*, 67–83.

38. Ibid., 387; Carlos Manani Condori, *Taraqu 1866–1935: Masacre, guerra y renovación en la biografía de Eduardo Nina Qhispi* (La Paz, 1991), 22–24; Hera-

clio Bonilla, "Peru and Bolivia," in Leslie Bethell, ed., *Spanish America after Independence c. 1820–70* (Cambridge, 1987), 254–255.

39. The process in Bolivia was more drawn out, as detailed in Sánchez-Albornóz, *Indios y tributo en el Alto Perú*, and Platt, *Estado boliviano y ayllu andino.* Indeed, the 1874 Law of Exvinculation and monetary reform, far from abolishing the tribute, involved attempts to increase revenue from the Indian tributaries. See Platt, *Estado tributario y librecambio en Potosí*, and Platt, "Andean Experience of Bolivian Liberalism."

40. Mark Van Aken, "The Lingering Death of Indian Tribute in Ecuador," *Hispanic American Historical Review* 61.3 (1981): 429–459; Guerrero, "Curagas y tenientes políticos."

41. In Bolivia, along similar lines, the Road Service Act was passed in 1880 and compulsory military service was introduced in 1882, but "Indian" identity remained unambiguous through the continued importance of tribute. See Silvia Rivera Cusicanqui, *Oprimidos pero no vencidos: Luchas del campesinado aymara y quechwa* (La Paz, 1984).

42. Gootenberg, "Population and Ethnicity in Early Republican Peru"; Rory Miller, "Peru, Bolivia and Chile 1830–1920," *AHILA Handbuch des Geschichte Lateinamerikas* (Stuttgart, 1992). Herbert S. Klein, however, notes that in highland Bolivia, population growth was faster during the period of economic recession (1780–1830) than later in the century. See Klein, *Haciendas and "Ayllus": Rural Society in the Bolivian Andes in the Eighteenth and Nineteenth Centuries* (Stanford, 1993).

43. Erick D. Langer, "La comercialización de la cebada en los ayllus y las haciendas de Tarabuco (Chuquisaca) a comienzos del siglo XX," in Harris et al., *Participación indígena*, 583–602.

44. Piel ("Articulaciones de la reserva andina," 330) mentions that the woolproducing Indian communities of the Titicaca region in Southern Peru tried to get direct access to market and rebelled in 1867–1868, but they failed and were repressed again. Nelson Manrique makes clear the strength of middlemen in his *Colonialismo y pobreza campesina: Caylloma y el valle del Colca, siglos XVI–XX* (Lima, 1985), 200–203.

45. Manuel Burga and Wilson Réategui, *Lanas y capital mercantil en el sur: La Casa Ricketts 1895–1935* (Lima, 1981).

46. Silvia Rivera Cusicanqui, "La expansión del latifundio en el altiplano boliviano: Elementos para la caracterización de una oligarquía regional," *Avances* (La Paz) 2 (1987): 112. Mining had been a major source of income until the building of railways. Juan Van Kessel, for example, notes that almost all the local Indians

worked as arrieros around the nitrate mines in the 1870s. See his *Holocausto al progreso: Los aymaras de Tarapaca* (Amsterdam, 1980), 242; see also Platt, Chapter 9 in this volume.

47. José Tamayo Herrera, *Historia social e indigenismo en el altiplano* (Lima, 1982); Piel, "Articulaciones de la reserva andina"; Deborah Poole, "Landscapes of Power in a Cattle-rustling Culture of Southern Andean Peru," *Dialectical Anthropology* 12 (1988): 367–398.

48. The rapid expansion of Indian marketplaces in the Bolivian altiplano after the 1953 agrarian reform took many people by surprise, so engrained was the notion that Indians were resistant to markets. See Katherine Barnes de Marschall, "La formación de nuevos pueblos en Bolivia: Proceso e implicaciones," *Estudios Andinos* 1.3 (1970): 23–38; David Preston, "New Towns: A Major Change in the Rural Settlement Pattern in Highland Bolivia," *Journal of Latin American Studies* 2.1 (1970): 1–27; Xavier Albó, *¿Bodas de plata? O requiem por una reforma agraria* (La Paz, 1979), 36–37.

49. Henri Favre, "The Dynamics of Indian Peasant Society and Migration to Coastal Plantations in Central Peru," in Kenneth Duncan and Ian Rutledge, eds., *Land and Labour in Latin America: Essays on the Development of Agrarian Capitalism in the Nineteenth and Twentieth Centuries* (Cambridge, 1977), 253–268. The theme of highland communities breaking the "restrictions" imposed by their traditional ties to valley pueblos recurs in several other accounts of central Peru—for example, Carlos Samaniego, "Peasant Movements at the Turn of the Century and the Rise of the Independent Farmer," in Norman Long and Bryan Roberts, eds., *Peasant Cooperation and Capitalist Expansion in Southern Peru* (Austin, 1978); Barbara Bradby, "Resistance to Capitalism in the Peruvian Andes," in David Lehmann, ed., *Ecology and Exchange in the Andes* (Cambridge, 1982), 97–122.

50. Alberto Flores Galindo, *Los Mineros de la Cerro de Pasco 1900–1930* (Lima, [1974] 1983), 21; Olivia Harris and Xavier Albó, *Monteras y guardatojos: Campesinos y mineros en el norte de Potosí* (La Paz, 1975); Florencia E. Mallon, *The Defense of Community in Peru's Central Highlands: Peasant Struggle and Capitalist Transition, 1860–1940* (Princeton, 1983), 73–74. By contrast in mid-century, Peruvian plantation enterprises imported black and Chinese workers because of the difficulties of attracting labor from the highlands; see Michael Gonzales, "Capitalist Agriculture and Labour Contracting in Northern Peru 1880–1905," *Journal of Latin American Studies* 12 (1980): 291–315.

51. Rivera Cusicanqui, "Expansión del latifundio"; Mallon, *Defense of Community;* Erick D. Langer, *Economic Change and Rural Resistance in Southern Bolivia, 1880–1930* (Stanford, 1989).

52. Nils Jacobsen, *Mirages of Transition: The Peruvian Altiplano, 1780–1930* (Berkeley, 1993), ch. 6. Manrique, *Colonialismo y pobreza campesina;* Platt, Chapter 9 in this volume.

53. Taller de Historia Oral Andina (THOA), *El indio Santos Marka T'ula* (La Paz, 1984), 155.

54. Ramiro Condarco, *Zarate, el terrible Willka* (La Paz, 1965); Platt, *Estado boliviano y ayllu andino;* Tamayo Herrera, *Historia social e indigenismo,* ch. 3; Mallon, *Defense of Community;* Rivera Cusicanqui, *Oprimidos pero no vencidos;* THOA, *El indio Santos Marka T'ula;* Flores Galindo, *Buscando un Inca,* ch. 5; Condori, *Taraqu 1866–1935;* Jacobsen, *Mirages of Transition,* ch. 6.

55. In 1918: Hernán Ibarra, "La identidad devaluada de los 'Modern Indians,'" in Ileana Almeida et al., eds., *Indios: Una reflexión sobre el levantamiento indígena de 1990* (Quito, 1990), 319–349; Nelson Manrique notes a comparable attempt to abolish Indian fiestas in Huancayo, in *Yawar Mayu: Sociedades terratenientes serranas, 1879–1910* (Lima, 1987), 46–47.

56. Thomas Davies, *Indian Integration in Peru: A Half Century of Experience 1900–1948* (Lincoln, Neb., 1970).

57. Thérèse Bouysse-Cassagne and Thierry Saignes, "El cholo: Actor olvidado de la historia," *Revista UNITAS* 5 (1992): 23.

58. Jacobsen, *Mirages of Transition,* 146.

59. Contreras, "Estado republicano y tributo indígena"; also Hünefeldt, *Lucha por la tierra.* Langer, *Economic Change and Rural Resistance,* 53–54, indicates that some landowners transferred their peons from Indian to mestizo status as a favor.

60. Alberto Flores Galindo, *Aristocracia y plebe, Lima 1760–1830* (Lima, 1984); Rosanna Barragán, *Espacio urbano y dinamica étnica: La Paz en el siglo XIX* (La Paz, 1990).

61. Conversely, once mestizo identity was achieved, mestizos might actively proclaim their kinship with Indians in order to claim land in Indian communities. See Manrique, *Colonialismo y pobreza campesina.*

62. Platt ("Andean Experience of Bolivian Liberalism") shows how, in Chayanta, the 1874 law making mestizo occupation of Indian land illegal led to an uneasy alliance between them and the local Indians. This was ruptured after the 1899 war, since the liberal/mestizo camp took power and provided mestizos with opportunity for consolidating their holdings. By contrast, the *tinterillos,* or legal clerks, of the rural pueblos were mestizos who sometimes championed the Indian cause. See Ibarra, "Identidad devaluada de los 'Modern Indians'"; Ricardo Godoy, "State, Ayllu, and Ethnicity in Northern Potosí, Bolivia," *Anthropos* 80 (1985): 58–59. Rivera Cusicanqui (*Oprimidos pero no vencidos*) notes the growing con-

flict between Indians and mestizos as a result of the latter's growing monopoly of trade/transport with the expansion of the railways in the early twentieth century in the altiplano.

63. Poole's "Landscapes of Power," a vivid account of *gamonalismo* in Chumbivilcas, emphasizes the alternation between violent aggression toward the Indians at one moment and recognition of their cultural similarity and identification in the next.

64. Xavier Albó, Thomas Greaves, and Godofredo Sandoval, *Chukiyawu: La cara aymara de La Paz*. Vol. 3. *Cabalgando entre dos mundos* (La Paz, 1983); Xavier Albó and Mathias Preiswerk, *Los señores del Gran Poder* (La Paz, 1986), 83–85. Frank Salomon explores the complexity of the ritualized expression of the "inner Indian" by urban Quichua speakers in Quito in his "Killing the Yumbo: A Ritual Drama in Northern Quito," in Norman E. Whitten Jr., ed., *Cultural Transformations and Ethnicity in Modern Ecuador* (Urbana, 1981), 162–208.

65. Magnus Mörner quotes the words of a priest of Puno criticizing the educational work of the Seventh Day Adventists in the early years of the century: "God has ordained that you should dedicate yourselves to pasturing your flocks and not to learning to read, which only grieves your fathers and mothers. This is why you suffer misfortunes and why, year after year, your harvests are so poor." Mörner, *The Andean Past: Land, Societies and Conflicts* (New York, 1985), 185. Nils Jacobsen notes that some hacendados hired thugs to destroy rural schools in Southern Peru in "Free Trade, Regional Elites and the Internal Market in Southern Peru 1895–1932," in Joseph Love and Nils Jacobsen, eds., *Guiding the Invisible Hand: Economy, Liberalism and the State in Latin American History* (New York, 1988), 159.

66. Benjamin S. Orlove, "The History of the Andes," in Benjamin Orlove and David Guillet, eds., *Convergences and Differences in Mountain Economies and Societies*, Special Issue of *Mountain Research and Development* 5.1 (1985): 55.

67. Herbert S. Klein, "Bolivia from the War of the Pacific to the Chaco War," in Leslie Bethell, ed., *Cambridge History of Latin America* (Cambridge, 1986), 5:553–586.

68. Marie-Danièle Demelas, "Darwinismo a la criolla: El darwinismo social en Bolivia 1809–1910," *Historia Boliviana* (Cochabamba) 1.2 (1981): 55–82; Charles Hale, "Political and Social Ideas in Latin America 1870–1930," in Leslie Bethell, ed., *Cambridge History of Latin America* (Cambridge, 1985), 4:367–441.

69. Jorge Flores Ochoa, "Mistis and Indians: Their Relations in a Microeconomic Region of Cuzco," *International Journal of Comparative Sociology* 15.3–4 (1974): 190. Indeed, Fernando Fuenzalida reports the complaints of sierra mistis

in Peru after the agrarian reform that their meat consumption had seriously declined. See his "Poder, etnía y estratificación social en el Perú rural," *Perú Hoy* (1971): 38 and 41.

70. José María Arguedas, *Las comunidades de España y del Perú* (Lima, 1968); Benjamin S. Orlove and Ricardo Godoy, "Sectoral Fallowing Systems in the Central Andes," *Journal of Ethnobiology* 6.1 (1986): 169–204; Ricardo Godoy, "The Evolution of Common Field Agriculture in the Andes: A Hypothesis," *Comparative Studies in Society and History* 33 (1991): 395–414.

71. Pierre Van Den Berghe and George Primov, *Inequality in the Peruvian Andes: Class and Ethnicity in Cuzco* (Columbia, Mo., 1977); William Carter and Xavier Albó, "La comunidad aymara: Un mini-estado en conflicto," in Xavier Albó, ed., *Raíces de América: El mundo aymara* (Madrid, 1988); Antoinette Fioravanti-Molinié, "The Andean Community Today," in John V. Murra, Nathan Wachtel, and Jacques Revel, eds., *Anthropological History of Andean Polities* (Cambridge, 1986), 342–358. The Confederación de Nacionalidades Indígenas del Ecuador (CONAIE) also stresses that the community is an essential organizational principle. See Fernando Rosero, "Defensa y recuperación de la tierra: Campesinado, identidad etnocultural y nación," in Almeida et al., eds., *Indios: Una reflexión sobre el* levantamiento indígena (423).

72. Peter Gose, "Work, Class and Culture in Huaquirca, a Village in the Southern Peruvian Andes," Ph.D. dissertation (University of London, 1986); José Sánchez-Parga, "Estrategias de supervivencia," in Manuel Chiriboga et al., eds., *Estrategias de supervivencia en la comunidad andina* (Quito, 1984), 9–57.

73. Peruvian attempts at cooperative production and commercialization processes in the agrarian reform were premised on the assumption that collective organization in the rural communities applied to all areas of economic activity. Their failure is discussed by Cristóbal Kay, "Achievements and Contradictions of the Peruvian Agrarian Reform," *Journal of Development Studies* 18.2 (1982): 141–170. Since 1980 there has been a gradual dissolution of many of the cooperatives, along with some shift of identity from *cooperativas comunales* to *empresas comunales*. See Rodrigo Sánchez, *Organización andina: Drama y posibilidad* (Hunacayo, 1987), ch. 5. Anthropologists have argued that most cases of successful collective ethnic intervention in markets are found where ethnic groups have minority/outsider status and can corner a niche in the wider division of labor. See Abner Cohen, *Two-dimensional Man: An Essay on the Anthropology of Power and Symbolism in Complex Society* (Berkeley, 1974).

74. David Guillet, "Land Tenure, Ecological Zone and Agricultural Regime in the Central Andes," *American Ethnologist* 8 (1981): 139–156; Enrique Mayer,

"Production Zones," in Shozo Masuda, Izumi Shimada, and Craig Morris, eds., *Andean Ecology and Civilization* (Tokyo, 1985), 45–84; Jürgen Golte and Marisol de la Cadena, "La codeterminación de la organización social andina," *Documento de Trabajo*, no. 13 (Lima, 1986); Marisol de la Cadena, *Cooperación y conflicto* (Lima, 1989); Bruno Kervyn and Equipo del Cedep Ayllu, "Campesinos y acción colectiva: La organización del espacio en comunidades de la sierra sur del Perú," *Revista Andina* 7.1 (1989): 7–60. Galo Ramón emphasizes the importance of Indian peasants' collective response to natural disasters in "El comportamiento de las comunidades de Cangahua frente a los riesgos agricolas," in Manuel Chiriboga et al., *Estrategias de supervivencia en la comunidad Andina* (Quito, 1984), 125–153. Ricardo Godoy, however, points out that collective decisions can also be responsible for ecological degradation. See his "Ecological Degradation and Agricultural Intensification in the Andean Highlands," *Human Ecology* 12.4 (1984): 359–383, and *Mining and Agriculture in Highland Bolivia: Ecology, History, and Commerce among the Jukumanis* (Tucson, 1990).

75. Cecilia Blondet notes the very selective use of mutual aid among migrants to Lima in "Establishing an Identity: Women Settlers in a Poor Lima Neighbourhood," in Elizabeth Jelin, ed., *Women and Social Change in Latin America*, trans. D. Ann Zammit and Marilyn Thomson (London, 1990), 12–46; Xavier Albó, Thomas Greaves, and Godofredo Sandoval also make clear that, for all the apparent continuity of form in the celebration of fiestas among Aymara migrants to La Paz, the social relations are profoundly different from those around which religious feasts are organized in the countryside, with far less emphasis on mutuality and equal participation and far more on competition and exclusivity. See their *Chukiyawu: La cara aymara de La Paz* (La Paz, 1983) 3:44–48.

76. One important early organization was named *mink'a*—a form of mutual aid. See Xavier Albó, "From MNRistas to Kataristas to Katari," in Steve J. Stern, ed., *Resistance, Rebellion, and Consciousness in the Andean Peasant World, 18th to 20th Centuries* (Madison, 1987), 379–419; Rivera Cusicanqui, *Oprimidos pero no vencidos*. In Peru another organization is called *Minga*. The concept of ayllu is also of great importance.

77. Penelope Harvey suggests that Indian identity is closely associated with a sense of moral superiority in the Cuzco region; by contrast, "the most distinctive feature of misti work methods is the employment of others" ("Language and the Power of History: The Discourse of Bilinguals in Ocongate," Ph.D. dissertation [University of London, 1987], 30–33).

78. Otavalo's weaving industry survived and prospered thanks to certain colonial policies and, in the twentieth century, their ability to undercut the price of

imported tweeds. See Phelan, *Kingdom of Quito;* Frank Salomon, "Weavers of Otavalo," in Norman E. Whitten Jr., ed., *Cultural Transformations and Ethnicity in Modern Ecuador* (Urbana, 1981): 420–449.

79. Golte and de la Cadena, "Codeterminación de la organización social andina"; Benjamin S. Orlove, "Stability and Change in Highland Andean Dietary Patterns," in Marvin Harris and Eric Ross, eds., *Food and Evolution: Toward a Theory of Human Food Habits* (Philadelphia, 1987).

80. Alberto Figueroa, *Capitalist Development and the Peasant Economy in Peru* (Cambridge, 1984). However, Raul Hopkins and Ricardo Barrantes argue that price policies are not definitive in "El desafío de la diversidad: Hacia una tipología de la agricultura campesina," in Efrain González and Bruno Kervyn, eds., *La lenta modernización de la economía campesina* (Lima, 1991), 71. According to their argument, technical limitations such as the absence of irrigation affect the possibilities for commercialization of highland crops even where prices and demand are favorable.

81. Gilles Rivière, "Sabaya: Structures socio-économiques et représentations symboliques dans le Carangas, Bolivie," Ph.D. dissertation (Paris, 1984).

82. José María Arguedas, "Evolución de las comunidades indígenas," in *Formación de una cultura indoamericana* (Mexico City, 1975), 139. There are a number of theories as to why this fertile and strategically located region retained an independent Indian population. Apart from those discussed by Arguedas, Mallon's (*Defense of Community,* 39) interesting hypothesis is that the very fertility of the valley allowed profitable intensive small-scale agriculture, so that haciendas only expanded in the surrounding highlands where extensive methods were employed using a captive labor force.

83. Sánchez, *Organización Andina,* 156; however, he emphasizes that this communal enterprise is unique in Peru.

84. de la Cadena, *Cooperación y conflicto.*

85. Albó, *¿Bodas de Plata?;* Joel Jurado, "Tendencias estructurales del campesinado en el Perú," *Allpanchis* 34 (1989): 63–115; Simón Pachano, "Transformación de la estructura agraria: Personajes, autores y escenarios," in Manuel Chiriboga, ed., *El problema agrario en el Ecuador* (Quito, 1988), 389–410. Albó ("From MNRistas to Kataristas to Katari," 406) notes that much local mobilization of Bolivian peasants in the 1980s was concerned with the prices of agricultural products, inputs, and transport.

86. Godoy, "Ecological Degradation and Agricultural Intensification"; Sánchez-Parga, "Estrategias de supervivencia," 86.

87. Enrique Tandeter's study of the importance of the Potosí market in times of dearth at the turn of the nineteenth century shows that this use of the labor

market is of some historical depth. See his "Crisis in Upper Peru, 1800–1805," *Hispanic American Historical Review* 71.1 (1991): 35–69.

88. González and Kervyn ("Lenta modernización"), writing of the Cuzco region make clear that the increased reliance on chemical inputs is a defensive reaction to declining yields, and that many of the changes are ecologically inefficient.

89. The Chapare region in Bolivia today, for example, shares a lot in common with Potosí in the seventeenth century as a place where fortunes may be made and lost, where the rigors and risks of the work are coupled with the massive intake of artificial stimulants and conspicuous consumption, and where Indians and non-Indians from all regions congregate and interact and are in the process transformed (Thierry Saignes, personal communication).

90. Linda Seligmann writes of cholas/market women as brokers moving between two worlds. See her "To Be In Between: The Cholas as Market Women," *Comparative Studies in Society and History* 31.4 (1989): 694–721. Marisol de la Cadena (Chapter 11 in this volume) refers to the de-Indianization of the Cuzco region and quotes an informant's statement that these days "the women are more Indian than the men." She emphasizes the fluidity and volatility of ethnic categories in contrast to their ideological fixity. In Chitapampa because of its proximity to the city of Cuzco, most men are now in a process of transition ("en proceso" is the term used locally) to mestizo status.

91. Fuenzalida, "Poder, etnia y estratificación social"; François Bourricaud, "Indian, Mestizo and Cholo as Symbols in the Peruvian System of Stratification," in Nathan Glazer and Daniel P. Moynihan, eds., *Ethnicity: Theory and Experience* (Cambridge, Mass., 1975), 350–387; Harvey, "Language and the Power of History"; de la Cadena, Chapter 11 in this volume.

92. Aníbal Quijano, *Dominación y cultura: Lo cholo y el conflicto* (Lima, 1980).

93. Hugo Sanmartin Arzabe, *El palenquismo: Movimiento social, populismo, informalidad política* (La Paz, 1991); José Morales Saravia and Godofredo Sandoval, *Jach'a uru: ¿La esperanza de un pueblo?* (La Paz, 1991).

94. Nelson Manrique, "Time of Fear," *NACLA Report on the Americas* 24.4 (1990): 35.

95. Carlos I. Degregori, "How Difficult It Is to Be God," *Critique of Anthropology* 11.3 (1991): 233–250.

96. Taller de Historia Oral Andina (THOA) and Silvia Rivera Cusicanqui, "Indigenous Women and Community Resistance: History and Memory," in Elizabeth Jelin, ed., *Women and Social Change in Latin America* (London, 1990), 177.

97. Niels Fock quotes Abner Cohen's work on ethnicity to argue that while Indians correspond to the concept of an ethnic group, mestizos are better characterized as a regional group, directly linked to the national level. See his "Eth-

nicity and Alternative Identification: An Example from Cañar," in Norman E. Whitten, ed., *Cultural Transformations and Ethnicity in Modern Ecuador* (Urbana, 1981), 412.

98. For example in the 1590s. The Bolivian state repeated the maneuver under President Melgarejo in 1866.

99. Thomas Abercrombie, "To Be Indian, To Be Bolivian: 'Ethnic' and 'National' Discourses of Identity," in Greg Urban and Joel Sherzer, eds., *Nation-States and Indians in Latin America* (Austin, 1991), 95–130; Xavier Albó, "El retorno del indio," *Revista Andina* 18 (1991): 299–366. However, unlike most other parts of Latin America, there is historical precedent for general Indianist politics in the Andes, as evidenced by the recurrent theme of the Inca state and by the large-scale organization and network of alliances achieved by some political movements. See THOA, *El indio Santos Marka T'ula;* Steve J. Stern, "The Age of Andean Insurrection 1742–1782: A Reappraisal," in Stern, *Resistance, Rebellion and Consciousness,* 34–93.

100. Sendero Luminoso perhaps represents today a particularly dramatic case of such illegality. Hernando de Soto also emphasizes the illegality of most entrepreneurial activity by migrants in Lima. See *El otro Sendero: La revolución informal* (Bogotá, 1987).

101. This change of terminology was adopted in the Bolivian Agrarian Reform Law in 1953 and in the Peruvian Agrarian Reform Law in 1969.

Glossary

✤

Aym. = Aymara   Q. = Quechua   Sp. = Spanish

abarcas (Sp.) sandals

abasca everyday woolen cloth

agregado (Sp.) migrant incorporated into an *ayllu* (q.v.) or *hacienda.* (q.v.) different from his place of birth

aguardiente (Sp.) brandy, liquor

aguayos (Aym.) shawls, carrying cloths

alcabala (Sp.) sales tax

alpargates leather shoes

al partir (Sp.) sharing or sharecropping

altiplano (Sp.) high Andean plain (c. 4000 m.) extending south from Lake Titicaca

anexo (Sp.) satellite village

apiri (Aym.) carrier (used for unskilled mineworker)

arrieraje; arriero (Sp.) droving; drover

arroba (Sp.) weight of approx 25 lbs.

artesanía (Sp.) handicrafts

astucia (Sp.) astuteness, sharp practice

audiencia (Sp.) viceregal court and governing body

awqaruna (Q.) soldier people, who according to myth dominated the central and southern Andes before Inca rule

ayllu (Q.) territorial group organized in a segmentary system and a rule of endogamy

ayni (Aym. & Q.) reciprocal exchange of like for like

azogue (Sp.) mercury

azogueros (Sp.) large mine owners who refined using mercury

baja (Sp.) carry mineral from minehead to refinery

bajador (Sp.) worker who transports the mineral

barreta (Sp.) iron bar

bayeta (Sp.) baize, homespun woolen cloth

botija (Sp.) earthenware jug

cachcoa unidentified food-plant

cacique   Carib word used by Sp. to refer to Indian chief or lord

cacique gobernador   (Sp.) Indian governor of a large tribute-paying unit

cacicazgo   lordship, chiefship

cajón   (Sp.) packing case

camino real   (Sp.) royal highway

campesino   (Sp.) peasant

canasta familiar   (Sp.) family staple foods

casta   (Sp.) *lit.*, caste: the mixed-race population and those who had been classified as such

cavi   (Q.) dried *oca* (q.v.)

chacra   (Q.) cultivated field; *chacra de comunidad* communal field

chaquira   shell beads

ch'aqu   (Aym.) edible lime-rich earth (see also *phasa*)

ch'arki or charqui   (Aym. & Q.) dried llama or other meat

chicha   (Sp.) maize beer

cholaje   (Sp.) the *cholo* (q.v.) population

cholo   (Aym. Q. & Sp.) in colonial law a person three-quarters Indian and one-quarter white; also used generally of an Indian in transition to mestizo status

chullpa   (Aym.) pre-Inca population; also their monumental tombs

chuño, ch'uñu   (Aym. & Q.) dehydrated potato

cobrador   (Sp.) see *hilacata*

collas   a pre-Inca kingdom on the northern end of L. Titicaca; also used to refer in general to the population of the Titicaca region

collque haque   see *qullqi jaqi*

colono   (Sp.) serf, tenant farmer

compadre   (Sp.) *lit.*, co-parent,

through becoming the godparent of a partner's child; *compadrazgo* system of co-parenting

comunidad   (Sp.) peasant community

cordillera   (Sp.) mountain range

corregidor   (Sp.) magistrate, administrator of a province

corregimiento   (Sp.) unit administered by *corregidor*

criados   (Sp.) service Indians; retainers

curaca, curaga   variants of *kuraka* (q.v.)

efectos de Castilla   (Sp.) goods imported from Europe (mainly Spain)

efecto de la tierra   (Sp.) goods imported from other colonial provinces in the Americas

encomendero   (Sp.) Spanish beneficiary of a grant (*encomienda*) to the tribute and services of a group of Indians

enganche   (Sp.) *lit.*, hook: system of labor-recruitment through debt bondage

en proceso   (Sp.) in the process of moving from Indian to mestizo status

estancia   (Sp.) ranch, herding community, remote Indian hamlet

fanega   (Sp.) measure of land and of volume, which varied by region but was generally equivalent to about 1.6 bushels

feria   (Sp.) fair

feria mercantil   (Sp.) wholesale fair

forastero   (Sp.) stranger; also used to refer to Indians living away from their village of origin *gamonal* (Sp.) local boss

gobernador (Sp.) governor

guaranga (Aym. & Q.) *lit.*, one thousand: an Inca administrative unit of about 1,000 tributaries

guía (Sp.) customs declaration

hacienda (Sp.) private landed estate

hacendado (Sp.) estate owner

hilacata (Aym.) local Indian headman responsible for collecting tribute as *cobrador*

hatun runa or *jatunruna* (Q.) Indian tribute payer (males 18–50 years of age)

huiñapu (Aym. & Q.) fermented maize for making beer

illa (Aym. & Q.) sacred amulet with generative powers

indígena (Sp.) indigenous

indigenista (Sp.) intellectual taking a pro-Indian stance

ingenio (Sp.) mill in which ore was ground and refined

jarana (Aym.) resting place

justicia mayor (Sp.) chief judge

kamayujkuna (Q.) authorities; people in charge

katarista follower of Túpac Katari, the Aymara insurrectionary leader of the 1780s, or of the Indianist movement named after him in the 1970s

khipu (Q.) knotted cords that stored information

kula ritualized exchange system in Melanesia

kuraka (Q.) (*pl.*, *kuraqkuna*) Indian lord

lacayote form of squash or pumpkin

liga de mercaderes (Sp.) merchant league

llactaruna (Q.) seasonal migrant

llallawa (Aym.) ritual term for unusual tuber, fruit, or mineral thought to embody powerful fertility

llamero (Sp.) drovers who transport goods with their llama herds

luki (Aym. & Q.) bitter potato, used for making *ch'uña* (q.v.)

maíz blanco (Sp.) soft white maize

mallku (Aym.) lord, Indian leader

mancha india (Sp.) *lit.*, Indian stain: The regions of highland S. Peru with dense Indian population

manta (Aym.) communal field cultivated in rotation

marahaque (Aym.) Indian contracted for a year's personal service

marka (Aym.) Indian town with its population and territory

maxua (Q.) Andean tuber (*Tropaeolum tuberosum*)

mercaderes (Sp.) merchants

mestizaje (Sp.) condition of *mestizo* (q.v.)

mestizo (Sp.) *lit.*, person of mixed race

mindala (*pl.*, mindaláes) North Andean exchange specialist

mink'a (Aym. & Q.) exchange of labor for goods (or money)

misti (Q.) variant of *mestizo*

mita, mit'a (Aym. & Q.) turn of work, rotative labor

mitayo rotative Indian laborer

mitmaq, mitima (Q.) (*pl.*, mitmaqkuna or mitimaes) colonist sent to occupy distinct ecological niches by ethnic group or by state.

morocho   (Sp.) dark-colored hard maize

mote, mut'i   (Aym. & Q.) boiled yellow maize

mullu   (Q.) pink *spondylus* shell

mozo   (Sp.) *lit.*, youth, servant: refers to Indian man who has started transition to mestizo

natural   (Sp.) lit., native: Indian residing at place of birth

obraje   (Sp.) textile workshop

oca   (Q.) Andean tuber (*Oxalis tuberosa*)

oidor   (Sp.) judge

olluco   (Q.) Andean tuber known also as *papalisa* (*Ullucus tuberosus*)

ordenanza   (Sp.) decree

originario   (Sp.) see *natural* (*originario* is more common from eighteenth century)

pachamama   (Aym. & Q.) earth deity, earth mother

padrón   (Sp.) cantonal register of tributaries

papalisa   see *olluco*

páramo   (Sp.) high humid moor, typical of highland Ecuador

parcialidad   (Sp.) moiety; refers to the divisions of Andean groups into upper (*hanansaya*) and lower (*hurinsaya*) moieties

pesos ensayados   (Sp.) minted coins

phaqhara   (Aym.) flower; used in libations to refer to the fertility of livestock

phasa   (Aym.) edible lime-rich white earth, eaten with baked potatoes.

phaxsima   (Aym.) like the moon; used in libations to refer to silver/ money

pito   (Aym.) ground *quinoa* (q.v.) or other grain

principal   (Sp.) Indian leader

pueblo   (Sp.) rural town

pueblo real   (Sp.) term used for Indian districts in Cochabamba

pulpería   (Sp.) food store

puna   (Q.) high-altitude arid steppes, typical from C. Peru to S. Bolivia and N. Argentina

q'ara   (Aym.) *lit.*, peeled, bare: Indian term to refer to non-Indians, especially mestizos

qhapaqñan   (Q.) state highway

quebrada   (Sp.) mountain gorge through which stream flows down to the central valleys

quichua, quishwa   (Q.) temperate valley

quinoa   (Q.) high Andean grain

quintal   (Sp.) four *arrobas* (q.v.), i.e., 100 lbs weight

quipu   (Q.) see *khipu*

quiteño   (Sp.) from Quito, referring to high-quality cloth

qullqi   (Aym. & Q.) silver, money

qullqi jaqi or runa   (Aym. & Q.) *lit.*, money people: refers to wealthy Indians who commuted *mita* (q.v.) service through money

q'uwa   (Aym. & Q.) aromatic herb burnt in offerings to earth deities

repartimiento de efectos/mercancías (Sp.) distribution of goods, usually by *corregidor* (q.v.) or his agent, which Indians were forced to buy

repartimiento de efectos/mercancías (Sp.) distribution of goods, usually

394

by *corregidor* or his agent, which Indians were forced to buy

repartos (Sp.) goods

rescatador, rescatiri (Sp. & Aym.) intermediary who buys from producer

ropa de la tierra (Sp.) cloth/clothing woven locally in the Andean region

sabio (Sp.) wise, one who has been educated

serranía, sierra (Sp.) mountainous region, mountain range

subdelegado (Sp.) highest appointed official of a *partido*, the subdivision of a *corregimiento*

sullu (Aym. & Q.) dried llama or sheep fetus used in ritual offerings

supay (Aym. & Q.) devil

suyu (Q.) plot of land allocated for cultivation

tambo (Q.) posting house, inn

tarea (Sp.) *lit.*, task: parcel of land (see *suyu*)

taure, tawri (Q.) Andean bean (*Lupimus albus*)

Tawantinsuyu (Q.) *lit.*, four parts: Inca term for their state

tiangues (*pl., tiangueces*) Nahuatl word used by Spanish to refer to market-like gatherings in Quito region

tijara (Aym.) see *yapa*

tío/tía (Sp.) uncle/aunt; refers to the spirit owners of the mines who are represented as devils

tocuyo (Sp.) coarse, unbleached cotton cloth

tomin (Sp.) coin of the value of 2 *reales*

tonel (Sp.) barrel, cask

trapiche (Sp.) small human-powered mill for refining ore; *trapichero* miller

t'ula (Aym. & Q.) shrub found in certain *puna* (q.v.) ecotypes (*Lepidophylum quadrangulare*)

veintena (Sp.) twentieth part of harvest allocated to the church

visita (Sp.) *lit.*, visit: house-to-house inspection for tax and census purposes

visitador (Sp.) inspector

wak'a, huaca (Q.) sacred place of origin

wanu (Aym.) manure

wayra (Aym.) wind; refers to wind-powered mills for refining ore

xalca, jalka (Q.) high arid region, *puna* (q.v.)

yana (Q.) individual retainer of lord or state detached from the *ayllu* of origin under the Incas

yanacona (Q.) Indian dependant, service Indian miner, or agricultural laborer no longer attached to an *ayllu*, but often bound to a Spanish master

yapa (Aym.) extra amount added by trader to what is sold

yatiri (Aym.) *lit.*, one who knows: ritual specialist

yunga, yunka (Aym. & Q.) tropical valley

Selected Bibliography

❖

Archive Abbreviations

ACMS   Archivo Castillo Muro Sime (Lambayeque)
ACT   Actas del Cabildo de Trujillo (Trujillo)
ADA   Archivo Departamental de Ayacucho (Ayacucho)
AGI   Archivo General de las Indias (Seville)
    AL   Audiencia de Lima
    J   Justicia
    P   Patronato
AGN   Archivo General de la Nación (Buenos Aires)
AHMC   Archivo Histórico Municipal de Cochabamba
AHLP   Archivo Histórico de la Paz (La Paz)
AHP   Archivo Histórico de Potosí (Potosí)
    PDC   Prefectura Departamental-Correspondencia
    PDE   Prefectura Departamental-Expedientes
ANB   Archivo Nacional de Bolivia (Sucre)
    EC   Expediente Colonial
    MF   Ministerio de Finanzas
    MH   Ministerio de Hacienda
ANCR   Archivo Notorial Carlos Rivadeneira (Lambayeque)
ANP   Archivo Nacional del Perú (Lima)
    RA   Real Academia
    R   Residencia
ART   Archivo Regional de Trujillo (Trujillo)
    CoAG   Corregimiento, Asuntos de Gobierno
    CoO   Corregimiento, Ordinario
    CoP   Corregimiento, Pedimiento
    CoR   Corregimiento, Residencia

Selected Bibliography

BARH   Biblioteca de la Academia Real de Historia (Madrid)
BNB   Biblioteca Nacional de Bolivia (Sucre)
BNE   Biblioteca Nacional de España (Madrid)
BNP   Biblioteca Nacional del Perú (Lima)
BPR   Biblioteca del Palacio Real (Madrid)
CVU   Colección Vargas Ugarte (Lima)
YULAC   Yale University Latin American Collection (New Haven)

Abercrombie, Thomas. "To Be Indian, to Be Bolivian: 'Ethnic' and 'National' Discourses of Identity." In Greg Urban and Joel Sherzer (eds.), *Nation-States and Indians in Latin America*. Austin, 1991. 95–130.

Adorno, Rolena. "Images of *Indios Ladinos* in Early Colonial Peru." In Kenneth J. Adrien and Rolena Adorno (eds.), *Transatlantic Encounters: Europeans and Andeans in the Sixteenth Century*. Berkeley, 1991. 232–270.

Adrien, Kenneth J. *Crisis and Decline: The Viceroyalty of Peru in the Seventeenth Century*. Albuquerque, 1985.

Adrien, Kenneth J. "Spaniards, Andeans and the Early Colonial State in Peru." In Kenneth J. Adrien and Rolena Adorno (eds.), *Transatlantic Encounters: Europeans and Andeans in the Sixteenth Century*. Berkeley, 1991. 121–150.

Alberti, Giorgio, and Enrique Mayer (eds.). *Reciprocidad e intercambio en los Andes peruanos*. Lima, 1974.

Albó, Xavier, and Josep M. Barnadas. *La cara campesina de nuestra historia*. La Paz, 1984.

Albó, Xavier (ed.). *Raíces de América: El mundo aymara*. Madrid, 1988.

Alchon, Suzanne Austin. *Native Society and Disease in Colonial Ecuador*. Cambridge, 1991.

Appleby, Gordon. "Exportation and Its Aftermath: The Spatioeconomic Evolution of the Regional Marketing System in Highland Puno, Peru." Ph.D. dissertation. Stanford University, 1978.

Arguedas, José María. *Las comunidades de España y del Perú*. Lima, 1968.

Arze, Silvia et al. (eds.). *Etnicidad, economía y simbolismo en los Andes*. La Paz, 1992.

Arze Aguirre, René. "El cacicazgo en las postrimerías coloniales." *Avances* (La Paz) 1 (1978): 47–50.

Assadourian, Carlos Sempat. *Modos de producción, capitalismo y subdesarrollo en América Latina*. Buenos Aires and Mexico City, 1973.

Assadourian, Carlos Sempat. "La producción de la mercancía dinero en la formación del mercado interno colonial: El caso del espacio peruano, siglo XVI." In Enrique Florescano (ed.), *Ensayos sobre el desarrollo económico de México y América Latina (1500–1975)*. Mexico City, 1979. 223–292.

Assadourian, Carlos Sempat et al. *Minería y espacio económico en los Andes, siglos XVI–XX*. Lima, 1981.

Assadourian, Carlos Sempat. *El sistema de la economía colonial: Mercado interno, regiones y espacio económico.* Lima, 1982.

Assadourian, Carlos Sempat. "Dominio colonial y señores étnicos en el espacio andino." *HISLA: Revista Latinoamericana de Historia Económica y Social* (Lima) 1 (1983): 7–20.

Assadourian, Carlos Sempat. "La crisis demográfica del siglo XVI y la transición del Tahuantinsuyo al sistema mercantil colonial." In Nicolás Sánchez Albornoz (ed.), *Población y mano de obra en América Latina.* Madrid, 1985. 69–93.

Babb, Florence. *Between Field and Cooking Pot: The Political Economy of Market-women in Peru.* Austin, 1989.

Baker, Paul T., and Michael Little (eds.). *Man in the Andes.* Stroudsberg, 1976.

Bakewell, Peter J. "Registered Silver Production in the Potosí District, 1550–1735." *Jahrbuch für Geschichte von Staat, Wirtschaft und Gesellschaft Lateinamerikas* 12 (Cologne, 1975): 67–103.

Bakewell, Peter J. *Miners of the Red Mountain: Indian Labor in Potosí, 1545–1650.* Albuquerque, 1984.

Bakewell, Peter J. *Silver and Entrepreneurship in Seventeenth-Century Potosí: The Life and Times of Antonio López de Quiroga.* Albuquerque, 1988.

Barnes de Marschall, Katherine. "La formación de nuevos pueblos en Bolivia: Proceso e implicaciones." *Estudios Andinos* 1.3 (1970): 23–38.

Barragán, Rossana. *Espacio urbano y dinámica étnica: La Paz en el siglo XIX.* La Paz, 1990.

Barragán, Rossana. "Aproximaciones al mundo 'chulu' y 'huayqui.'" *Estado y Sociedad* (La Paz) 8 (1991): 68–88.

Bastien, Joseph. *Mountain of the Condor.* New York, 1978.

Basto Girón, Luís J. *Las mitas de Huamanga y Huancavelica.* Lima, 1954.

Blondet, Cecilia. "Establishing an Identity: Women Settlers in a Poor Lima Neighbourhood." In Elizabeth Jelin (ed.), *Women and Social Change in Latin America.* Trans. D. Ann Zammit and Marilyn Thomson. London, 1990. 12–46.

Bolton, Ralph, and Enrique Mayer (eds.). *Andean Kinship and Marriage.* Washington, D.C., 1977.

Bonilla, Heraclio (ed.). *Las crisis económicas en la historia del Perú.* Lima, 1986.

Bonilla, Heraclio. "Peru and Bolivia." In Leslie Bethell (ed.), *Spanish America after Independence c. 1820–70.* Cambridge, 1987. 239–282.

Bonilla, Heraclio. "The Indian Peasantry and 'Peru' in the War with Chile." In Steve J. Stern (ed.), *Resistance, Rebellion, and Consciousness in the Andean Peasant World, 18th to 20th Centuries.* Madison, 1987. 219–231.

Bonilla, Heraclio (ed.). *Los Andes en la encrucijada: Indios, comunidades y estado en el siglo XIX.* Quito, 1991.

Bourque, Susan C., and Kay B. Warren. *Women of the Andes: Patriarchy and Social Change in Two Peruvian Towns.* Ann Arbor, 1981.

Bourricaud, François. "Indian, Mestizo and Cholo as Symbols in the Peruvian System of Stratification." In Nathan Glazer and Daniel P. Moynihan (eds.), *Ethnicity: Theory and Experience.* Cambridge, Mass., 1975. 350–387.

Bouysse-Cassagne, Thérèse. *La identidad aymara: Aproximación histórica, siglos XV–XVI.* La Paz, 1987.

Bradby, Barbara. "Resistance to Capitalism in the Peruvian Andes." In David Lehmann (ed.), *Ecology and Exchange in the Andes.* Cambridge, 1982. 97–122.

Brading, David A., and Harry E. Cross. "Colonial Silver Mining: Mexico and Peru." *Hispanic American Historical Review* 52.4 (1972): 545–579.

Brush, Stephen. *Mountain, Field and Family: The Economy and Human Ecology of an Andean Valley.* Philadelphia, 1977.

Buechler, Hans C. *The Masked Media: Aymara Fiestas and Social Integration in the Bolivian Highlands.* The Hague, 1980.

Buechler, Judith-Maria. "Las negociantes-contratistas en los mercados bolivianos." *Estudios Andinos* 5.1 (1976): 57–76.

Burchard, Roderick. "Coca y trueque de alimentos." In Giorgio Alberti and Enrique Mayer (eds.), *Reciprocidad e intercambio en los Andes peruanos.* Lima, 1974. 209–251.

Burga, Manuel. *Nacimento de una utopía: Muerte y resurrección de los Incas.* Lima, 1988.

Burga, Manuel, and Wilson Réategui. *Lanas y capital mercantil en el sur: La Casa Ricketts 1895–1935.* Lima, 1981.

Burkett, Elinor C. "Indian Women and White Society: The Case of Sixteenth-Century Peru." In Asunción Lavrin (ed.), *Latin American Women: Historical Perspectives.* Westport, Conn., 1978. 101–128.

Caballero, José María. *Economía agraria de la sierra peruana antes de la Reforma Agraria de 1969.* Lima, 1981.

Caillavet, Chantal. "La adaptación de la frontera septentrional del imperio: Territorio Otavalo, Ecuador." *Revista Andina* 3.2 (1985): 403–423.

Calderón, Fernando, and Jorge Dandler (eds.). *Bolivia: la fuerza histórica del campesinado: Movimientos campesinos y etnicidad.* Cochabamba, 1984.

Calderón, Fernando, and Alberto Rivera. *La Cancha: Una gran feria campesina en la ciudad de Cochabamba.* Cochabamba, 1985.

Calderón, Fernando, and Alberto Rivera. *La mina urbana: Los ladrilleros de Jaihuayco.* Cochabamba, 1985.

Cárdenas, Victor Hugo. "La lucha de un pueblo." In Xavier Albó (ed.), *Raíces de América: El mundo aymara.* Madrid, 1988. 495–532.

Carmagnani, Marcello. *El salariado minero en Chile colonial: El Norte Chico, 1690–1800.* Santiago, 1963.

Carter, William, and Mauricio Mamani. *Irpa Chico: Individuo y comunidad en la cultura aymara.* La Paz, 1982.

Casaverde, Juvenal. "El trueque en la economía pastoril." In Jorge Flores Ochoa (ed.), *Pastores de puna: Uywamichiq Punarunakuna.* Lima, 1977. 171–192.

Castelli, Amalia et al. (eds.). *Etnohistoria y antropología andina*. Lima, 1981.

Centro Andino de Acción Popular (CAAP). *Estrategias de supervivencia en la comunidad andina*. Quito, 1984.

Céspedes, Guillermo. "Lima y Buenos Aires: Repercusiones económicas y políticas de la creación del Virreinato del Plata." *Anuario de Estudios Americanos* (Seville) 3 (1946): 669–873.

Chiriboga, Manuel et al. (eds.). *Estrategias de supervivencia en la comunidad andina*. Quito, 1984.

Chiriboga, Manuel (ed.). *El problema agrario en el Ecuador*. Quito, 1988.

Chocano, Magdalena. *Comercio en Cerro de Pasco a fines de la época colonial*. Lima, 1982.

Choque Canqui, Roberto, "Los caciques aymaras y el comercio en el Alto Perú." In Olivia Harris, Brooke Larson, and Enrique Tandeter (eds.), *La participación indígena en los mercados surandinos*. La Paz, 1987. 357–378.

Choque, Roberto. "Pedro Chipana: Cacique comerciante de Calamarca." *Avances* (La Paz) 1 (1978): 28–32.

Cobb, Gwendoline, B. "Supply and Transportation for the Potosí Mines, 1545–1640." *Hispanic American Historical Review* 29.5 (1949): 25–45.

Cohen, Abner. *Two-dimensional Man: An Essay on the Anthropology of Power and Symbolism in Complex Society*. Berkeley, 1974.

Cole, Jeffrey. *The Potosí Mita, 1573–1700: Compulsory Indian Labor in the Andes*. Stanford, 1985.

Collier, George A., Renato I. Rosaldo, and John D. Wirth (eds.). *The Inca and Aztec States, 1400–1800: Anthropology and History*. New York, 1982.

Collins, Jane L. *Unseasonal Migrations. The Effects of Rural Labor Scarcity in Peru*. Princeton, 1988.

Contreras, Carlos. *Mineros y Campesinos en los Andes*. Lima, 1988.

Contreras, Carlos. "Estado republicano y tributo indígena en la sierra central en la post independencia." *Revista de Indias* 48.182–183 (1988): 517–550.

Cook, Noble David (ed.). *Tasa de la visita general de Francisco de Toledo*. Lima, 1975.

Cook, Noble David. *Demographic Collapse: Indian Peru, 1520–1620*. Cambridge, 1981.

Cooper, Frederick et al. *Confronting Historical Paradigms: Peasants, Labor, and the Capitalist World-System in Africa and Latin America*. Madison, 1993.

Crespo Rodas, Alberto. "La 'mita' de Potosí." *Revista Histórica* (Lima) 22 (1955–56): 169–182.

Cushner, Nicolas P. *Lords of the Land: Sugar, Wine and Jesuit Estates of Coastal Peru, 1600–1767*. New York, 1980.

Custred, Glynn. "Llameros y comercio interregional." In Giorgio Alberti and Enrique Mayer (eds.), *Reciprocidad e intercambio en los Andes peruanos*. Lima, 1974. 252–289.

Davies, Thomas. *Indian Integration in Peru: A Half Century of Experience 1900–1948*. Lincoln, Neb., 1970.

de la Cadena, Marisol. "Cooperación y mercado en la organización comunal andina." *Revista Andina* 4.1 (1986): 31–58.

de la Cadena, Marisol. *Cooperación y conflicto*. Lima, 1989.

del Río, Mercedes. "Simbolismo y poder en Tapacarí." *Revista Andina* 8.1 (1990): 77–106.

de Janvry, Alain. *The Agrarian Question and Reformism in Latin America*. Baltimore, 1981.

de Soto, Hernán. *The Other Path: The Invisible Revolution in the Third World*. London, 1989.

Deere, Carmen Diana. "Peasant Production, Proletarianization, and the Sexual Division of Labor in the Andes." *Signs* 7.2 (1981): 338–360.

Degregori, Carlos I. "How Difficult It Is to Be God." *Critique of Anthropology* 11.3 (1991): 233–250.

Demelas, María D. "Darwinismo a la criolla: El darwinismo social en Bolivia 1809–1910." *Historia Boliviana* (Cochabamba) 1.2 (1981): 55–82.

Deustua, José. "Mining Markets, Peasants, and Power in Nineteenth-Century Peru." *Latin American Research Review* 29.1 (1984): 29–54.

Deustua, José. *La minería peruana y la iniciación de la república, 1820–1840*. Lima, 1986.

DeWind, Josh. *Peasants Become Miners: The Evolution of Industrial Mining Systems in Peru*. New York, 1987.

Diez de San Miguel, Garci. *Visita hecha a la provincia de Chucuito* [1567]. Ed. Waldemar Espinoza Soriano. Lima, 1964.

Dobyns, Henry F. "An Outline of Andean Epidemic History to 1720." *Bulletin of the History of Medicine* 37 (1963): 493–515.

Dollfus, Olivier. *El reto del espacio andino*. Lima, 1981.

Duncan, Kenneth, and Ian Rutledge (eds.). *Land and Labor in Latin America: Essays on the Development of Agrarian Capitalism in the Nineteenth and Twentieth Centuries*. Cambridge, 1977.

Escobar, Filomón. "El neoliberalismo apunta de muerte a las culturas originarias." *Autodeterminación* (La Paz) 9 (1991): 43–50.

Espinoza Soriano, Waldemar. "El alcalde mayor de indios." *Anuario de Estudios Americanos* (Seville) 17 (1960): 183–300.

Espinoza Soriano, Waldemar. "El 'Memorial' de Charcas: 'Crónica' inédita de 1582." *Cantuta: Revista de la Universidad Nacional de Educación* (Chosica, Peru, 1969): 1–35.

Falk Moore, Sally. *Power and Property in Inca Peru*. New York, 1958.

Favre, Henri. "The Dynamics of Indian Peasant Society and Migration to Coastal Plantations in Central Peru." In Kenneth Duncan and Ian Rutledge (eds.), *Land and Labour in Latin America: Essays on the Development of Agrarian Capitalism in the Nineteenth and Twentieth Centuries*. Cambridge, 1977. 253–268.

Fifer, Valerie. *Bolivia: Land, Location and Politics Since 1825.* Cambridge, 1972.

Figueroa, Alberto. *Capitalist Development and the Peasant Economy in Peru.* Cambridge, 1984.

Fioravanti-Moliniè, Antoinette. "Multi-leveled Andean Society and Market Exchange: The Case of Yucay (Peru)." In David Lehmann (ed.), *Ecology and Exchange in the Andes.* Cambridge, 1982. 211–230.

Fisher, John. *Government and Society in Colonial Peru: The Intendant System 1784–1814.* London, 1970.

Flores Galindo, Alberto. *Arequipa y el sur andino, siglos XVII–XIX.* Lima, 1977.

Flores Galindo, Alberto. *Los mineros de la Cerro de Pasco 1900–1930.* Lima, [1974] 1983.

Flores Galindo, Alberto. *Aristocracia y plebe, Lima 1760–1830.* Lima, 1984.

Flores Galindo, Alberto. *Buscando un Inca: Identidad y utopía en los Andes.* Havana, 1986.

Flores Galindo, Alberto (ed.). *Comunidades campesinas: Cambios y permanencias.* Chiclayo, 1988.

Flores Ochoa, Jorge. "Mistis and Indians: Their Relations in a Micro-economic Region of Cuzco." *International Journal of Comparative Sociology* 15.3–4 (1974): 182–192.

Flores Ochoa, Jorge (ed.). *Pastores de puna: Uywamichiq Punarunakuna.* Lima, 1977.

Fock, Niels. "Ethnicity and Alternative Identification: An Example from Cañar." In Norman E. Whitten (ed.), *Cultural Transformations and Ethnicity in Modern Ecuador.* Urbana, 1981. 402–419.

Fonseca, César. *Sistemas económicos andinos.* Lima, 1973.

Fuenzalida, Fernando. *Perú, Hoy.* Mexico City, 1971.

Garavaglia, Juan Carlos. *Mercado interno y economía colonial.* Mexico City, 1983.

Geertz, Clifford. *Peddlers and Princes.* Chicago, 1963.

Gelman, Jorge. "Los caminos del mercado: Campesinos, estancieros, y pulperos en una región del Río de la Plata colonial." *Latin American Research Review* 28.2 (1993): 89–118.

Glave, Luís Miguel, and María Isabel Remy. *Estructura agraria y vida rural en una región andina: Ollantaytambo entre los siglos XVI y XIX.* Cuzco, 1983.

Glave, Luís Miguel. "El Virreinato Peruano y la Llamada 'Crisis General' del Siglo XVII." In Heraclio Bonilla (ed.), *Las crisis económicas en la historia del Perú.* Lima, 1986. 95–138.

Glave, Luís Miguel. "Trajines: Un capítulo en la formación del mercado interno colonial." *Revista Andina* (Cuzco) 1.1 (1983): 9–67.

Glave, Luís Miguel. *Trajinantes: Caminos indígenas en la sociedad colonial, siglos XVI–XVII.* Lima, 1989.

Glave, Luís Miguel. "Tambos y caminos y andinos en la formación del mercado interno colonial." In Segundo Moreno Yañez and Frank Salomon (eds.), *Repro-*

ducción y transformación de las sociedades andinas, siglos XVI–XX. Quito, 1991. 1:285–348.

Godoy, Ricardo. "State, Ayllu, and Ethnicity in Northern Potosí, Bolivia." *Anthropos* 80 (1985): 53–65.

Godoy, Ricardo. *Mining and Agriculture in Highland Bolivia: Ecology, History, and Commerce among the Jukumanis.* Tucson, 1990.

Golte, Jürgen. *La racionalidad de la organización andina.* Lima, 1980.

Golte, Jürgen. *Repartos y rebeliones: Túpac Amaru y las contradicciones de la economía colonial.* Lima, 1980.

Gootenberg, Paul. *Between Silver and Guano: Commercial Policy and the State in Postindependence Peru.* Princeton, 1989.

Gootenberg, Paul. "Population and Ethnicity in Early Republican Peru: Some Revisions." *Latin American Research Review* 26.3 (1991): 109–157.

Gootenburg, Paul. *Imagining Development: Economic Ideas in Peru's "Fictitious Prosperity" of Guano, 1840–1880.* Berkeley, 1993.

Greenfield, Sidney M., et al. (eds.). *Entrepreneurs in Cultural Context.* Albuquerque, 1979.

Grieshaber, Erwin P. "Survival of Indian Communities in Nineteenth-Century Bolivia." Ph.D. dissertation, University of North Carolina, 1977.

Grieshaber, Erwin P. "Survival of Indian Communities in Nineteenth-Century Bolivia: A Regional Comparison." *Journal of Latin American Studies,* 12.2 (1980): 223–269.

Guerrero, Andrés. "Curagas y tenientes políticos: La ley de la costumbre y la ley del estado (Otavalo 1830–1875)." *Revista Andina* 7.2 (Cuzco, 1989): 321–366.

Guerrero, Andrés. *La semántica de la dominación: El concertaje de indios.* Quito, 1991.

Guillet, David. "Land Tenure, Ecological Zone and Agricultural Regime in the Central Andes." *American Ethnologist* 8 (1981): 139–156.

Halperin, Rhoda, and James Dow (eds.). *Peasant Livelihood: Studies in Economic Anthropology and Cultural Ecology.* New York, 1977.

Harris, Olivia, and Xavier Albó. *Monteras y guardatojos: Campesinos y mineros en el Norte de Potosí.* La Paz, 1975.

Harris, Olivia. "Complementarity and Conflict: An Andean View of Men and Women." In J. S. LaFontaine (ed.), *Sex and Age as Principles of Social Differentiation.* New York, 1978. 21–40.

Harris, Olivia. "Labour and Produce in an Ethnic Economy, Northern Potosí, Bolivia." In David Lehmann (ed.), *Ecology and Exchange in the Andes.* Cambridge, 1982. 70–96.

Harris, Olivia. "The Dead and the Devils among the Bolivian Laymi." In Maurice Bloch and Jonathan Parry (eds.), *Death and the Regeneration of Life.* Cambridge, 1982. 45–73.

Harris, Olivia, and Thérèse Bouysse-Cassagne. "Pacha: En torno al pensamiento aymara." In Thérèse Bouysse-Cassagne et al., *Tres reflexiones sobre el pensamiento queshwaymara*. La Paz, 1986. 11–59.

Harris, Olivia, Brooke Larson, and Enrique Tandeter (eds.). *La participación indígena en los mercados surandinos: Estrategias y reproducción social, siglos XVI–XX*. La Paz, 1987.

Harrison, Regina. *Signs, Songs, and Memory in the Andes: Translating Quechua Language and Culture*. Austin, 1989.

Hartmann, Roswith. "Mercados y ferias prehispánicas en el área andina." *Boletín de la Academia Nacional de Historia* (Quito) 54.118 (1971): 214–236.

Hart-Terre, Emilio. *Negros e indios: Un estamento social ignorado del Perú colonial*. Lima, 1973.

Harvey, Penelope. "Language and the Power of History: The Discourse of Bilinguals in Ocongate." Ph.D. dissertation. University of London, 1987.

Hirschman, Albert O. *Rival Views of Market Society*. Cambridge, Mass., 1992.

Humphrey, Caroline. "Barter and Economic Disintegration." *Man* (N.S.) 20 (1985): 48–72.

Hünefeldt, Christine. *Lucha por la tierra y protesta indígena: Las comunidades indígenas del Perú entre colonia y república*. Bonn, 1982.

Hyslop, John. *Inka Settlement Patterns*. Austin, 1990.

Hyslop, John. *The Inca Road System*. New York, 1984.

Iasaki Cauti, Fernando. "Ambulantes y comercio colonial: Iniciativas mercantiles en el Virreynato Peruano." *Jahrbuch für Geschichte von Staat, Wirtschaft und Gesellshaft Lateinamerikas* 24 (1987): 179–212.

Ibarra, Hernán. "La identidad devaluada de los 'Modern Indians.'" In Ileana Almeida et al. *Indios: Una reflexión sobre el levantamiento indígena de 1990*. Quito, 1990. 319–349.

Iguinéz, Javier (ed). *La cuestión rural en el Perú*. Lima, 1983.

Isaacman, Allan. "Peasants and Rural Social Protest in Africa." In Frederick Cooper et al., *Confronting Historical Paradigms*. Madison, 1993. 205–317. Reprinted from *Journal of African Studies* 33.2 (1990): 1–120.

Isbell, Billie Jean. "La influencia de los migrantes en los conceptos sociales y políticos tradicionales: Estudio de un caso peruano." *Estudios Andinos* 3.3 (1974): 81–103.

Isbell, Billie Jean. *To Defend Ourselves: A View through the Andean Kaleidoscope*. Austin, 1978.

Jackson, Robert. "The Decline of the Hacienda in Cochabamba, Bolivia: The Case of the Sacaba Valley, 1870–1929." *Hispanic American Historical Review* 69 (1989): 259–281.

Jacobsen, Nils. "Livestock Complexes in Late Colonial Peru and New Spain: An Attempt at Comparison." In Nils Jacobsen and Hans-Jürgen Puhle (eds.), *The Economies of Mexico and Peru during the Late Colonial Period*. Berlin, 1986. 113–142.

Jacobsen, Nils. "Free Trade, Regional Elites and the Internal Market in Southern Peru 1895–1932." In Joseph Love and Nils Jacobsen (eds.), *Guiding the Invisible Hand: Economy, Liberalism and the State in Latin American History.* New York, 1988. 145–176.

Jacobsen, Nils. *Mirages of Transition: The Peruvian Altiplano, 1780–1930.* Berkeley, 1993.

Johnson, Lyman J., and Enrique Tandeter (eds.). *Essays on the Price History of Eighteenth-Century Latin America.* Albuquerque, 1990.

Joseph, Gilbert. "On the Trail of Latin American Bandits: A Reexamination of Peasant Resistance." *Latin American Research Review* 25.3 (1990): 7–53.

Journal of Peasant Studies. Special Issue. "Everyday Forms of Peasant Resistance in South-East Asia." 13.2 (January 1986).

Kay, Cristóbal. "Achievements and Contradictions of the Peruvian Agrarian Reform." *Journal of Development Studies* 18.2 (1982): 141–170.

Keith, Robert G. *Conquest and Agrarian Change: The Emergence of the Hacienda System on the Peruvian Coast.* Cambridge, Mass., 1976.

Kervyn, Bruno, and Equipo del Cedep Ayllu. "Campesinos y acción colectiva: La organización del espacio en comunidades de la sierra sur del Perú." *Revista Andina* 7.1 (1989): 7–60.

Kicza, John (ed.). *The Indian in Latin American History: Resistance, Rebellion and Acculturation.* Wilmington, 1993.

Klein, Herbert S. *Bolivia: The Evolution of a Multi-Ethnic Society.* New York, 1982.

Klein, Herbert S. "Bolivia from the War of the Pacific to the Chaco War." In Leslie Bethell (ed.), *Cambridge History of Latin America.* Cambridge, 1986. 5:553–586.

Klein, Herbert S. *Haciendas and "Ayllus": Rural Society in the Bolivian Andes in the Eighteenth and Nineteenth Centuries.* Stanford, 1993.

Krech, Shepard. "The State of Ethnohistory." *Annual Review of Anthropology* 20 (1991): 345–375.

Kubler, George. *The Indian Caste of Peru 1795–1940.* Washington, D.C., 1952.

Lagos, María L. *Autonomy and Power: The Dynamics of Class and Culture in Rural Bolivia.* Philadelphia, 1994.

Laite, Julian. *Industrial Development and Migrant Labor in Latin America.* Austin, 1981.

LaLone, Darrel. "Historical Contexts of Trade and Markets in the Peruvian Andes." M.A. thesis. University of Michigan, 1978.

Langer, Erick D. "La comercialización de la cebada en los ayllus y las haciendas de Tarabuco (Chuquisaca) a comienzos del siglo XX." In Olivia Harris, Brooke Larson, and Enrique Tandeter (eds.), *La participación indígena en los mercados surandinos.* La Paz, 1987. 583–602.

Langer, Erick D. "Espacios coloniales y economías nacionales: Bolivia y el norte argentino." *Siglo XIX* 2 (1987): 135–160.

Langer, Erick D. *Economic Change and Rural Resistance in Southern Bolivia, 1880–1930.* Stanford, 1989.

Langer, Erick D. "Economic Geography and Ethnic Economies: Indian Trade in the Andes." In Lance H. Grahan (ed.), *Indian Trade in the Americas: A Comparative Perspective.* Lincoln, forthcoming.

Langer, Erick D., and Viviana E. Conti. "Circuitos comerciales tradicionales y cambio económico en los Andes centromeridionales, 1830–1930." *Desarrollo Económico* (Buenos Aires) 31.121 (1991): 91–111.

Larson, Brooke. "Caciques, Class Structure and the Colonial State in Bolivia." *Nova Americana* (Turin) 2 (1979): 197–235.

Larson, Brooke. "Rural Rhythms of Class Conflict in Eighteenth-Century Cochabamba." *Hispanic American Historical Review* 60.3 (1980): 407–430.

Larson, Brooke. "Producción doméstica y trabajo femenino indígena en la formación de una economía mercantil colonial." *Historia Boliviana* 3.2 (1983): 173–187.

Larson, Brooke. *Colonialism and Agrarian Transformation in Bolivia: Cochabamba, 1550–1900.* Princeton, 1988.

Larson, Brooke. "Explotacíon y economía moral en los andes del sur andino: Hacia una reconsideración crítica." In Segundo Moreno Yañez and Frank Salomon (eds.), *Reproducción y transformación de las sociedades andinas, siglos XVI–XX.* Quito, 1991. 2:441–480.

Larson, Brooke, and Robert Wasserstrom. "Consumo forzoso en Cochabamba y Chiapas durante la época colonial." In Manuel Miño Grijalva (ed.), *La formación de América Latina: La época colonial.* Mexico City, 1992. 166–213.

Lears, Jackson. "The Concept of Cultural Hegemony: Problems and Possibilities." *American Historical Review* 90.3 (1985): 567–593.

Lehmann, David (ed.). *Ecology and Exchange in the Andes.* Cambridge, 1982.

Lewinski, Liliana. "Una plaza de venta atomizada: La Cancha de Oruro, 1803 y 1812." In Olivia Harris, Brooke Larson, and Enrique Tandeter (eds.), *La participación indígena en los mercados surandinos.* La Paz, 1987. 445–470.

Lockhart, James. *Spanish Peru, 1532–1560: A Colonial Society.* Madison, 1968.

Lockhart, James. "Trunk Lines and Feeder Lines: The Spanish Reaction to American Resources." In Kenneth J. Adrien and Rolena Adorno (eds.), *Transatlantic Encounters: Europeans and Andeans in the Sixteenth Century.* Berkeley, 1991. 90–120.

Long, Norman, and Bryan Roberts (eds.). *Peasant Cooperation and Capitalist Expansion in Southern Peru.* Austin, 1978.

Long, Norman, and Bryan Roberts. *Miners, Peasants and Entrepreneurs: Regional Development in the Central Highlands of Peru.* Cambridge, 1984.

López Beltrán, Clara. *Estructura económica de una sociedad colonial: Charcas en el siglo XVII.* La Paz, 1988.

MacCormick Adams, Robert. "Anthropological Perspectives on Ancient Trade." *Current Anthropology* 15 (1974): 239–258.

MacCormick, Sabine. *Religion in the Andes: Vision and Imagination in Early Colonial Peru.* Princeton, 1991.

Macera, Pablo. "Feudalismo colonial americano: El caso de las haciendas peruanas." In *Trabajos de historia,* 4 vols. Lima, 1977. 3:139–227.

Maletta, Héctor. "Peru: ¿País campesino? Aspectos cuantitativos de su mundo rural." *Análisis* (Lima) 6 (1978): 3–51.

Mallon, Florencia E. *The Defense of Community in Peru's Central Highlands: Peasant Struggle and Capitalist Transition, 1860–1940.* Princeton, 1983.

Mallon, Florencia E. "Indian Communities, Political Cultures, and the State in Latin America." *Journal of Latin American Studies* 24 (1992): 35–53.

Mannheim, Bruce. *The Language of the Inka Since the European Invasion.* Austin, 1991.

Manrique, Nelson. *Colonialismo y pobreza campesina: Caylloma y el valle del Colca, siglos XVI–XX.* Lima, 1985.

Manrique, Nelson. *Mercado interno y región: La sierra central, 1820–1930.* Lima, 1987.

Manrique, Nelson. *Yawar Mayu: Sociedades terratenientes serranas, 1879–1910.* Lima, 1988.

Martínez Alier, Juan. *Los huacchilleros del Perú.* Lima, 1973.

Martínez Alier, Juan. "Relations of Production in Andean Haciendas: Peru." In Kenneth Duncan and Ian Rutledge (eds.), *Land and Labour in Latin America.* Cambridge, 1977. 141–164.

Masuda, Shozo, Izumi Shimada, and Craig Morris (eds.). *Andean Ecology and Civilization: An Interdisciplinary Perspective on Andean Ecological Complementarity.* Tokyo, 1985.

Matos Mar, José (ed.). *Hacienda, comunidad y campesinado en el Perú.* Lima, 1976.

Mauss, Marcel. *The Gift: Forms and Functions of Exchange in Archaic Societies.* New York, 1967.

Mayer, Enrique. "Mestizo e indio: El contexto social de las relaciones interétnicas." In Fernando Fuenzalida et al., eds., *El indio y el poder en el Perú rural.* Lima, 1970. 87–152.

Mayer, Enrique. "Un carnero por un saco de maíz." *Revista del Museo Nacional* (Lima) 37 (1971): 184–196.

Mayer, Enrique. "Las reglas del juego en la reciprocidad andina." In Giorgio Alberti and Enrique Mayer (eds.), *Reciprocidad e intercambio en los Andes peruanos.* Lima, 1974. 37–65.

Mayer, Enrique. "Production Zones." In Shozo Masuda, Izumi Shimada, and Craig Morris (eds.), *Andean Ecology and Civilization.* Tokyo, 1985, 45–84.

Mendez, Cecilia. "Los campesinos, la independencia y la iniciación de la república. El caso de los Iquichanos realistas: Ayachucho, 1825–1828." In Henrique Urbano (ed.), *Poder y violencia en los Andes.* Cuzco, 1991. 165–188.

Mintz, Sidney. "Internal Market Systems as Mechanisms of Social Articulation."

In Vernon Ray (ed.), *Proceedings of the 1959 Annual Spring Meeting of the American Ethnological Society.* Madison, 1959. 20–30.

Mitchell, William P. *Peasants on the Edge: Crop, Cult, and Crisis in the Andes.* Austin, 1991.

Mitre, Antonio. *Los patriarcas de la plata: Estructura socioeconómica de la minería boliviana en el siglo XIX.* Lima, 1981.

Moreno Cebrián, Alfredo. *El corregidor de indios y la economía peruana del siglo XVIII: Los repartos forzosos de mercaderías.* Madrid, 1977.

Moreno Yañez, Segundo. *Sublevaciones indígenas en la audiencia de Quito.* Quito, 1985.

Moreno Yañez, Segundo, and Udo Oberem (eds.). *Contribución a la etnohistoria ecuatoriana.* Otavalo, 1981.

Moreno Yañez, Segundo, and Frank Salomon (eds.). *La reproducción y transformación de las sociedades andinas, siglos XVI–XX.* Quito, 1991. 2 vols.

Mörner, Magnus. *Race Mixture in the History of Latin America.* Boston, 1967.

Mörner, Magnus. *Perfil de la sociedad rural del Cuzco a fines de la colonia.* Lima, 1978.

Mörner, Magnus. *The Andean Past: Land, Societies and Conflicts.* New York, 1985.

Murra, John V. "Herds and herders in the Inca state." In Anthony Leeds and Andrew Vayda (eds.), *Man, Culture, and Animals: The Role of Animals in Human Ecological Adjustments.* Washington, D.C., 1965. 185–215.

Murra, John V. "Herds and Herders in the Inca State." In Anthony Leeds and Andrew Vayda (eds.), *Man, Culture, and Animals: The Role of Animals in Human Ecological Adjustments.* Washington, D.C., 1965. 185–215.

Murra, John V. "El 'control vertical' de un máximo de pisos ecológicos en las economías de las sociedades andinas." In Iñigo Ortíz de Zúñiga, *Visita a la provincia de León de Huánuco* [1562]. 2 vols. Huánuco, 1967 and 1972. 2:429–476. Reprinted in Murra, *Formaciones económicas y políticas.*

Murra, John V. *Formaciones económicas y políticas del mundo andino.* Lima, 1975.

Murra, John V. "Aymara Lords and Their European Agents at Potosí." *Nova Americana* (Turin) 1 (1978): 231–244.

Murra, John V. *The Economic Organization of the Inca State.* Greenwich, Conn., [1955] 1979. Spanish edition: *La organización económica del estado inca.* Mexico, 1978.

Murra, John V. " 'El Archipiélago Vertical' Revisited." In Shozo Masuda, Izumi Shimada, and Craig Morris (eds.), *Andean Ecology and Civilization: An Interdisciplinary Perspective on Andean Ecological Complementarity.* Tokyo, 1985, 3–13.

Murra, John V. "The Limits and Limitations of the 'Vertical Archipelago' in the Andes." In Shozo Masuda, Izumi Shimada, and Craig Morris (eds.), *Andean Ecology and Civilization.* Tokyo, 1985. 15–20.

Murra, John V. "The Expansion of the Inka State: Armies, War and Rebellions."

In John V. Murra, Nathan Wachtel, and Jacques Revel (eds.), *Anthropological History of Andean Polities*. Cambridge, 1986. 49–58.

Murra, John V. *Visita de los valles de Sonqo en los yunka de coca de La Paz (1568–70)*. Madrid, 1992.

Murra, John V. " 'Nos Hazen Mucha Ventaja': The Early European Perception of Andean Achievement." In Kenneth J. Adrien and Rolena Adorno (eds.), *Transatlantic Encounters: Europeans and Andeans in the Sixteenth Century*. Berkeley, 1991. 73–89.

Nash, June. *We Eat the Mines and the Mines Eat Us: Dependency and Exploitation in the Bolivian Tin Mines*. New York, 1979.

Nugent, Guillermo. *El laberinto de la choledad: Formas del conocimiento social*. Lima, 1991.

O'Phelan Godoy, Scarlett. *Rebellions and Revolts in Eighteenth-Century Peru and Upper Peru*. Cologne, 1985.

Orlove, Benjamin S. "Reciprocidad, desigualdad y dominación." In Giorgio Alberti and Enrique Mayer (eds.), *Reciprocidad e intercambio en los Andes peruanos*. Lima, 1974. 290–321.

Orlove, Benjamin S. *Alpacas, Sheep and Men: The Wool Export Economy and Regional Society in Southern Peru*. New York, 1977.

Orlove, Benjamin S. "Ricos y pobres: La desigualdad en las comunidades campesinas." *Estudios Andinos* (Lima) 8.15 (1979): 5–20.

Orlove, Benjamin S., and Glyn Custred (eds.). *Land and Power in Latin America: Agrarian Economies and Social Processes in the Andes*. New York, 1980.

Orlove, Benjamin S. "Barter and Cash Sale on Lake Titicaca: A Test of Competing Approaches." *Current Anthropology* 27.2 (1986): 85–106.

Orlove, Benjamin S., and Ricardo Godoy. "Sectoral Fallowing Systems in the Central Andes." *Journal of Ethnobiology* 6.1 (1986): 169–204.

Ortíz de Zuñiga, Iñigo. *Visita a la provincia de León de Huánuco* [1562], 2 vols. (Huánuco, 1967, 1972).

Ossio, Juan (ed.). *Ideología mesiánica del mundo andino*. Lima, 1973.

Parry, Jonathan, and Maurice Bloch (eds.). *Money and the Morality of Exchange*. Cambridge, 1989.

Pease, Franklin. *Del Tawantinsuyo a la historia del Perú*. Lima, 1978.

Pease, Franklin. "The Formation of Tawantinsuyu: Mechanisms of Colonization and Relationships with Ethnic Groups." In George A. Collier et al. (eds.), *The Inca and Aztec States, 1400–1800*. New York, 1982. 173–198.

Pease, Franklin. "Cases and Variations of Verticality in the Southern Andes." In Shozo Masuda et al. (eds.), *Andean Ecology and Civilization*. Tokyo, 1985. 141–160.

Pease, Franklin. *Curacas, reciprocidad y riqueza*. Lima, 1992.

Phelan, John L. *The Kingdom of Quito in the Seventeenth Century*. Madison, 1967.

Piel, Jean. "Las articulaciones de la reserva andina al estado y al mercado desde

1820 hasta 1950." In Jean Pierre Deler and Yves Saint-Geours (eds.), *Estados y naciones en los Andes*. Lima, 1986. 1:323–336.

Platt, Tristan. *Espejos y maíz: Temas de la estructura simbólica andina*. La Paz, 1975. English edition: "Mirrors and Maize: The Concept of *Yanantin* among the Macha of Bolivia." In John V. Murra, Nathan Wachtel, and Jacques Pevel (eds.), *Anthropological History of Andean Polities*. Cambridge, 1986.

Platt, Tristan. "Acerca del sistema tributario pre-toledano en el Alto Perú." *Avances* (La Paz) 1 (1978): 33–44.

Platt, Tristan. *Estado boliviano y ayllu andino: Tierra y tributo en el norte de Potosí*. Lima, 1982.

Platt, Tristan. "The Role of the Andean *Ayllu* in the Reproduction of the Petty Commodity Regime in North Potosí (Bolivia)." In David Lehmann (ed.), *Ecology and Exchange in the Andes*. Cambridge, 1982. 27–69.

Platt, Tristan. "Religión andina y conciencia proletaria: Qhuyaruna y ayllu en el norte de Potosí." *HISLA*, (Lima) 2 (1983): 47–74.

Platt, Tristan. "Liberalism and Ethnocide in the Southern Andes." *History Workshop Journal* (London) 17 (1984): 3–18.

Platt, Tristan. *Estado tributario y librecambio en Potosí durante el siglo XIX*. La Paz, 1986.

Platt, Tristan. "The Andean Experience of Bolivian Liberalism, 1825–1900: Roots of Rebellion in 19th-Century Chayanta (Potosí)." In Steve J. Stern (ed.), *Resistance, Rebellion, and Consciousness in the Andean Peasant World, 18th to 20th Centuries*. Madison, 1987. 280–323.

Platt, Tristan. "Divine Protection and Liberal Damnation: Exchanging Metaphors in Nineteenth-Century Potosí (Bolivia)." In Roy Dilley (ed.), *Contesting Markets: Analyses of Ideology, Discourse, and Practice*. Edinburgh, 1992. 131–158.

Polanyi, Karl. *The Great Transformation: The Political and Economic Origins of Our Time*. Boston, [1944] 1957.

Polanyi, Karl. *The Livelihood of Man*. New York, 1977.

Polanyi, Karl et al. (eds.). *Trade and Market in the Early Empires: Economies in History and Theory*. Chicago, 1957.

Polo de Ondegardo, Juan. "Informe al licenciado Briviesca de Muñatones sobre la perpetuidad de las encomiendas en el Perú [1516]." *Revista Histórica* (Lima) 13 (1940): 125–196.

Polo de Ondegardo, Juan. "Relación de los fundamentos acerca del notable daño que resulta de no guardar a los indios sus fueros [1571]." In *Colección de libros y documentos referentes a la historia del Perú*. 4 vols. (Lima 1916), 3: 45–188. Also published in *Colección de documentos inéditos relativos al descubrimiento, conquista y organización de las antiguas posesiones españoles de América y Oceania*, 1st ser., (Madrid, 1872), 3: 5–177.

Poma de Ayala, Felipe Guaman. *Nueva corónica y buen gobierno* [1615]. 3 vols. Ed. John V. Murra and Rolena Adorno. Mexico City, 1980.

Poole, Deborah. "Landscapes of Power in a Cattle-rustling Culture of Southern Andean Peru." *Dialectical Anthropology* 12 (1988): 367–398.

Powers, Karen. "Indian Migration and Socio-political Change in the Audiencia of Quito, 1534–1700." Ph.D. dissertation. New York University, 1990.

Powers, Karen. "Resilient Lords and Indian Vagabonds: Wealth, Migration, and the Reproductive Transformation of Quito's Chiefdoms, 1500–1700." *Ethnohistory* 38 (1991): 225–249.

Preston, David. "New Towns: A Major Change in the Rural Settlement Pattern in Highland Bolivia." *Journal of Latin American Studies* 2.1 (1970): 1–27.

Quijano, Aníbal. *Dominación y cultura: Lo cholo y el conflicto.* Lima, 1980.

Ramírez, Susan E. "Retainers of the Lords or Merchants: A Case of Mistaken Identity?" *Senri Ethnological Studies* 10 (1982): 123–136.

Ramírez, Susan E. "Social Frontiers and the Territorial Base of Curacazgos." In Shozo Masuda, Izumi Shimada, and Craig Morris (eds.), *Andean Ecology and Civilization: An Interdisciplinary Perspective on Andean Ecological Complementarity.* Tokyo, 1985. 423–442.

Ramírez, Susan E. *Provincial Patriarchs: Land Tenure and the Economics of Power in Colonial Peru.* Albuquerque, 1986.

Ramírez, Susan E. "The '*Dueño de Indios*': Thoughts on the Consequences of the Shifting Bases of Power of the '*Curaca de los viejos antiguos*' under the Spanish in Sixteenth-Century Peru." *Hispanic American Historical Review* 67.4 (1987): 575–610.

Ramírez, Susan E. "Tribute." In *The World Turned Upside Down: Essays on Cross-Cultural Contact in Sixteenth-Century Peru.* Stanford, 1995.

Ramón, Galo. "El Ecuador en el espacio andino: Idea, proceso y utopía." *Allpanchis* (Cuzco) 35–36 (1990): 517–578.

Rappaport, Joanne. *The Politics of Memory: Native Historical Interpretation in the Colombian Andes.* Cambridge, 1990.

Rasnake, Roger. *Domination and Cultural Resistance: Authority and Power among an Andean People.* Durham, 1988.

Rivera Cusicanqui, Silvia. "El mallku y la sociedad colonial en el siglo XVII: El caso de Jesús de Machaca." *Avances* (La Paz) 1 (1978): 7–27.

Rivera Cusicanqui, Silvia. "La expansión del latifundio en el altiplano boliviano: Elementos para la caracterización de una oligarquía regional." *Avances* (La Paz) 2 (1978): 95–118.

Rivera Cusicanqui, Silvia. *Oppressed but Not Defeated: Peasant Struggles among the Aymara and Quechwa in Bolivia.* Geneva, 1987. Spanish edition: *Oprimidos pero no vencidos: Luchas del campesinado aymara y quechwa.* La Paz, 1984.

Rivera Cusicanqui, Silvia. "Liberal Democracy and Ayllu Democracy in Bolivia: The Case of Northern Potosí." *Journal of Development Studies* 26.4 (1990): 97–121.

Roberts, Bryan. *Cities of Peasants.* London, 1979.

Robinson, David J. (ed.). *Studies in Spanish American Population History.* Boulder, 1981.

Robinson, David J. (ed.). *Migration in Colonial Spanish America.* Cambridge, 1990.

Rodríguez Ostria, Gustavo, and Humberto Solares Serrano. *Sociedad Oligárquica, Chicha y Cultura Popular.* Cochabamba, 1990.

Romano, Ruggiero, and Genevieve Tranchard. "Una encomienda de coca." *HISLA* (Lima) 1 (1983): 57–88.

Roseberry, William. "Beyond the Agrarian Question in Latin America." In Frederick Cooper et al. (eds.), *Confronting Historical Paradigms.* Madison, 1993. 318–368.

Rostworowski de Diez Canseco, María. *Etnía y sociedad: Costa peruana prehispánica.* Lima, 1977. 2nd ed.: *Costa peruana prehispánica.* Lima, 1989.

Sahlins, Marshall. *Stone Age Economics.* Chicago, 1972.

Saignes, Thierry. "De la filiation à la résidence: Les ethnies dans les vallées de Larecaja." *Annales ESC* (Paris) 33.5–6 (1978): 1160–1181.

Saignes, Thierry. "Políticas étnicas en Bolivia colonial, siglos XVI–XIX." *Historia Boliviana* (Cochabamba) 3.1 (1983): 1–30.

Saignes, Thierry. "Las étnias de Charcas frente al sistema colonial (siglo XVII): Ausentismo y fugas en el debate sobre la mano de obra indígena (1595–1665)." *Jahrbuch für Geschichte von Staat, Wirschaft und Gesellschaft Lateinamerikas* (Cologne) 21 (1984): 27–75.

Saignes, Thierry. *Los Andes orientales: Historia de un olvido.* Cochabamba, 1985.

Saignes, Thierry. "Politique du recensement dans les Andes coloniales: Décroissance tributaire ou mobilité indigène?" *Histoire, Economie, Société* (Paris) 4 (1987): 435–468.

Salas de Coloma, Miriam. "Crisis en desfase en el centro-sur este del virreinato peruano: Minería y manufactura textil." In Heraclio Bonilla (ed.), *Las crisis económicas en la historia del Perú.* Lima, 1986. 139–166.

Salomon, Frank. "Weavers of Otavalo." In Norman E. Whitten Jr. (ed.), *Cultural Transformations and Ethnicity in Modern Ecuador.* Urbana, 1981. 420–449.

Salomon, Frank. "Systèmes politiques aux marchés de l'empire." *Annales ESC* 33.5–6 (1978): 967–990.

Salomon, Frank. "Andean Ethnology in the 1970s: A Retrospective." *Latin American Research Review* 17.2 (1982): 75–128.

Salomon, Frank. "The Dynamic Potential of the Complementarity Concept." In Shozo Masuda, Izumi Shimada, and Craig Morris (eds.), *Andean Ecology and Civilization.* Tokyo, 1985. 511–531.

Salomon, Frank. "The Historical Development of Andean Ethnology." *Mountain Research and Development* 5.1 (1985): 79–98.

Salomon, Frank. *Native Lords of Quito in the Age of the Incas.* Cambridge, 1986.

Salomon, Frank. "Ancestor Cults and Resistance to the State in Arequipa, ca. 1748–1754." In Steve J. Stern (ed.), *Resistance, Rebellion, and Consciousness in the Andean Peasant World, 18th to 20th Centuries.* Madison, 1987. 148–165.

Salomon, Frank, and George L. Urioste (eds.). *The Huarochirí Manuscript: A Testament of Ancient and Colonial Andean Religion.* Austin, 1991.

Samaniego, Carlos. "Location, Social Differentiation and Peasant Movements in the Central Sierra of Peru." Ph.D. dissertation. University of Manchester, 1974.

Sánchez Albornoz, Nicolás. *The Population of Latin America: A History.* Berkeley, 1974. Spanish edition: *La población de América Latina: Desde los tiempos precolombinos al año 2000,* 2nd ed. Madrid, 1977.

Sánchez Albornoz, Nicolás. *Indios y tributos en el Alto Perú.* Lima, 1978.

Sánchez Albornoz, Nicolás. "Mita, migraciones y pueblos: variaciones en el espacio y en el tiempo: Alto Perú, 1575–1692." *Historia Boliviana* (Cochabamba) 3.1 (1983): 31–46.

Santamaría, Daniel J. "La participación indígena en la producción y comercio de coca, Alto Perú 1780–1810." In Olivia Harris, Brooke Larson, and Enrique Tandeter (eds.), *La participación indígena en los mercados surandinos.* La Paz, 1987. 425–444.

Scott, James C. *The Moral Economy of the Peasant: Rebellion and Subsistence in Southern Asia.* New Haven, 1976.

Scott, James C. *Weapons of the Weak: Everyday Forms of Peasant Resistance.* New Haven, 1985.

Seligmann, Linda. "To Be in between: The Cholas as Market Women." *Comparative Studies of Society and History* 31.4 (1989): 694–721.

Silverblatt, Irene. *Moon, Sun and Witches: Gender Ideologies and Class in Inca and Spanish Peru.* Princeton, 1987.

Smith, Carol A. "How Marketing Systems Affect Economic Opportunity in Agrarian Societies." In Rhoda Halperin and James Dow (eds.), *Peasant Livelihood.* New York, 1977. 117–146.

Smith, Gavin A. *Livelihood and Resistance: Peasants and the Politics of Land in Peru.* Berkeley, 1989.

Spalding, Karen. "Social Climbers: Changing Patterns of Mobility among the Indians of Peru." *Hispanic American Historical Review* 50 (1970): 645–664.

Spalding, Karen. "Kurakas and Commerce: A Chapter in the Evolution of Andean Society." *Hispanic American Historical Review* 53 (1973): 581–599.

Spalding, Karen. *De indio a campesino: Cambios en la estructura social del Perú colonial.* Lima, 1974.

Spalding, Karen. "Hacienda-Village Relations in Andean Society to 1830." *Latin American Perspectives* 2:1 (1975): 107–121.

Spalding, Karen. "Exploitation as an Economic System: The State and the Extraction of Surplus in Colonial Peru." In George A. Collier, Renato Rosaldo, and John Wirth (eds.), *The Inca and Aztec States, 1400–1800.* New York, 1982. 321–342.

Spalding, Karen. *Huarochirí: An Andean Society under Inca and Spanish Rule.* Stanford, 1984.

Stern, Steve J. *Peru's Indian Peoples and the Challenge of the Spanish Conquest: Huamanga to 1640.* Madison, 1982.

Stern, Steve J. "The Struggle for Solidarity: Class, Culture and Community in Highland Indian America." *Radical History Review* 27 (1983): 21–45.

Stern, Steve J. "New Directions in Andean Economic History: A Critical Dialogue with Carlos Sempat Assadourian." *Latin American Perspectives* 12.1 (1985): 133–148.

Stern, Steve J. "New Approaches to the Study of Peasant Rebellion and Consciousness: Implications of the Andean Experience." In Steve J. Stern (ed.), *Resistance, Rebellion, and Consciousness in the Andean Peasant World, 18th to 20th Centuries.* Madison, 1987. 3–28.

Stern, Steve J. (ed.). *Resistance, Rebellion, and Consciousness in the Andean Peasant World, 18th to 20th Centuries.* Madison, 1987. Spanish edition: *Resistencia, rebelión y conciencia campesina en los Andes, siglos XVIII al XIX.* Lima, 1990.

Stern, Steve J. "Feudalism, Capitalism, and the World-System in the Perspective of Latin America and the Caribbean." In Frederick Cooper et al., *Confronting Historical Paradigms: Peasants, Labor, and the Capitalist World System in Africa and Latin America.* Madison, 1993. 23–83. Reprinted from *American Historical Review* 93.4 (October 1988): 829–872.

Stern, Steve J. "Paradigms of Conquest: History, Historiography, and Politics." *Journal of Latin American Studies* 24 (1992): 1–34.

Stutzman, Ronald. "El Mestizaje: An All-Inclusive Ideology of Exclusion." In Norman E. Whitten, Jr. (ed.), *Cultural Transformations and Ethnicity in Modern Ecuador.* Urbana, 1981. 45–94.

Taller de la Historia Oral Aymara (THOA). *El indio Santos Marka T'ula.* La Paz, 1984.

Taller de la Historia Oral Aymara (THOA) and Silvia Rivera Cusicanqui. "Indigenous Women and Community Resistance: History and Memory." In Elizabeth Jelin (ed.), *Women and Social Change in Latin America.* London, 1990. 151–183.

Tandeter, Enrique. "Forced and Free Labour in Late Colonial Potosí." *Past and Present* (London) 93 (1981): 98–136.

Tandeter, Enrique. "La producción como actividad popular: 'Ladrones de minas' en Potosí." *Nova Americana* (Turin) 4 (1981): 43–65.

Tandeter, Enrique, and Nathan Wachtel. "Prices and Agricultural Production: Potosí and Charcas in the Eighteenth Century." In Lyman J. Johnson and Enrique Tandeter (eds.), *Essays on the Price History of Eighteenth-Century Latin America.* Albuquerque, 1990. 201–276. Spanish edition: *Precios y producción agraria: Potosí y Charcas en el siglo XVIII.* Buenos Aires, 1983.

Tandeter, Enrique. *Coercion and Market: Silver Mining in Colonial Potosí, 1692–1826.* Albuquerque, 1993. Spanish edition: *Coacción y mercado: La minería de la plata en el Potosí colonial, 1692–1826.* Buenos Aires, 1992.

Taussig, Michael. *The Devil and Commodity Fetishism in South America.* Chapel Hill, N.C., 1980.

Tepaske, John J., and Herbert S. Klein. *The Royal Treasures of the Spanish Empire in America: Peru*. Durham, N.C., 1982.

Thomas, R. Brook. "Adaptación humana y ecología de la puna." In Jorge Flores Ochoa (ed.), *Pastores de puna: Uywamichiq Punarunakuna*. Lima, 1977. 87–112.

Thompson, E. P. "The Moral Economy of the English Crowd in the Eighteenth Century." *Past and Present* (London) 50 (1971): 76–136.

Thurner, Mark. "Peasant Politics and Andean Haciendas in the Transition to Capitalism: An Ethnographic History." *Latin American Research Review* 28.3 (1993): 41–82.

Thurner, Mark. "From Two Nations to One Divided: The Contradictions of Nation-Building in Andean Peru—The Case of Huaylas." Ph.D. dissertation. University of Wisconsin, 1993.

Tomoeda, Hiroyasu, and Luís Millones (eds.) *500 años de mestizaje en los Andes*. Osako, 1992.

Tord, Javier. "El corregidor de indios del Perú: Comercio y tributos." *Historia y Cultura* (Lima) 8 (1974): 187–198.

Tord, Javier, and Carlos Lazo. *Hacienda, comercio, fiscalidad y luchas sociales (Perú colonial)*. Lima, 1981.

Urban, Greg, and Joel Sherzer (eds.). *Nation-States and Indians in Latin America*. Austin, 1991.

Urbano, Henrique (ed.). *Violencia y poder en los Andes*. Cuzco, 1991.

Vallee, Lionel. "La ecología subjetiva como elemento esencial de la verticalidad." *Revista del Museo Nacional* (Lima) 37 (1971): 169–173.

Van Aken, Mark. "The Lingering Death of Indian Tribute in Ecuador." *Hispanic American Historical Review* 61.3 (1981): 429–459.

Van Den Berghe, Pierre, and George Primov. *Inequality in the Peruvian Andes: Class and Ethnicity in Cuzco*. Columbia, Mo., 1977.

Vilar, Pierre. *History of Gold and Money, 1450–1920*. London. 1976.

Wachtel, Nathan. *La visión des vaincus: Les Indiens du Pérou devant la conquête espagnol, 1530–1570*. Paris, 1971.

Wachtel, Nathan. *Sociedad e ideología: Ensayos de historia y antropología andinas*. Lima, 1973.

Wachtel, Nathan. "Hommes de l'eau: Le problème uru (XVI–XVII siècle)." *Annales ESC* 33.5–6 (1978): 1127–1159.

Wachtel, Nathan. "The Mitimaes of the Cochabamba Valley: The Colonization Policy of Huayna Cápac." In George A. Collier, Renato Rosaldo, and John Wirth (eds.), *The Inca and Aztec States, 1400–1800*. New York, 1982. 199–235. Spanish edition: "Los mitimas del valle de Cochabamba: La política de colonización de Wayna Capac." *Historia Boliviana* (Cochabamba) 1.1 (1981): 21–57.

Wachtel, Nathan. *Le retour des ancêtres: Les indiens urus de Bolivie, XXe–XVIe siècles*. Paris, 1990.

Walker, Charles. "La historiografía en inglés sobre los Andes: Balance de la década del 80." *Revista Andina* 9.2 (1991): 513–528.

Walker, Charles. "Peasants, Caudillos and the State in Peru: Cusco in the Transition from Colony to Republic, 1780–1840." Ph.D. dissertation. University of Chicago, 1992.

Webster, Steven. "Una comunidad quechua indígena en la explotación de múltiples zonas ecológicas." *Revista del Museo Nacional* (Lima) 37 (1971): 174–183.

Webster, Steven. "Native Pastoralism in the South Andes." *Ethnology* 12.2 (1973): 115–133.

Whitten, Norman E. Jr. (ed.). *Cultural Transformations and Ethnicity in Modern Ecuador.* Urbana, 1981.

Wightman, Ann W. *Indigenous Migration and Social Change: The Forasteros of Cuzco, 1570–1720.* Durham, N.C., 1990.

Zavala, Silvio (ed.). *El servicio personal de los indios en el Perú.* 3 vols. Mexico City, 1978–1979.

Zavaleta Mercado, René (ed.). *Bolivia, Hoy.* Mexico City, 1983.

Zulawski, Ann. "Social Differentiation, Gender and Ethnicity: Urban Indian Women in Colonial Bolivia, 1640–1725." *Latin American Research Review* 25.2 (1990): 93–113.

Zulawski, Ann. *"They Eat from Their Labor": Work and Social Change in Colonial Bolivia.* Pittsburgh, 1995.

Contributors

Carlos Sempat Assadourian is Professor of Economics and History at the Colegio de México. He is the author of *El sistem de la economía colonial: Mercado interno, regiones, y espacio económico* (1982).

Marisol de la Cadena is Assistant Professor of Anthropology at the University of North Carolina at Chapel Hill and has written *Cooperación y conflicto* (1989).

Olivia Harris is Senior Lecturer and Chair of the Anthropology Department at Goldsmith's College of the University of London. She is the author of *La economía étnica* (1985).

Brooke Larson is Associate Professor of History at the State University of New York, at Stony Brook, and Director of Latin American and Caribbean Studies. She is the author of *Colonialism and Agrarian Transformation in Bolivia: Cochabamba, 1550–1900* (1988).

Rosario León, an anthropologist, is the Bolivian Director of the Forest, Trees, and People Program of the United Nations. She is also a research associate of the Centro de Estudios de la Realidad Económica Social (CERES), in Cochabamba.

John V. Murra is Professor Emeritus of Anthropology at Cornell University. He is the author of *Formaciones económicas y políticas del mundo andino* (1975) and *The Economic Organization of the Inca State* (1979).

Tristan Platt is Professor of Anthropology at St. Andrew's University in Scotland and the author of *Estado boliviano y ayllu andino: Tierra y tributo en el Norte de Potosí* (1982).

Susan E. Ramírez is Professor of History at DePaul University in Chicago and has written *Provincial Patriarchs: Land Tenure and the Economics of Power in Colonial Peru* (1986) and *The World Turned Upside Down: Essays on Cross-Cultural Contact in Sixteenth-Century Peru* (1995).

Contributors

Thierry Saignes served as Directeur d'Etudes C.N.R.S., Institut des Hautes Etudes d'Amerique Latine, in Paris. He wrote *Los Andes orientales: Historia de un olivido* (1985).

Steve J. Stern, Professor of History and Director of Latin American Studies at the University of Wisconsin, at Madison, has written *Peru's Indian Peoples and the Challenge of Conquest* (1982; 1992).

Enrique Tandeter is Professor and Chairman of the History Department at the University of Buenos Aires. He is the author of *Coercion and Markets: Silver Mining in Colonial Potosí, 1692–1826* (1993). His collaborators, Vilma Milletich, María Matilda Ollier, and Beatríz Ruibal, are research historians.

Index

❖

Index

Index

Index

Library of Congress Cataloging-in-Publication Data

Ethnicity, markets, and migration in the Andes : at the
crossroads of history and anthropology / edited by Brooke
Larson, Olivia Harris, and Enrique Tandeter.
  p.   cm.
Includes bibliographical references and index.
ISBN 0-8223-1633-1. — ISBN 0-8223-1647-1 (pbk.)
  1. Indians of South America—Commerce—Andes Region.
2. Indians of South America—Andes Region—Economic
conditions.   3. Indians of South America—Andes Region—
Migrations.   4. Economic history.   5. Ethnohistory—Andes
Region.   6. Mercantile system—Andes Region—History.
7. Andes Region—Economic conditions.   8. Andes
Region—History.   I. Larson, Brooke   II. Harris, Olivia.
III. Tandeter, Enrique.
F2230.1.C75E85   1995
330.98—dc20   95-864
                                                      CIP